First World War
and Army of Occupation
War Diary
France, Belgium and Germany

52 DIVISION
Headquarters, Branches and Services
Commander Royal Artillery
1 April 1918 - 31 May 1919

WO95/2890/2

The Naval & Military Press Ltd
www.nmarchive.com
Published in association with The National Archives

Published by

The Naval & Military Press Ltd

Unit 10 Ridgewood Industrial Park,
Uckfield, East Sussex,
TN22 5QE England
Tel: +44 (0) 1825 749494

www.naval-military-press.com

www.nmarchive.com

This diary has been reprinted in facsimile from the original. Any imperfections are inevitably reproduced and the quality may fall short of modern type and cartographic standards.

© **Crown Copyright**
Images reproduced by permission of The National Archives, London, England, 2015.

Contents

Document type	Place/Title	Date From	Date To
Heading	WO95/2890/2 Commander Royal Artillery		
Heading	52nd Division C.R.A. Apr 1918-May 1919		
Heading	52nd Divisional Artillery Arrived Marseilles From Egypt 12.4.18 C.R.A 52nd (Lowland) Division April 1918.		
War Diary	Moascar	01/04/1918	02/04/1918
War Diary	Alexandria	03/04/1918	04/04/1918
War Diary	At Sea	05/04/1918	11/04/1918
War Diary	Marseilles	12/04/1918	14/04/1918
War Diary	Sailly-Flibeaucourt	16/04/1918	26/04/1918
War Diary	Frohen	27/04/1918	27/04/1918
War Diary	Willeman	28/04/1918	28/04/1918
War Diary	Crequy	29/04/1918	30/04/1918
Operation(al) Order(s)	52nd Divisional Artillery Order No. 3	28/04/1918	28/04/1918
Operation(al) Order(s)	52nd Divisional Artillery Order No. 2	27/04/1918	27/04/1918
Operation(al) Order(s)	52nd Divisional Artillery Order No. 1	26/04/1918	26/04/1918
Heading	War Diary Of 52nd D.A. H.Q. From 1st May 1918 To 31st May 1918 Vol IV		
War Diary	Crequy	01/05/1918	04/05/1918
War Diary	Aux Rietz	05/05/1918	06/05/1918
War Diary	Chateau D'Acq	07/05/1918	10/05/1918
War Diary	Villers Au Bois	11/05/1918	31/05/1918
Miscellaneous	Daily Report	12/05/1918	12/05/1918
Miscellaneous	Daily Report 6.am 12/5/18 To 6.am 13/5/18	13/05/1918	13/05/1918
Miscellaneous	242nd A.F.A Brigade Group (2)	13/05/1918	13/05/1918
Miscellaneous	Daily Report 6.0 am 13/5/18 To 6.am 14/5/18.	13/05/1918	13/05/1918
Miscellaneous	Daily Report 6.0 am 14/5/18 To 6.am. 15/5/18	15/05/1918	15/05/1918
Miscellaneous	52nd Brigade (7) 242nd Brigade (7)	14/05/1918	14/05/1918
Miscellaneous	Daily Report 6.0 am 15/5/18 To 6.0.am 16/5/18	16/05/1918	16/05/1918
Miscellaneous	242nd Army Bde (7) 52nd Army Bde (7)	16/05/1918	16/05/1918
Miscellaneous	Daily Report 52nd Divisional Artillery	17/05/1918	17/05/1918
Miscellaneous	Daily Report 52nd Divisional Artillery	18/05/1918	18/05/1918
Miscellaneous	52nd.D.A. No. B.M.303.	17/05/1918	17/05/1918
Miscellaneous	52nd.DA. No. BM.309	18/05/1918	18/05/1918
Miscellaneous	52nd Div'l. Artillery Mutual Support Scheme		
Miscellaneous	Daily Report 52nd Divisional Artillery	19/05/1918	19/05/1918
Miscellaneous	52nd Divisional Artillery	18/05/1918	18/05/1918
Miscellaneous	Daily Report 52nd Divisional Artillery	20/05/1918	20/05/1918
Miscellaneous	All Recipients 52nd D.A.no.b.M.282	20/05/1918	20/05/1918
Miscellaneous	Daily Report 52nd Divisional Artillery	21/05/1918	21/05/1918
Miscellaneous	All Recipients 52nd D.A. No. B.M.282	20/05/1918	20/05/1918
Miscellaneous	Daily Report 52nd Divisional Artillery	22/05/1918	22/05/1918
Operation(al) Order(s)	Operation Order No. 8 by Brigadier General E. Harding Newman CMG DSO Commanding 52nd Divisional Artillery		
Miscellaneous	Daily Report 52nd Divisional Artillery	23/05/1918	23/05/1918
Miscellaneous	Daily Report 52nd Divisional Artillery	24/05/1918	24/05/1918
Miscellaneous	242nd Brigade 52nd Brigade	23/05/1918	23/05/1918
Miscellaneous	Daily Report 52nd Divisional Artillery	25/05/1918	25/05/1918

Operation(al) Order(s)	Operation Order No. 9 by Brigadier General E. Harding Newman CMG., DSO Commanding 52nd Divisional Artillery	24/05/1918	24/05/1918
Miscellaneous	Amendment To Operation Order No. 9	24/05/1918	24/05/1918
Operation(al) Order(s)	Operation Order No. 10 by Brigadier General E. Harding Newman CMG., DSO Commanding 52nd Divisional Artillery	24/05/1918	24/05/1918
Miscellaneous	Daily Report 52nd Divisional Artillery	26/05/1918	26/05/1918
Operation(al) Order(s)	Operation Order No. 11 by Brigadier General E. Harding Newman CMG., DSO Commanding 52nd Divisional Artillery	25/05/1918	25/05/1918
Miscellaneous	Barrage Table To Accompany 52nd D.A.O.O.no.11		
Miscellaneous	Amendment To Operation Order No. 11	25/05/1918	25/05/1918
Miscellaneous	Amendment To Operation Order No. 10	25/05/1918	25/05/1918
Miscellaneous	Daily Report 52nd Divisional Artillery	27/05/1918	27/05/1918
Miscellaneous	242nd.Brigade (8) 52nd Brigade (12)	26/05/1918	26/05/1918
Miscellaneous	Bombardment Table A. For Field Artillery		
Miscellaneous	Daily Report 52nd Divisional Artillery	29/05/1918	29/05/1918
Miscellaneous	All Recipients Of 52nd D.A. No. B.M. 303	27/05/1918	27/05/1918
Miscellaneous	Daily Report 52nd Divisional Artillery	29/05/1918	29/05/1918
Miscellaneous	Amendment No. 1 To 52nd D.A. No BM 457	28/05/1918	28/05/1918
Miscellaneous	Daily Report 52nd Divisional Artillery	30/05/1918	30/05/1918
Miscellaneous	Daily Report 52nd Divisional Artillery	31/05/1918	31/05/1918
Miscellaneous	Daily Report 52nd Divisional Artillery	01/06/1918	01/06/1918
Heading	HQ R A 52d Vol 3 June 1918		
Heading	War Diary Of Headquarters 52nd Divisional Artillery From 1st June 1918 To 30th June 1918 Volume V Part VI		
War Diary	Villers Au Bois	01/06/1918	30/06/1918
Heading	June 1918 Appendices To War Diary H Q R A 52 Divn		
Miscellaneous	Daily Report 52nd Divisional Artillery	01/06/1918	01/06/1918
Miscellaneous	Daily Report 52nd Divisional Artillery	03/06/1918	03/06/1918
Miscellaneous	52nd D.A. No.B.M./516.	02/06/1918	02/06/1918
Miscellaneous	Bombardment Table To Accompany 52nd D.A. No.B.M./516.		
Miscellaneous	Daily Report 52nd Divisional Artillery	04/06/1918	04/06/1918
Operation(al) Order(s)	Operation Order No. 13 by Brigadier General E. Harding Newman CMG., DSO Commanding 52nd Divisional Artillery	03/06/1918	03/06/1918
Miscellaneous	Daily Report 52nd Divisional Artillery	04/06/1918	04/06/1918
Miscellaneous	Daily Report 52nd Divisional Artillery	06/06/1918	06/06/1918
Miscellaneous	Daily Report 52nd Divisional Artillery	07/06/1918	07/06/1918
Miscellaneous	Daily Report 52nd Divisional Artillery	08/05/1918	08/05/1918
Miscellaneous	Daily Report 52nd Divisional Artillery	09/06/1918	09/06/1918
Miscellaneous	Daily Report 52nd Divisional Artillery	10/06/1918	10/06/1918
Miscellaneous	Daily Report 52nd Divisional Artillery	11/06/1918	11/06/1918
Miscellaneous	52nd.DA.No.53/A.	10/06/1918	10/06/1918
Miscellaneous	Daily Report 52nd Divisional Artillery	12/06/1918	12/06/1918
Operation(al) Order(s)	Operation Order No. 14 by Brigadier General E. Harding Newman CMG., DSO Commanding 52nd Divisional Artillery	11/06/1918	11/06/1918
Miscellaneous	Daily Report 52nd Divisional Artillery	13/06/1918	13/06/1918
Miscellaneous	Daily Report 52nd Divisional Artillery	14/06/1918	14/06/1918
Miscellaneous	52nd.D.A.No.73/A.	13/06/1918	13/06/1918
Miscellaneous	Right Group 16th Bde RGA D.T.M.O.	13/06/1918	13/06/1918
Miscellaneous	Daily Report 52nd Divisional Artillery	15/06/1918	15/06/1918

Type	Description	Date From	Date To
Miscellaneous	All Recipients 52nd DA. O.O. No. 14.	14/06/1918	14/06/1918
Operation(al) Order(s)	Operation Order No. 15 by Brigadier General E. Harding Newman CMG., DSO Commanding 52nd Divisional Artillery	11/06/1918	11/06/1918
Miscellaneous	Table "A"		
Miscellaneous	Table "B"		
Diagram etc	Diagram		
Map	Tracing For HA		
Miscellaneous	Daily Report 52nd Divisional Artillery	15/06/1918	15/06/1918
Miscellaneous	Daily Report 52nd Divisional Artillery	16/06/1918	16/06/1918
Miscellaneous	Daily Report 52nd Divisional Artillery	17/06/1918	17/06/1918
Miscellaneous	Daily Report 52nd Divisional Artillery	19/06/1918	19/06/1918
Miscellaneous	Daily Report 52nd Divisional Artillery	20/06/1918	20/06/1918
Miscellaneous	All Recipients 52nd D.A. O.O.No. 14	19/06/1918	19/06/1918
Miscellaneous	Daily Report 52nd Divisional Artillery	21/06/1918	21/06/1918
Miscellaneous	Distribution Of Guns		
Operation(al) Order(s)	52nd Divisional Artillery Order No. 16	21/06/1918	21/06/1918
Diagram etc	Diagram		
Operation(al) Order(s)	52nd Divisional Artillery Order No. 17	21/06/1918	21/06/1918
Miscellaneous	Daily Report 52nd Divisional Artillery	22/06/1918	22/06/1918
Miscellaneous	Daily Report 52nd Divisional Artillery	23/06/1918	23/06/1918
Miscellaneous	Right Group Left Group	23/06/1918	23/06/1918
Miscellaneous	Daily Report 52nd Divisional Artillery	24/06/1918	24/06/1918
Miscellaneous	To All Recipients Of O.O.18	24/06/1918	24/06/1918
Operation(al) Order(s)	52nd Divisional Artillery Order No. 18	24/06/1918	24/06/1918
Map	Identification Trace For Use With Artillery Maps		
Miscellaneous	Daily Report 52nd Divisional Artillery	25/06/1918	25/06/1918
Operation(al) Order(s)	52nd Divisional Artillery Order No. 19	24/06/1918	24/06/1918
Miscellaneous	Daily Report 52nd Divisional Artillery	26/06/1918	26/06/1918
Miscellaneous	Daily Report 52nd Divisional Artillery	27/06/1918	27/06/1918
Miscellaneous	Daily Report 52nd Divisional Artillery	28/06/1918	28/06/1918
Miscellaneous	52nd Divisional Artillery Instructions No. 1	28/06/1918	28/06/1918
Map	Field Artillery-Outpost & Black Barrages		
Miscellaneous	Daily Report 52nd Divisional Artillery	29/06/1918	29/06/1918
Miscellaneous	To All Recipients Of 52nd Divisional Artillery Order No. 1	29/06/1918	29/06/1918
Operation(al) Order(s)	52nd Divisional Artillery Order No. 20	30/06/1918	30/06/1918
Miscellaneous	Daily Report, 52nd Divisional Artillery	30/06/1918	30/06/1918
Miscellaneous	Daily Report 52nd Divisional Artillery	01/07/1918	01/07/1918
Heading	War Diary Of 52nd Divisional Artillery For July 1918 Vol 4		
Heading	War Diary Of Headquarters 52nd Divisional Artillery From 1st July 1918 To 31st July 1918 Volume-IV Part-VII		
War Diary	Villers Au Bois	01/07/1918	21/07/1918
War Diary	Cuvigny	22/07/1918	31/07/1918
Miscellaneous	Daily Report, 52nd Divisional Artillery	02/07/1918	02/07/1918
Miscellaneous	To All Recipients Of 52nd D.A. Instructions No. 1	01/07/1918	01/07/1918
Miscellaneous	Daily Report 52nd Divisional Artillery	03/07/1918	03/07/1918
Miscellaneous	To All Recipients Of 218/M	02/07/1918	02/07/1918
Operation(al) Order(s)	52nd Divisional Artillery Order No. 21	02/07/1918	02/07/1918
Miscellaneous	Daily Report 52nd Divisional Artillery	04/07/1918	04/07/1918
Miscellaneous	Reference 52nd Division Order No. 113	05/07/1918	05/07/1918
Miscellaneous	Daily Report 52nd Divisional Artillery	07/07/1918	07/07/1918
Miscellaneous	Daily Report 52nd Divisional Artillery	06/07/1918	06/07/1918
Miscellaneous	Daily Report 52nd Divisional Artillery	05/07/1918	05/07/1918

Miscellaneous	Daily Report 52nd Divisional Artillery	08/07/1918	08/07/1918
Miscellaneous	Daily Report 52nd Divisional Artillery	09/07/1918	09/07/1918
Miscellaneous	Daily Report 52nd Divisional Artillery	10/07/1918	10/07/1918
Miscellaneous	52nd Divisional Artillery Defence Scheme		
Miscellaneous	Disposition Statement		
Miscellaneous	Field Artillery S.O.S. Lines		
Miscellaneous	Mutual Support		
Miscellaneous	Brown Line		
Miscellaneous	Green Line		
Miscellaneous	Ecurie Switch		
Miscellaneous	List Of Observation Posts And How Manned		
Miscellaneous	Orders For Anti-Tank Guns		
Miscellaneous	Heavy Artillery Counter Preparation And S.O.S. Points		
Miscellaneous	Yellow Cross Gas Shell Bombardments		
Miscellaneous	Action For Ecurie Switch		
Map	La Targette		
Miscellaneous	Daily Report 52nd Divisional Artillery	11/07/1918	11/07/1918
Miscellaneous	Recipients Of 52nd D.A. Order No. 22	11/07/1918	11/07/1918
Operation(al) Order(s)	52nd Divisional Artillery Order No. 22	11/07/1918	11/07/1918
Miscellaneous	Tasks.		
Miscellaneous	Daily Report 52 Divisional Artillery 6 am 11th to 6 am 12th July 1918	12/07/1918	12/07/1918
Operation(al) Order(s)	52nd Divisional Artillery Order No. 23	12/07/1918	12/07/1918
Miscellaneous	Daily Report 52nd Divisional Artillery	13/07/1918	13/07/1918
Miscellaneous	To All Recipients Of D.A Order No. 22	13/07/1918	13/07/1918
Miscellaneous	Daily Report 52nd Divisional Artillery	14/07/1918	14/07/1918
Operation(al) Order(s)	52nd Divisional Artillery Order No. 24	14/07/1918	14/07/1918
Map	Map To Accompany 52nd Div Arty Order No. 24		
Operation(al) Order(s)	52nd Divisional Artillery Order No. 25	14/07/1918	14/07/1918
Miscellaneous	52nd D.A. No. M/302		
Miscellaneous	Heavy Artillery Counter Preparation And S.O.S. Points		
Miscellaneous	Daily Report 52nd Divisional Artillery	15/07/1918	15/07/1918
Miscellaneous	52nd DA. No. R/306	15/07/1918	15/07/1918
Miscellaneous	52nd D.A. No.M/309	15/07/1918	15/07/1918
Map	Map B		
Miscellaneous	Harassing Fire Boundaries Etc		
Miscellaneous	Daily Report 52nd Divisional Artillery	16/07/1918	16/07/1918
Miscellaneous	Daily Report 52nd Divisional Artillery	17/07/1918	17/07/1918
Miscellaneous	Daily Report 52nd Divisional Artillery	18/07/1918	18/07/1918
Miscellaneous	52nd D.A. No. M/321	17/07/1918	17/07/1918
Miscellaneous	Disposition Statement		
Miscellaneous	Mutual Support		
Miscellaneous	Heavy Artillery Counter Preparation And S.O.S. Points		
Miscellaneous	Daily Report 52nd Divisional Artillery	19/07/1918	19/07/1918
Miscellaneous	9th Brigade R.F.A. 242nd Army Bde R.F.A.	19/07/1918	19/07/1918
Miscellaneous	242nd Brigade	20/07/1918	20/07/1918
Operation(al) Order(s)	52nd Divisional Artillery Order No. 26	20/07/1918	20/07/1918
Miscellaneous	Table 'B' Reliefs		
Miscellaneous	Table 'A' (1)		
Miscellaneous	52nd Divisional Artillery Defence Scheme		
Miscellaneous	Appendix 'B'		
Miscellaneous	List Of Observation Posts And How Manned		
Miscellaneous	Daily Report 52nd Divisional Artillery	20/07/1918	20/07/1918
Operation(al) Order(s)	52nd Divisional Artillery Order No. 27	20/07/1918	20/07/1918
Miscellaneous	Daily Report Right Divisional Artillery, VIII Corps.	21/07/1918	21/07/1918
Operation(al) Order(s)	52nd Divisional Artillery Order No. 28	23/07/1918	23/07/1918

Operation(al) Order(s)	52nd Divisional Artillery Order No. 29		
Miscellaneous	52nd D.A. Relief Order	29/07/1918	29/07/1918
Miscellaneous	Table 'A'		
Miscellaneous	52nd D.A. No, A/398.	31/07/1918	31/07/1918
Heading	HQ R A52D Vol 5 August 18		
Heading	D.A.G G.H.Q. 3rd Echelon		
Heading	War Diary Of 52nd Divisional Artillery. H.Q. From 1st August 1918.To 31st August 1918 Volume-V, Part-VIII		
War Diary	Etrun	01/08/1918	01/08/1918
War Diary	Maroeuil	02/08/1918	16/08/1918
War Diary	Aubigny	17/08/1918	21/08/1918
War Diary	Beaumetz-Les-Loges	22/08/1918	23/08/1918
War Diary	Blairville	24/08/1918	30/08/1918
War Diary	Fontain-Lez-Croisilles	31/08/1918	31/08/1918
Heading	Appendices To War Diary Of 52nd Divisional Artillery H.Q. For August 1918		
Miscellaneous	52nd D.A. No. X/414.	03/08/1918	03/08/1918
Miscellaneous	52nd Divisional Artillery Intelligence Summary 6 am. August 1st to 6 am. August 2nd 1918.	01/08/1918	01/08/1918
Miscellaneous	52nd Divisional Artillery Instructions No. 2	01/08/1918	01/08/1918
Miscellaneous	52nd Divisional Artillery Instructions No. 3	01/08/1918	01/08/1918
Miscellaneous	Left Divisional Artillery (XVII Corps) Intelligence Summary 6 am. 2nd August to 6 am. 3rd August 1918.	03/08/1918	03/08/1918
Miscellaneous	52nd D.A. No.Z/404.	02/08/1918	02/08/1918
Miscellaneous	Left Divisional Artillery (XVII Corps) Intelligence Summary From 6 am. 3rd to 6 am. 4th August 1918.	04/08/1918	04/08/1918
Miscellaneous	(XVII Corps) Left Divisional Artillery Intelligence Summary 6 am. 4th to 6 am. 5th August 1918.	05/08/1918	05/08/1918
Miscellaneous	Left Divisional Artillery (XVII Corps) Intelligence Summary 6 am. 5th to 6 am. 6th August 1918.	06/08/1918	06/08/1918
Miscellaneous	52nd D.A. No, A/423	04/08/1918	04/08/1918
Miscellaneous	52nd D.A.No. Z/427/2	05/08/1918	05/08/1918
Miscellaneous	My G.2/1/22 Of August 4th:-	05/08/1918	05/08/1918
Miscellaneous	52nd D.A.No. A/438.	05/08/1918	05/08/1918
Miscellaneous	52nd D.A.No M/440.	05/08/1918	05/08/1918
Miscellaneous	Left Divisional Artillery (XVII Corps) Intelligence Summary.	07/08/1918	07/08/1918
Miscellaneous	9th Brigade (5) 56th Brigade (5)	06/08/1918	06/08/1918
Miscellaneous	Left Divisional Artillery XVII Corps Intelligence Summary 6 am. 7th to 6 am. 8th August 1918.	08/08/1918	08/08/1918
Miscellaneous	Left Divisional Artillery XVII Corps Intelligence Summary 6 am. 8th to 6 am. August 9th 1918.	09/08/1918	09/08/1918
Miscellaneous	Right Group Centre Group. Left Group.	08/08/1918	08/08/1918
Map	Map		
Miscellaneous	52nd Divisional Artillery Mutual Support	08/08/1918	08/08/1918
Miscellaneous	Reference 52nd Divisional Artillery	08/08/1918	08/08/1918
Miscellaneous	Reference 52nd Division Order No. 119	08/08/1918	08/08/1918
Miscellaneous	Left Divisional Artillery XVII Corps Intelligence Summary 6 am. 9th to 6 am. 10th August 1918.	10/08/1918	10/08/1918
Miscellaneous	Provisional Defence Instructions Left Sector XVII Corps	08/08/1918	08/08/1918
Miscellaneous	Left Divisional Artillery XVII Corps Intelligence Summary 6 am. 10th to 6 am. 11th August 1918.	11/08/1918	11/08/1918
Miscellaneous	Left Divisional Artillery XVII Corps Intelligence Summary 6 am. 11th to 6 am. 12th August 1918.	12/08/1918	12/08/1918

Miscellaneous	Left Divisional Artillery XVII Corps Intelligence Summary 6 am. 12th to 6 am. 13th August 1918.	13/08/1918	13/08/1918
Miscellaneous	Left Divisional Artillery XVII Corps Intelligence Summary 6 am. 13th to 6 am. 14th August 1918.	14/08/1918	14/08/1918
Operation(al) Order(s)	52nd Divisional Artillery Order No. 30	13/08/1918	13/08/1918
Miscellaneous	Table "A" Issued With 52nd D.A Order No. 30		
Miscellaneous	Left Divisional Artillery XVII Corps Intelligence Summary 6 am. 14th to 6 am. 15th August 1918.	15/08/1918	15/08/1918
Operation(al) Order(s)	52nd Divisional Artillery Operation Order No. 31	14/08/1918	14/08/1918
Operation(al) Order(s)	52nd Divisional Artillery Order Number 32	14/08/1918	14/08/1918
Miscellaneous	Centre Group 52nd Divisional Artillery	15/08/1918	15/08/1918
Miscellaneous	52nd. D.A.C	15/08/1918	15/08/1918
Operation(al) Order(s)	52nd Divisional Artillery Order No. 33	16/08/1918	16/08/1918
Operation(al) Order(s)	52nd Divisional Artillery Operation Order No. 34	21/08/1918	21/08/1918
Miscellaneous	Amendment To Operation Order No. 34	21/08/1918	21/08/1918
Operation(al) Order(s)	52nd Divisional Artillery Order No 33	31/08/1918	31/08/1918
Heading	War Diary Of Headquarters Royal Artillery 52nd Division From 1st September 1918 To 30th September 1918 Volume., V. Part-IX.		
War Diary	Fontaine Les Croissiles	01/09/1918	03/09/1918
War Diary	Pronville	04/09/1918	10/09/1918
War Diary	Croissilles	11/09/1918	16/09/1918
War Diary	Queant	17/09/1918	27/09/1918
War Diary	Moeuvres	28/09/1918	28/09/1918
War Diary	Cantaing	29/09/1918	30/09/1918
Heading	Appendices To War Diary Of Headquarters Royal Artillery 52nd Division For September 1918.		
Operation(al) Order(s)	57th Divisional Artillery Operation Order No. 30	01/09/1918	01/09/1918
Operation(al) Order(s)	57th Division Order No. 119	01/09/1918	01/09/1918
Operation(al) Order(s)	57th Divisional Artillery Operation Order No. 31		
Operation(al) Order(s)	52nd Divisional Artillery Order No. 35	17/09/1918	17/09/1918
Miscellaneous	52nd Divisional Artillery Intelligence Summary 6.0 am 17th to 6.0 am 18th Sept. 1918	18/09/1918	18/09/1918
Miscellaneous	52nd Divisional Artillery Intelligence Summary 6.0 am Sept 18th to 6.0 am Sept 19th Sept 18	19/09/1918	19/09/1918
Miscellaneous	52nd Divisional Artillery Intelligence Summary 6.0 am 19th Sept to 6.0 am 20th Sept	20/09/1918	20/09/1918
Miscellaneous	Right Group Left Group	19/09/1918	19/09/1918
Operation(al) Order(s)	52nd Divisional Artillery Order No. 36	19/09/1918	19/09/1918
Miscellaneous	Table To Accompany 52nd Divisional Artillery Order No. 36		
Miscellaneous	52nd Divisional Artillery Intelligence Summary 6 a.m. 20th Sept to 6 am 21st Sept. 1918	21/09/1918	21/09/1918
Miscellaneous	52nd Divisional Artillery Intelligence Summary Of Intelligence 6 a.m. 21st Sept to 6 a.m. 22nd Sept 1918	22/09/1918	22/09/1918
Operation(al) Order(s)	52nd Divisional Artillery Order No. 37	21/09/1918	21/09/1918
Miscellaneous	52nd Divisional Artillery Intelligence Summary 6 am Sept. 22nd to 6 am Sept 23rd 1918.	23/09/1918	23/09/1918
Miscellaneous	52nd Divisional Artillery Intelligence Summary 6 am 23rd Sept to 6 am 24th Sept 1918.	24/09/1918	24/09/1918
Miscellaneous	52nd Divisional Artillery Intelligence Summary 6 am Sept. 25th to 6 am 26th Sept1918.	26/09/1918	26/09/1918
Operation(al) Order(s)	52nd Divisional Artillery Order No. 38	25/09/1918	25/09/1918
Miscellaneous	Advance Table		
Operation(al) Order(s)	57th Divisional Artillery Operation Order No. 39	30/09/1918	30/09/1918

Heading	War Diary Of 52nd Divisional Artillery Headquarters Volume-V Part-X From-1st October 1918 To-31st October 1918		
War Diary	Cantaing	01/10/1918	08/10/1918
War Diary	Awoingt	09/10/1918	09/10/1918
War Diary	Cagnoncles	10/10/1918	10/10/1918
War Diary	Avesnes Les Aubert	11/10/1918	11/10/1918
War Diary	St. Aubert	12/10/1918	20/10/1918
War Diary	Mont St Eloi	21/10/1918	24/10/1918
War Diary	Blanche Maison	25/10/1918	26/10/1918
War Diary	Frais Marais	27/10/1918	31/10/1918
Heading	Appendices To War Diary Of 52nd Divisional Artillery Headquarters October 1918.		
Operation(al) Order(s)	52nd Divisional Artillery Order No. 40	03/10/1918	03/10/1918
Miscellaneous	9th Brigade Group Tasks		
Operation(al) Order(s)	52nd Divisional Artillery Order No. 41	07/10/1918	07/10/1918
Miscellaneous	Addendum No 1 52nd Divisional Artillery Order No. 42	15/10/1918	15/10/1918
Miscellaneous	Amendment No 1 To 52nd Divisional Artillery Order No 42	15/10/1918	15/10/1918
Operation(al) Order(s)	52nd Divisional Artillery Order No. 42	15/10/1918	15/10/1918
Operation(al) Order(s)	52nd Divisional Artillery Order No. 43	17/10/1918	17/10/1918
Operation(al) Order(s)	52nd Divisional Artillery Order No. 44	18/10/1918	18/10/1918
Operation(al) Order(s)	52nd Divisional Artillery Order No. 45.	23/10/1918	23/10/1918
Miscellaneous	Administrative Instructions No. 13	19/10/1918	19/10/1918
Operation(al) Order(s)	52nd Divisional Artillery Order No. 46	25/10/1918	25/10/1918
Operation(al) Order(s)	52nd Divisional Artillery Order No. 47	31/10/1918	31/10/1918
Miscellaneous	March Table		
Heading	War Diary Of 52nd D.A. H.Q. From 1st November 1918 To 30th November 1918 Vol: V. Part XI		
War Diary	Frais Marais	01/11/1918	02/11/1918
War Diary	Sameon	03/11/1918	08/11/1918
War Diary	Mont De Perulwelz	09/11/1918	09/11/1918
War Diary	Sirault	10/11/1918	17/11/1918
War Diary	Ghlin	19/11/1918	19/11/1918
War Diary	Casteau	25/11/1918	30/11/1918
Heading	Appendices To War Diary Of 52nd D.A., H.Q. For November 1918		
Miscellaneous	Amendment No.1 To 52nd Divisional Artillery Order No. 49	03/11/1918	03/11/1918
Operation(al) Order(s)	52nd Divisional Artillery Order No. 49	03/11/1918	03/11/1918
Operation(al) Order(s)	52nd Divisional Artillery Order No. 48	03/11/1918	03/11/1918
Operation(al) Order(s)	52nd Divisional Artillery Order No. 50	04/11/1918	04/11/1918
Miscellaneous	52nd Divisional Artillery Daily Report	05/11/1918	05/11/1918
Operation(al) Order(s)	52nd Divisional Artillery Order No. 51	05/11/1918	05/11/1918
Miscellaneous	Daily Report-52nd Divisional Artillery	05/11/1918	05/11/1918
Miscellaneous	Daily Report-52nd Divisional Artillery	06/11/1918	06/11/1918
Operation(al) Order(s)	52nd Divisional Artillery Order No. 52	07/11/1918	07/11/1918
Miscellaneous	Table Of Tasks		
Miscellaneous	Daily Report-52nd Divisional Artillery	07/11/1918	07/11/1918
Operation(al) Order(s)	52nd Divisional Artillery Order No. 53.	11/11/1918	11/11/1918
Heading	War Diary Of Headquarters Royal Artillery 52nd Division From 1st December 1918 To 31st December 1918 Part XII. Vol VI		
War Diary	Casteau	01/12/1918	11/12/1918
War Diary	Thieusies	12/12/1918	31/12/1918

Heading	War Diary Of Headquarters Royal Artillery 52nd Division From 1st January 1919 Ro 31st January 1919 Part I Vol VI		
War Diary	Thieusies	01/01/1919	31/01/1919
Heading	War Diary Of Headquarters Royal Artillery 52nd Division From February 1st 1919 To February 28th 1919 Part II Vol VI		
War Diary	Thieusies	01/02/1919	28/02/1919
Heading	War Diary Of Headquarters R.A., 52nd (Lowland) Division From 1st March To 31st March 1919 Vol 5-Part 3.		
War Diary	Thieusies	01/03/1919	21/03/1919
War Diary	Soignies	22/03/1919	31/03/1919
Heading	War Diary Of Headquarters 52nd (Lowland) Divisional Artillery From 1st April 1919 To 30th April 1919 Vol 13		
War Diary	Soignies	01/04/1919	30/04/1919
Heading	War Diary Of Headquarters Royal Artillery 52nd (Lowland) Division From May 1st 1919 To May 31st 1919 Part V Vol VI		
War Diary	Soignies	01/05/1919	31/05/1919

WO/95/2690/2

Commando Leger Afdeling

52ND DIVISION
—————————C. R. A.

APR 1918-MAY 1919

52nd Divisional Artillery.

Arrived MARSEILLES from EGYPT 12.4.18.

C. R. A.

52nd (Lowland) DIVISION

APRIL 1918.

Army Form C. 2118.

WAR DIARY
OR
INTELLIGENCE SUMMARY.
(Erase heading not required.)

Instructions regarding War Diaries and Intelligence Summaries are contained in F. S. Regs., Part II, and the Staff Manual, respectively. Title pages will be prepared in manuscript.

Hour, Date, Place.		Summary of Events and Information.	Remarks and references to Appendices.
MOASCAR April 1st		Reorganisation continued	
	2nd	entrained Moascar R.	
ALEXANDRIA	3rd	embarked as follows:–	
		H.M.T. MANITOU – 149 R.A. 35th Bde, NRC 100 1 Sectn	
		H.M.T. KINGSTONIAN. 9th Bde, 133 & 134 T.M.B'ies 35th Bde D.A.C.	
	4th	sailed from port	
AT SEA	5th		
	6th		
	10th	} nil	
	11th		
		H.M.T. KINGSTONIAN torpedoed – casualties 2 Kilned,	
		4 drowned. all transferred to H.M.T. Gala	
MARSEILLES	12th	82nd Bde Bt'y arrived.	
	13th	149 R.A. 105th Bde entrained, DAC entrained in 2 cars	
		train, while 133 & 134 TM B'ies	
	14th	9th F.A.Bde entrained.	
SARLY-PINSAUCOURT 16th		35th Bde arrived NOYELLES & sent out parties on	
		Army Pat School	
		DAC detrained.	
	17th	DAC. 6 points at PONT-LE-GRAND	
		9th Bde. arrived MORBANNE train 6 billets at	
		Pont de GRAND LANGER	

Army Form C. 2118.

WAR DIARY
OR
INTELLIGENCE SUMMARY.

(Erase heading not required.)

Instructions regarding War Diaries and Intelligence Summaries are contained in F. S. Regs., Part II, and the Staff Manual, respectively. Title pages will be prepared in manuscript.

Hour, Date, Place.	Summary of Events and Information.	Remarks and references to Appendices.
SAILLY-FLIBEAUCOURT, 18"	military duties	
19"	" "	
20"	" "	
21"	" "	
22"	" "	
23"	" " ordered to be ready to move 28"	
24"	" " " " "	
25"	" " " " " 27"	
26"	" M.T.M. Bgs went to T.M. School VALHEUREUX	
27"	Bde marched to FROHEN area	
28"	" " " WILLEMAN	
29"	" " CRÉQUY — ordered remain till	
30"	further orders	
	NIL	

FROHEN.
WILLEMAN.
CRÉQUY.

Watson Lt Col
for GSO 2nd Army

Lal Chand & Sons, Calcutta—No. 20 Army C.—15-9-15—21,500 Bks

S E C R E T.   52nd Divisional Artillery   Copy No. 6
                Order No.3.

Reference 250,000 map France, sheet III.   28th April, 1918.
----

1.   The Divisional Artillery will march to the CREQUY Area in square K1 tomorrow.

2.   Units will billet in area as below :-

      Headquarters R.A.   -   COUPELLE VIEILLE.
      56th Brigade R.F.A.   -   - do -
         Accommodation - Officers 36, Other Ranks 979.
      56th Brigade R.F.A. will please arrange Headquarters billet.
      Divisional Ammn. Column.   -   EMBRY.
         Accommodation - Officers 27, Other Ranks 974.
      9th Brigade R.F.A.   -   CREQUY.
         Accommodation - Officers 40, Other Ranks 1000.

3.   Billeting Lorry will leave 9th Brigade R.F.A. at 9.30 a.m. tomorrow 29th instant, pick up the 56th Brigade R.F.A. party at OEUF and then D.A.C. party at WILLEMAN.
      It will then proceed direct to new billeting area and parties will carry on in communication with the Maires concerned.
      Billeting certificates will be given to the Maires direct.
      Lorry will remain with 9th Brigade R.F.A. tomorrow night.

4.   Routes will be as under :-

      56th Brigade R.F.A. start 10.0 a.m. from OEUF and proceed via BEAUVOIR - BLANGY - RUISSEAUVILLE to COUPELLE NEUVE.

      9th Brigade R.F.A. start 10.0 a.m. from LINZEUX and proceed via WILLEMAN - VIEIL HESDIN - GRIGNY - AUCHY - FRESSIN to CREQUY.

      Headquarters R.A. start 10.0 a.m. from WILLEMAN and proceed via NOYELLE - BLANGY and thence same route as 56th Brigade R.F.A.

      D.A.C. start 9.45 a.m. from WILLEMAN and FRESNOY and march via VIEIL HESDIN - HESDIN - LA LOGE - LE BIEZ to EMBRY.

5.   There are no latrine arrangements except some at CREQUY. Units must make their own.

6.   Water for horses from adjacent streams.

7.   Ration and baggage wagons will accompany units under their own arrangements.

8.   Units will arrange their own halts.

9.   This office will close at the Chateau WILLEMAN at 8.0 a.m. and reopen at COUPELLE VIEILLE on arrival.

10.   Acknowledge.

                                                    Captain R.A.
                                     Brigade Major R.A., 52nd Division.
C.C.
      Issued at 4.30 p.m.
      Copy No. 1 to 9th F.A. Bde.
             2   56th   "
             3   D.A.C.
             4   Area Comdt., Wail.
             5   S.C.
           6-7   Records.

SECRET.   59nd Divisional Artillery.   Copy No...7.
                              Order No.5.

Reference 250,000 map France, Sheet III   27th April, 1918.

1.   The Divisional Artillery will march to WILLEMAN Area at
the Southern edge of square 12 tomorrow.

2.   Billets will be as below :-
        Headquarters R.A.   -   Chateau WILLEMAN.
        9th Brigade R.F.A.   -   LINZEUX, accommodation Officers
                                        21, Other ranks 1200.
        56th Brigade R.F.A.   -   OEUF, accommodation Officers
                                        37, Other Ranks 2000.
        Divisional Amm. Column -   WILLEMAN (less Chateau),
                                        Accommodation Officers 15, Other
                                        Ranks 800, and FRESNOY, accom-
                                        modation Officers 8, Other R.400.

        Billeting Lorry will start from 9th Brigade R.F.A. at 9.30
a.m., pick up remaining billeting parties and proceed to new area.
        Units will carry on their billeting arrangements without
further orders in direct communication with the MAIRES concerned.
        Lorry will remain with 9th Brigade R.F.A. tomorrow night.

3.   Routes will be as follows :-
        56th Brigade R.F.A. start 10.0 a.m. and march via WAVANS -
NOEUX - EUDRE - HARAVESNES - FILLIEVRES to OEUF.

        Divisional Ammunition Column start 10.0 a.m. and march via
BEAUVOIR - AUXI LE CHATEAU - QUOEUX - HAUT MAISNIL - road junction
S.E.GALAMETZ - WAIL to WILLEMAN.

        9th Brigade R.F.A. start 10.0 a.m. from BEALCOURT and follow
same route as 56th Brigade R.F.A. to LINZEUX.

4.   Units will arrange to hand in their own billeting certifi-
cates direct to the Maires concerned through their Interpreters.

5.   Water reported as good for men and horses.

6.   Units will arrange their own halts as they desire.

7.   Ration and baggage wagons will accompany Units under their
own arrangements.

8.   Headquarters R.A. will accompany 56th Brigade R.F.A. as
far as FILLIEVRES and thence direct to WILLEMAN.

9.   This office will close here at 9.0 a.m. tomorrow morning
and reopen at the Chateau at WILLEMAN on arrival.

10.   Acknowledge.

                                                Captain R.A.
                                        XXXXXXXXXXXXXX B.... R.A., 59nd.Divn.

Issued at 6.0 p.m.
Copy No.1 to 9th Brigade R.F.A.
     "   2   56th   "
     "   3   D.A.C.
     "   4   Area Comdt., Wail. FROHEN
     "   5   S.C.
     "   6-7   Records.

C.C.

SECRET.　　　　　62nd. DIVISIONAL ARTILLERY.　　　Copy No. 5

ORDER No. 1.

Reference 250,000 map of FRANCE, sheet III.　　　26th April, 1918

1. The Divisional Artillery will march to FROHEN Area tomorrow XX 27th instant.

2. Units will march independently by routes as under. Headquarters R.A. will march with 56th Brigade R.F.A.

3. 56th Brigade R.F.A. start 9.0 a.m. and march via LE TITRE - DOMVAST - BRAILLY - GUESCHART - NEUILLY LE DIEU - AUXI LE CHATEAU to FROHEN LE GRAND.

4. Divisional Ammunition Column start 9.0 a.m. and march via BUIGNY - NEUILLY L'HOPITAL - AGENVILLERS - YVRENCH - HIERMONT - MAIZICOURT to FROHEN LE PETIT.

5. 9th Brigade R.F.A. start 9.45 a.m. and march via BUIGNY - MILLENCOURT - ST.RIQUIER - BEAUMETZ - LE MEILLARD to FROHEN LE PETIT.

6. Billeting parties with Interpreters will report to Staff Captain at cross roads opposite church at FROHEN LE GRAND by 2.0 p.m.

7. March discipline is to be strictly supervised and care taken that during halts bridges, cross roads, etc., are not blocked.

8. Administrative Orders re transport, rations and maps will issue later.

9. Units will make their own arrangements re halts, watering and feeding.

10. Acknowledge.

11. This Office will close at 7.30 a.m. 27th instant at BAILLY LE SEC and reopen at FROHEN LE GRAND on arrival.

　　　　　　　　　　　　　　　　　　　　　　Captain R.A.
C.C.　　　　　　　Brigade Major R.A., 62nd Division.

Issued to D.R. at 12.15 p.m.

Copy No. 1　to 9th Bde. R.F.A.
　　　　2　　　56th　　"
　　　　3　　　D.A.C.
　　　　4　　　S.C.
　　　　5-6. Records.

Vol 2

Confidential

War Diary
52nd D.A.
of
Vol. IX
Pt. VI

From
1st May 1918
To
31st May 1918

Army Form C. 2118.

WAR DIARY
or
INTELLIGENCE SUMMARY.
(Erase heading not required.)

MAY 1918.

Instructions regarding War Diaries and Intelligence Summaries are contained in F.S. Regs., Part II. and the Staff Manual respectively. Title pages will be prepared in manuscript.

Place	Date	Hour	Summary of Events and Information	Remarks and references to Appendices
CREQUY.	1/5/.		Warning Order to move to XVlll Corps.	S/A
	2/5/.		Warning Order cancelled.	S/A
	3/5/.		D.A.C. moved from EMBRY to CREQUY.	S/A
	4/5/.		52nd Division less R.A. to relieve 4th Canadian Division and join XVlll Corps. Party of Officers and men sent to 51st D.A. to study conditions. Orders received for R.A. Staff, less Staff Captain, to relieve Headquarters 5th Canadian D.A.	S/A
AUX RIETZ.	5/5/.		Headquarters Royal Artillery arrived. 2/Lt. CROFT joined from 24th D.A.C. as acting Staff Captain.	S/A
	6/5/.		Assumed Command of 65th and 242nd Army Artillery Brigades, supporting the 11th Canadian Infantry Brigade under the 15th Div'l Artillery.	S/A
CHATEAU D'ACQ.	7/5/.		Moved to CHATEAU D'ACQ and joined 52nd Division who assumed Command of 157th Infantry Bde Line.	S/A
	7/8/5. night.		157th Infantry Brigade relieved 11th Canadian Infantry Bde.	S/A
	8th.		155th Infantry Bde relieved 153rd Infantry Bde.	S/A
	9/5/.		52nd Army Artillery Brigade came under orders of 52nd Div'l Artillery.	S/A
	10/5/.		Brig:General E.HARDING NEWMAN C.M.G., D.S.O. and R.A. Staff 14th Division took over Command of the Artillery supporting 52nd Division. C.R.A. and Staff 52nd Division remaining under instruction.	S/A

Army Form C. 2118.

WAR DIARY
or
INTELLIGENCE SUMMARY.

(Erase heading not required.)

MAY 1918.

Place	Date	Hour	Summary of Events and Information	Remarks and references to Appendices
VILLERS AU BOIS.	11th.		Our front line and supports in B.4,10 and 16 were bombarded from 8.50pm.to 10.40pm. The fire which was heaviest at 9.45pm.appeared to come chiefly from the FRESNOY GROUP. T.Ms also reported to have taken part. Probably all calibres up to 21cm were used. The remainder of the night was very quiet. During the day we engaged and dispersed small parties at U.19.b.2.0, C.2.b.1.7 and T.18.d.7.4 and checked several registrations. Harassing fire was carried out during the night according to programme. Our planes were active in the afternoon when the visibility had improved. For Daily Report vide Ap. I.	Ap. I.
do.	12th.		Hostile artillery quieter than during the previous 24 hours,and activity chiefly confined to the evening. 80 rounds of PHOSGENE Gas were fired into B.7.c. between 7.15pm.and 8.pm. and 300 rounds 15cm into A.12.a.,B.7.d.&.c. between 7.30pm.and 10.45pm. A 21cm How.was reported firing as late as 11.30pm.which is unusual on this front. During the day movement was again engaged at U.19.b.,and U.20.d.9.5 - U.26.b.9.5. At night a programme of harassing fire on selected targets including the active hostile battery DW.40 was carried out as usual. For Daily Report vide Orders regarding the re-grouping of the Field Artillery covering the 52nd.Division sent out See B.M.247. vide Ap. III	Ap. II. Ap. III.

Army Form C. 2118.

WAR DIARY
or
INTELLIGENCE SUMMARY.
(Erase heading not required.)

MAY 1918.

Instructions regarding War Diaries and Intelligence Summaries are contained in F.S. Regs., Part II. and the Staff Manual respectively. Title pages will be prepared in manuscript.

Place	Date	Hour	Summary of Events and Information	Remarks and references to Appendices
VILLERS AU BOIS.	13th		Hostile fire considerably less than on the 12th, probably on account of the high wind and rain and consisted chiefly of small area shoots at a slow rate of fire. B.8. continues to receive an undue share of attention, 185 rds being fired into it during the period under review. No gas reported. Evening and night very quiet. During the day movement in U.20.b. was engaged by 18-pounders; otherwise our fire was NIL. During the evening and night we carried out harassing fire as usual. Targets engaged included the hostile battery U.V.20 at U.20.b.90.50 which was intermittently engaged with 18-pdr.H.E. For Daily Report vide	Appx IV.
	14th		Hostile Artillery much quieter to-day than yesterday. Two cases of probable registration and two probably three cases of H.V. guns reported. No area or destructive shoots. At 9.15 p.m. a large calibre H.V. gun fired 1 rd. possibly meant for Division H.Q. which fell at W.30.central. Between 7 p.m. and dawn some 1,000 rds of gas shell were fired into T.19.,T.20 and T.25 - nature not known. Visibility was very good, so our forward guns were able to carry out a fair amount of sniping. Small parties at U.27.a.65.73 and in U.19.b. & d.,S.2.,& C.8. were engaged and dispersed - several hits claimed. During the night we carried out harassing fire on selected targets. Our aeroplanes were very active all day. They were heavily engaged by A.A. and M.G. even when well on our side of the line.	

Army Form C. 2118.

MAY 1918.

WAR DIARY
or
INTELLIGENCE SUMMARY.

(Erase heading not required.)

Instructions regarding War Diaries and Intelligence Summaries are contained in F. S. Regs., Part II. and the Staff Manual respectively. Title pages will be prepared in manuscript.

Place	Date	Hour	Summary of Events and Information	Remarks and references to Appendices
VILLERS AU BOIS.	15th		Considerable movement was observed during the day.	
			For Daily Report vide	Appx IV
			For purposes of co-ordination with H.A. and D.A's on either flank, zones for harassing fire have been allotted, see 52nd D.A. No.BM.252, vide	Appx IV
			Enemy activity slightly more active. This was chiefly confined to what is believed to have been counter battery shoots on A.12.a.17 and A.18. About 100 rds 77mm and 4.2 Hows were fired in an area shoot on S.30.b.& c.	
			During the day 100 rds 15 cm were fired into T.19.c. & d. and from 4.20 - 5 p.m. 100rds 77mm and 10.5cm at our trenches in B.9.b. and B.10.a. Three cases of H.V.G. reported, but no registrations. Night quiet.	
			During the day one 18-pounders engaged roads and tracks in U.3.c. and U.19.b. and road at T.18.d.85.65.	
			Several N.F. Calls were received but all out of range.	
			During the night harassing fire was carried out on roads and tracks in T.6., T.12 & U.26 and on other selected targets. Our 'planes were active all day.	
			For Daily Report vide.	
			Another scheme for harassing fire sent out to-day - see 52nd D.A. No.BM.269	Appx IV

P.T.O.

Army Form C. 2118.

WAR DIARY
or
INTELLIGENCE SUMMARY.
(Erase heading not required.)

MAY 1918.

Place	Date	Hour	Summary of Events and Information	Remarks and references to Appendices
VILLERS AU BOIS	15th		Orders issued with regard to a "Gas Beam" attack to be carried out on the XVIIIth Corps front from T.29.b. to N.25.b. on the night of May 16th/17th or the first night after upon which the wind is favourable. See 52nd D.A. No.B.M. 232	Appx VIII
	16th		The forward gun of A/52 was engaged by the enemy at 7, 8 and 11 a.m. and noon to 2.15pm and short bursts 2.15pm - 4 p.m. About 350 rds 10.5cm and 15cm Hows were fired.	Appx IX
			At 7 a.m. an E.A. seems to have been ranging the 2 10.5cm Hows. which were accurate for a short time, but then distributed their fire. No damage was done.	
			During the night the enemy fired about 300 rds on the N.& W. outskirts of VIMY and after midnight directed harassing fire between THELUS and FARBUS.	
			A working party at T.5.c.55.73 was engaged and 2 hits observed. Movement was also fired on at U.19.d.9.5., U.25.a.20.10, B.6.c.25.90 and in U.21.c. Harassing fire was carried out on roads, tracks and centres of activity by day and by night. For Daily Report vide 52nd D.A. location statement vide	
			9th and 56th Brigades RFA, 52nd Div. moved to VILLERS AU BOIS area. 52nd D.A.C. less S.A.A. Section moved to ESTREE CAUCHIE	
	17th		The enemy Artillery were less active than usual. The night was exceptionally quiet. Our Artillery engaged movement at U.25.a.20.10 U.20.a.30.05. Harassing fire was	

P.T.O.

Army Form C. 2118.

WAR DIARY
or
INTELLIGENCE SUMMARY.
(Erase heading not required.)

MAY 1918.

Place	Date	Hour	Summary of Events and Information	Remarks and references to Appendices
VILLERS AU BOIS.	17th		directed on roads, tracks and centres of activity by day and night.	SMS
			Left Group fired in response to a Test S.O.S. at 2.29am.	SMS
			Our 'Planes very active all day, particularly between 6pm and 8pm. Hostile A.A. very active. For Daily Report vide	APP X
	18th		Orders regarding S.O.S. barrage lines on 52nd Div. front sent out - see 52nd DA.No.BM.307 [handwritten] vide APP XII [handwritten] APP XB
			Enemy Artillery resumed its normal activity after a quiet day yesterday. VIMY was shelled considerably. The tank in VIMY Station appears to be used as a datum point.	
			THELUS was shelled during the night.	
			Movement was engaged by our Artillery in U.19.a.,U.20.a. and U.25.a. During the night harassing fire was directed on Roads and tracks in T.6.,T.30.,U.7.,13.,25., & B.6.	SMS
			Hostile Battery positions U.14.d.20.10.,U.14.d.30.70.,U.16.d.15.30. & O.25.d.6.O. were harassed by 18-pdrs during the night.	Appx II Sub APPXT-H
			10.5pm. Test S.O.S. Call received and answered. For Daily Report vide	
			Enemy is suspected to be using a 60-pdr.	
			Mutual Support scheme for 52nd D.A. sent out - see 52nd D.A.No.B.M.319 vide	
	19th		Hostile activity. Artillery was active during the morning on VIMY and on the LONE TREE (T.27.c.O.8.) Fairly quiet throughout the afternoon and night. The Artillery positions at THELUS were molested throughout the day.	

P.T.O.

Army Form C. 2118.

WAR DIARY
OR
INTELLIGENCE SUMMARY.

(Erase heading not required.)

Instructions regarding War Diaries and Intelligence Summaries are contained in F. S. Regs., Part II, and the Staff Manual, respectively. Title pages will be prepared in manuscript.

MAY 1918.

Hour, Date, Place.	Summary of Events and Information.	Remarks and references to Appendices.
VILLERS AU BOIS 19th	M.@ By day 18-pdrs fired on H.Q. and occupied area T.5.b.& c. on M.G.emplacements T.4.b., on T.M. and dugouts T.5.d. and on tracks in T.13.d. During the night 18-pdrs harassed hostile batteries U.8.c,8.5. and U.9.b.5.2., which had been engaged by heavy Artillery during the day. Harassing fire was also directed on B.5.c.55.95 and on tracks an/centres of activity in N.34.d.,U.7.,15,19, T.24. & B.6. For Daily Report vide	Apdx ﬁ: Sh. Sh
20th	General activity of hostile Artillery less than yesterday and chiefly confined to the morning. VIMY and vicinity received a large share of the shelling. The R.G.A. Batteries in A.12 were again shelled with what is believed to be 60-pdrs. No Gas reported. During the day 18-pdrs fired 100 rds on tracks, T.5.b. T.5.d., T.12.a. and engaged movement in U.15.c. Many N.F.Calls were received but all were out of range. P.T.O.	

Army Form C. 2118.

WAR DIARY
OR
INTELLIGENCE SUMMARY.

(*Erase heading not required.*)

MAY 1918.

Instructions regarding War Diaries and Intelligence Summaries are contained in F. S. Regs., Part II. and the Staff Manual, respectively. Title pages will be prepared in manuscript.

Hour, Date, Place.	Summary of Events and Information.	Remarks and references to Appendices.
VILLERS AU BOIS.	**20th.** Hostile Battery U.26.c.45.15. was engaged in the night and also tracks and roads in U.13., 7.b. T.6. ARLEUX and approaches by 18-pdrs. 4.5"Hows engaged Trench junctions and selected points U.13. & U.7. ARLEUX and approaches. At 8.55 pm 18-pdrs and 4.5"Hows engaged Hostile battery U.Y.57 in response to Zone Call. 52nd D.A. No.BM.371 sent out to all recipients of 52nd D.A. No.B.M.282 vide Daily Report show	app XIII app XIII-A S/S
	21st Hostile Artillery still quiet. 100rds 15cm were fired at the dug-outs at B.8.a.2.2. Where much movement has taken place of late. No other large shots were reported. A 77mm Battery appeared to register B.2.a.9.7. where the trench goes under the road and Railway. The foot of VIMY Ridge in B.2. & B.2.b. was registered at 7 pm by 77mm Batteries. At 12.45 a.m. 12 rds Blue Cross Gas shell were fired into S.30.d. Night otherwise very quiet. During the day our 18-pdrs engaged movement in U.20.c.& U.13.d Bm 378 round cancelled B.M.p.3.T.O. B.M. i vide	S/S app XIII-B

Army Form C. 2118.

WAR DIARY
OR
INTELLIGENCE SUMMARY.   MAY 1918.

(Erase heading not required.)

Instructions regarding War Diaries and Intelligence Summaries are contained in F. S. Regs., Part II, and the Staff Manual, respectively. Title pages will be prepared in manuscript.

Hour, Date, Place.	Summary of Events and Information.	Remarks and references to Appendices.
VILLERS AU BOIS. 21st	and selected targets. Hostile Battery U.W.58 U.8.d.45.25 engaged at 5.35 p.m. in answer to Zone Call. Many N.F.Calls received during the day but only the above within range. During the night harassing fire was carried out on hostile battery U.W.95,(U.15.c.45.20) and on roads and tracks. For Daily Report vide Operation Order No.8 sent out with orders for the relief of the 65th Army Brigade by the 56th Brigade RFA (52nd Div.) on nights 22nd/23rd and 23rd/24th, vide	AppxIV S/18 AppxIV S/18
22nd	Hostile Artillery has been more active again during the last 24 hours. Three heavy shoots have been reported. 6am-9am About 200rds 15cm were fired into S.24.d. 5.45am-11.45am 550rds chiefly 10.5cm and a few 15cm fell in T.19.a. This was no doubt intended to catch our forward guns. 2am-3.30am (23rd) 300rds 10.5cm H.E. and Gas fired into A.6.c. VIMY was intermittently shelled with 10.5cm and ROCLINCOURT	S/18

P.T.O.

Army Form C. 2118.

WAR DIARY
OR
INTELLIGENCE SUMMARY.

(Erase heading not required.)

MAY 1918.

Instructions regarding War Diaries and Intelligence Summaries are contained in F. S. Regs., Part II, and the Staff Manual, respectively. Title pages will be prepared in manuscript.

Hour, Date, Place.	Summary of Events and Information.	Remarks and references to Appendices.
VILLERS AU BOIS 22nd	by H.V.G. during the day. An H.V.G. fired some 200rds into our back areas during the night - exact locality not known. In the course of the day our 18-pdrs engaged movement at special points. During the night harassing fire was carried out by 18-pdrs and 4.5"Hows. on roads, tracks, trenches and railways. For Daily Report vide	S F/A
23rd	A quiet day. Hostile Artillery attempted a destructive shoot on 146th H.B. and also included 122nd Bty's forward gun in an area harassing shoot. The gun was put temporarily out of action. At 8 p.m. a working party at U.20.b.6.2. was fired on by our Artillery. During the night harassing fire was brought to bear on roads, tracks and T.M's. For Daily Report vide. A list of areas for concentrated bombardments by heavy and Field Artillery with instructions, sent out. See BM418 vide. 52nd D.A.C. less S.A.A.Section moved to VILLERS AU BOIS.	appx IV S F/A S F/A appx V S F/A appx VI S F/A
24th	Hostile Artillery activity was above normal. 10.5cm,15cm & 21cm P. T. O.	

Army Form C. 2118.

WAR DIARY
OR
INTELLIGENCE SUMMARY.
(Erase heading not required.)

MAY 1918.

Instructions regarding War Diaries and Intelligence Summaries are contained in F. S. Regs., Part II, and the Staff Manual, respectively. Title page will be prepared in manuscript.

Hour, Date, Place.		Summary of Events and Information.	Remarks and references to Appendices.
VILLERS AU BOIS.	24th.	Hows. and 10cm Guns were very active on THELUS area to the N.E. during the day. FARBUS WOOD was also shelled considerably in the course of the afternoon. Our 18-pdrs engaged movement during the day at various points. Harassing fire was carried out on tracks, roads, Railways, trenches and O.T's in T.6.,T.24.,T.30.,U.7.,U.13.,U.19., U.26.b.,O.1.a,O.3.o., B.6.a.	
		10.8pm Right Group fired in response to a Test S.O.S. sent at 10.5pm.	
		Considerable individual movement during the day was observed round ROUVROY Trench,U.20.b.,U.11.a., and U.25.a. For Daily Report vide	Appx XVIII S/A
		Orders regarding 9th Brigade moving up into positions now in preparation on night 25th/26th, issued. See O.O. No.9 vide.	Appx XIV S/A
		Amendment to above order sent out altering 25/26 to 27/28, vide O.O. No.10 issued.28th Bty.RFA to go into action on night 25th/26th for special operation vide.	Appx XV S/A
	25th	Enemy activity greater than on the 24th. Four enemy batteries	Appx XVI S/A

P.T.O.

Army Form C. 2118.

WAR DIARY
OR
INTELLIGENCE SUMMARY.

(Erase heading not required.)

Week MAY 1918

Hour, Date, Place.	Summary of Events and Information.	Remarks and references to Appendices.
VILLERS AU BOIS 25th	carried out an area harassing shoot on THELUS and vicinity, A.18.b. B.7.& B.13. between 9am and 11.30am. Probably 1,000rds were put over. 200 15cm were fired into THELUS and A.6.c.& d. The shelling appeared to come from the ROUVROY and BOIS BERNARD Groups. From 1.30pm to 7.30pm some 250 rds of 10.5cm were fired into T.20.& T.26.	S/A
	4pm to 6pm 200rds 77mm (100rds that was PHOSGENE Gas) were fired into B.1. During the afternoon both 18-pdrs and 4.5"Hows checked registrations. No sniping targets were observed.	S/A
	During the night harassing fire was carried out on roads, tracks, etc. For Daily Report vide	
	Operation Order regarding a projectore Gas attack issued. See O.O. No.11 vide	
	Amendment to O.O. No.11 (Altering 26th/ to 28th in para.1) vide	appx XXIII S/A
	Amendment 1 to O.O.No.10 (Altering 25th/26th to 27th/28th) vide	appx XXIV S/A
26th	Enemy Artillery still very active. In the afternoon, VIMY and GOULOT WOOD received a good deal of attention and a 15cm H.V.Gun fired on the areas A.5.,A.11. for the first time. P.T.O.	appx XXV S/A

Army Form C. 2118.

WAR DIARY
OR
INTELLIGENCE SUMMARY.
(Erase heading not required.)

MAY 1918.

Instructions regarding War Diaries and Intelligence Summaries are contained in F. S. Regs., Part II, and the Staff Manual, respectively. Title pages will be prepared in manuscript.

Hour, Date, Place.	Summary of Events and Information.	Remarks and references to Appendices.
VILLERS AU BOIS. 26th.	9am to 9.45am. Left Brigade carried out harassing fire on roads and tracks, in Brigade zone. At 3.30pm Right Brigade in conjunction with 16th Brigade RGA. carried out a 5 minutes hurricane bombardment. Concentration of fire observed to be very effective. By night harassing fire was carried out, the Right Brigade including in their targets a number of reported M.G's. For Daily Report vide 52nd D.A.B.M.457 sent out cancelling B.M.416 and a new list of areas for concentrated bombardments by Heavy and Field Artillery issued vide	appx V + VI S/S. appx V + VII S/S
27th	Enemy Artillery has been exceptionally quiet. During the day, a 24cm naval gun fired intermittently around Div. H.Q. Some 200rds were fired on VIMY during the night including a few rds 77mm Gas Shell. Fragments of Gas Shell fired during the night 26th/27th on A.6.c. are identified as 8" Yellow Cross. Enemy replied with 6 10cm shells on T.25.d. to each burst of fire during the night from forward gun in T.25.b. For Daily Report vide	appx V + VIII S/S P.T.O.

Army Form C. 2118.

WAR DIARY
OR
INTELLIGENCE SUMMARY.

(*Erase heading not required.*)

Instructions regarding War Diaries and Intelligence Summaries are contained in F. S. Regs., Part II, and the Staff Manual, respectively. Title pages will be prepared in manuscript.

MAY 1918.

Hour, Date, Place.		Summary of Events and Information.	Remarks and references to Appendices.
VILLERS AU BOIS.	27th.	Amendment to 52nd D.A. No.B.M.303 sent out vide	Appx. XXIV SFA
	28th.	Hostile Artillery still less active than usual. There were a certain number of small shoots in the morning and B.7.and FARBUS WOOD received a certain amount of shelling. No Gas Reported.	
		H.V.Gun still active on back areas.	SFA
		One of our 18-pdr batteries engaged a hostile battery observed firing from U.20.a. One explosion was caused. At 9.29pm Left Group fired in response to a Test S.O.S. During the night Brigades harassed Batteries which were at the same time being engaged with Lethal Gas by Corps C.B's.	
		Our 'planes were very active all day. For Daily Report vide Amendment No.1 to 52nd D.A. No.B.M.457 sent out vide	Appx XX SFA Appx XXII SFA
	29th	Enemy Guns still fairly quiet. VIMY received a good deal of spasmodic shelling. Also S.8.(S.E. of FARBUS).	
		An H.V. Gun fired several rounds into the VILLERS AU BOIS area between 7.45 p.m. and 11.30 p.m.	SFA
		P.T.O.	

Army Form C. 2118.

WAR DIARY
OR
INTELLIGENCE SUMMARY.

(Erase heading not required.)

MAY 1918.

Instructions regarding War Diaries and Intelligence
Summaries are contained in F. S. Regs., Part II,
and the Staff Manual, respectively. Title pages
will be prepared in manuscript.

Hour, Date, Place.	Summary of Events and Information.	Remarks and references to Appendices.
VILLERS AU BOIS. 29th.	At 8pm. our Artillery engaged what appeared to be a camouflaged tank at U.20.c.7.8. Several rounds appeared O.K.	Appx XXII S/A
	By night Gas Bombardment carried out on Coy. H.Q. at C.1.a. 25.80 and on Coy. H.Q. C.1.c.48.95.	
	Harassing fire was carried out on roads, tracks etc.	
	At midnight the Right Group engaged a number of selected targets in support of a raid by the Infantry at 3,5,a,45.18.	
	Enemy replied with M.G. fire. For Daily Report vide	
30th	Hostile Artillery remained quiet during the day. H.V.Guns continued to be active on back areas.	Appx XXIII S/A
	A few rounds 10.5cm Gas were fired on FARBUS in the afternoon.	
	During the day our Artillery carried out some registrations.	
	Harassing fire was brought to bear on selected roads, tracks etc.	
	For Daily Report vide	
	P.T.O.	

Army Form C. 2118.

WAR DIARY
OR
INTELLIGENCE SUMMARY.

(Erase heading not required.)

Instructions regarding War Diaries and Intelligence Summaries are contained in F. S. Regs., Part II, and the Staff Manual, respectively. Title pages will be prepared in manuscript.

MAY 1918.

Hour. Date, Place.	Summary of Events and Information.	Remarks and references to Appendices.
VILLERS AU BOIS. 31st.	Hostile activity still below normal.	
	100rds 10.5cm and 15cm fell in B.14 (TOMMY ALLEY) between 9 & 9.30am. Some Gas was fired into VIMY and Right Btn. during the night.	
	H.V.Guns continue to harass back areas. Portions of 21cm shell with false cap were found at CHATEAU D'ACQ. This is a new Gun in this area. Our 4.5"Hows. fired 75 rds on wire at T.12.c.5.7. & T.11.a.	Appx XXXIV S/S
	Harassin fire was carried out during the night on roads, tracks, Railways in T.8.& 24, U.7.,13.,19.,25 & 26 & C.1.	
	For Daily Report vide	

S.F. Muirhead
Brigadier General,
52nd (Lowland) Division.

DAILY REPORT.
6.AM.11/5/18 to 6.AM.12/5/18.
----

1. OUR ACTIVITY.

   (a) <u>Operations</u>. During the day we engaged and dispersed small
                    parties at U.19.b.2.0, C.2.b.1.7., and T.18.d.7.4
                    and checked several registrations, and at night
                    carried out a programme of harassing fire.
                    Total rounds expended :-
                       18.Pdrs. 1528.   4.5"Hows. 160

   (b) <u>Aerial</u>.   Our planes were active in the afternoon when
                    the visibility had improved.

2. <u>HOSTILE ACTIVITY</u>.

                    Hostile artillery quiet except for a bombardment
   of our front line and supports in B.4., 10 and 16 from 8.50pm
   to 10.40pm. The fire which was heaviest at 9.45pm. appeared
   to come chiefly from the FRESNOY Group. T.Ms also
   reported as participating.
                    Some Gas was used but no definite details as
   to calibres used or damage done yet received.
                    12. Midnight to 6.am. very quiet.

Date. Time.	No.of Rds.	Calibre.	Area shelled.	Direction.	Remarks.
11th.9-11am.	24	15.cm.	LONG WOOD, B.15.a.	?	1 rd. every 5 minutes.
" 11.45am.	10	15cm	A.12.c.&.d.	64°TB.(S)	from B.7.b.6.3.
" do.	20	77mm	F.L. in B.10.c.&.d.	74°TB.(S)	from B.7.b.6.3.
" do.	25	15cm	A.12.a.		
" 11.45am-12 noon.	6	H.V.G.	Area W.of VIMY(?)	?	
3.0.pm	5	77mm.	T.14.a.		
3.20pm.) to 3.50pm.)	?	77mm.	T.23.a.		Rapid rate.
3.45pm.	10	15cm	A.12.c.&.d.	64°TB(S)	from B.7.b.6.3.
3.45pm.	10	15cm	A.12.a.		
4.0pm.	30	77mm	A.6.c.		
4.15-4.30pm.)	8	10.5cm	STATION WOOD B.2.c	BOIS VILAIN	(S).
8.50-10.40pm.	?	Probably all Cal. up to 21.cm.	(Front line & (trenches in (B.4, 10 and 16		
10.30pm to 12 midnight.)	50	15cm	T.12.d.		

   (b) <u>WORK</u>.   New loophole or O.P. slit reported in CHEZ
                    BONTEMPS.

   (c) <u>MOVEMENT</u>.   U.19.b.2.0.) Small parties engaged and
                    C.2.b.1.7.)   dispersed.
                    T.18.d.7.4.)

   (d) <u>Aerial</u>.   Two E.A. picked up on wireless but none seen.

3. GENERAL.

                    <u>Visibility</u> - very poor until 2.pm. Fair from 2.pm.
                         to 5.pm.

                                                        (signed)
                                                        Lieut. R.A.
12th. May, 1918.   Reconnaissance Officer 52nd.Div'l.Arty.

War Diary.
App II

DAILY REPORT
6.AM.12/5/18 to 6.AM.13/5/18.

1. OUR ACTIVITY.
   (a) Operations. During the day movement was engaged at U.19.b. and U.20.d.9.5. - U.26.b.9.5. and several registrations checked.
   At night a programme of harassing fire on selected targets, including the active hostile battery UW.40, was carried out as usual.
   Total rounds expended.
   18.Pdrs - 900.   4.5"Hows - 100.

   (b) Aerial. Our planes active from 4.pm, when visibility became good, to dusk.
   At 3.10pm. a machine, nationality unknown, came down in flames in the ROCLINCOURT Area.

2. HOSTILE ACTIVITY.
   Hostile artillery quieter than during the preceding 24 hours and activity chiefly confined to the evening.
   Eighty rds. of phosgene gas were fired into B.7.c. between 7.15pm and 8pm. and 300 rds. of 15cm into A.12.a. B.7.d. and c. between 7.30pm. and 10.45pm.
   A 21cm How was reported firing as late as 11.30pm. which is unusual on this front.

Date.	Time.	No. of Rds.	Calibre.	Area shelled.	Direction. Remarks.
12th.	10.am -11.am.	100	77mm	Front line T.17.c.	
	2.40pm.	4	10.5cm	T.26.a.	
	Noon-7.30pm.	50	10.5 & 15cm	S.24.c.	
	4.30pm.	42	10.5 & 15cm	T.19.a.&.b.	
	5.30-6.0pm.	30	15cm	B.8.c.	T.15 area.
	5.30pm.	15	10.5cm	B.8.a.2055.	69°GB from B.8.d.2.2.
	5.45pm.	15	15cm	B.8.a.&.c.	NEUVIREUIL.
	7.0-7.40pm.	100	10.5cm	S.30.b.	
	7.15-8.0pm.	80	10.5cm Gas	B.7.c.4060	Phosgene Gas
	7.30pm	30	10.5cm	?	93°TB(S) from B.8.a.3.1.
	7.30-10.45pm	300	15cm.	A.12.a., B.7.d.&.c.	
	8.10pm.	20	10.5cm	?	97°TB. from B.8.a.3.1.(S)
	8.30-11.30pm	60	21cm.	A.11.b.& A.12.a.	
	8.30-9.34pm.	?	10.5cm	B.7.c.&.b.	70°TB.(S) from B.8.a.2.2.
13th.	12.5am.	68	10.5cm	A.7.a.	NEUVIREUIL (S)
	5.10-6.am.	30	21cm.	A.11.b.& A.12.a.	62°GB(F) from B.8.a.3515.

   (b) WORK Nil.

   (c) 3.5pm. Working party of 7 men observed at U.20.c.5.0. dispersed by 18.Prs.
   3.30pm. Individual movement seen in U.24.a. and U.19.c.
   5.15-6pm. Parties of 2 & 3 walking from C.8.c.&.d. towards NEUVIREUIL.
   6.20pm. 20 men with packs on parapet C.8.a.65.00 to C.8.c. 7.2. (disappeared).
   6.28pm. 14 men with packs on parapet C.8.c.90.25 disappeared at C.8.c.65.00 when fired on.
   7.15pm. 8 men observed at C.10.b.7.6.
   8.5pm. Train was observed in BILLY MONTIGNY moving in the direction of HARNES. Another was seen at 8.10pm.
   During the afternoon a large amount of dust visible on BILLY MONTIGNY -IZELLES QUERCHIN Road indicating movement of transport in a southerly direction.

   (d) E.A. None observed.
   4 Balloons up in the afternoon.

Continued

3. <u>GENERAL</u>.   10.30pm. Enemy sent up Golden and Red Rockets near MERICOURT. No action followed. These were fired by double Greens. Still no action.
Two parties with packs being seen in C.8.c. may indicate a local relief.

<u>Visibility</u>- Dawn to 4.pm. Poor.
              4.pm. to dusk - Good.

[signature]
Lieut.R.A.

13th.May,1918.   Reconnaissance Officer 52nd.Div.Arty.

SECRET.

B.M.247.

appd III

To,
    242nd A.F.A. Brigade Group (2)
    52nd A.F.A. Brigade.
    52nd Division G.S. (4)

Reference 52nd Division No.G.R.5/2/88 forwarded under this Office No. B.M.242, dated May 13th, 1918.

1.   The Field Artillery covering the 52nd Division will be regrouped into 2 Groups as follows :-

	Commander.	Batteries.
(a).	O.C. 242nd Army Brigade R.F.A.	242nd Brigade. 504th Battery. 505th Battery.
(b).	O.C. 52nd Army Brigade R.F.A.	52nd Brigade. 465th Battery. 466th Battery.

2.   Above grouping will come into force at 8-0 PM, May 14th. All details to be arranged by Brigade Commanders concerned.

3.   H.Q. 65th Army Brigade R.F.A. will remain in its present location.

4.   R.A. Brigades to acknowledge.

                                       Major R.A.
                        Brigade Major R.A., 52nd Division.

13/5/18.

DAILY REPORT
6.0am.13/5/18 to 6.am.14/5/18.

1. OUR ACTIVITY.
   (a) Operations. During the day movement in U.20.b. was engaged by 18.Pdrs.: otherwise our fire was nil, owing to the light being too poor for checking registrations and no other targets offering themselves.
   During the evening and at night we carried out harassing fire as usual. Targets engaged included the hostile battery U.V.20 at U.20.b.90.50, which was intermittently engaged with 18.Pr.H.E.
   Total number of rounds fired :-
      18.Pdr. 950   4.5"How. 160.

   (b) Aerial. Our machines very active from dawn until 11.30am when the rain commenced.

2. HOSTILE ACTIVITY.
   (a) Artillery. Hostile fire considerably less than on the 12th, probably on account of the high wind & rain and consisted chiefly of small area shoots at a slow rate of fire. B.8 continues to receive an undue share of attention, 185 rds. being fired into it during the period under review. No gas reported. Evening and night very quiet.

Date.	Time.	No.ofRds.	Calibre.	Area shelled.	Direction.	Remarks.
13th.	9am.	12	15cm	A.6.c.		60°GB from A.6.c.93.35(S)
	9am-12 noon	25	10.5cm	T.13.d.		
	ditto.	30	15cm	B.2.c.		
	9.20am.	10	77mm	T.26.c.		
	10.0am.	15	77mm	S.24.d.		ROUVROI (S).
	10.0am.	6	77mm	S.8.c.&.d.		do (S).
	10.15am	A few.	10.5cm	Front line in B.10.a.		
	11am-1.pm	40	10.5cm	B.8.a.&.c.		56°TB from B.7.b.6.3.(S)
	1.50pm-2.pm.	4	10.5cm	FARBUS STA.) B.2.d.)		FRESNOY (S).
	3.30.pm.	30	10.5cm	B.8.c.		NEUVIREUIL (S)
	5.25-6.55pm	50	10.5cm	FARBUS WOOD &) B.8.c.)		do. (S)
	7.10-9.15pm	25	10.5 or 15cm	B.8.c.		56°TB from B.7.b.6.3.
	10.30pm.	12	77mm	B.2.c.		
14th.	2.45am.	20	15cm	Road in B.8.a.&.b.		
	4.45am.	20	15cm	ditto.		

FLASHES & SMOKE PUFFS.
   13th.10.57am. Smoke puffs of 10.5cm How.spotted 56°15' TB.from B.8.a.35.15.
   2.30pm. Faint flashes of 10.5cm How on 92°40'TB from B.8.a.35.15 during shelling of BAILLEUL.

   (b) Work. Timber, chiefly pit props, is being dumped at U.19.d.8534.

   (c) Movement. 6.20am. Man on horse dismounted at U.25.a.25.15 and disappeared behind FRESNOY Park.
      6.30am. Four trains seen moving South beyond IZEL LES EQUERCHIN.
      7.15am. Eight men on road U.19.d.8.4.
      7.45am. 6 men left U.19.b.4.4. and went to trench at U.19.d.45.85.
      3 men on road at B.6.c.7.4.

P.T.O.

(c) Movement.(contd).
  8.am.-10.am. Movement on road in IZEL.- Appeared to be transport going south.
  9.35am. 4 horsed wagon halted at U.16.c.0.6. unloaded, and moved off to IZEL.
  10.12am. Another wagon unloaded at same spot.
  10.30am. Five men in IZEL - HOF.
  10.55am. Train going South behind MERICOURT.
  4.30pm. Three men carrying dixies left CHEZ BONTEMPS.
  5.30pm. Three men at U.19.d.7.7.
  Note. 5 Trains and movement, believed transport, observed moving South.

(d) Aerial. Two low flying E.A. crossed our lines between 9am. and 9.15am.
  7 Balloons were up at 6.45am.

3. GENERAL.
  13th. 8.am. Big volumes of white smoke having appearance of exploded Dump, but probably smoke screen, seen in front of SALAUMINES. Continued until 10.30.am.
  During morning Colliery at 0.33.a.95.80 shewed sign of being worked by enemy. Smoke seen issuing from stacks and steam emerging from two other points.
  Much smoke (dense white cloud) at BILLY MONTIGNY 38°TB from B.8.a.20.15 probably screen to conceal flashes.

  Visibility. Dawn to 11.am. Fair.
  11.am. to dusk. Very poor.

Lieut.R.A.
Reconnaissance Officer 52nd.Div'l.Arty.

War Diary.
appx V
D 36

DAILY REPORT.
6.0.AM.14/5/18 to 6.0.AM.15/5/18.

1. OUR ACTIVITY.
   (a) Operations. The visibility being very good our forward guns were able to carry out a fair amount of sniping of individual movement. Small parties at T.27.a.65, U.19.b.and d.,C.2 & C.8.were engaged and dispersed. Several hits claimed.

   Between 2.pm. and 6pm. our Left Group fired 40 rds.18.Pr. on the CROSS ROADS in U.3.c.

   4.5"Hows.checked their Zero line.

   Three N.F. targets were received during the afternoon but were all out of range.

   During the night we carried out harassing fire on -

   Dugouts and Trench - T.29.d.9.9 - T.30.c.4.5.
   Roads & Tracks - B.6.
   Trenches in - C.1,C.2,C.7 and C.8 to catch suspected relief.
   Tracks,Trenches &)- T.18,U.13, T.5 and 6.
   centres of activity)

   Total number of rounds expended -
   18.Pdr. 1177.   4.5"How. 147.

   (b) Aerial. Our machines very active all day. Heavily engaged by A.A. and M.Gs even when well on our side of the line.

2. HOSTILE ACTIVITY.
   (a) Artillery. Hostile guns quieter during the day than on the 13th. Two cases of probable registration and two, possibly three, cases of HV.Gun reported. No area or destructive shoots.

   At 9.15pm.a large calibre HV Gun fired 1 rd. possibly meant for,Div.HQ.,which fell at W.30.central.

   The night was not so quiet.

   Between 7.0.PM & dawn - some 1000 rds.of Gas Shell were fired into T.19,T.20 & T.25.Nature not known.

Date.	Time.	No.of Rds.	Calibre.	Area shelled.	Direction.	Remarks.
14th.	During morning.	10	10.5cm	T.25.c.& B.16.		
	9.20am.	12	77mm.	Road at B.8.b.2.8	62°GB from	
	10.15am.	10	77mm.	Rly.Crossing at B.8.b.5.8.	)B.7.b.6.3.)(S).	Probably registration.
	12 noon.	5	TM.(?)	Trs.in B.4.c.& B.10.a.		
	1.30pm.	6	15cm	CT.at T.25.b.8.7.		
	do.	12	10.5cm	A.11.a.		Very long range
	1.45pm.	20	15cm.	T.19.d.		
	2.15pm.	?	TM.(?)	Trs.in B.4.c.& B.10.a.		
	2.45-3.30pm.	50	10cm HVG	B.7.c.	60°-70°GB a.8.2.(S).	Possibly two separate guns from B.7. firing.
	3.50pm.	?	TM.(?)	Trs.B.4.c.& B.10.a.		
	4.0pm.	30	10.5cm	T.13.c.& T.19.a.		
	8.45pm. to 9.30pm.	24	10.5cm	T.19.d.		
15th.	12.m.n. to 12.10am	10	15cm	B.8.c.	NEUVIREUIL(S)	
	12.30-1.0.am.	50	10.5cm	WILLERVAL	BOIS en T.(S)	
	4.30am.	20	77mm	B.3.b.		

Page. 2.

FLASHES. 14th. 4.pm. 10cm H.V.G. on 62°GB from B.8.a.3.1.
     8.45pm. Calibre unknown on 56°GB from B.7.b.6.3.
     6.45pm. "   " on 70°GB from " appeared to be engaged by H.A. shortly afterwards.

(b) Work. Nil.

(c) Movement. Considerable movement was observed during the morning and engaged. ULSTER TRENCH, U.19.c.&.d. and Main Road U.19.b.&.d. seemed chief centres of activity.
  A good deal of movement in U.26.b.8.7.(QUARRY) also about House C.5.b.0.9 all day.
  Horses came up to the latter spot, and later returned to IZEL at a fast pace.
  Two motor lorries seen on road at U.10.b.00.60 moving in direction of HENIN-LEITARD.
  4.45pm. Ration Party (2 carried a hot food container) on Track by WEST COPSE U.27.a.80.75.
  6. 5pm. About 40 men left trenches in C.2 and C.8 and went N.E. in small parties.
  6.20pm. Twenty men moved from FRESNES-ROUVROY line to Sunken Road U.22.
  6.30pm. Considerable movement in C.2, C.8., men going out with packs on, and men entering from N.E. with packs. An inter-Battalion relief seemed to be taking place; Right Group opened up harassing fire from forward guns and H.A. were informed.
  7.25pm. A long Passenger Train left LENS travelling S.E.
  7-9.pm. Movement of small groups walking to and from trenches in front of Left Group - engaged.

(d) Aerial. Three enemy machines crossed our lines high up at 7.15pm. but were driven back by A.A. fire.
  6 enemy balloons up from 8.30am onwards.

3. GENERAL. 4.30pm. Signalling Lamp in action on 40°GB from B.7.b.6.3.
    7.30pm. Smoke observed all along ARLEUX TRENCH, B.5. about 40 puffs lasting about 5 secs.
  Visibility - Very Good.

                Lieut.R.A.

15th.May,1918.   Reconnaissance Officer 52nd.Div'l.Arty.

S E C R E T.

52nd.D.A.No.BM.252.

52nd. Brigade (7)
242nd. Brigade (7)

App VI

HARASSING FIRE.

1.   For purposes of co-ordination with Heavy Artillery and D.A's on either flank Zones for harassing fire have been allotted. The Zones for Field Artillery has been extended as far East as possible.

2.   The following Zones for Field Artillery covering the 52nd. Division Front will come into force forthwith :-

(i)   Northern Boundary.T.3.b.4.0 to N.36.a.0.0.
      Eastern Boundary N.36.a.0.0 to U.21 central to C.3.d.0.0.
      Southern Boundary B.6.c.0.0.to C.3.d.0.0.

(ii) Dividing Line between 242nd.Bde.on the North, and 52nd.Bde, on the South, will be T.18.c.8.7 to U.14.d.60.45.

3.   Harassing Fire will be carried out under the orders of Brigade Commanders, the following principles being observed.

(i)   Harassing Fire will be carried out during hours of darkness, and also on misty days when the mist is of sufficient density to conceal enemy movement. This especially applies to misty mornings and evenings.
(ii) Only forward guns and howitzers will be employed.
(iii) Fire will be in quick bursts at irregular intervals extending over the whole period of darkness. Times and objectives to be frequently varied. At least four objectives will be allotted to each gun nightly.
(iv) Full use to be made of enfilade fire on Roads etc.
(v)   Objectives will be engaged up to the eastern Boundary of Brigade Zones.
      Only H.E.(106 fuze if available) will be used by 18.Pdrs. at ranges over 5,500 yards.
(vi) Where Brigades are in possession of them, air recuperator guns only will be employed as forward Guns.

4.   Until further orders the following amounts of ammunition will be expended nightly on harassing fire. More may be fired by Brigades if desired -

	18.Pr.	4.5"How.
52nd. Brigade	500	80
242nd. Brigade	500	80

P.T.O.

Page.2.

5. Recent re-Grouping and allotment of Zones will necessitate a redistribution of forward guns.

(i) It is suggested that the personnel of the 468 Battery gun at T.13.d.20.75 and 465 Battery Gun at T.19.b.60.90 should change places with the personnel of B/242 Gun at T.26.a.25.25 and C/242 gun at T.26.c.58.48 respectively. Brigade Commanders will arrange mutually regarding redistribution.

(ii) O.C.52nd.Bde will select, and move into as soon as possible, positions further forward for the gun of C/52 at B.1.a.8.3 and the howitzer of D/52 at B.13.b.8.3.

(iii) Proposed action to be taken regarding this para. will be reported to this office by last D.R. May 15th.

6. Previous Orders regarding Harassing Fire are cancelled.

7. F.A.Brigades to ACKNOWLEDGE.

S.F. Burne

for Major R.A.
Brigade Major R.A.
52nd.Div'l.Artillery.

14th.May,1918.

Copies to :-

65th.Bde RFA)
52nd.Divn.G.S.)
155th.Inf.Bde.) For
156th.Inf.Bde.) information.
157th.Inf.Bde)
R.O.)

War Diary

DAILY REPORT
6.0.A.M. 15/5/18 to 6.0.A.M. 16/5/18.

1. OUR ACTIVITY.

(a) **Operations.** During the day our 18.Prs. engaged roads & tracks in U.5.c. and U.19.b. and road at T.18.d. 85.65. No fleeting opportunities offered themselves. Several N.F. calls received but all out of range.

During the night harassing fire was carried out on roads and tracks in T.6 - T.12 - U.26 and on -

Hostile Battery   - U.27.b.08.52.
"   "   - U.15.c.95.45.
Road & Dugouts   - T.29.b.3.0.-T.29.d.45.38.
Road Junction   - U.13.b.25.65.
T.M. Emplacement - T.18.d.12.63.
Road & Dugouts   - T.18.d.85.65.
Track   - T.24.b.40.50.-T.24.b.85.90.
HQ. Dugouts   - T.12.c.25.84.

Total number of rounds fired -
18.Pounder 1154.   4.5"Howr. 107.

(b) **Aerial.**   Our planes active from dawn to dusk.

2. HOSTILE ACTIVITY.

(a) **Artillery.**   Enemys guns slightly more active than yesterday - chief activity confined to what is believed to have been counter-battery shoots on A.12, A.18 and A.18 - details not known.

From 1.15-1.45pm. 77mm and 4.2 Hows. carried out an area shoot on S.30.b.&.c.- about 100 rds. fired.

During the day 100 rds. of 15cm were fired into T.19.c.&.d. and from 4.20pm-5.pm. 100 rds. of 77mm & 10.5cm at our trenches in B.9.b. and B.10.a.

At 11.pm. 20 rds. of 77mm Gas, nature not known were fired in T.19.c.&.d. Three cases of H.V.G. reported but no registrations.

Night quiet but at about 4.pm. heavy firing opened in the Corps on our right.

Date.	Time.	No. of Rds.	Calibre.	Area shelled.	Direction.	Remarks.
15th.	7.30am & intermittently - 4.0.p.m.	100	15cm	T.19.c.&.d.		
	10.15-11.am.	20	10.5cm	B.4.c.		
	11.15am-12 noon	10	10cm HVG	FARBUS STA.	NEUVIREUIL.	
	12.15pm.	3	15cm HVG	T.23.b.		Air bursts.
	During morning	?	10cm HVG	S.29.		High air bursts
	1.15-1.45pm.	100	77mm and 10.5cm	S.30.b.&.c.		Area shoot.
	4.0.pm.	4	10.5cm	T.10.a.4.1.		
	4.20.pm.	100	77mm and 10.5cm	Front trenches in B.9.b.&.B.10.a.		
	6.15.pm.	20	77mm.	S.18.c.		
	6.45.pm.	12	77mm.	T.10.c.7.5.		
	During the day	50	10.5cm	A.12.c.		60°GB from A.6.c.93.33.
	ditto.	80	15cm	A.12.a.		
	11.0.pm	20	77mm Gas	T.19.c.&.d.		Nature not known.
16th.	12.m.n. to 3.a.m.	?	10.5cm	T.19.d.&.T.20.d.		Intermittent fire.

P.T.O.

Page 2.

FLASHES. 9.20.am. A.A.guns on 67°30' GB from S.8.a.35.15.
11.5am.&.5.15pm.15cm How.on 73°30' GB from A.6.b.41.79.
12.20pm. 77mm(?) on 76°GB from A.6.b.41.79 -believed to be at U.19.b.8.2.
12.30pm. Section 10.5cm Hows.on 73°GB from A.6.b.8.7.
15cm how.on 68°GB from A.6.b.8.7.
3.pm.and 4.25pm. 15cm How.on 62°GB from A.6.b.41179 - Flash to report 25 secs.
Calibres unknown on 72°30',73°,73°10' G.Bs.from A.6.b.41.79. These hows appeared to be doing counter-battery work on A.12, A.17 and A.18.
During the afternoon 15cm How.in U.15.c. thought to be No.94 fired 8 rounds.

(b) **Work.** Nil.

(c) **Movement.** 9.0.am.12 men going East in U.26.a.2.9.
Individual movement in U.19.c.&.d.,U.20.c.,t.21.c. and d. during morning.
1.30pm.30 men(in 2's and 3's) going South in U.26.central.

(d) **Aerial.** E.A. crossed our lines at high altitudes at intervals during the day. Five Artillery machines operated patrolled behind their lines in the evening - possibly to spot flashes.
A.A.not so active as usual of late.
Four Balloons up.

3. **GENERAL.** 7.15pm.Lamp signalling from C.6.c.0.2.
11.50pm.Searchlight seen on 48°GB from S.22.b.75.50
Visibility - Very good.

G.P.Crew

14th.May.1918. Reconnaissance Officer 52nd.Div¹ l.Artillery.
Lieut.R.A.

SECRET.   52nd.DA.No.BM282.

242nd.Army Bde (7)
52nd.Army Bde   (7)   appd VIII
65th.Army Brigade
D.T.M.O.

1.   A "Gas Beam" attack will be carried out on the 18th.Corps front from T.9.b. to N.25.b. on the Night of May 16th/17th., or the first night after, upon which the wind is favourable.

2.   The Gas will be discharged at three Tramway heads from the trucks on which the cylinders are loaded.

3. PRECAUTIONS FOR TROOPS IN THE LINE.   If the Gas Beam attack is ordered -
   (a) The outpost line between VESTA TILLY in T.10.c.and N.20.a. 0.4 and troops in the line of resistance between T.2.b.9.9 and N.32.c.8.6. and between N.25.d.9.7 and N.19.c.5.5 in AGUE and N.19.b.1.6 in AMULET, will be withdrawn by 12 midnight.
   (b) Troops forward of a line drawn through T.11.c.0.0 -T.15.b.0.7 - T.1.b.9.9.- N.25.c.0.8 - N.13.c.0.0.-N.13.b.5.5. will wear box respirators from 12 midnight until orders for their removal is given by an Officer. This should in no case be given until Zero plus 30 minutes, and then only if the trench system is reported clear of Gas.
   (c) B.G.C.157th.Inf.Bde will arrange to re-occupy the lines of resistance and outpost on the first possible opportunity, reporting by Priority wire when completed.
   (d) The Divisional Gas Officer of the Divisions concerned, assisted by the Anti-Gas personnel of Units, should make arrangements for -
       (i) Clearing Dugouts and cellars by means of fires, etc. immediately after completion of discharge.
       (ii) Clearing trenches, saps, etc. by means of flappers, etc. immediately after completion of discharge.
       (iii) Troops should not re-occupy trenches, etc. until qualified anti-gas personnel have declared them to be safe.

4. ARTILLERY & MACHINE GUNS. Artillery action, which might cause retaliation, will be avoided, otherwise artillery fire and machine gun fire will be normal until 2 hours after discharge, and should cover the noise made by the trucks on the railway, and the noise of the discharge of cylinders, which is equal to about two rifle shots fired together.

                                                            P.T.O.

5. **WIND LIMITS.** Cylinders can be discharged in any winds between W.N.W. to S.W. of velocity not less than 6.m.p.h. or more than 15 m.p.h.

Decision will be given at 1.pm. daily as to whether the operation will be carried out.

Code Words will be used as follows:-

"Gas Beam attack will take place tonight" - ASTI.
No message will be sent at 1.pm. if no attack is to take place. To cancel "Gas Beam attack previously ordered" the word CHIANTI will be sent.

6. **ZERO HOUR.** Zero Hour will be at 12 midnight or as soon after as the trucks are reported to be in position.

7. **RATIONS.** On the day it is decided to discharge the Gas Beam, light railways will be closed to ammunition and food supply from 12 noon onwards. Two days supply will, therefore, be taken up on May 15th. There will then be 1 days's supply in hand for use on the day following the night upon which the Gas is discharged.

Care will be taken that no transport, other than is normal, is employed for the distribution of these rations on the night of the Operation.

8. **ACKNOWLEDGE.**

(signed) Major RA
Brigade Major R.A.
52nd. Div'l. Artillery.

16th. May, 1918.

Line.	Railway Base.	Siding.	Power Heads.	Discharge Points.
1.	LENS.	X.12.c.41.56 - X.12.c.07.47.	DORIS DUMP - T.8.d.80.95.	T.9.b.45.60 to T.3.d.30.07.
2.	LENS.	X.12.a.96.42 - X.12.a.65.10.	ADEPT DUMP - N.31.d.50.35.	N.32.d.92.62 to N.32.d.42.60.
3.	AIX NOULETTE.	R.21.d.99.46 - R.21.d.85.25.	M.30.d.57.44.	N.25.b.92.88 to N.25.b.50.58.

DAILY REPORT
52ND DIVISIONAL ARTILLERY.
6.0.A.M.16/5/18 to 6.A.M.17/5/18.

1. OUR ACTIVITY.

(a) **Operations.** A working party at T.5.c.55.73 was engaged & two hits observed. Movement was also fired on at U.19.d.9.5., U.25.a.20.10., B.6.c.25.90 and in U.21.c.
Harassing fire was carried out on roads, tracks and centres of activity by day and by night.
Total number of rounds fired -
18.Pounders - 996.   4.5"Hows - 150.

(b) **Aerial.**   Our aircraft very active.

2. HOSTILE ACTIVITY.

(a) **Artillery.** The enemy fired about 300.rds.during the night on the N. and W.outskirts of VIMY and after midnight directed harassing fire between THELUS & FARBUS. The forward gun of A/52 was engaged by the enemy during the day as under :-
Time. 7.0am., 8.0.am to 11.am., Noon to 2.15pm. & short bursts 2.15pm to 4pm.
Bty shelled. A/52.Forward Gun - T.27.c.0.8.
Calibre. 10.5cm and 15cm Hows.
No.of Rds. Approx.350.
Direction. 10.5cm hows. from direction of MERICOURT.
           15cm   "   "   "   "   MERICOURT & BOIS BERNARD.
Ranging. At 7.am.an aeroplane seems to have been ranging the two 10.5cm Hows which were accurate for a short time but then distributed their fire.
Damage. Nil.

Date.	Time.	No.of Rds	Calibre.	Area shelled.	Direction.	Remarks.
16th.	7.am.	20	10.5cm	T.19.a.&.d.	MERICOURT.	
	7-10am.	-	15cm	T.19.c.		
	9-10am.	10	77mm	T.19.d.	do.	
	10-12.noon	5	77mm	T.19.c.		
	10.15am.	4	10.5cm	T.16.c.		
	10.30am.	41n	10.5cm	T.9.c.		
	12.30pm-5.pm.	50	10.5cm	S.29.c.	64°GB.from S.29.c.8427.	
	1.-3.pm.	18	77mm	T.19.a.		
	1.35-1.38pm	5	10.5cm(Gun)?		64°TB from B.1.c.73.92.	
	1.55-4.30pm.	50	77mm	B.3,B.10.		Front line.
	3.15pm.	6	10.5cm	T.7.b.&.a.		
	3 - 5.30pm.	12	77mm	T.25.a.		
	3.30pm.	10	15cm	T.8.c.		
	4.40-5.40pm.	250	77 & 10.5cm	B.10.a.2095 B.4.c.7.2.	Flashes from B.1.c.7392 4.25pm.74°.F. to R.21 secs. 5.10pm.70°10', 70°20'.F.to R. 18 secs. 5.35pm. 71°10'. The Btys stoped when engaged by our heavies. Dumps went up on the bearing 70°10' from B.1.c.7392 and continued to burn for 30 minutes.	
	6.-6.30pm.	5	10.5cm	T.17.c.-T.3.d.		Front line.
	ditto	6	T.M.	ditto.		
	8.10.p.m.	8	10.5cm	S.29.c.	67°GB from S.29.c.84.27	
	8.pm.-1.am.	300	10.5cm 15.cm	T.19.a. S.24.c.		

P.T.O.

(b) **Work.** Nil.

(c) **Movement.** 12.40pm. Working party T.5.c.55.73-dispersed by 18.Pdrs.
5.0pm. Party of fire entered dugout in U.20.c.
6.30pm. Movement about U.19.d.9.5 fired on by 18.Pounders.
7.15pm. Working party about U.19.d.9.5. dispersed by 18.Pdrs.

(d) **Aerial.** Between 11.am.and noon 2.E.A. flew high over our lines.

3. **GENERAL.** Dummy flashes observed on Chalk Mound ACHEVILLE when 10.5cm Gun, whose actual flash was observed 64°GB from B.1.c.73.92 (ROUVROY), fired.
10.40.am. Helio on slag heap O.33.c.
At 4.pm. a spherical propaganda balloon fell in our lines B.3.b.
5.pm. "N.F. T.H. ARLEUX" received. No flash seen by F.O.Os.
11.45pm. to midnight. Large number of Red Flares breaking into 2 green sent up between OPPY & ARLEUX. No action.

A.F.Dufton
Lieut.RA
for Reconnaissance Officer 52nd.Div.Arty.

17th.May,1918.

War Diary

Appx X

DAILY REPORT
52ND DIVISIONAL ARTILLERY
6.0.AM.17/5/18 TO 6.0.AM.18/5/18.

1. **OUR ACTIVITY.**
   (a) **Operations.** Movement was engaged at U.25.a.2.1., U.20.a.80.05.
   Harassing fire was directed on roads, tracks and centres of activity by day and night.
   Left Group fired in response to a test SOS 2.29.am. Total number of rounds fired -
   18.Pounders 902.   4.5"Hows. 290.

   (b) **Aerial.** Our planes very active all day particularly between 6.pm. and 8.pm.
   Hostile A.A. were active.

2. **HOSTILE ACTIVITY.**
   (a) **Artillery.** The enemy artillery was less active than usual, 193 rds. being reported as compared with 790 yesterday.
   The night was exceptionally quiet.
   VIMY STATION was registered by 77mm.

Date.	Time.	No. of Rds.	Calibre.	Area shelled.	Direction.	Remarks.
17th.	8.30-9.30am	12	15cm	T.19.c.		
	10.0am	3	10.5cm	B.8.a.	63°GB.from B.7.b.8.3.	
	10.15am	4	AA(2)	-	74°GB.from B.1.a.7592.	
	10.40am	6	10.5cm	T.10.c.4.8.		
	10.45am	8	77mm	T.18.c.central.		
	11.0am	6	10.5cm	T.16.b.&.c.		
	11.15am	12	10.5cm	T.22.a.		
	11.40am	4	10.5cm	T.22.b.		
	11.45am	4	10.5cm	T.9.d.9.9.		
	12.30pm.	10	10.5cm How	TIRED ALLEY.		
	12.45pm.	8	77mm	T.20.a.		Apparently registering VIMY STATION.
	2 - 6pm.	50	15cm	A.2.a.		
	4.50pm.	6	10.5cm	T.16.c.		
	6.45pm.	6	10.5cm	T.3.a.		
	6.45-7.20pm.	50	10.5cm	T.9.b.		
	7.40pm.	10	10.5cm How	A.11.		One shell PHOSGENE.

   (b) **Work.** Nil.

   (c) **Movement.** During afternoon a good deal of movement in U.21.c.
   6.15pm. Party of six in U.20.b.
   6.15-6.30pm. Movement at U.25.a.2.1. and U.20.a.80.05 engaged by 18.Pounders.
   6.15-6.30pm. Six men at U.26.b.
   8.30pm. Two men without packs walked from U.19.c.1.7 to T.24.d.4.2.

   (d) **Aerial.** 5 hostile Balloons up. Two bombing planes passed over between 10. and 10.30pm.

3. **GENERAL.** Fire in MERICOURT caused by Heavy Artillery.
   10.am. 4 Horizontal Flares seen close together at GB.95° from S.22.b.63.57.
   10.40am. Light car at 49°GB. from B.8.a.20.15.
   12.20pm. Smoke at B.12.b.4.5.

A.F.Drufton
Lieut.R.A.
Reconnaissance Officer 52nd.Div.Arty.

18th. May, 1918.

S E C R E T.   52nd.D.A.No.B.M.303.

242nd. Brigade (7)
52nd. Brigade (7)
65th. Brigade   )
52nd.Divn.G.S.   )
155th.Inf.Bde.   )
156th.Inf.Bde.   ) For
157th.Inf.Bde.   ) information.
20th.D.A.   )
15th.D.A.   )
XVlll Corps H.A.)
18th.Brigade RGA)

Appx X-A

1. The 18.Pounder S.O.S. barrage lines on 52nd.Division Front will consist of three barrages as follows :-

(i) <u>YELLOW BARRAGE</u>.   B.10.b.95.80-B.5.c.40.10-B.5.a.40.05. Gap
B.5.a.42.45-T.29.c.58.40. Gap.
T.29.c.85.95-T.23.d.3.0.-T.17.b.70.20 -
T.10.central - T.4.c.0.6.

The initial barrage will come down on above line for two minutes after which it will drop back on to the :-

(ii) <u>RED BARRAGE</u>.   B.10.b.95.80-T.28.d.9.0.-T.29.c.18.40. Gap
T.29.c.58.90-T.23.d.3.0.-T.23.b.5.3.-
T.17.c.95.25.-T.17.a.10.25.-T.10.a.00.00 -
T.9.central - T.3.d.00.00.

(iii) In the event of the message "S.O.S.BLUE" being received guns concerned will drop back on to the :-

BLUE BARRAGE.   T.23.d.3.0. - T.23.c.42.70.-T.17.c.1.0. -
T.16.d.50.90.-T.9.c.45.68.-T.3.c.45.00.

2.   52nd.&.242nd.Army Bdes RFA will be responsible for those portions of above barrage which lie within their Brigade Zones. Bde Commanders will allot objectives for 4.5"Howrs., several objectives being allotted to each Howitzer.

P.T.O.
Continued.

3. Rates of fire for S.O.S. will be as follows:-

	18.Prs.	Hows.	
First five minutes	4	3	rds. per gun per minute.
Next " "	3	2	--do--
" " "	2	1	--do--
Until situation develops or fresh orders are received	1	½	--do--

4. All guns firing Shrapnel for S.O.S. will have 40 rds. per gun ready set in the gun pit.

5. F.A. Brigades to ACKNOWLEDGE.

[signature]

Major RA
Brigade Major RA
17th. May, 1918.   52nd. Divisional Artillery.

S E C R E T.　　　　　　　　　　52nd.DA.No.BM.309

242nd.Brigade (?)
52nd.Brigade (?)
65th.Brigade
52nd.Divn.GS.　　)
155th.Inf.Bde.　)
156th.Inf.Bde.　)For
157th.Inf.Bde.　)information.
R.A. 18th.Corps　)
XVIII Corps HA　)
16th.Bde RGA　　)

COUNTER PREPARATION.

1. Counter Preparation is the Artillery action to be taken during an intense hostile bombardment which is evidently the prelude to an attack. Its object is the destruction of the enemy's trench system, including M.Gs and T.Ms, from which the Infantry attack will be launched, and the killing of the troops while coming up to, and in, their assembly places.

2. Counter Preparation will be ordered by the C.R.A., or, if communications are cut, by Brigade Commanders.

3. Following will be the procedure in the event of Counter Preparation being ordered.

(i) 18.Pdrs. Commencing on the "YELLOW" S.O.S. barrage line,
(a) will search back 700 yards in 100 yard lifts, sweeping on the traverse but not moving trails. No gun to shoot over a range of 7000 yards.
(b) 4.5" Hows. will conform to 18.Pr. lifts, searching communication trenches, destroying trench junctions, M.G. and T.M. emplacements and probable assembly places. Brigade Commanders will allot several objectives for each howitzer.

(ii) (a) Fire will be in rapid bursts at irregular intervals. At least 6 bursts per hour.
(b) Ammunition. 18.Prs.-40 rds. per gun per hour.
　　　　　　　　4.5" Howrs.-30　"　" How per hour.

(c) As it is impossible to foretell how long the hostile bombardment will last Brigade Commanders must control the rate of fire so that an undue proportion of the ammunition at positions shall not be expended before the attack commences. For this purpose, during Counter Preparation, ammunition at gun positions must not be allowed to drop below 400 rds. per 18.Pr. or 300 rds. per How. at the position.

4. Previous orders regarding Counter Preparation are cancelled.
5. F.A. Brigades to ACKNOWLEDGE.

　　　　　　　　　　　　　　　　　　Major RA
　　　　　　　　　　　　　　　　Brigade Major R.A.
　　　　　　　　　　　　　　　　52nd. Divisional Artillery.

12th. May, 1918.

52ND DIV'L. ARTILLERY MUTUAL SUPPORT SCHEME.

SECTOR.	CALL SENT OR RECEIVED.	ASSISTING ARTILLERY.	GUNS.	NATURE.	ZONE OF ASSISTANCE.
Division on our Left.	HELP AVION	242nd.Army Bde Group.	10	18.Pdrs.	T.4.a.55.65 - N.33.d.45.55.
Left Inf.Bde 52nd.Divn.	HELP MIRICOURT.	20th.D.A.	6	18.Pdrs.	T.3.central - T.9.central (not to be put down until 2 minutes after SOS has been put up.)
		52nd.Army Bde RFA	2 6	4.5"Hows 18.Pdrs.	T.4.d.00.90.- T.4.a.50.60. Barrage from T.17.d.0.2 to T.17.c.60.65.
Right Inf. Bde.52nd.Div	ASSIST PLUMER.	242nd.Army Bde RFA	12	18.Pdrs.	Barrage from T.23.d.5.0. to T.17.d.0.2.
		do. Div.Arty on our Right.	3 12 3	4.5"How. 18.Pdrs. 4.5"How.	On points T.29.b.6.5.,T.29.b.70.85.,T.23.d.85.00 B.5.c.50.65 - B.5.a.30.70. B.5.c.55.90., B.5.a.55.15.,B.5.a.6.5.
Division on our Right.	ASSIST OPPY.	52nd.Army Bde RFA	12 3	18.Pdrs. 4.5 Hows.	B.17.a.65.60 -B.17.d.35.60. B.17.b.10.50 -B.17.b.50.00.
Division on our Right.	ASSIST ARLEUX.	52nd.Army Bde RFA	12 3	18.Pdrs. 4.5"Hows.	B.11.a.60.65 -B.5.c.20.75. B.5.c.30.20 - B.11.a.80.80.

In addition to above should the attack come astride the 52nd.Division inter Brigade Boundary the 242nd.Army Bde RFA will arrange to superimpose the fire of their left 18.Pounder Battery on the barrage line from T.29.a.5.0. - T.23.b.5.3.

The above Support to be given only when the tactical situation permits.

DAILY REPORT
52ND DIVISIONAL ARTILLERY
6.0.AM.18/5/18 TO 6. .A.M.19/5/18.

1. OUR ACTIVITY.
   (a) <u>Operations</u>. Movement was engaged in U.19.a.,U.20.a. and
      U.25.a.   During the night Harassing fire was
      directed on roads and tracks in T.6,T.30,U.7,13,25
      and B.6.
         Hostile battery positions U.14.d.20.10,U.14.d.
      30.70.,U.18.d.15.30 & O.25.d.6.0. were harassed by
      18.Prs.during the night.
         10.5pm.TEST S.O.S. Call received & answered.
        Total rounds fired-18.Prs.1050. 4.5"Hows. 200

   (b) <u>Aerial</u>.   Our planes active all day.

2. HOSTILE ACTIVITY.
         Enemy artillery resumed its normal activity
after a quiet day yesterday.
      VIMY was shelled considerably. The Tank in
VIMY Station appears to be used as a datum point. THELUS was
shelled during the night and the front line in B.10.a.&.c. was
bombarded in the early morning.

Date.	Time.	No.of Rds.	Calibre.	Area shelled.	Direction.	Remarks.
18th.	9.30-10.30am	50	10cm HVG	F.12.a.&.c.		
	During Day.	50	15cm)	A.11.b.		
		50	10.5cm)	A.12.a.&.b.		
		20	HV Gun.)			
	10.0am-noon.	20	10.5cm	B.5.		
	11.15am.	10	77mm	B.8.a.		
	11.0am.	6	T.M.	T.3.d.,T.9.b.	MERICOURT.	
	12.30pm.	6	10.5cm	T.15.d.central.		
	12.10-1.0pm.	25	15cm(2)	A.12.	64°45' GB.from B.1.a.7392	
	1.30-2.30pm	40	15cm)10cm Gun)	A.12.c.&.d.	48°50' GB from B.1.a.7392 Flash to report 25 secs.	
	2.0-3.0pm.	56	10.5cm	VIMY Sta.(T.19.d.)		
	3.15pm.	3	77mm	S.30.a.		
	do.	10	10.5cm	T.19.c.	ROUVROY.	
	3.0pm.	20	10.5cm	T.19.c.	FRESNOY.	
	3.0-4.0pm	50	15cm	VIMY STA.(T.19.d.)		Registration.
	5.0pm.	4	10.5cm	T.13.b.7.7.		
	8.0-8.30pm	100	15cm	A.11.b.,A.12.a.&.b.		
	10.30pm.	20	15cm How	THELUS.	NEUVIREUIL.	
	2.45-3am.(19th)	200	T.M.)77mm)10.5cm)	B.10.a.&.c.		Red,double Red & Green lights from enemys lines.
19th.	3-5.30am.	50	10.5cm How	THELUS.		

FLASHES. 10.30am.AA.(2) 61°20' GB from B.1.a.73.92. F.to R. 25 secs.
       2.30.pm.One flash at U.19.b.70.55.
       2.30-2.45pm.4 flashes observed about U.13.a.20.35.
       4.45-5.20pm.Flashes from suspected 60.Pr.69°30'from
          B.1.a.73.92. F. to R. 18 secs.
       5.53pm. Flash of battery firing on T.18.c. 52°GB from
          T.17.c.9.2.
       8.45pm.&.3.20am.Flashes of 10.5cm How. 80°GB from B.1.a.8.5.

P.T.O.

Page.2.

(b) <u>Work.</u>   NIL.

(c) <u>Movement.</u>   Slight movement engaged in T.19.a.&.U.25.a.
       1.35pm.3 men in FRESNOY TRENCH U.19.c.05.70.
       1 Man on Bicycle on FRESNOY Road U.19.c.20.80.
       1.58pm.1 man on MONTREAL Road entered BOIS
        VILAIN U.19.b.15.25.

(d) <u>Aerial.</u>   NIL.

3. <u>GENERAL.</u>   { Enemy suspected to be using a 60.Pdr.
     Flash seen 69°30' GB. from B.1.a.75.92. Flash to
{ report 18 secs.
    12.50pm. Lamp seen at T.29.d.45.45.
    10.15-10.25pm. Numerous double Red & Green lights
     in MERICOURT Sector.
    2.45-3.0am. Numerous Double Red & Green lights
     opposite B.10 during bombardment.

19th.May,1918.   Lieut.R.A.
          Reconnaissance Officer 52nd.Div.Arty.

S E C R E T.   52nd.D.A.No.B.M.319.

52nd.Divisional Artillery.
18th.May,1918.

Herewith Mutual Support Scheme for 52nd.Divisional Artillery.

Note that the Call for Right Inf.Brigade Front of 52nd.Division has been altered to "ASSIST PLUMER."

Please cancel all previous copies.

S.F. Burne
for

Major RA
Brigade Major RA
52nd.Div'l.Artillery.

Copies to :-
- 242nd.Army Bde RFA (7)
- 52nd. "   "   " (7)
- 65th. "   "   " (1)
- 52nd.Division GS. (1)
- 155th.Inf.Bde.   (1)
- 156th.Inf.Bde.   (1)
- 157th.Inf.Bde.   (1)
- 15th.D.A.   (1)
- 20th.D.A.   (1)
- R.A.XVlll Corps   (1)
- XVlll Corps H.A.   (1)
- 16th.Brigade RGA   (1)

DAILY REPORT
52ND DIVISIONAL ARTILLERY.
6.0.AM.19/5/18 TO 6.0.AM.20/5/18.

=1. OUR ACTIVITY.

(a) Operations. By day 18.Pdrs.fired on H.Q.and Occupied area T.5.b.&.c., on M.G.emplacements T.4.b., on T.M. and dugouts T.5.d. and on tracks in T.13.d.
During the night 18.Prs.harassed hostile batteries U.8.c.8.3 & U.9.b.5.2 which had been engaged by Heavy Arty during the day. Harassing fire was also directed on B.5.c.55.95 and on tracks & centres of activity in N.34.d., U.7,13,19 T.24 and B.6.
Total number of Rds.fired :-
18.Pdrs, 953.   4.5"Hows. 226.

(b) Aerial.   Our aircraft active.

2. HOSTILE ACTIVITY.

(a) Artillery. Active during the morning on VIMY,   . and on the LONE TREE(T.27.c.0.8). Fairly quiet during the afternoon and throughout the night.
The artillery positions at THELUS were unmolested throughout the day.

Date.	Time.	No.of Rds.	Calibre.	Area shelled.	Direction.	Remarks.
19th.	6.0am	100	15cm	T.19.d.		
	7.30-11.30am	150	Various chiefly 15cm	T.27.c.0.8.	115°GB from T.27.d.6.3.	
	8.0am.	50	10.5cm	T.19.c.		
	9.0am	30	15cm	do.		
	9.15-10.30am	50	10.5cm	B.2.a.	90°GB.from B.8.a.20.15	
	9.30am.	6	10.5cm	S.21.d.		
	9.50-10.15am	30	10.5cm	B.10.a.&.c.		
	10.15-11am.	9	15cm	T.19.c.		
	11.35am.	50	15cm	T.19.c.		
	12.45pm.	20	15cm	A.12.a&.		
	2.30pm.	-	10.5cm	T.16.b.		Appeared to be registering with SMOKE shell
	2.45pm.	3	77mm	T.13.d.		
	5.40pm.	10	10.5cm	B.10.a.		NEUVIREUIL.
	7.0pm.	10	10.5cm	B.10.a.		do.
	9-9.30pm.	30	77mm	B.4.d.	90°GB.from B.8.a.20.15	
20th.	12.30am.	12	10.5cm	B.8.a.		At gun fire.
	During night.	50	15cm	A.11.b., A.12.a.&.b.		
	ditto.	6	10.5cm	T.22.b.		BLUE CROSS.

(b) Work.   Nil.
(c) Movement. 9.0am.Working party in front of ACHEVILLE.
2.50pm.One man walking near CHEZ BONTEMPS(U..20)
4.0pm.Individuals at B.6.c.
5.15pm.   "   " T.30.d.6.8.
5.35pm.Movement in U.19.

(d) Aerial. 9.30am.E.A.dropped 10 bombs on S.22.d.

3. GENERAL. 5.35pm.Large explosion in SALLAUMINES.
4.45am.Two small parachutes,which when first seen in distance carried lights,drifted over our lines. One fell about THELUS, the other about VIMY. Probably used by enemy for testing the wind.

A.F.Dutton
Lieut.RA.
for Reconnaissance Officer 52nd.Div'l.Arty.

20th.May,1918.

SECRET.   52nd.DA.No.BM.371.

To
   All Recipients 52nd.D.A.No.B.M.282.

                  Reference para.4 of B.M.282 dated 16/5/18.

1.   From Zero plus 2 Hours to Zero plus 5 Hours harassing fire will be carried out vigorously on the whole Corps Front.

2.   During this period the expenditure of ammunition for all natures will be treble that which would be normally expended for the same period under 52nd.D.A.No.B.M.269 (Harassing Fire).

3.   The following total amounts of ammunition will therefore be expended on harassing fire on Zero night :-

BRIGADE.	8.30.PM. to ZERO.		ZERO plus 2 Hours to ZERO plus 5 Hours.	
	18.Pr.	4.5"How	18.Pdr.	4.5"How.
52nd. Brigade.	325	80	150	40
242nd. Brigade.	325	80	150	40

4.   F.A. Brigades to ACKNOWLEDGE.

                                               Major RA
                                         Brigade Major R.A.,
                                        52nd.Divisional Artillery.
30th.May,1918.

DAILY REPORT
52ND DIVISIONAL ARTILLERY.
6.0.AM.20/5/18 to 6.0.AM.21/5/18.

1. OUR ACTIVITY.

(a) Operations. During the day 18.Prs.fired 100 rds on Tracks in T.5.b., T.5.d., T.12.a., and engaged movement in U.13.c.
    4.5"Hows checked registrations.
    Numerous N.F. targets received but all out of range.
    During the night 18.Pdrs.engaged –
        Hostile Battery U.26.c.45.15
        Tracks & Roads in U.13,7 and T.6.
        ARLEUX and approaches.
    4.5"Hows engaged –
    Trench junctions & selected points U.15 & U.7.
    ARLEUX and approaches.
    At 8.55pm.18.Prs. and 4.5"Hows engaged hostile battery U Y 57. in response to zone call.
    Total number of rounds fired –
    18.Pdrs. 838.   4.5"Howrs. 217.

(b) Aerial. All machines active all day.

2. HOSTILE ACTIVITY.

(a) Artillery. General activity slightly less than on the 19th. and chiefly confined to the morning. No heavy area or destructive shoots reported. VIMY and vicinity received a large share of the shelling.
    The R.G.A.batteries in A.12 were again shelled with what is believed to be 60.Prs. No gas reported.
    Night quiet.

Date.Time.	No.of Rds.	Calibre.	Area shelled.	Direction.	Remarks.
20th.8.0.am.	50	15cm	S.30.b.		
9.10.am.	20	77mm	T.22.		
10.am.-5.20pm.	100	77mm	T.19 & 25.VIMY		
10.30.am.	30	15cm	T.19.c.VIMY.		
10.30.am.	20	10.5cm How	T.20		BOIS BERNARD (S)
11.am.-1.45pm.	20	15cm	B.10.a.		
11.am.- noon.	11	15cm	B.8.a.		
12 noon	12	10.5cm	T.25.b.		
Noon - 1.0pm.	50	4.1(?)Gun	A.12.		68°GB(S)from B.1.a.7394. Believed to be 60.Pdr.
During morning	–	HV.Gun.	ROCLINCOURT(?)Area.		
12 noon-2.0pm.	30	77mm	T.25.a.& c.		
12.30pm	20	10.5cm	S.29.d., S.30.c.		
2. 5pm	8 (2)	10.5cm How	– –		66°50' GB from B.1.a.7394. (Flash and smoke). Flash to report 19 secs.
2.10-2.50pm.	10	77mm	T.15.d.–		78°GB(S)from S.25.c.7.8
2.10.p.m.	20	10.5cm	A.6.b.		71°GB(F)from A.6.b.8070.
5.45-6.30pm.	8	H.E.Air bursts.	T.17.a.		

TRENCH MORTAR. B.5.b.2.2. reported by the Infantry.

(b) Work. Nil.

P.T.O.

Page.2.

(c) Movement. Few men on Road B.6.c. during afternoon.
6.30pm. A certain amount of movement in U.13.c. This was fired on by 18.Prs and enemy disappeared very quickly.

3. GENERAL. 4.45.pm. Holiograph signalled from VITRY-EN-ARTOIS.

Visibility - Fair.

21st.May,1918.

Lieut.R.A.
Reconnaissance Officer 32nd.Div.Arty.

S E C R E T.   52nd.DA.No.BM.378.

To
    All Recipients 52nd.D.A.No.B.M.282.

    This office No.B.M.371 dated 20th.inst. is cancelled and the following substituted -

    Reference para.4 of B.M.282 dated 16/5/18.

1. From Zero plus 2 Hours to Zero plus 5 Hours harassing fire will be carried out vigorously on the whole Corps Front.

2. During this period the expenditure of ammunition for all natures will be treble that which would be normally expended for the same period, under 52nd.DA.No.B.M.269 (Harassing Fire).

3. The following total amounts of ammunition will therefore be expended on harassing fire on Zero Night:-

BRIGADE.	8.30.PM.to ZERO Plus 2 Hours.		Zero plus 2 Hours to Zero plus 5 Hours.	
	18.Pdr.	4.5"How.	18.Pdr.	4.5"How.
52nd.Brigade.	240	60	400	120
242nd.Brigade.	240	60	400	120

4. F.A.Brigades to ACKNOWLEDGE.

                          Major RA
                        Brigade Major R.A.
20th.May,1918.   52nd.Div'l.Artillery.

W.D.
apped+iv

DAILY REPORT
52ND DIVISIONAL ARTILLERY.
6.0.AM.21/5/18 to 6.0.AM.22/5/18.

1. **OUR ACTIVITY.**

   (a) <u>Operations.</u> By day 18.Pdrs engaged :-
   Movement in ... (U.20.c.
   (U.15.d.
   Selected Points in (T.5.c.&.d.
   (T.12.a.
   Hostile Bty (UW.58, U.8.d.45.25.
   (Zone Call received at 5.35pm.
   4.5"Howitzers engaged :-
   Railhead - T.18.d.
   May N.F. Calls received during the day but only UW.58 within range.
   By night harassing fire was carried out on -
   Hostile Battery - UW.95, U.15.c.45.20.
   Roads & Tracks in (U.13.
   (U.19.d. (?)
   (U.20.d.
   (U.25.a.
   (T.30.d.
   (T.6.
   (U.7.
   Tracks at - (N.34.d.00.20.
   (N.34.d.50.90.
   Trench - T.4.b.00.50 - N.34.d.00.15.

   (b) <u>Aerial.</u> Our machines active throughout the day.

2. <u>HOSTILE ACTIVITY.</u>   Hostile guns still quiet - amount of shelling about the same as on the 20th. 100 rounds of 15cm were fired at the Dugouts at B.8.a.2.2 where much movement has taken place of late. No other large shoots reported. A 77mm battery appeared to register B.2.a.9.7. where trench goes under Road & Railway.
   At 7.pm. 77mm batteries are reported to have registered the Foot of VIMY RIDGE in B.2 and B.8.b. No further developements from this during the night.
   At 12.45am. 12 rds.of BLUE CROSS Gas shell were fired into S.30.d.
   Night very quiet.

Date.	Time.	No.of Rds.	Calibres.	Area shelled.	Direction.	Remarks.
21st.	8-10.am	100 HE	15cm	Dugout B.8.a.2.2	77°(S)GB.from B.8.a.2015	
	9.0.am.	30	15cm	T.19.c.		
	10.15.am.	10	10.5cm	F.L.in B.4.		Slow rate.
	11.10.am.	3	10.5cm	T.9.b.		
	11.30-12.15pm.	50	4.1 Gun	Dugouts & Road B.8.a.		M.P.1.well over wood.
	11.45.am.	3	10.5cm	T.9.b.2.3.		
	2.45.p.m.	12	10.5cm	T.9.b.		
	3.0.p.m.	3	10.5cm	B.3.d.	ACHEVILLE(S)	
	3.10.p.m.	20	10.5cm	T.2.d.		
	4-4.15p.m.	6	77mm	Road B.2.a.9.7		Registration(?)
	5.58.p.m.	Flash & Smoke of Heavy Gun			69°15'GB from B.1.a.75.94 (S).	
	During Day.	50	15 & 10.5 cm.	B.7.c.		
	11.30.pm.	8	15cm	B.7.b.		
22nd.	12.45am.	12	10.5cm	S.30.d.		Blue Cross.
	1.0.am.	5	15cm	B.7.b.		
	5.45.-7.45.am.	50	15cm	T.19.a.45.85.		

(b) <u>Work.</u> Nil.

P.T.O.

Page 2.

(c) <u>Movement.</u> 12 noon. Parties of men seen around Quarry in
U.26.b.80.70.
During afternoon individual movement around
same spot.
3.30.pm. Enemy working party of 12 men seen at
U.13.d.8.8. Dispersed by 18.Pounders.
Movement around CHEZ BONTEMPS also fired on.
Slight movement during day along FRESNES -
ROUVROY Line in U.21.c., U.27.a.

(d) <u>Aerial.</u> E.A. inactive during day but several bombing
machines passed over to our back areas during the
early part of the night.
One Balloon up from 10.am. to 11.am.

3. <u>GENERAL.</u> 5.0.pm. Dump exploded by heavies in MERICOURT.
<u>Visibility-</u> Only fair on account of haze.

C.H.Pluim

22/5/28.
Lieut.R.A.,
Reconnaissance Officer 52nd.Div.Arty.

SECRET.   COPY No. 36

OPERATION ORDER NO.8
BY
BRIGADIER GENERAL E.HARDING NEWMAN., CMG., DSO
COMMANDING 52ND DIVISIONAL ARTILLERY.

Reference Maps - LENS CANAL & FOOTHILL, 1/20,000.

1.   H.Q. and batteries of 56th.Brigade RFA (52nd.DA.) will relieve H.Q. and Batteries of 65th.Army Brigade RFA in the line as follows -
   (i) Night May 22nd/23rd. - 1 Section per battery.
   (ii) Night May 23rd/24th. - H.Q. and 2 sections per battery.

2.   (i) The 527th.(4.5"How) Battery will relieve the 504th.Battery.

   (ii) Guns will not be exchanged.

   (iii) There will be no movement of horses or vehicles East of the ARRAS-SOUCHEZ Road before 9.15.pm. each night.

3.   (i) Commands will pass on completion of relief Night May 23rd/24th.

   (ii) Completion of reliefs each night to be wired to this office.

4.   On completion of relief -

   (i) The Batteries relieving the 466th. and 465th. batteries will remain under the orders of O.C.52nd.Brigade RFA

   (ii) H.Q.56th.Bde RFA, remaining 18.Pr.battery and 527th.(How) Bty of 56th.Bde RFA will form a sub-group under O.C.242nd.Army Bde RFA.

5.   (i) All further details will be arranged by Bde Commanders concerned

   (ii) O.C.56th.Bde RFA will submit a copy of his orders for the Relief to this office as soon as possible.

   (iii) Orders for the relief of batteries of 65th.Army Bde RFA will be issued by Os.C.52nd. and 242nd.Army Bdes RFA for the batteries of their respective Groups.

6.   (i) On relief 65th.Army Bde RFA will withdraw to billets at their present Wagon Lines.

   (ii) Wagon Lines of 56th.Bde RFA will remain as at present.

7.   65th.Army Bde RFA will be in First Army Reserve from 8.0.am. on May 24th.

8.   O.C.65th.Army Bde RFA will carry on with present reconnaissance etc. of Brown and Green Line and ECURIE SWITCH Positions until further orders.

9.   Field Artillery Brigades to ACKNOWLEDGE.

                                                     Major R.A.
                                                     Brigade Major R.A.
Issued at 1.15.PM. May 21st. 1918.   52nd. Divisional Artillery.
   Copies 1-7 to 242nd.Bde.   8-14 to 52nd.Bde.   15-17 to 65th.Bde.
       18-22 to 56th.Bde.   23 to 9th.Bde.   24 to D.T.M.O.
       25 to 52nd.Div.G.S.   26 to 155th.I.B.   27 to 156th.I.B.
       28 to 157th.I.B.   29 to RA.18 Corps.   30 to S.C.R.A.
       31 to R.O.R.A.   32 to O i/c RA.Signals.
       33 to 16th.Bde RGA   34 to General MUSGRAVE.
   35/36 to War Diary.   37 File.   38/39 War Diary(14 DA)
       40 to File(14 DA)   41 B.M.R.A.

DAILY REPORT
52ND DIVISIONAL ARTILLERY.
6.0.AM.22/5/18 TO 6.0.AM.23/5/18.

1. OUR ACTIVITY.
(a) Operations. During the day 18.Pdrs engaged -
Movement - (at T.24.b.8.5.working party.
(in U.20.b.
(in T.3.c.
(at U.19.d.1.8.

During the night harassing fire was carried out on -
18.Pounders -
Roads & Tracks in (U.19.b.
(U.20.
(U.25.
(T.30.
(C.1.a.
(T.6.
Trenches - (B.5.d.30.80) At request
(B.5.c.55.95.) of Infantry.

4.5" Howrs.
Trenches - (B.5.d.30.85.) At request of
(B.5.c.55.95.) Infantry.
Tracks- (T.30.d.
(C.1.a.
Railways, Roads & Tracks- (U.7.
(U.13.

Total number of rounds expended :-
18.Pounders.   4.5" Howrs.
829   200

(b) Aerial. Usual fine weather activity. Enemy A.A. very active in the afternoon and especially between 7.pm. and 8.pm.

2. HOSTILE ACTIVITY.
(a) Artillery. Hostile guns more active than during the previous 24 hours. Three heavy shoots reported.
From 6.am.-9.am. some 200 rds. of 15cm were fired in S.24.d. From 5.45am.-11.45am. 350 rds., chiefly 10.5cm, some 15cm were fired in T.19.a. No doubt an area shoot intended to catch our forward guns in that area. No damage done. details given below.
From 2.am.-3.30am. 23rd. 200 rds. of 10.5cm HE and Gas (nature not yet reported) fired into A.0.c. B.7.b. and B.8.a. were also intermittently shelled with H.E. and Gas.(nature not yet reported), at 10.30pm. and 1.30.am.
VIMY was intermittently shelled with 10.5cm and ROCLINCOURT by H.V.G. during the day. A H.V. Gun fired some 20 rds. into our back areas during the night-exact locality not known.

Shoot on Forward Guns.
Time. 5.45am.-11.45am. and 2.30.pm.
(short bursts of fire).
Btys shelled. 527 Bty - single Howr.
B/56. - single Gun.
Calibre. 10.5cm.& 15cm Hows. a little Gas.
No. of Rds. Approx.350.
Directions. 38°GB.(S)from A.6.b.8.7.
110°GB "   "   "
55°GE "   " S.23.c.7.8.
Method of Observation. Not known.
Damage. Nil.

Continued.

Page. 2.

Date.	Time.	No.of Rds.	Calibre.	Area shelled.	Direction.	Remarks.
22nd.	5.45am -11.45.am	350	15cm & 10.5cm	T.19.a.		
	6 - 9.am.	200	15cm	S.24.d.		
	8.0am.	?	15cm Gun(?)	Back areas.	69°GB(F) from B.1.c.7394. F. to R. 28 secs.(approx)	
	8 - 9.am.	30	10.5cm	T.19.c.		
*	9.45-10.30am	15	10.5cm	VIMY		
	1 - 4.pm.	12	77mm	T.19.c.		
	2-2.45.p.m.	50	21cm	S.24.c.		
	4 - 5.pm.	50	10.5cm	S.24.c.		
	6.15.pm.	6	10.5cm	T.26.c.		
	10-11.30pm	50	10.5cm	S.24.c.		
	10.30pm.) 1.35am. &) 3.30am)	40	10.5cm HE & Gas.	B.7.b. & B.8.a.	BOIS BERNARD (S)	Nature of gas not yet reported.
* Repeated at	1.30-2.15pm.	20	10.5cm)	VIMY.	ROUVROY Group (S).	
	Again at 2.40-2.55pm	10	do.)			
	11.30pm & 3.10.am.	10	HVG.	Back areas- details not yet reported.	DROCOURT (S).	
23rd.	2.am.-3.30am.	200	Gas & HE 10.5cm	A.6.c.		Nature of Gas not yet reported.

TRENCH MORTAR - at B.5.a.55.10 active.

(b) Work. Nil.

(c) Movement. During day working party seen at T.24.b.5.5. This was fired on repeatedly by 18.Prs. and dispersed but always returned to work again. Nature of work could not be seen.
Some movement in U.20.b. and 21.c.
Movement at 6.pm.in U19.d. fired on.

(d) Aerial. One E.A. over B.13 at a 1000 feet(?) at 5.30am.
Bombing machines very active from 10.pm. - 12 midnight. No reports of bombs on this Div'l.Area.

3. GENERAL. Helio at 12.15.pm.64°GB. from B.1.c.73.92.
12.30pm.-1.pm.Dumps of shells & charges along DROCOURT -ROUVROY Road exploding intermittently.
Visibility- Fair.

C.K. Peen.

Lieut.R.A.,

23/5/18.   Reconnaissance Officer 52nd.Div.Arty,

DAILY REPORT
52ND DIVISIONAL ARTILLERY
6.0.A.M. 23/5/18 TO 6.A.M. 24/5/18.

War Diary
appx XVI

1. **OUR ACTIVITY.**
   (a) Operations.   At 8.pm. a working party at U.20.b.6.2 was fired on.
   During the night harassing fire was directed on Roads, Tracks and T.Ms.
   Total number of rounds expended :-

18.Pounders.	4.5"Howrs.
1378	360.

   (b) Aerial.   Several observation machines up during the day.

2. **HOSTILE ACTIVITY.**
   (a) Artillery.   A quiet day. Enemy attempted a destructive shoot on 146 H.B. and also included the Forward Gun of 122 Battery in an Area harassing shoot- details below -
   Time. 3.30 - 6.30.pm.
   Battery Shelled. Single Gun 122 Bty.-FFA
   Calibre. 10.5cm.
   No. of Rds. 150.
   Direction. Flash reported 70°GB from B.1.a.73.92.
   Flash to report 25 secs but not known if this was the battery engaging the area.
   Method of Observation. Not known.
   Damage. Slight. Gun temporarily out of action.

Date.	Time.	No.of Rds.	Calibre.	Area shelled.	Direction.	Remarks.
23rd,	7-8am	50	15cm	A.12.d.	77°GB from B.7.b.8.3.	
	3.30-6.30pm	150	10.5cm	B.8.d.8.7.		On Forward Gun 122 Bty,
	7-8pm.	50	21cm	A.6.c.		
	8-8.30pm.	20	15cm	(THELUS (A.12.a.8.8.		

   (b) Work. Nil.

   (c) Movement. 12.10pm. Movement in Trench U.20.b.
   1.30pm.   "   about U.26.b.
   4.15pm.   "   on road in U.8.d.
   5.30pm.   "   of individuals along FRESNOY-CHEZ BONTEMPS Road.
   do.   Men busy round pole & tin shed at U.1.a.90.80. Possibly a wireless station.
   7.20pm. Movement of individuals along trench U.21.b.3.6.
   8.0.pm. Working party at U.20.b.6.2.-fired on.
   8.15pm. 20 men at C.8.a.0.4 engaged by heavies & dispersed.
   8.32pm. Party of 20 or 30 at C.15.d.1.2 dispersed by Heavies.

   (d) Aerial. 8.30am. Two balloons up, descended 9.0.am.
   9.30am. 2 E.A. passed over A.5.d.-engaged by A.A. and M.G. fire.
   21.15am. 2 E.A. passed over our lines flying low.
   11.0am. 4 E.A. very high over B.13.

3. **GENERAL.**   Visibility- Poor until 6.pm.
   Good from 6.pm. - dusk.

A.J.Dufton
for
Lieut.R.A.,
Reconnaissance Officer 52nd.Div.Arty..

24th, May, 1918.

SECRET.

B.M.416.

242nd.Brigade (8)	52nd.Divn.G.S. (1)
52nd. Brigade (12)	155th.Inf.Bde (1)
D.T.M.O. (5)	156th.Inf.Bde (1)
14th.Bde RGA (1)	157th.Inf.Bde (1)
XVlll Corps HA (1)	52ndBn.M.G.C. (1)
R.A.XVlll Corps (1)	

1. Following is a list of areas for concentrated Bombardments by Heavy and Field Artillery :-

CODE NAME.	AREA.	
CHARLIE	C.1.c.55.80 Area with 200 Yards radius.	
TOM.	U.19.b.40.10 to U.19.b.30.60.	TRENCH.
BOB.	T.18.c.85.70 to T.18.d.60.70.	T.M.EMPLACEMENT.
DICK.	T.12.d.00.35 to T.12.c.80.60.	TRENCH.
REX.	T.5.b.00.20 to T.4.a.40.15.	ROAD & H.Q.
HARRY.	U.7.d.00.20.	H.Q.
EMMA.	Southern half of MERICOURT.	
VIC.	ACHEVILLE Central.	
LUX.	ARLEUX.	
NUT.	FRESNOY.	
MAB.	MABEL CORONS.	

2. (i) Bombardments will be ordered by C.R.A. as much notice as possible being given. When bombardments are ordered the Code Word will be sent followed by the Zero hour e.g. "TOM 11.am.".

   (ii) Duration of each Bombardment - 5 Minutes.
   Rates of fire per gun per minute :-
   18.Pdrs. - 3 rounds.
   4.5"Hows. - 2 rounds.

   (iii) When the objective is a Village, Field Artillery fire will be directed on the Eastern exits of the Village.
   For other objectives searching & sweeping fire will be directed on areas 100 yards on either side of, and distant from, the centre of the objective.

   (iv) Watches will be synchronised with F.A.Bdes and H.A. from this Office.

3. Co-operation of M.Gs in above bombardments is being arranged by 52nd.Division G.S. as required.

4. F.A.Brigades to ACKNOWLEDGE.

Major R.A.
Brigade Major R.A.
52nd.Divisional Artillery.

23rd.May,1918.

DAILY REPORT
52ND DIVISIONAL ARTILLERY
6.0.A.M. 24/5/18 TO 6.0.A.M. 25/5/18.

1. OUR ACTIVITY.

(a) Operations. 18.Pdrs. engaged movement during the day.
During the night harassing fire was carried out on Tracks, Roads, Railways, trenches and C.Ts in T.6, T.24, T.30, U.7, U.13, U.19, U.26.b, C.1.a., C.3.c. and B.6.c.
10.8pm. Right Group fired in response to a Test SOS sent at 10.5pm.

(b) Aerial. No flying owing to weather.

2. HOSTILE ACTIVITY.

Hostile artillery was again slightly above normal.
Enemy 10.5cm, 15cm and 21cm Hows and 10.cm Guns being extremely active on THELUS and Area to N.E. throughout the day. FARBUS WOOD was also shelled considerably during the afternoon.

Date	Time	No.of Rds	Calibre	Area shelled	Direction	Remarks
24th.	9.0am to 6.0pm	800	10.5cm How	THELUS & Area to N.E.		65° from B.1.c.7392. Flash to Report 22 secs.
			15cm How			71° GB from B.1.c.73.92 Flash to Report 25 secs.
			21cm How			79° GB.from B.7.b.8.3.(S) 85° GB.from A.6.d.9.2.(S) 62° GB.from B.7.b.5272(S)
	5-7pm.	40	10cm Gun	ditto.		70° GB.from B.1.c.7392. Flash to Report 19 secs.
	1-2.30pm.	200	77mm 10.5cm How	FARBUS WOOD B.8.a.&.c.		
	4-4.15pm.	60	10.5cm How	ditto.		
	5.45-6.40pm.	80	10.5cm How	ditto.		65° GB.from B.1.c.73.92 Flash to Report 22 secs.
	4.45pm.	10	10.5cm	S.24.central		
	6.45pm.	30	77mm	B.2.d.& B.1.c.		Behind OPPY.
25th.	1.35am.	10	77mm	B.1.b.		GAS (not identified).
	3.55am.	30	10.5cm	VIMY STA.		

(b) Work. Nil.

(c) Movement. Considerable individual movement during the day round ROUVROY Trench, U.20.b., U.11.a. and U.25.a.

(d) Aerial. Nil.

3. GENERAL. Visibility - Bad.

25th. May, 1918.

Lieut. RA
for Reconnaissance Officer 52nd. DA.

SECRET.
COPY NO. 10

Appx XIX

OPERATION ORDER NO.9.
BY
BRIGADIER GENERAL E. HARDING NEWMAN., C.M.G., DSO.
COMMANDING 52ND DIVISIONAL ARTILLERY.

Reference 1/20,000 Map Sheets 36c.SW & 51b.NW.

1. (a) 9th.Brigade RFA, less 28th.Battery RFA will move up into action to positions now under preparation in Squares B.7 and 13 and A.18 on Night 25th/26th.May.

   (b) One gun per battery will be moved on into forward positions as soon as the latter are prepared.

   (c) Separate orders will be issued for 28th.Battery RFA.

2. No movement E. of ARRAS-SOUCHEZ Road before 9.15.p.m.

3. No wagons will be taken up. 600 rds. per 18.Pr.Battery and 450 rounds per Howr.Battery will be sent up by light railway under arrangements to be made by S.C.R.A.

4. (a) The Brigade will form a sub-group under Lt.Colonel R. MARRYAT., D.S.O. Commanding 52nd.Army Bde RFA.

   (b) 9th.Bde H.Q. will function as Sub-Group H.Q.

5. Wagon Lines will remain as at present.

6. Completion of move will be reported by wire to this office.

7. F.A.Brigades to ACKNOWLEDGE.

Major R.A.
Brigade Major R.A.
52nd.Divisional Artillery.

Issued at 8.PM.
24th.May,1918.

Copies 1 -5 to 9th.Bde RFA
       6 to 52nd.Army Bde RFA
   7 -8 to 242nd. " " "
      9 to D.T.M.O.
     10 to 52nd.Divn.G.
     11 to 155th.Inf.Bde.
     12 to 156th.Inf.Bde.
     13 to 157th.Inf.Bde.
     14 to R.A.XVIII Corps.
     15 to S.C.R.A.
     16 to R.O.R.A.
     17 to R.A.Signals.
     18 to 16th.Bde RGA
  19- 20 to War Diary.
  21- 22 to " " (14 DA)
     23 to File.
     24 to File (14 DA)
     25 to B.M.R.A.

SECRET.   COPY NO. 19

AMENDMENT to OPERATION ORDER NO.9.

Reference above quoted Order para.1.(a) –
for "25th/26th May" read "27th/28th May".

[signature]
Major R.A.
Brigade Major R.A.
52nd. Divisional Artillery.

24th. May, 1918.
Issued at

To All Recipients 52nd.D.A. O.O.NO.9.

S E C R E T.
COPY NO. 19

OPERATION ORDER NO. 10.
BY
BRIGADIER GENERAL E. HARDING NEWMAN., CMG., DSO.
Commanding 52nd. Divisional Artillery.

Reference Map 1/20,000.

1. 28th. Battery RFA will go into action on Night 25th/26th. May, for a special operation, at T.13.c.60.53.

2. Guns, personnel, and ammunition will be taken up by train under arrangements to be made by S.C.R.A.

3. No limbers or wagons to be taken, nor will ammunition be taken from vehicles. S.C.R.A. will arrange for 30 rds. H.E. per Gun from Dump.

4. On arrival in position they will come under the orders of O.C. 242nd. Bde RFA.

5. The battery will be withdrawn on completion of Operation, and will go into action with remainder of 9th Bde RFA under orders to be issued later.

6. 9th. and 242nd. Brigades to ACKNOWLEDGE.

Major R.A.
Brigade Major R.A.,
52nd. Divisional Artillery.

24th. May, 1918.
Issued at 8.PM.

Distribution as per Operation Order No.9 dated 24th. May, 1918.

DAILY REPORT
52ND DIVISIONAL ARTILLERY
6.0.AM.25/5/18 TO 6.0.AM.26/5/18.

1. **OUR ACTIVITY.**
    (a) <u>Operations</u>.   During the afternoon both 18.Pdrs. and 4.5"Hows.carried out some checking of registrations.
    No 'sniping' targets offered themselves.
    Several N.F.Calls received but all out of range.
    At night harassing fire was carried out on Roads,Tracks etc. in :-

    T.6.   U.26.   T.24.b.
    U.7.   U.19.a.   T.24.d.
    U.13.   U.19.b.   B.6.
    U.25.   T.30.

    The Left Bde fired in response to a 'TEST' SOS Call at 10.36.pm.
    Total number of rounds fired :-
    18.Pdrs. 783.   4.5"Howrs. 213.

    (b) <u>Aerial</u>.   Usual activity by our R.E.8 machines.

2. **HOSTILE ACTIVITY.**   Enemy's guns even more active than on 24th.
    From 9.am.to 11.30am. four enemy batteries carried out an Area harassing shoot on THELUS and vicinity, A.18,B.7,and B.13. One report puts total number of rounds fired at 1100,another report at 500 (Silent Period prevents investigation for the time being). From 6pm.to 8pm.a further 200 rounds of 15cm were fired into THELUS and A.6.c.and d. and at 5.15am.(26th) 100 rds.of 15cm and 10.5cm into A.6.c.
    No damage to any F.A. or G.A. batteries in the area so far as is known. The ROUVROY Group and BOIS BERNARD Group appear to be the offenders.
    In addition,from 1.30pm. to 7.30pm. some 250 rds of 10.5cm were fired into T.20 and T.26,probably to harass our Forward Guns. No damage reported.
    From 5pm.-6pm.100 rds.15cm were fired into T.9.d.
    During the   T.26 was subjected to bursts of 10.5cm probably on account of the harassing fire of our Forward Guns,and from 4pm.-6pm.some 200 rds. 77mm (100 of which were PHOSGENE Gas) were fired into B.1.

Date.	Time.	No.of Rds.	Calibre.	Area shelled.	Direction.	Remarks.
25th.	8.30-8.50am.	3	10.5cm	S.11.		
	9-11.30.am.	1100	(1) 21cm	A.6.c.&.d.	(1) 90°GB.from A.6.b.7.9.(S)	
			(2) 15cm	A.11,A.12	(2) 67°GB.from A.6.b.7.9.(S)	
				A.18,B.7	(2) 62°GB.from B.1.d.2.3.(S)	
			(3)10.5cm	B.13.		
			Some Gas.			
			(4)10cm HVG.			
	10.45am.	7	77mm	T.17.a.		
	12.30pm.	4	77mm	T.27.c.0.8.		
	12.30-2.pm.	40	77 & 10.5cm	VIMY STATION.		
	1.30-7.30pm.	250	10.5cm How.	T.20,26.	61°GB.from B.1.d.2.3.(F)	
	2.7pm.	Flash of 10.5cm Gun			68°GB.from B.1.c.73.92.	F.to R.20 secs.
	3.45pm.	10	15cm	T.25.a.		
	5.0-6.0pm.	100	15cm	T.9.d.		
	6.0-8.0pm.	200	15cm	A.6.c.&.d.	72°GB.from B.1.d.2.3(S).	
	6.50-7.15pm.	20	10cm Gun	A.12.	79°,71°30',69°15' from B.1.c.73.92.	F. to R. 18, 19, 19 secs.

Continued.

Page 2.

Date.	Time.	No. of Rds.	Calibre.	Area shelled.	Direction.	Remarks.
	8.30pm & throughout night.	? Bursts.	Area shoot. 10.5cm How	T.26.	FRESNOY	99-102°GB. from B.1.d. 2.3.(S). 86°GB. from A.6.b.7.9. (S).
	9-9.30pm.	?	77mm	B.2.c.& d.		
	4.0am.-6.am. (26th).	200 (100 of which, Gas Phosgene).	77mm.	B.1.		60°GB. from B.1.c.73.92. (S).
	5.15.a.m.	100	15cm & 10.5cm.	A.6.c		

(b) Work. Nil.

(c) Movement. Nil.

(d) Aerial. No E.A. seen.

3. GENERAL. Visibility - Very poor during morning.
Slightly better during afternoon.

C.S.Plean
Lieut.RA.
Reconnaissance Officer 52nd.Div.Arty.

26th.May,1918.

Date.	Time.	No. of Rds.	Calibre.	Area shelled.	Direction.	Remarks.
	8.30pm & throughout night.	? Area shoot. Bursts.	10.5cm How	T.26.		FRESNOY. 99°-102°GB.from B.1.d. 2.3.(S). 86°GB. from A.6.b.7.9. (S).
	9-9.30pm.	?	77mm	B.2.c.&.d.		
	4.0am.-6.am. (26th).	200 (100 of which, Gas, Phosgene).	77mm.	B.1.		60°GB.from B.1.c.73.92. (S).
	5.15.a.m.	100	15cm & 10.5cm	A.6.c.		

(b) **Work.** Nil.

(c) **Movement.** Nil.

(d) **Aerial.** No E.A. seen.

3. **GENERAL.** <u>Visibility</u> - Very poor during morning. Slightly better during afternoon.

C.S. Phen
Lieut.RA.

26th.May,1918. Reconnaissance Officer 52nd.Div.Arty.

SECRET.   COPY No. 38

OPERATION ORDER NO. 11.
BY
BRIGADIER GENERAL E. HARDING NEWMAN., CMG., DSO.
COMMANDING 52ND DIVISIONAL ARTILLERY.

Appx XXIII

Reference Map 1/20,000.

1. A Projector Gas Attack will take place on the 26th.inst., or on the first favourable day afterwards, with the object of surprising and gassing the enemy occupying dugouts in the Embankment in Square N.34.c.

2. 'F' Special Company R.E. will carry out the Operation.

3. The following are the Targets -

   (i)   N.34.d.10.10 - N.34.c.80.30.
   (ii) N.34.c.80.30 - N.34.c.55.45.
   (iii) N.34.c.55.45 - N.34.c.30.65.
   (iv) N.34.c.30.65 - N.34.c.00.85.

   150 Projectors will be fired on each Target, making 600 in all.

4. The projectors will be fired from T.9.b.4.8 and material will reach this position by the CARIBOU Line.

5. (a) Projectors can be discharged in winds between S. and W.N.W. through W.
   (b) At 6.30pm. on May 26th. and daily afterwards if necessary, the Code Word "MYSTERY" or "SHIP" will be wired to Artillery Units concerned.
   "MYSTERY" means "Gas will be projected".
   "SHIP"   "   "GAS will NOT be projected."

6. Zero Hour will be 11.PM.
   The Projectors will be fired at ZERO.

7. (i) The action of the 52nd.D.A., 20th.D.A. and 16th.Bde RGA is shown on Barrage Table attached.

   (ii) The Barrage will commence at Zero minus 3 Minutes, and will cease at Zero Plus 2 minutes.

   (iii) Rates of fire for the whole period :-
      18.Pdrs. - 3 rds. per gun per minute.
      4.5"Howrs - 2 rds. per How per minute.
      6"Hows.   - 1 rd per How per minute.
      60.Pdrs. - 1 rd per gun per minute.

8. A proportion of Machine Guns will open fire from Zero minus 3 minutes to Zero Plus 2 minutes engaging O.Ps and trenches in T.4.a. and b.

9. Watches will be synchronised at 5.30.PM. on May 26th. at 155th.Inf.Bde HQ. at S.23.c.3.4.

10. F.A.Brigades, 20th.D.A. & 16th.Bde RGA to ACKNOWLEDGE.

S.F. Surue
for Major RA
Brigade Major RA
52nd. Divisional Artillery.

25th. May, 1918. Issued 11.AM.
Copies 1-7 to 242nd.Bde.   8-14 to 52nd.Bde.   15-16 to 9th.Bde
17-21 to 16 Bde RGA   22-27 " 20th.DA   28 to 52nd.Div.G.
29 to 155 Inf.Bde   30 to 156th.I.B.   31 to 157th.Inf.Bde
32 to 15th.D.A.   33 to 18 Corps HA   34 to RA.18 Corps.
35 to D.T.M.O.   36 to S.C.R.A.   37/38 War Diary.
39 to File.   40/41 War Diary (14 DA)   42 File (14 DA)
43 to B.M.R.A.

BARRAGE TABLE to accompany 52ND D.A.O.O.NO.11.

TIME.	BRIGADE.	SERIAL NO.	GUNS. NO.& NATURE.	OBJECTIVE.
Zero minus 3 minutes to Zero plus 2 minutes.	242nd.Bde.	1.	4 -18.Pdrs.	Trench T.4.a.40.75 to N.34.c.80.00.
	do.	2.	2 -4.5"Hows.	Trench at N.34.c.80.00.
	52nd.Bde.	3.	4— 18.Pdrs.	Trench T.4.b.00.45 to N.34.d.00.10.
	do.	4.	1 -4.5"How.	Trench at T.4.b.00.90.
	20th.D.A.	5.	2 -18.Pdrs.	Trench N.33.d.70.30 to N.34.c.10.60.
	do.	6.	2 -18.Pdrs.	Trench T.4.a.13.78 to N.34.c.30.50.
	do.	7.	1 -4.5"How.	Trench N.34.c.13.20.
	do.	8.	1 -4.5"How.	Trench at N.34.c.00.50.
	16 Bde RGA	9.	12-6"Howrs. 2 -60.Prs.	MERICOURT ROAD T.4.b.60.70 to T.5.c.90.60 (60 Pdrs. searching Eastern exits of Village).
Zero Minus 3 mins to Zero minus 1 min.	242nd.Bde. (28th.Bty)	10.	6 -18.Pdrs.	Trench T.4.b.00.45 to T.4.a.40.75.
	20th.D.A.	11.	6 -18.Pdrs.	Trench T.4.a.13.78 to N.33.d.70.30.
Zero Minus 1 minute to Zero.	Serial Nos. 10 & 11.			Lift 100 Yards.
Zero to Zero plus 2 mins.	Serial Nos. 10 & 11.			Lift 100 Yards.

SECRET.   War Diary   COPY NO. 37

Appx XXIV

AMENDMENT to OPERATION ORDER NO. 11.

Reference para 1 of above quoted Order - for "26th inst" read "28th inst".

S. F. Dunne

for Brigade Major R.A., Major R.A.
52nd Division.

25/5/18.
Issued at 1.15pm.
To all recipients of 52nd D.A. O.O.NO.11.

War Diary APPX X

SECRET.   COPY NO. 19

AMENDMENT to OPERATION ORDER NO.10.

Reference para 1 of above quoted order – for " 25/28th May" read "27/28th May.

S.F. Burne for
Brigade Major R.A. Major R.A., 52nd Division.

25/5/18.

Issued at 1.15pm.

To all recipients 52nd D.A. O.O.10.

War Diary.
Appx XXVI

DAILY REPORT
53ND DIVISIONAL ARTILLERY.
6.0.AM.26/5/18 TO 6.0.AM.27/5/18.

1. OUR ACTIVITY.

(a) **Operations.** From 9am.-9.45am. the Left Brigade carried out harassing fire on roads and tracks in Bde Zone.

During the afternoon some registrations were checked. Otherwise our guns were silent during the day.

At 8.30pm. the Right Bde in conjunction with 16th.Bde RGA carried out a five minutes hurricane Bombardment as follows :-

18.Pdrs. Trench B.6.d.30.75 to B.6.d.60.85 to B.6.d.60.50.

4.5"Hows. Trench Junction B.6.d.30.75.

16th.Bde RGA. SUNKEN ROAD B.6.b.central. to B.6.b.5.4.

Concentration of fire observed to be very effective.

16th.Bde RGA report -Several apparent O.Ks observed on Dugouts(in SUNKEN ROAD). Shrapnel burst average height 30'. All Guns well on target for line and range. One small fire observed which burnt for 10 minutes.

By night harassing fire was carried out as usual, the Right Bde including in their targets a number of reported M.Gs.

Total number of rounds fired :-
18.Pounders. 1045.   4.5"Howrs. 260.

(b) **Aerial.** Our machines active especially between 6.pm. and 8.pm.

2. HOSTILE ACTIVITY.

(a) **Artillery.** Enemy's guns still very active but the sum total of rounds reported is not nearly so great as that of the 25th.

Except for some Gas shelling early/this morning (27th) there were no area shoots during the period under review.

The morning was comparatively quiet but during the afternoon and evening scattered promiscuous shelling was almost continuous making it very difficult to report the number of rounds fired.

In the afternoon VIMY and GOULOT WOOD received a good deal of attention and a 15cm H.V.Gun fired on the areas A.5.,A.11 for the first time.

Gas shelling reported as follows :-
(a) 1.am-5.30am.some 200 rds.15cm and 10.5cm Green & Yellow Cross Gas and H.E. on A.6. c.&.d.and A.12.a.
(b) 2.0am-5.0.am.Continuous shelling with 10.5cm H.E. and 77mm Blue Cross Gas on B.2.c., B.8.a. & B.7.b.
(c) 4.45am-5.15am.Intermittent shelling with 77mm H.E.& Gas(nature unknown) of T.25.a.

At 5.am.a 24cm HVG. commenced to shell Divl.Hd.Qrs. with H.E. and Shrapnel at an intermittent rate - shelling continuing 12 noon 27th.

Continued....

Page.2.

Date.	Time.	No.of Rds.	Calibre.	Area shelled.	Direction.	Remarks.
26th.	7.47am	–	?	B.1.a.		73° GB.from Heavy Gun B.1.d.2.3.(S)
	7.30-8.30am.	50	15cm	VIMY STA.		
	8.45am.	–	15cm	A.6.c.		73° GB.from B.1.d.2.3.(S)
	10.55-11.50am	50	10.5cm	B.1.a.		62° GB.from B.1.d.2.3.(S)
	11.37am	–	15cm	B.1.a.		79° GB.from B.1.d.2.3.(S)
	2.40-3.15pm.	General shelling.	10.5cm	(Along foot of Ridge B.1.a. B.2,B.8 and VIMY & on both (sides of house.		76° GB.from B.1.c.73.92.(F) Flash to report 19 secs. 75°20' GB.from B.1.c.7392 Flash to report 20 secs. 79° GB.from B.1.c.73.92.(F) 62° GB.from B.1.d.2.3.
	3.30-5.0.pm.	30	15cm	A.4.b.&.d.		
	3.40 & 6.6pm.	–	8"Howr.	STATION WOOD. B.2.c.		90°20' GB.from B.1.c.7392 Flash to report 32 secs.
	4.0-6.0pm.	60	15cm	T.25.a.9.1.		
	4.10-6.0pm.	40/50.	4.1 or 15cm Gun.	Area A.5.		68°30' GB.from B.1.c.7392. F.to R.15 secs.
	4.57pm.	7	ditto.	do.		67°40' GB.from B.1.c.7392 F.to R. 23 secs.
	6.10pm.	–	15cm	B.1.a.		89° GB.from B.1.d.2.3.
	6.0.pm.	60	10.5cm How	B.1.a.		62° GB.from B.1.d.2.3.
	6.15pm.	6	10.5cm	T.13.d.		
	6.30pm.	5	15cm	T.19.b.		
	6.30pm.	12	10.5cm	T.13.c.		
	7-7.30pm.	20	15cm HVG	THELUS		68°30' GB.from B.1.c.7392.
27th.	1.0am-5.30am.	200	15 & 10.5cm	A.6.c.&.d. & .A.12.a.	FRESNOY.	Some Green & Yellow Cross Gas.
	2-5.am.	Continuous	77mm & 10.5cm	B.2.c.,B.8.a and B.7.b.		77mm Blue Cross Gas.
	2.5-3.5.am.	300 (approx)	10.5cm	B.10.		Gas.
	4.45-5.15am.	Some shelling.	77mm.	T.25.a.		Gas & H.E.

(b) WORK. NIL.

(c) MOVEMENT. 4 horsed wagon moved N.E. across U.28.a. at 7.30pm and halted at U.28.a.2.8.(approx).

(d) Aerial. No E.A. reported. A.A. very active.

3. GENERAL. Visibility- Poor in the morning. Improved after midday.

C.S.Puen
Lieut.RA
Reconnaissance Officer 52nd.D.A.

27th.May,1918.

SECRET.   B.M.457.

242nd. Brigade (8)   52nd. Divn. G.S. (1)
52nd. Brigade (12)   155th. Inf. Bde (1)
D.T.M.O.   (3)   156th. Inf. Bde (1)
16th. Bde RGA (1)   157th. Inf. Bde (1)
XVlll Corps HA (1)   52nd. Bn. M.G.C. (1)
R.A. XVlll Corps (1)

52ND D.A. No. B.M.416 DATED MAY 23RD 1918. IS CANCELLED
AND THE FOLLOWING SUBSTITUTED.

1. Following is a list of areas for concentrated Bombardments by Heavy and Field Artillery:-

CODE NAME.	AREA.
CHARLIE.	C.1.c.55.80 Area with 200 Yards radius.
TOM.	U.19.b.40.10 to U.19.b.30.60. TRENCH.
BOB.	T.18.c.85.70 to T.18.d.60.70. T.M. EMPLACEMENT.
DICK.	T.12.d.00.35 to T.12.c.80.60. TRENCH.
REX.	T.5.b.00.20 to T.5.a.40.15. ROAD & H.Q.
HARRY.	U.7.d.00.20. H.Q.
MERRY.	MERICOURT T.5.d.65.50 to 40.50.
VIC.	ACHEVILLE Central. 100 Yard Radius about T.18.d.75.60
LUX.	ARLEUX. Road B.5.b.90.25 to 58.65.
NUT.	FRESNOY. Area about U.25.c.5.4.
MAB.	MABEL CORONS. Road T.6.b.20.50 to 00.70.
JANE.	Trenches in Area T.24.c.40.85 - T.24.c.95.70 - T.24.c.70.10 - T.24.c.20.30.
ARTHUR.	Trenches & Road in Area T.24.c.90.20-T.24.d.10.80 - T.24.d.30.90 - T.24.d.50.10.
BILL.	Trenches in Area T.30.b.50.80 - U.25.a.35.90 - U.25.a.30.20 - T.30.b.60.20.
JIM.	Trenches & Road in Area U.25.b.20.10 - U.25.b.95.30 - U.25.d.95.60 - U.25.d.25.50.
FRANK.	Trenches in Area B.6.a.85.20 - B.6.b.30.60 - B.6.b.70.20 - B.6.d.10.80.

2.   Bombardments will be ordered by the C.R.A., as much notice as possible being given.
     When Bombardments are ordered the Code Word will be sent followed by the Zero Hour e.g. "TOM 11. AM."

3.   Duration of each Bombardment - 5 minutes.

4.   Rates of Fire Field & Heavy Artillery - RAPID.

Continued.

SECRET.

Page.2.

5. Number of Field & Heavy Guns and Howrs. at present available for each Bombardment are shewn in Table B.

6. (i) FIELD ARTILLERY.

    (a) Objectives for F.A.Brigades for each Bombardment are shewn in Bombardment Table A. attached.
    (b) Searching or sweeping fire will be employed according to the nature of the objective allotted.
    (c) All Forward Guns and Howitzers that can reach the Target will fire.

(ii) HEAVY ARTILLERY.

    (a) 16th.Bde RGA will arrange for Heavy Artillery co-operation in the Bombardments.
    (b) All Howrs. engaged will fire H.E. (106 Fuze) and each 60.Pr will fire 2 rds.H.E. and 3 rds.Shrapnel.
    (c) All Guns & Howrs. that can bear will shoot except those at the time being engaged by in C.B., Destructive, or Neutralisation Work.
    (d) Where the Target is given as a road or trench all batteries will distribute their fire along the target.
    When an area is given, all batteries will distribute on a N.&.S. rectangle across, and extending 100 Yards each side of the centre of the area.

7. SYNCHRONISATION. Two Hours before the time fixed for the Bombardment each Bde will send an Officer to H.Q.52nd.Army Bde RFA at A.6.c.6.7. to synchronise.
    For REX and EMMA Bombardments, in which 52nd.Bde do not shoot, watches will be synchronised at H.Q.242nd. Army Bde RFA at S.27.b.00.60.

8. F.A. and H.A.Brigades to ACKNOWLEDGE.

MERRY.

Major R.A.
Brigade Major R.A.,
52nd.Divisional Artillery.

26th.May.1918.

BOMBARDMENT TABLE A. FOR FIELD ARTILLERY.
(To accompany 22nd.D.A.No.B.M.457.)

CODE NAME.	BRIGADE.	OBJECTIVES.	
		18.POUNDERS.	4.5"HOWITZERS.
CHARLIE.	52nd.Bde	Trench C.1.a.4.0 to C.1.a. 25.20. Trench C.1.c.60.60 to C.1.c.60.45.	Trench Junction C.1.c.85.85.
TOM.	242nd.Bde	Trench U.19.b.25.60 to U.19.b.15.85.	Trench Junction U.19.b.20.80.
	52nd.Bde.	Trench U.19.b.40.20 to U.19.d.55.95.	Trench Junction U.19.d.55.95.
BOB.	242nd.Bde	Trench T.18.c.00.70 to T.18.b.10.00.	Road T.18.d.30.90 to T.18.d.40.70.
	52nd.Bde.	Trench T.18.d.60.55 to T.18.d.75.20.	Trench T.18.d.70.40.
DICK.	242nd.Bde	Trench T.12.c.65.60 to T.12.d.00.70.	Tr.Jnc.T.12.c.80.60. Tr.Jnc.T.12.d.10.80.
	52nd.Bde.	Trench T.12.d.00.30 to 20.10	
REX.	242nd.Bde	Trench T.5.a.40.30 to 80.50	Trench T.5.c.50.80 to T.5.a.65.00.
HARRY.	242nd.Bde	Track U.7.d.20.35 to 90.45	U.7.d.00.20.
	52nd.Bde.	Trench U.7.d.20.10 to U.13.b.75.80.	U.7.d.00.80.
EMMA. MERRY	242nd.Bde	Road T.5.d.60.50 to T.6.c.20.35. Road T.5.d.30.40 to 70.00	Road T.5.d.90.90. Road T.5.d.70.75.
VIC.	242nd.Bde	Road T.18.d.95.60 to U.13.a.40.00.	Trench T.18.d.85.85 to U.13.a.30.20.
	52nd.Bde.	Road T.13.d.80.25 to T.24.b.95.85. Road U.13.c.00.50 to 40.25	Road Junc.U.13.c.40.25
LUX.	52nd.Bde.	Road T.29.d.85.00 to T.30.c.10.00. Road B.6.a.00.10 to B.6.c.30.85.	Road Junc.T.29.d.9.0
MAB.	242nd.Bde	Track T.6.b.00.70 to T.6.a.80.90. Trench T.6.b.30.15-55.35.	Point N.36.d.80.00. Point T.6.b.50.70.
JANE.	242nd.Bde	Trenches T.24.c.50.80 to T.24.c.90.70.	Road T.24.d.10.75.
	52nd.Bde.	Trench T.24.c.45.15 to T.30.a.55.75.	Road T.24.c.95.15.
ARTHUR.	242nd.Bde	Trench T.24.d.30.80 to T.24.b.15.10.	Trench Jnc.T.24.d.3075
	52nd.Bde.	Trench T.24.d.10.20 to T.30.a.85.80.	Trench Jnc.T.24.d.4015
BILL.	242nd.Bde	Trench T.30.b.65.70 to T.24.d.50.00.	-
	52nd.Bde.	Trench T.30.b.60.20 to T.30.d.60.80. Trench U.25.a.20.40 to 85.00	Trench & Road Junc. U.25.a.50.25.

Continued....

TABLE "A" (Continued).

CODE NAME.	BRIGADE.	OBJECTIVES.	
		18.POUNDERS.	4.5"HOWITZERS.
JIM.	242nd.Bde	Trench U.25.b.50.10 to U.25.b.30.30.	-
	52nd.Bde.	Trench U.25.d.45.55 to U.25.d.25.35. Trench U.25.d.85.60 to U.26.c.20.65.	Trench Jnc.U.25.d.8560.
FRANK.	242nd.Bde	Trench B.6.b.05.30 to B.6.b.25.40.	-
	52nd.Bde.	Trench B.6.d.30.75 to B.6.d.60.85 to B.6.d.60.50	Trench Junction B.6.d.30.75.

TABLE "B".

1. **16TH BDE RGA.** No.of Guns and Howitzers that can fire in each Bombardment if not otherwise engaged as in para. 6(ii) (c).:-

    9.2 Hows ... 4
    8" Howrs ... 6
    6" Howrs ... 12
    60.Pr.Guns.. 12

2. **FIELD ARTILLERY.**

CODE NAME.	242ND BRIGADE.		52ND BRIGADE.	
	18.Pounders.	4.5"Howrs.	18.Pounders.	4.5"Howrs.
CHARLIE	-	-	5	1
TOM.	2	1	5	1
BOB.	4	2	5	1
DICK.	4	2	2	-
REX.	3	2	-	-
HARRY.	4	2	3	1
EMMA.	4	2	-	-
VIC.	4	2	5	1
LUX.	-	-	5	1
NUT.	2	-	5	1
HAB.	4	2	-	-
JANE.	3	1	5	1
ARTHUR.	3	1	5	1
BILL	3	-	5	1
JIM.	2	-	5	1
FRANK.	1	-	5	1

War Diary
Appx. XXVIII

DAILY REPORT
52ND DIVISIONAL ARTILLERY
6.0.AM.27/5/18 TO 6.0.AM.28/5/18.

=1. OUR ACTIVITY.

(a) **Operations.** By day 4.5 Hows. fired 40 rds. on CHEZ BONTEMPS U.20.c.50.85.
By night the hostile batteries O.31.d.42.40 and U.8.d.45.20 which had been engaged by Heavy Artillery, M.G. at B.5.a.45.18 and M.Gs at T.24.c.6.7 were harassed; the Roads and Tracks in U.7. and U.13 were swept by 18.Pdrs., and 4.5"Howrs fired on the Railway, H.Q etc. in T.6 and U.7.
Right Group fired at 11.31pm. in response to a "TEST" S.O.S. 11.29.pm.

(b) **Aerial.** Our aircraft was active all day.

2. HOSTILE ACTIVITY. Enemy artillery was extraordinarily quiet during the whole 24 hours.
During the day a 24cm. Naval Gun fired intermittently around Div. Headquarters.
Some 200 rds. were fired on VIMY during the night including a few rds. 77mm Gas shell.
Fragments of Gas Shell fired during the night 26th/27th. on A.6.c. are identified as 8" Yellow Cross.
Enemy replied with 6 -10.5cm shells on T.25.d. to each burst of fire during the night from Forward Gun in T.22.b.

Date.	Time.	No. of Rds.	Calibre.	Area shelled.	Direction.	Remarks.
27th.	5-5.30am	50	24cm. Naval Gun	W.24,30 & S.25	F.35.	Intermittent
	12.40-12.50pm	-	-	T.29.a., T.28.c.&.d.		Slight spasmodic shelling
	12.31pm.	-	-	T.14.	72°GB.(S) from B.1.d.2.3.	Slight spasmodic shelling
	3.0pm-5.0pm.	-	-	T.14.		
	3.15pm-3.30pm.	-	-	T.22.b.&.d.		Slight spasmodic shelling.
	11.pm.-12.1am.	30	77mm	T.26.		(Gas, nature
28th.	12.1-1.am	20	77mm	VIMY		(unknown.
	During Night.	200	15 & 10.5 cm	VIMY T.20.d.		
	do.	30	10.5cm	T.25.d.		

FLASH. 3.50pm-4.20pm. Flash HV Gun 86°GB. from B.7.b.6.3. Flash to report 28 secs.

(b) **Work.** Nil.

(c) **Movement.** Nil.

(d) **Aerial.** Enemy machines crossed our lines about 10.pm.
Three Observation Balloons were up during the day.

3. GENERAL. Visibility - Good.

A.J.Dufton
Lieut.R.A.
for Reconnaissance Officer 52nd.Div.Arty.

29th.May,1918.

SECRET.
==========

All recipients of 52nd D.A. No. B.M. 303 dated May 17th, 1918.

AMENDMENT TO 52nd D.A. No. B.M. 303.
====================================

1. Reference Para(11) "RED BARRAGE".

   Cancel last co-ordinate (T.3.d.00.00.) and add following co-ordinates:- T.9.b.00.60.- T.3.c. 45.00.

2. 242nd Army Brigade to ACKNOWLEDGE.

27/5/1918.

Major R.A.,
Brigade Major, R.A.,
52nd Divisional Artillery.

DAILY REPORT
52ND DIVISIONAL ARTILLERY
6.0.AM.28/5/18 TO 6.AM.29/5/18.

1. OUR ACTIVITY.
   (a) Operations.   An 18.Pdr.battery engaged with success
a hostile battery observed firing in U.26.a.
one explosion being caused. The Battery could
not be pin pointed but shoot was carried out
with G.O. Report states that battery appeared
to consist of 8 Guns.
            A few registrations were checked.
            No other firing during the day.
            At 9.29pm.the Left Group fired in response
to a TEST S.O.S.
            During the night Brigades harassed
Batteries which were at the same time being
engaged with Lethal Gas by Corps C.Bs.Targets
as follows:-
        LEFT GROUP.   RIGHT GROUP.
  U.W.94 - U.15.c.30.51.   UW.80. U.14.a.75.55.
  U.Y.25 - U.20.d.14.54.   UW.81. U.14.b.45.87.
  U.Y.57 - U.26.c.49.29.   UW.86. U.14.c.9.1.
           U.26.c.40.51.   U.20.a.85.00.
            Further harassing fire was carried out on
M.G at B.5.a.45.18.
    Batteries (U.W.1. - U.15.d.65.40.
              (U.W.58 - U.8.d.45.20.
    Tracks,Sunken Roads (T.24.   U.5.   U.25.
    Dugouts &c. in -   (T.11.   U.19.   T.18.
                        (O.1.   T.12.   U.13.
            Total number of rounds fired -
    18.Pounders - 1479 (approx). 4.5"Howrs- 400.

   (b) Aerial.   Our planes very active all day. A flight of
12 machines over the enemy's lines at 11.15am.were
heavily engaged by AA. but appeared to come
through unscathed.

2. HOSTILE ACTIVITY.
   (a) Artillery.   Hostile fire as on the 27th.still much less
than what has been usual of late.
            There were a certain number of small shoots
during the morning and B.7 and FARBUS WOOD received
a certain amount of attention but the afternoon &
night were exceptionally quiet.
            Five cases of registration are suspected.
            No gas reported.
            HV.Guns were active on Back Area but not to the
same extent as on 27th. Some 10 rounds on LA
TARGETTE and 20 rounds on NINE ELMS being the only
cases in the Div'l.Area.

Date.	Time.	No.of Rds.	Calibre.	Area shelled.	Direction.	Remarks.
28th.	8.25-9am	40	10.5.cm	FARBUS.	65°30'GB from B.1.c.7392 F.to R.20 secs.	
	10-10.30am.	25	15cm.	do.	78°GB.from B.14.a.8.6.(S) (C.A.43?)	Bursts of fire. Casualties in C/52 W.L.
	10-11.0am.	10	HV.Gs.	LA TARGETTE		
	do.	-	HV.Gun	- -	89°GB.from B.1.d.2.3. F.to R. 32 secs.	
	10.10-11.15am	20	15cm HVG	NINE ELMS.	89°GB.from B.1.d.2.3. F.to R. 25 secs.	
	10.15am.	20	15cm.	B.7.d.		
	10.30am.	10	77mm.	T.16.a.		Appeared to be registration.
	11-12.30.pm.	32	77mm	T.16.a.		ditto.

P.T.O.

Date.	Time	No.of Rds.	Calibre.	Area shelled.	Direction.	Remarks.
28th.	11.40-12.30pm	100	10.5cm or 15cm	B.7.c.& FARBUS WOOD	(69°GB.from B.14.a.8.6(S) (91°& 92° " B.1.c.7392(S) (F.to R. 31 secs.	
	12.15pm	6	10.5cm	T.19.c.		Appeared to be registration.
	1.0pm.	-	10.5 & 15 cm.	T.16.a.		ditto.
	1.15pm.	10	HVG	Back Areas.	81°30' GB.from B.14.a.8.6. (S).	
	2.pm.,5.30pm and 6.30.pm.	90	15cm	B.8.a.&.c. B.7.c.&.d.	69°(S)GB from B.14.a.8.6 83°(S)GB.from B.1.d.2.3	30 rds.each time.
	2.5.pm.	12	77mm	T.15.b.		
	2.30-.430pm.	5	10.5cm	T.16.b.		
	8.50-9.20pm.	100	10.5cm	B.7.c.	83/86°GB.(S)from B.1.d.2.3 (Eight flashes).	
	9.20pm.& at intervals during night.		77mm	T.22,T.28.d	81°GB.from B.1.c.73.92. at 9.20pm. F.to R. 18 secs.	

(b) Work. Nil.

(c) Movement. 8.0pm. 3 - 6 horsed wagons along track U.22.d., lost from view near EAST COPSE.

(d) Aerial. 9.15am. AA.active from U.28.c.1.9.
10.40am. Three flights of 5 EA.each over VIMY RIDGE.
6. 0pm. E.A.flew low over VIMY RIDGE from North to South.
10.30pm. AA.active on 90°GB.from B.14.a.8.6.
Five balloons up during the day.

3. GENERAL. 10.30am.Large clouds of smoke in DOUAI.
9.30.pm.Dump of charges burning 85°30'GB.from B.1.c.7392.
Visibility - Good.

29th.May,1918.

Lieut.R.A.
Reconnaissance Officer 52nd.Div.Arty.

S E C R E T.

          AMENDMENT NO.1.to 52ND.D.A.NO.BM.457
                Dated May 26th.1918.

Reference Code Names.

In all cases for "EMMA" read "MERRY".

                                        Major RA
                                 Brigade Major RA
28th.May,1918.   52nd.Divisional Artillery.

To
    All Recipients of above.

DAILY REPORT.
52ND DIVISIONAL ARTILLERY
6.0.AM.29/5/18 TO 6.AM.30/5/18.

1. **OUR ACTIVITY.**
   (a) **Operations.** By day registration and checking of lines.
   At 8 p.m. what appeared to be a camouflaged Tank was engaged at U.20.c.7.8. Several rounds appeared O.K., but light was failing rapidly.
   By night, Gas Bombardments were carried out on
       COY.HQ. - C.1.a.25.80.
       COY.HQ. - C.1.c.49.95.
   Harassing fire was carried out on roads, tracks etc.
   At midnight the Right Group engaged a number of selected targets in support of a raid by the Infantry at B.5.a.45.18 - enemy replied with M.G. fire.
   Total number of rounds fired -
   18-pounders - 1550. 4.5"How. 564.

   (b) **Aerial.** All classes of our 'planes very active.

2. **HOSTILE ACTIVITY.** Enemy's guns still fairly quiet. Shelling slightly less than on the 28th.
   VIMY received a good deal of spasmodic shelling also B.8 (S.E.FARBUS).
   From 11.am.-1.30pm. FARBUS was harassed with some 50 rounds of 10.5cm Gas - nature not known.
   Between 7.45pm and 11.30pm a H.V.Gun fired 4 rounds into the Area VILLERS AU BOIS - CHATEUA D'AC
   Shelling commenced again at 6.30 am 30th and continues - some 15 rounds have been fired up to the present (12 noon).

Date.	Time.	No.of Rds.	Calibre.	Area shelled.	Direction.	Remarks.
29th.	9.30-9.45am	40	10.5cm	B.8.c.& FARBUS WOOD.		
	9.45-10.15am	20	15 cm	B.1.c.		62°30'GB.from B.1.d.2.3 F. to R. 21 secs.
	10.45-11.30am	50	77 or 10.5cm	B.3.		
	11.20am	6	15 cm	T.17.d.		
	11.35am	4	10.5cm	T.8.a.9.9.		
	2.10pm	20	15 cm	T.19. VIMY		62°GB.(S)from B.1.d.2.3.
	2.30pm	8	15 cm	T.26.b. & d.		
	3-4.30pm	70	77 mm	B.8.& 9.		
	3.45pm	7	15 cm	T.2.central.		
	4.45pm	6	10.5cm	T.8.a.		
	During day	180	10.5cm	T.19.c. VIMY.		
	7.30-9 pm	80	15 cm	T.19.c.& d.VIMY.		
	8.30pm	?	15 cm	T.19.b.& d.		62°GB.from B.1.c.73.92. F. to R. 27 secs.
	10-10.15pm	24(Gas)	10.5cm	B.2.a.& c.		71°GB.(S)from B.1.c.7392
	9-9.30pm	Scattered	77 mm	B.10. & 16.		
	11pm-1.30am	50(Gas)	10.5cm	FARBUS.		

   (b) **Work.** NIL.
   (c) **Movement.** What appeared to be a camouflaged hostile Tank observed at U.20.c.70.80.
   7.30pm. 6 horsed teams & limbered wagons or guns seen passing up and down road, running through U.29.c.,U.28.d. to BOIS ENT. Our heavies engaged these with good effect.

   (d) **Aerial.** A number of bombing 'planes passed over during early part of night.

3. **GENERAL.** Visibility - very good.

30/5/18.
                                (sd) G.S.PEREN, Lieutenant, R.A.,
                           Reconnaissance Officer 52nd D.A.

DAILY REPORT
52ND DIVISIONAL ARTILLERY
6.0.AM.30/5/18 TO 6.AM.31/5/18.

APPX XXXIII

1. OUR ACTIVITY.
    (a) <u>Artillery</u>. Operations. During the day some registration was carried out & a few rounds were fired on suspected T.M.emplacement at B.5.central.
        Harassing fire at night was directed on Roads, Tracks in T.24,30, U.7,13,19 20,26,25,B.6 and on suspected T.M. B.5.central. 4.5"How.fired also on Railways and HQ.in T.6.
        Batteries fired in response to TEST S.OS. Rockets.
    Total number of rounds fired –
    18.Pounders - 762.   4.5"Hows.- 202.

    (b) <u>Aerial</u>.   Our machines were up all day & enemy AA.were not so active.

2. <u>HOSTILE ARTIVITY</u>.   Hostile artillery remained quiet during day.
    Approximately same number of rounds being fired as on previous day. HV.Guns continue to be active on back areas.
    A few rounds of 10.5cm Gas were fired on FARBUS in the afternoon.

Date.	Time.	No of Rds.	Calibre.	Area shelled.	Direction.	Remarks.
30th.	10-11am	25	10.5 cm.	T.9.b.		
	10.30-11.am.	60	10.5cm.	B.8.a.&.c.		
	11-12 noon.	25	10.5cm.	T.3.c.		
	12 noon-1.pm.	20	15cm.	T.25.b.		
	1.0.-1.30pm.	10	10.5cm(?)	T.26.c.6.3.		FRESNES.103°& 110°from B.1.d.2.3.(F).
	1.30-1.40pm.	8	77mm	B.4.d.4.4.		CREST WOOD.
	2.0-3.0pm.	20	77mm	T.9.a.		
	3.0-4.0pm.	35(Gas)	10.5cm	B.8.a.&.c.		86°30' from B.7.b.8.3.(GB)S. 81°GB.from B.14.a.8.6.(S)
	3.25pm.	Flash of heavy Howr. 90°30' from B.1.a.73.92.				F.to R.33 secs.
	3.30pm.	6	10.5cm	T.19.c.		
	4.0.-8.0pm.	A few.	77mm.	Front system.		
	6.50pm.	10	10.5cm	B.1.c.		59°GB.from B.1.d.2.3.(S).
	9.0pm.		15cm	-		81°GB.from S.23.c.7.8. (F).
	10.55pm.	10(Gas)	10.5cm	B.8.a.&.c.		
	10.50pm	10(Gas)	10.5cm	VIMY.		45°GB.from B.1.d.2.3. (S)
31st.	3.30-5.0am	50	10.5cm	T.22.		BOIS VILAIN.

    (b) <u>Work</u>. Nil.

    (c) <u>Movement</u>.   Working party in U.27.a. dispersed by H.A.

    (d) <u>Aerial</u>.   Hostile reconnaissance machines active during morning. One machine over at 8.pm.

3. GENERAL.
    Visibility - Fair.

31st.May,1918.

Lieut.RA.
Reconnaissance Officer 52nd.D.A.

DAILY REPORT
52ND DIVISIONAL ARTILLERY
6.0.AM 31/5/18 TO 6.AM 1/6/18.

War Diary
Appx XXXIV

1. **OUR ACTIVITY.**
   (a) <u>Artillery.</u> During the day some registration was carried out and 4.5" Hows fired 75 rounds on wire at T.12.c.3.7. and T.11.a.
   Harassing fire at night was directed on roads, tracks, railways, etc. in T.6. and 24. U.7.,13.,19., 25 and 26 and C.1.
   Total number of rounds fired -
   18 pounders - 755   4.5" Hows - 219.

   (b) <u>Aerial.</u> Our aeroplanes were busy all day.

2. **HOSTILE ACTIVITY.**
   (a) <u>Artillery.</u> Hostile fire continues to be below normal.
   Between 9 and 9.30 am enemy shelled B.14 (TOMMY ALLEY) with some 100 rounds of 10.5 and 15 cm.
   Some gas shells were fired into VIMY and the Right Battalion front during the night.
   H.V. guns continue to fire on rear areas. portions of 21 cm shell with false cap were found at CHATEAU D'ACQ. This H.V. gun is apparently new to this area.

Date.	Time.	No.of Rds.	Calibre.	Area shelled.	Direction.	Remarks.
31st.	9 - 9.30 am	100	10.5 & 15cm	TOMMY ALLEY B.14		Concentrated.
	10 am	6	10.5cm	T.16.b.		
	10.30am	8	10.5cm	T.15.a.		
	11.25am	8	77mm	T.27.c.& d.	DROCOURT.	
	12.59pm	20	10.5cm	T.27.a.	97° from B.1.d.2.3. Flash to Rport 20 secs.	
	1.10pm	16	10.5cm	B.1.a.&b.	WEST COPSE.	
	2.15pm	-	10 cm gun (F)		84° G.E.from B.1.d.2.3.	
	3.50pm	-	How.(F)		71° G.B.from B.1.a.35.00 (Very slow rate of fire)	
	4.30pm	6	10.5cm	T.23.a.		
	5 pm.	6	15 cm	T.19.c.		
	6.30pm	20	10.5cm	S.30.a.		
	10-10.30pm	40(app)	Gas, (Lach & Sneezing)	VIMY T.19 & B.1.	54° G.B. B.7.b.8.3.	
	11 pm	18	77mm	B.8.a.	62° from B.7.b.8.3.	
	11.30pm		10 cm HV.gun	T.27.		
	9pm to 1am	Continuous	15cm	T.19.c & d.		Gas & H.E. Green cross reported.
	2am to 3.30am	do	10.5cm	T.25.a.& b.		

   FLASHES. 11am to 12 noon Flashes seen at approx. C.6.c.6.5. from B.7.b.8.3.
   3pm to 4pm enemy battery observed firing at U.15.c.20.50.

   (b) <u>New Work.</u>   N I L .

   (c) <u>Movement.</u>   6.30pm some movement near CHEZ BONTEMPS.

   (d) <u>Aerial.</u>   Active during early morning.
   An aeroplane dropped 3 bombs on wagon lines A.7.b. about mid-day.
   3 Observation balloons up.

3. **GENERAL.**   Infantry report T.M's active at B.5.a.94.64 and B.5.b.05.05.
   Visibility - Good.

1st June 1918.

Lieutenant R.A.,
Reconnaissance Officer 52nd D.A.

No R.g 52 D
/W 3
June 1918

On His Majesty's Service.

D.A.G.
3rd Echelon

CONFIDENTIAL

O.H.M.S.
SECOND ARMY.

CONFIDENTIAL.

ORIGINAL.
******

WAR DIARY.
of
HEADQUARTERS 52ND DIVISIONAL ARTILLERY.

From :-
1st JUNE 1918.   To :-
                   30th JUNE 1918.

Volume V,
Part VI.

WAR DIARY
OR
INTELLIGENCE SUMMARY.

(Erase heading not required.)

HEADQUARTERS 52nd Div. ARTY. Army Form C. 2118.

JUNE 1918.

Sheet 1. Volume 38.

Army Form C. 2118.

Instructions regarding War Diaries and Intelligence Summaries are contained in F. S. Regs., Part II, and the Staff Manual, respectively. Title pages will be prepared in manuscript.

Hour. Date. Place.	Summary of Events and Information.	Remarks and references to Appendices
VILLERS AU BOIS. 1/6/18.	Enemy Artillery has shown more activity than during the previous few days. 100 rds 15 cm. How. were fired at the junction of the PLANK Rd. with TRIED ALLEY (B.13.b.2.6.) causing damage to an empty pit belonging to C/52.	
	A considerable amount of Gas was fired around battery areas during the early morning.	
	Our guns carried out some registration by day. 40 rds of 18-pdr. were fired into ACHEVILLE and U.13.c. and 80 rds 4.5" How. on trenches and wire.	
	By night harassing fire was directed on to various selected targets including M.G. and T.M. emplacements.	
	Enemy A.A. guns were less active than usual on our 'planes who were out patrolling all day along our front. For Daily Report vide Appx. 1.	Appx. 1.
	Operation Order No.12 sent out. 28th Battery to withdraw to wagon lines by rail on night 2nd/3rd and move into action at B.7.c.3.2. on night 3rd/4th. vide	Appx. 2.

Army Form C. 2118.

WAR DIARY

HEADQUARTERS 52ND DIV. ARTY.

OR

INTELLIGENCE SUMMARY.

JUNE 1918.

Sheet 2. Volume 38.

(Erase heading not required.)

Instructions regarding War Diaries and Intelligence Summaries are contained in F. S. Regs., Part II, and the Staff Manual, respectively. Title pages will be prepared in manuscript.

Hour. Date. Place.	Summary of Events and Information.	Remarks and references to Appendices
VILLERS AU BOIS. 2/6/18.	Enemy Arty. was quieter again than during the previous 24 hours. 77mm guns were more active than usual from BOIS-EN-T. In the afternoon our 18-pdrs fired 40 rds on T.5.d. & T.11.a. Harassing fire was brought to bear on tracks, roads, M.G. & T.M. emplacements as# selected. At 1 a.m. a 5 minute barrage was brought down in conjunction with the gas projection on N.34.c. At 7p.m. 6" Newton Trench Mortars fired 10 rds on M.G. at B.5.a.0.2. Three hits are reported. A ground haze prevented much aerial activity or possibility of observing ground movement. For Daily Report vide Orders regarding bombardments to take place on certain dates sent out with attached bombardment table - see 52nd D.A. No.BM/516, vide	Appx.3. Appx.4.
3/6/18.	Hostile Artillery has been more active, particularly on B.1. BOIS DE BONVAL S.30.c. was persistently shelled during the morning. The night was quiet. 10 rds 77mm gas were fired on MERSEY ALLEY. At 12 noon 5 minutes intense bombardment of ACONITE and ACACIA trenches (U.7.d. & U.13.b.) was carried out in conjunction with the 16th Brigade R.G.A. Harassing fire at night was directed on Roads,	

Army Form C. 2118.

WAR DIARY
INTELLIGENCE SUMMARY.

HEADQUARTERS 52ND DIV. ARTY.

JUNE 1918.

Sheet 3.

(Erase heading not required.)

Instructions regarding War Diaries and Intelligence Summaries are contained in F. S. Regs., Part II, and the Staff Manual, respectively. Title pages will be prepared in manuscript.

Hour. Date. Place.	Summary of Events and Information.	Remarks and references to Appendices
VILLERS-AU-BOIS. 3/6/18.	and tracks in MERICOURT (T.5.) and on other selected targets. For Daily Report vide	Appx. 5.
	0.0. 12/1 cancelling 0.0.12 sent out vide	Appx. 6.
	0.0.13 sent out vide	Appx. 7.
4/6/18.	Hostile Arty. has been less active again. 150 rds 15 cm were fired on Area between fARBUS and VIMY and THELUS was also shelled during the morning. 77mm fired 100 rds on Left Battalion trenches in the morning. A 15 cm How. registered Trench junction at T.15.a. 80.70. Afternoon and night were quiet.	
	In response to NF. Call at 2 p.m. 18-pdrs and 4.5" Hows. fired on hostile battery U.19.b.5.3. ACHEVILLE and CHEZ BONTEMPS were fired on in the afternoon for instructional shoots.	
	5.20 p.m. & 5 minutes intense bombardment in conjunction with 16th Bde. RGA was carried out on FRESNOY Tr., FOOT ALLEY and CORD Tr. (C.1.a. & C.) 10.16 p.m. Test S.O.S. received by Left Group.	
	11.20 p.m. 8 18-pdrs and 4 4.5" Hows fired in co-operation with raid on Railway embankments in N.33.d. and N.34.c. by 20th Div.	

Army Form C. 2118.

WAR DIARY
HEADQUARTERS 52ND DIV. ARTY.
JUNE 1918.   Sheet 4.

INTELLIGENCE SUMMARY.
(Erase heading not required.)

Instructions regarding War Diaries and Intelligence Summaries are contained in F.S. Regs., Part II, and the Staff Manual, respectively. Title pages will be prepared in manuscript.

Hour. Date. Place.	Summary of Events and Information.	Remarks and references to Appendices
VILLERS-AU-BOIS. 4/6/18.	Harassing fire at night was carried out on selected targets including the hostile battery which was engaged during the day. For Daily Report vide	Appx. 8.
5/6/18.	15 cm and 21 cm Hows. were persistently active on THELUS area during the morning and at 9.45 p.m. Harassing fire from 77 mm and 15 cm How. was directed on our trenches at intervals. A base plate of a H.V. shell which fell in W.30 at 9 p.m. measured 193mm and 65mm thick. This varies from the 21cm and 24 cm naval gun which have previously fired into this area. At 11 a.m. & 5 minutes intense bombardment of dugouts, Roads, RUPERT and UNTIDY trenches (U.25.d. & U.26.c.) was carried out in conjunction with 16th Bde. RGA. During the afternoon CHEZ BON TEMPS, ACHEVILLE church and various points were fired on for registration and for instructional shoots. At night harassing fire was directed on selected targets. 12.59 a.m. a Test S.O.S. was received and responded to by the Right Group. Our 'planes Very active and enemy A.A. was more active against them than usual. For Daily Report vide	Appx. 9.

Army Form C. 2118.

WAR DIARY

HEADQUARTERS 52ND DIV. ARTY.

OR

INTELLIGENCE SUMMARY. JUNE 1918.

Sheet 5. Volume 38.

(Erase heading not required.)

Instructions regarding War Diaries and Intelligence Summaries are contained in F. S. Regs., Part II, and the Staff Manual, respectively. Title pages will be prepared in manuscript.

Hour. Date. Place.	Summary of Events and Information.	Remarks and references to Appendices
VILLERS-AU-BOIS. 6/6/18.	Enemy Arty. has shown greater activity. THELUS area was again heavily shelled. In the evening a short intense bombardment was directed against the area North of WILLERVAL. H.V. gun fired on LA TARGET during the day and in the vicinity of Chateau D'ACQ at night. 10.5 and 15cm fired 200 rds on C/56's forward gun - no damage to gun but all ammunition blown up. At 9.30 p.m. a 5 minutes intense bombardment on U.18.d. and U.24.b., T.M's., Roads, ACCLOY, ACACIA and ACCENT trs. was carried out in conjunction with 16th Bde. RGA Selected targets were harassed during the night. 12.15 p.m. 6" T.M's fired 10 rds searching for hostile T.M. at B.5.cent. For Daily Report vide Appx.10.	
7/6/18.	Hostile Arty. has been quieter than during the previous 24 hours. The night was particularly quiet. THELUS and area was heavily shelled in the morning. 100 rds Blue Cross gas shell were fired into T.25.& B.1. at night. Several points at which movement was observed were engaged by our Arty. during the day. At 9 p.m. 18-pdrs and 4.5"Hows. fired on T.M. emplacements at B.5.b.05.05 in conjunction with T.M's.	

Army Form C. 2118.

WAR DIARY
OR
INTELLIGENCE SUMMARY.

(Erase heading not required.)

HEADQUARTERS 52ND DIV. ARTY.

JUNE 1918.

Sheet 6.

Instructions regarding War Diaries and Intelligence Summaries are contained in F. S. Regs., Part II, and the Staff Manual, respectively. Title pages will be prepared in manuscript.

Hour. Date. Place.	Summary of Events and Information.	Remarks and references to Appendices
VILLERS-AU-BOIS. 7/6/18.	By night increased harassing fire was directed against selected targets	
	10.14 p.m. a Test S.O.S. was received and responded to by Left Group. For Daily Report vide	Appx. 11.
8/6/18.	Hostile Arty. has been very quiet throughout the whole 24 hours. 5 p.m. LL Call N.28.b.90.40. - N.29.a.00.70 received by Left Group who fired 20 rds 18-pdr. and 20 rds 4.5" How in response. During the night harassing fire was again directed against selected targets. 11.24 p.m. Right Group received and answered a Test S.O.S. call. For Daily Report vide	Appx. 12.
9/6/18.	During the day enemy Arty. was much more active. The aera N. of VIMY was shelled with 15 cm during the morning and the area round THELUS with 15cm & 21cm. A heavy battery position S.W. of THELUS was heavily shelled. The night was quiet. During the day 4.5" Hows. fired 50 rds on wire in front of MERIZ tr., 30 rds on MERIM tr. and 150 rds on MEGRIN tr. Harassing fire on selected targets was carried out at night. For Daily Report vide	Appx. 13.

Army Form C. 2118.

WAR DIARY
HEADQUARTERS 52ND DIV. ARTY.
OR
INTELLIGENCE SUMMARY. Sheet 7.

JUNE 1918.

(Erase heading not required.)

Instructions regarding War Diaries and Intelligence Summaries are contained in F. S. Regs., Part II, and the Staff Manual, respectively. Title pages will be prepared in manuscript.

Hour. Date. Place.	Summary of Events and Information.	Remarks and references to Appendices
VILLERS-AU-BOIS. 10/6/18.	Enemy Arty. has been quieter again. During the morning a section of 10.5cm Hows. fired on the area about the Railway embankment in T.26.c. and B.2.b. This was probably intended for the forward guns. The pit of A/52 F.G. was hit twice - no damage done to the gun. FARBUS, VIMY and THELUS were all shelled during the day. Our 18-pdrs fired 22 rds on enemy working party in U.20.c. and 20 rds on movement in T.6. Movement in U.21.c. was also engaged. Harassing fire by night was directed on Roads, tracks and centres of activity. For Daily Report vide 52nd D.A. No.53/A sent out with reference to a Bombardment on June 12.	Appx.14. vide Appx.15.
11/6/18.	No heavy shelling by hostile Arty. reported today. 150 rds 15cm fell in T.19.c.& d. during the night. 140 rds suspected Gas fell in VIMY between 10pm and 10.30pm. Our fire was confined to checking registrations. At 8.22pm TK. T.18.a.2.2. was received. 3 Forward guns opened fire. During the night harassing fire was carried out on selected targets.	

Army Form C. 2118.

WAR DIARY
or
INTELLIGENCE SUMMARY.

HEADQUARTERS 52ND DIV. ARTY.

JUNE 1918.

Sheet 8.

(Erase heading not required.)

Instructions regarding War Diaries and Intelligence Summaries are contained in F. S. Regs., Part II, and the Staff Manual, respectively. Title pages will be prepared in manuscript.

Hour. Date. Place.	Summary of Events and Information.	Remarks and references to Appendices
VILLERS-AU-BOIS. 11/6/18.	Right Group answered test S.O.S. at 1.22am. For Daily Report vide	Appx.16.
12/6/18.	O.O. No.14 sent showing composition of Right Group from 10am June 18 vide Appx.17. Hostile Arty. has been very quiet during the day and night. Our Arty. did no firing during the day. At 7.40 p.m. a working party at U.19.d.55.97. was scattered. Harassing fire was carried out during the night on selected targets. For Daily Report vide	Appx.18.
13/6/18.	Enemy Arty. still quiet. A destructive shoot was attempted on one of our F.G's. but without success. Intermittent fire all day and night in T.13. No gas was reported. Night was on the whole quiet. During the afternoon our 4.5" Hows. fired 40 rds on Tr. junction T.18.c.90.75. and movement in T.&6.c.was engaged by 18-pdrs. At 6.15pm and 8.15pm the Right Group and 16th Bde.RGA.carried out 3 minute bombardments on selected areas in T.24. For Daily Report vide 52nd D.A. No.73/A. reference a Bombardment sent out vide Orders for bombardment on the 14th sent out. See 52nd D.A.No.78/A vide	Appx.19. Appx.20. Appx.21.
14/6/18.	Enemy Arty. has been very quiet except for one attempted destructive	

Army Form C. 2118.

WAR DIARY HEADQUARTERS 52ND DIV. ARTY.

INTELLIGENCE SUMMARY.

JUNE 1918.

Sheet 9.

(Erase heading not required.)

Instructions regarding War Diaries and Intelligence Summaries are contained in F. S. Regs., Part II, and the Staff Manual, respectively. Title pages will be prepared in manuscript.

Hour. Date. Place.	Summary of Events and Information.	Remarks and references to Appendices
VILLERS-AU-BOIS. 14/6/18.	shoot on C/52's F.G. and 130 rds 15cm on T.26.c.⊃ At 3pm Right Group, 16th Bde.RGA. and 4.6" Newton T.M's carried out a 5 minute bombardment of the enemy's wire - M.P.I. reported well on the wire. 50 rds 18-pdr. were fired on Trench junctions during the afternoon in T.18. 7.10pm A small party moving towards CHEZ BONTEMPS was dispersed. 12.25am - 12.55am Right Group assisted in operation by Division on our Right by sweeping from B.6.c.15.65. along ARLEUX main street to Cross Roads B.5.b.60.65. with 270 rds. Harassing fire was also carried out during the night. For Daily Report vide 52nd D.A. O.O.14/1 sent out postponing O.O. No.14 vide O.O. No.15 issued for bombardment of ARLEUX salient vide	Appx.22. Appx.23. Appx.24.
15/6/18.	15cm and 10.5cm Hows. active all day on forward gun area near the Railway embankment in T.26. and B.2. Otherwise hostile Arty. was quiet. Our Arty. engaged movement in T.6.c. and U.1.a.	

Army Form C. 2118.

WAR DIARY
INTELLIGENCE SUMMARY.

HEADQUARTERS 52ND DIV. ARTY.

JUNE 1918 Sheet 10.

(Erase heading not required.)

Instructions regarding War Diaries and Intelligence Summaries are contained in F. S. Regs., Part II, and the Staff Manual, respectively. Title pages will be prepared in manuscript.

Place	Hour. Date.	Summary of Events and Information.	Remarks and references to Appendices
VILLERS-AU-BOIS.	15/6/18.	Harassing fire at night was carried on Roads, tracks and trenches as selected. Left Group received and answered Test S.O.S. at 12.11a.m. For Daily Report vide	Appx. 25.
	16/6/18.	A very quiet day. Several small shoots were carried out by the enemy artillery. A H.V.gun worried A.17. during the morning but was silenced by our H.V.guns. Movement around dugout at T.6.d.35.78 and in U.1.b. was engaged and scattered. Harassing fire on selected targets was carried out during the night. For Daily Report vide	Appx. 26.
	17/6/18.	Enemy artillery quiet except for shelling of THELUS from 6 a.m. - 8.30 a.m. with 100 rds 15 cm. Night quiet. 4.5"Hows. fired 250 rds during the day on wire T.12.c.10.00.- T.4.d.9.1. 11.23pm Right Group responded to Test S.O.S. Harassing fire on selected targets was carried out at night. For Daily Report vide	Appx. 27.

Army Form C. 2118.

WAR DIARY HEADQUARTERS 52ND DIV. ARTY.
or
INTELLIGENCE SUMMARY.

JUNE 1918.   Sheet 11.

(Erase heading not required.)

Instructions regarding War Diaries and Intelligence Summaries are contained in F. S. Regs., Part II, and the Staff Manual, respectively. Title pages will be prepared in manuscript.

Hour. Date. Place.	Summary of Events and Information.	Remarks and references to Appendices
VILLERS-AU-BOIS. 18/6/18.	Quiet all day. A few rds Gas Shell were fired.	
	18-pdrs fired on movement in T.6.d. and U.25.c. 4.5"Hows.	
	registered with balloon observation on brick stacks in T.11.a.	
	Harassing fire brought to bear on selected targets.	
	For Daily Report vide	Appx. 28.
19/6/18.	Again a very quiet day. At 7.35pm 40 rds 77mm were fired at	
	intense rate at movement on the Ridge about B.1.a. and S.30.d.	
	18-pdrs engaged movement during the day.	
	At 11.15pm Test S.O.S. was received and answered by Left Group.	
	Harassing fire was directed against selected targets in the night.	
	For Daily Report vide	Appx. 29.
	52nd D.A. No.14/2 cancelling No.0.0.14 sent out vide	Appx. 30.
20th.	Again the enemy guns have been very quiet.	
	4.5" Hows fired 50 rds. on wire at T.12.c.10.00, T.4.d.90.10	
	T.11.c.80.20 and T.18.c.70.80. Movement was engaged by 18-pdrs.	
	Harassing fire was carried out by night.	

Army Form C. 2118.

WAR DIARY
OR
INTELLIGENCE SUMMARY.

HEADQUARTERS. 52nd DIVISIONAL ARTILLERY.
JUNE 1918.

SHEET 12.

(*Erase heading not required.*)

Instructions regarding War Diaries and Intelligence Summaries are contained in F. S. Regs., Part II, and the Staff Manual, respectively. Title pages will be prepared in manuscript.

Hour. Date. Place.	Summary of Events and Information.	Remarks and references to Appendices
VILLERS-AU-BOIS. 20/6/18.	At 8.30pm 6" T.M. fired on T.M. at B.5 central, and on ARLEUX loop B.5.d.1.6 obtaining several direct hits in trenches. For Daily Report vide	
21/6/18.	52nd D.A. Order No.16, re Counter Preparation, issued vide.	Appendix 31.
	52nd D.A. Order No.17, re moves of Batteries and Command of Right Group issued vide	Appendix 32.
	Enemy heavy Artillery inactive, vide Daily Report	Appendix 33.
22/6/18.	Quiet day, vide Daily Report	Appendix 34.
23/6/18.	Warning Order, re proposed gas bombardment N.W. of MERICOURT issued vide	Appendix 35.
	Enemy Artillery remained quiet except for Field gun activity on "forward gun" area. For Daily Report vide	Appendix 36.
24/6/18.	52nd D.A. Order No. 18, re gas shell bombardment issued vide	Appendix 37.
	9.30pm. 4.5" Hows. carried out gas shell bombardment N.W. of MERICOURT in conjunction with 20th D.A. and H.A.	Appendix 38.
	77mm guns continue to be active on "forward gun" area. For Daily Report vide	Appendix 39.

Army Form C. 2118.

WAR DIARY
OR
INTELLIGENCE SUMMARY.

HEADQUARTERS 52nd DIV. ARTY. JUNE 1918.

SHEET 13.

(Erase heading not required.)

Instructions regarding War Diaries and Intelligence Summaries are contained in F. S. Regs., Part II, and the Staff Manual, respectively. Title pages will be prepared in manuscript.

Hour, Date, Place.	Summary of Events and Information.	Remarks and references to Appendices
VILLERS-AU-BOIS. 24/6/18.	25 rounds, 21cm Yellow Cross gas shell fired on A.18.c. 52nd D.A. Order No.19, re moves of batteries, issued vide	Appendix 40.
25/6/18.	Very quiet day. Heavy Artillery of enemy remained inactive and activity of field guns dropped to normal. For Daily Report vide	Appendix 41.
26/6/18.	H.Q. 9th Brigade R.F.A. took over command of Right Group at noon. Quiet day. For Daily Report vide	Appendix 42.
27/6/18.	Hostile artillery quiet all day except for some shelling of area by Railway Embankment. For Daily Report vide	Appendix 43.
28/6/18.	52nd D.A. Instructions No.1, issued, re BLACK LINE and S.O.S. Barrages.	Appendix 44.
	Quiet day. A few rounds Blue Cross Gas fired on A.6.c. For Daily Report vide	Appendix 45.
29/6/18.	Detail of Heavy Artillery barrage for BLACK LINE issued vide	Appendix 46.
	52nd D.A. Order No.20 re proposed gas projection on ARLEUX issued vide	Appendix 47.

Army Form C. 2118.

WAR DIARY
OR
INTELLIGENCE SUMMARY.

HEADQUARTERS 52nd DIV. ARTY.

JUNE 1918.

SHEET 14.

(Erase heading not required.)

Instructions regarding War Diaries and Intelligence Summaries are contained in F. S. Regs., Part II, and the Staff Manual, respectively. Title pages will be prepared in manuscript.

Hour. Date. Place.	Summary of Events and Information.	Remarks and references to Appendices
VILLERS-AU-BOIS. 29/6/18.	At night harassing fire was increased to catch a suspected relief N. of ACHEVILLE.	
	77mm rather more active than usual on Embankment area. 10.5cm How. and 15cm How. were inactive. For Daily Report vide	Appendix 48.
30/6/18.	10.5cm Hows. fired 500 rounds at the rate of about 30 rounds per minute on the Embankment area. For Daily Report vide	Appendix 49.

[signature]

Brig: General RA.
Commanding R.A., 52nd (Lowland) Division.

June 1918   Original

Appendices
to
War Diary

H.Q., R.A.
82n Divn

DAILY REPORT
52nd DIVISIONAL ARTILLERY.
6 am 1/6/18 TO 6.am 2/6/18.

1. **OUR ACTIVITY.**
   (a) **Artillery.** By day some registration was carried out.
   18 pounders fired 40 rounds into ACHEVILLE and
   U.13.c., and 4.5" Hows. 80 rounds on trenches
   and wire.
   By night fire was directed by 18.Prs.on roads
   and tracks in T.6 and U.13.
   on B.5.a.53.18 - B.5.a.92.20.
   and on M.G.Empl. at B.5.c.60.95, B.5.a.60.50.,
   B.5.a.79.69, & B.5.a.71.75.
   By 4.5"Howrs.- On T.M.Empl. at B.5.a.92.64 and
   B.5.b.05.05. and on centres of
   activity in T.5 and T.6.
   Total rounds fired -
   18.Pounders - 992. 4.5"Hows. 287.

   (b) **Aerial.** Our aeroplanes were active along the front and
   were less fired on by AA. than usual.

2. **HOSTILE ACTIVITY.**
   (a) **Artillery.** The enemy guns were slightly more active than
   during the previous days.
   15cm Hows.fired 100 rds.at the junction of the
   Plank Road with TIRED ALLEY (B.13.b.2.6.) causing
   damage to one empty pit of C/52.
   A considerable amount of Gas was fired on
   Battery Areas during early morning.

Date.	Time.	No.of Rds.	Calibre.	Area shelled.	Direction.	Remarks.
1st.	7.30-9am.	100	15cm	B.13.b.		
	During Day.	-	15cm	T.19.c.,T.25.d.		
	9.0am	40	10.5cm	B.8.		68°GB.(S)from B.1.1.2.3.
	9.5am	20	do.	B.2.a.		90°GB.from B.1.d.2.3. F. to R. 18 secs.
	9.30-11.15am	50	do.	B.2.		98°GB.from B.1.d.2.3. F. to R. 18 secs.
	11.45am.		15 cm.	B.2.		68°GB.from B.1d.2.3.
		20	10.5cm	B.2.		80°GB.(S)from B.1.c.73.92.
	12.7-12.47pm	35	10cm Gun	?		63°GB.from B.1.d.2.3. F. to R. 18 secs.
	1.15pm.	40	10.5cm	B.14.b.2.1.	OPPY.	
	1.20pm.	-	77mm	B.8.d.		73°GB.from B.1.d.2.3.(S)
	1.35-1.45pm.	12	10.5cm	S.29.a.9.3.		
	2.40pm.	30	15cm	S.30.a.		
	During afternoon	40	10.5cm	S.29.b.2.5.		
	5.5pm.	25	77mm	S.24.b.		
	9.40pm.	10	10cm Gun	VIMY.		35°GB.from B.1.c.73.92. F. to R. 24 secs.
2nd.	1.30am.	100	10.5cm	B.8.a.&.b.		
	2.15-3.15am.	200	do.	B.13,B.1.& B.7.		91°,80° & 78°(F) from B.1.c.7392. GAS,Blue X and Green X.
	3.10-3.25am.	60	do.	B.1.central.	NEUVIREUIL.	

FLASH. 10.40am.Flash of 15cm How.possibly firing on A.18 was
observed 90°GB.from B.1.c.73.92. F. to R. 30 secs.
(b) **Work.** Nil.
(c) **Movement.** 6.30pm, 3 men at B.12.
(d) **Aerial.** 1 E.A. over Ridge at 10.20am.
5 Observation Balloons up.

3. **GENERAL.** Visibility - Fair.

Lieut.R.A.
Reconnaissance Officer 52nd.D.A.

one day

Appx 3.

DAILY REPORT
52ND DIVISIONAL ARTILLERY.
6.0.AM.2ND.TO 6.0.AM.3RD JUNE 1918.

1. OUR ACTIVITY.
    (a) Operations.   During the afternoon 18#.Prs.fired 40 rds. on T.5.d. & T.11.a.
    Harassing fire at night was directed on Tracks & Roads in T.6,U.7 & 13 and on
    B.5.a.53.18 - B.5.a.92.24
    On M.G.emplacements - B.5.c.6095, B.5.a.6.5., B.5.a.79.69 and B.5.a.71.75 and
    On T.M.emplacements - B.5.a.92.64 & B.5.b.05.05.
    At 1.0.am, a five minute barrage was put down in conjunction with the GAS PROJECTION on N.34.c.
    Total rounds fired -
    18.Pounders - 987.   4.5"Howrs. 274.
    At 7pm. 6" Newton T.M. fired 10 rounds on M.G. at B.5.a.0.2. Three hits were reported.

    (b) Aerial.   Activity below normal possibly on account of haze.

2. HOSTILE ACTIVITY.
    (a) Artillery.   Hostile artillery was fairly quiet, fewer rds. being fired than during the previous 24 hours.
    77mm Guns from BOIS-EN-T. were more in evidence than they have been lately.

Date.	Time.	No.of Rds.	Calibre.	Area shelled.	Direction.	Remarks.
2nd.	Throughout morning.	40	77mm	FARBUS.	WEST COPSE	(S).
	7 - 9am.	50	77mm	B.3.d.		
	9.5-12.20pm.	25	15cm	B.8.a.& b.		
		60	10.5cm		C.8.d.	(S).
	10.am.	30	15cm	T.19.c.9.7.	74°GB.from S.22.b.6560.	
	do.	6	10.5cm	T.15.b.		
	10.30am.	12	10.5cm	S.24.b.		
	11.am.	9	15cm	T.19.c.		
	1.25-1.45pm.	10	10cm Gun	B.3.b.	BOIS-EN-T.	
	2.20pm.	40	77mm	B.8.		
	3.30-5.0.pm.	15	10.5 & 15cm	T.19.c.		
	3.30-5.0.pm.	15	ditto	T.15.d.		
	5.10-5.20pm.	20	77mm	B.2.c.	BOIS-EN-T.	
	5.25-5.45pm.	30	77mm	Front line B.4 & T.28.	do.	
	9.50-10.30pm.	50(Gas)	10.5cm	T.19.c.	78°GB.from S.22.b.6560.	
	10-10.30pm.	30	15cm	T.19.c.	87°GB.from S.22.b.6560.	
	10.30pm	100	77mm	B.8.d.		
	11.30pm	70	10.5cm	B.3.d.		
	6.pm.-4.am.(3rd)Intermittent.		15cm	S.30.a.		

FLASH. 7.30pm. Flash of 8" How.(firing in A.18 ?) 90°50' from B.1.c.73.92. Flash to report 32 secs.
    These two Hows.seem to be in houses in IZEL LES EQUERCHIN.
    (b) Work. Nil.
    (c) Movement. 4pm. Movement about C.7.a.
    6-8pm. Individual movement about U.20.b.00.85.
    (d) Aerial. A few E.A. flying very high at 6.30pm.

3. GENERAL. Visibility- Fair, rather hazy.

3rd.June,1918.

for Reconnaissance Officer 52nd.D.A.
Lieut.R.A.

appx 4.

242nd Army Brigade, RFA.   52nd D.A. No.B.M./516.
52nd Army Brigade, RFA.
16th Brigade R.G.A.
52nd Division G.S.
155th Inf. Bde.
156th Inf. Bde.
157th Inf. Bde.
R.O.R.A.
D.T.M.O.
----

1. Bombardments will take place on dates specified according to Bombardment Table attached.

2. Zero hour for each Bombardment will be notified later.

3. Each Bombardment will last from Zero hour to Zero plus 5 minutes.

4. Rates of fire :-
        18-pounders and 4.5" Hows. - Intense.

        6", 8", & 9.2" Hows.   )
        60-pounders.   ) - Rapid.

5. An officer from each Brigade or Group will synchronise watches two hours before Zero at H.Q. Right Group, A.8.c.6.7. An officer will be sent with a watch from 52nd D.A. H.Q. for this purpose.

6. F.A. Groups and 16th Brigade R.G.A. to acknowledge.

                              S. F. Burne
                                 Major R.A.,
                            Brigade Major R.A.,
2nd June, 1918.   52nd Division.

BOMBARDMENT TABLE TO ACCOMPANY 52nd D.A. No.B.M./516.

Date.	Unit.	Number and Nature of Guns.	Objective.
June 3rd	16th Bde. RGA	2 — 9.2" Hows. 3 — 8" " 6 — 6" " 6 — 60-Pdrs	) ACONITE Trench U.7.d.00.20 to U.7.d.25.10.)))
		2 — 9.2" Hows. 3 — 8" " 6 — 6" " 3 — 60-Pdrs.	) Trench U.13.b.60.90 — U.13.b.50.75 — U.13.b.90.85.)) ACACIA Trench U.13.b.25.35 — U.13.b.90.90.)
	Left Group	(3 — 18-Pdrs. (1 — 4.5" How.	) ACONITE Trench U.7.d.25.10 — U.13.b.60.90.)
	Right Group	(3 — 18-Pdrs. (1 — 4.5" Hows.	))
June 4th	16th Bde. RGA	4 — 9.2" Hows. 6 — 8" " 12 — 6" "	) FRESNOY Trench C.1.a.40.10 — C.1.c.60.30.))
		3 — 60-Pdrs. 3 — 60-Pdrs.	FOOT ALLEY C.1.c.65.65 — C.1.a.25.50 — C.1.c.90.90 CORD Trench and Trench C.1.c.50.80 — C.1.cc.00.75.
	Right Group	2 — 18-Pdrs. 5 — 18-Pdrs. 1 — 4.5" How.	Trench C.1.a.10.30 — C.1.a.25.50. FOOT ALLEY C.1.c.65.65 — C.1.c.90.90 Trench junction C.1.c.60.30.

P.T.O.

Page.2.

Date.	Unit.	Number and Nature of Guns.	OBJECTIVE.
June 5th.	16th.Bde R.G.A.	2 - 9.2" Hows. 2 - 9.2"Howrs. 3 - 8" Hows. 6 - 6" Hows.	Dugouts U.25.d.40.90. RUPERT TRENCH U.25.b.60.00. - U.25.d.80.60.
		3 - 8" Howrs. 6 - 6" Howrs. 2 - 60.Pounders 10 - 60.Pounders	} Trenches U.26.c.25.65. - U.26.c.50.55 - U.26.c.40.35. } Trench U.25.d.45.70 - U.25.d.70.75. Trench U.25.d.80.60 - U.26.c.35.55.
	Left Group.	1 - 18.Pounder.	Road U.25.d.40.90 - U.25.b.60.00.
	Right Group.	2 - 18.Pounders 3 - 18.Pounders 1 - 4.5" Howr.	Road U.25.d.40.90 - U.25.b.60.00. Trench U.25.d.80.60 - U.26.c.35.55. DUGOUTS U.25.d.40.90.
June 6th.	16th.Bde R.G.A.	4 - 9.2" Hows. 6 - 8" Howrs. 12 - 6" Howrs. 6 - 60.Pounders 6 - 60.Pounders.	T.Ms and Trenches T.18.d.40.10 - T.18.d.50.10 - T.18.d. 65.15 - T.24.b.85.80. ACCLOY Trench T.24.b.30.90 - T.18.d.65.15. ACACIA Trench T.18.d.80.87 - U.13.a.30.20.
	Left Group.	3 - 18.Pounders 1 - 4.5" Howr.	ACCENT Trench T.18.d.20.50 - T.18.d.40.70. T.M. T.13.d.40.10.
	Right Group.	5 - 18.Pounders . 1 - 4.5" Howr.	ROAD T.24.b.65.70 - T.24.b.95.85. T.M. T.18.d.63.15.

DAILY REPORT
52ND DIVISIONAL ARTILLERY.
6.0.A.M. 3/6/18 TO 4/6/18 6.0.AM.

appx 5.

1. OUR ACTIVITY.
   (a) Operations.   At 12 noon a 5 minute intense Bombardment of
                    ACONITE & ACACIA Trenches (U.7.d. and U.13.b.) was
                    carried out in conjunction with 16th.Bde RGA.
                    Harassing fire at night was directed on Roads
                    and Tracks in MERICOURT (T.5),T.6,U.7,13,19,25,30
                    B.6,C.1 and on B.6.c.4.9 and B.5.central.
                    Total rounds fired -
                    18.Pounders 911.   4.5"Howrs. 261.

   (b) Aerial.   Our machines were active throughout the day.

2. HOSTILE ACTIVITY.
   (a) Artillery.   Hostile Field Guns have been more active,
                    particularly on B.1. BOIS DE BONVAL(S.30.c.) was
                    persistently shelled during the morning.
                    The night was quiet.
                    10 rds.Gas 77mm(nature not reported) were fired on
                    MERSEY ALLEY.

Date.	Time.	No.of Rds.	Calibre.	Area shelled.	Direction.	Remarks.
3rd.	9-9.30am	300	77mm	S.30.c.& A.6.c.		
	do.	250	77mm	B.1.		
			10.5cm	Area shoot.	80°GB.(S)from B.7.b.8.3.	
	10.5am	7	15cm	BRANDON TR. T.29.b.		
	10.15-2.30pm	350	15cm	BOIS DE BONVAL S.30.c.	93°GB.(S)from A.5.b.8.7.	
	9.25am & 1.15pm	20	77mm	CANADA Tr.T.21.a.		
	10.45am	6	77mm	GERTIE Tr.T.14.c.		
	Noon	8	10.5cm	FARBUS.		
	1.0.pm	12	15cm	B.8.d.		
	2.0.pm	12	77mm	PLUMER Tr.		
	During afternoon	20	77mm	DORIS Trench.		
	During Day	12	77mm	VIMY STATION.		
4th.	4.20am-4.50am	30	15cm	S.30.a.	76°GB.(S)from S.23.c.7.8.	
	5.25-6.30am	70	15cm	T.26.c.	65°GB.(S) from B.1.c.7392. 74°GB.(S) from B.7.b.8.3.	

   FLASHES. 11.30am.Flashes 70°,89°GB.from A.6.b.8.8.
            12.20-12.35pm.15cm How.101°GB.from B.7.b.8.3. F.to R. 20 secs.
            6.15pm.Flash 77mm. 52°GB.from B.8.a.3.2. F.to R. 13 secs.
   4th.   5.25am.67°GB.from B.1.d.2.3. F. to R. 15 secs.

   (b) Work.   NIL.
   (c) Movement. Slight individual movement in U.19.d.
                8.pm.Large number of men entered trench at C.7.c.5065.
   (d) Aerial. One or two E.A. crossed our lines flying high.during
                day.

3. GENERAL.   9.15pm.4 white lights near NEUVIREUIL.They were
               stationary & in a straight line facing our lines at
               intervals (from the Ridge) of half a degree
               Visibility - Good.

                                                    Lieut.R.A.
4th.June,1918.   Reconnaissance Officer 52nd.Div.Arty.

SECRET.   COPY No. 16

OPERATION ORDER NO. 13.
BY
BRIGADIER GENERAL E. HARDING NEWMAN., CMG., DSO.
COMMANDING 52ND DIVISIONAL ARTILLERY.

1. 28th. Battery will move from present position to position already prepared at B.7.c.3.2. on Night 3rd/4th. June.

2. S.C.R.A. will make arrangements for trucks, withdrawal of ammunition and supply of ammunition for new position.

3. Completion of Move to be reported to this office by Brigades concerned.

4. On completion of para.1. the Field Artillery covering the 52nd. Division will be constituted as follows :-

LEFT GROUP.   Commander - Lt.Col. COCKRAFT., D.S.O.

242nd. Army Bde RFA)	4 - 18.Pr. Batteries.
B/56.)	
527th. Battery (4.5" Howrs))	2 - 4.5" How. Batteries.

RIGHT GROUP. Commander - Lt.Col. MARRYAT., D.S.O.

52nd. Army Bde RFA)	
A/56.)	8 - 18.Pr. Btys.
C/56.)	
9th. Bde RFA (Sub-Group under)	2 - 4.5" How. Btys.
Lt.Col. COTTER., CIE., DSO.))	

5. F.A. Brigades to ACKNOWLEDGE.

S.F. Aime

Major RA
Brigade Major R.A.
52nd. Div'l. Artillery.

3rd. June, 1918.
Issued at 1.PM.

```
Copies 1 - 2 to 242nd. Army Bde RFA
       3    to 52nd.  "    "   "
       4 to 52nd. DAC.
       5 to D.T.M.O.
       6 to 16th. Bde RGA
       7 to 52nd. Divn. G.
       8 to 155th. Inf. Bde.
       9 to 156th. Inf. Bde.
      10 to 157th. Inf. Bde.
      11 to R.A. 18th. Corps.
      12 to O i/c RA Signals.
      13 to S.C.R.A.
      14 to R.O.R.A.
   15/16 to War Diary.
      17 to File.
   18/19 to War Diary (14 DA)
      20 to File (14 DA)
      21 to B.M.R.A.
```

DAILY REPORT
52ND DIVISIONAL ARTILLERY
6.0.AM.4TH TO 6.0.AM.5TH JUNE 1918.

1. OUR ACTIVITY.
   (a) Operations. 2.pm. 18.Prs. and 4.5"Howrs fired on hostile
   Battery U.19.b.5.3. in response to FF.Call.
   ACHEVILLE & CHEZ BONTEMPS were fired on in the
   afternoon for instructional shoots.
   5.20pm. A five minute intense bombardment in
   conjunction with 16th.Bde RGA was carried out on
   FRESNOY Trench,FOOT ALLEY and CORD Trench (C.1.a.
   &.c.): 10.15pm. TEST S.O.S. received by Left Group.
   11.20pm.8-18.Prs.and 4-4.5"Howrs.fired in
   co-operation with Raid on Railway Embankment in
   N.33.d. & N.34.c. by 20th.Division.
   Harassing fire at night was directed on Roads,
   Tracks,Tramways & HQ.in T.6 and U.7,13 and 19.,
   on FRESNOY TRENCH,FOOT ALLEY & on the hostile Bty
   U.19.b.5.3. which was reported by aeroplane and
   rengaged during the day.
   Total rounds fired :-
   18.Pounders. 1317   4.5"Howrs. 358.

   (b) Aerial. Our aeroplanes were very active and enemy AA.
   were more active than usual.

2. HOSTILE ACTIVITY.
   (a) Artillery. Hostile artillery was less active than on the
   previous day. 15 cm Hows.fired 150 rounds on Area
   between FARBUS & VIMY and also shelled THELUS during
   the morning.
   Field Guns fired about 100 rounds on trenches of
   Left Battalion in the morning.
   The Trench Junction T.15.a.8.7 was registered by
   15cm How.
   The afternoon and night were quiet.

Date.	Time.	No.of Rds.	Calibre.	Area shelled.	Direction. Remarks.
4th.	6-9.15am	150	15cm	B.2,8,T.25 & T.26.c. & d.	63°GB.from B.1.d.2.3.
	8.20am.	20	10.5cm	B.2.c.	
	9.0am.	4	do.	T.20.b.	
	9.15am.	30	77mm	B.8.a.&.b.	FRESNOY.
	9.45am.	4	77mm	T.21.a.	
	10.0am.	6	77mm	T.20.b.	
	10.20am.	30	10.5cm	VIMY(T.19.c)	64°,64°30' from B.1.a.3500.
	do.	6	77mm	T.20.b.	
	10.30am.	8	do.	T.15.a.	
	10.40am.	10	15cm	T.15.a.8.7.	73°GB.(F)from S.22.b.8765. Registration.
	10.30-11.0am.	12	77mm	T.13.d.	
	10.45-11.15am.	35	77mm	T.15.a.	
	11.15am.	20	10.5cm	T.15.a.8.7.	
	12.40pm	12	10.5cm	T.26.c.	65°GB.from B.1.c.7392. F. to R. 19 secs.
	3.45pm.	20	77mm	T.3.b.	
	4.0pm.	30	10.5cm	S.30.b.&.T.19.c.	
	9.40pm.	80	10.5cm 77mm.	T.8.d.	
5th.	6.50am.	6	77mm	T.8.d.	

FLASHES. During morning.45°,48° & 60°GB.from B.8.a.3.2. F. to R.
23,21 & 22 secs.
AA.Flash 64°30'GB. from B.1.a.35.00.- U.28.c.2.8.
5.40 & 8.10pm.Flashes of 10cm Guns firing on Back Areas
1. 68°GB.from B.1.c.7392. F.to R.29 secs.
2. 64°GB.from do. F. to R.21 secs.

P.T.O.

Page 2.

(b) <u>Work</u>. Fresh work is visible at U.26.b.8.7.(see (c) below).

(c) <u>Movement</u>. Throughout the day one or two men at intervals
came out of a dugout T.29.b.5.5.
Working party at U.26.b.8.7.
12 noon. Party in C.2.b.
4.15pm. Two men got out of BERNARD TRENCH in
U.8.c. and disappeared to rear.

(d) <u>Aerial</u>.   2 E.A. over our lines from 5.45am and 7.0am.

3. <u>GENERAL</u>.

8.10am. Two Trains, going North, one South.
2.15pm. Several explosions at T.30.d.8.7. caused by
heavy artillery.
11.35pm. Single Red & Single Green flares sent up by
enemy on commencement of shelling (20th.Divn
Raid).
Some Red bursting into 2 Red,& Green bursting
into 2 Green also used.

<u>Visibility</u>-   Good during day, fair during early
morning.

A.F.Dufton
Lieut.RA
Reconnaissance Officer 52nd.Div.Arty.

DAILY REPORT
52ND DIVISIONAL ARTILLERY.
6.0.AM.5TH TO 6.AM.6TH JUNE 1918.

War Diary
app 9

1. OUR ACTIVITY.
   (a) Operations.   At 11.am. a 5 minute intense bombardment of dugouts, road, RUPERT & UNTIDY Trenches (U.25.d. and U.26.c.) was carried out in conjunction with 16th. Bde RGA.
   During the afternoon CHEZ BONTEMPS, ACHEVILLE CHURCH and various points were fired on for registration & for instructional shoots.
   At night harassing fire was directed on Roads, Tracks and selected points in T.18, 30.c.&.d., U.7, 13, 19, 25, 26.a.&.c.
   12.59.am. a TEST SOS was received and responded to by the Right Group.
   Total rounds fired -
   18.Pounders - 1016.   4.5"Howrs. 273.

   (b) Aerial.   Our aeroplanes were very active throughout the day. Hostile AA Guns were more active than usual.

2. HOSTILE ACTIVITY.
   (a) Artillery.   15cm and 21cm Hows were persistently active on THELUS Area during the morning and at 9.45pm.
   Harassing fire from 77mm Guns and 15cm Hows. was directed on our trenches at intervals.
   A base plate of a HV Shell which fell in W.30 about 9.pm. is 195mm in diameter and 65 mm. thick. These measurements differ from those of the 21cm and the 24 cm. Naval shell which have been fired in this area.

Date.	Time.	No.of Rds.	Calibre.	Area shelled.	Direction.	Remarks.
5th.	6.45-7.45am	30	10.5cm	B.7.		
	6.50am.	6	77mm	T.8.d.		
	7.15am.	4	77mm	do.		
	8.30-10.30am.	40	10.5cm	B.9.&.10.		
	9.30-12.30pm.	250	A few 8") 15cm)	THELUS Area.		72°GB.from B.1.d.2.3. F. to R.18 secs. 76°GB.from B.7.b.6.3. F. to R.18 secs.
	9.40am.	5	15cm	T.19.c.		
	9.45am.	6	15cm	T.9.b.		
	10.0am.	6	15cm	T.16.a.		
	10.10am.	6	77mm	S.23.c.		
	10.15am.	13	15cm	T.10.a.		
	10.30am.	8	10cm Gun	S.23.a.		
	10.55am.	6	77mm	T.13.b.		
	11-11.20.am.	35	10 or 15 cm Gun.)	Vicinity of NINE ELMS A.17.		
	11.5.am.	4	10.5cm	T.17.a.		
	12 noon.	5	10.5cm	T.13.a.		
	12.15-12.40pm.	10	10.5cm	A.6.d.7.2.		
	12.30pm.	10	do.	S.30.c.&.29.d.		
	6.30-6.45p.m.	15	do.	T.25.c.		
	8-9.pm.	30	15cm	T.25.b.&.d.		
	9.35-10.15pm.	40	15cm	THELUS.		A cloud of smoke after each burst. 89°GB.from B.1.c.7392. F/R.22 secs.
	10.30pm.	12	10cm	T.19.b.&.c.		
6th.	10.pm-1.am.	Intermittent.	15cm	S.29.a.		
	3.45-4.30am.	2	15cm Gun	-		43°30'GB.from B.1.c.7392. F. to R. 25 secs.
	4.0-4.30am.	-	8" How.	THELUS.		90°30'GB.from B.1.c.7392. F. to R. 32 secs.

P.TO.

Page. 2.

FLASHES.   54°GB.from B.8.c.38.9&.   F. to R. 20 secs.
           44°GB.from B.14.a.8.6.   F. to R. 18 secs.
           56°GB.from B.7.b.6.3. at 2.15.pm.

(b) Work. Nil.

(c) Movement. 3-4.pm.15 men in small Groups wandered from
              U.25.b. into Quarry U.28.b.

(d) Aerial.   Three enemy Balloons up.
              6.15am.(6th.)5 E.A. patrolled front line.

3. GENERAL.   Visibility-   Good during day,poor during early
                            morning.

6th.June,1918.

A. J. Dufton
for Reconnaissance Officer 52nd.DIV.ARTY.
Lieut.RA

DAILY REPORT
52ND DIVISIONAL ARTILLERY
6.0.AM.6th TO 6.0.AM.7TH JUNE, 1918.

1. OUR ACTIVITY
    (a) Operations. At 9.30 p.m. a 5 minutes intense bombardment on U.18.d. and U.24.b. of T.Ms., roads, ACCLOY, ACACIA and ACCENT trenches was carried out in conjunction with 16th Brigade RGA.
        Harassing fire by night was directed on selected points, roads and tracks in T.6.,24.b.,U.7,13, 19.b.& c.
        Total rounds fired :-
        18-Pounders - 913   4.5" Hows. - 230.
        12.15pm 8" T.M. fired 10 rds searching for hostile T.M. at B.5.central.

2. HOSTILE ACTIVITY.
    (a) Artillery.   Enemy guns were more active.
        THELUS area was again heavily shelled.
        In the evening a short intense bombardment was directed on area N. of WILLERVAL.
        H.V. gun fired on LA TARGETTE during the day and in the vicinity of CHATEAU D'ACQ at night.
        A forward 18-Pounder was fired on for destruction as below :-
        Time   7.0 - 8.0 a.m.
        Bty.shelled   C/56 single gun.
        Calibre   10.5 and 15 cm.
        No.of rds   200.
        Method of observation   Not known.
        Damage   No damage to gun - all ammunition blown up.

Date.	Time.	No.of rds.	Calibre.	Area shelled.	Direction.	Remarks.
6th.	7 - 8am	200	10.5 & 15cm	T.25.c.		Destructive on C/56 F.G.
	7-8.30am	40	10.5 & 15cm	T.19.c.		
	8.30am	6	10.5cm	T.13.b.		
	9-10.30am	300	10.5 & 15cm	A.12 A.18 A.17.b.& d.	88°30' G.B. from B.1.c.73.92. 76°30' G.B.from B.8.a.3.2. F.to R. 21 & 16 secs.	
	11-11.20am	8	15cm	THELUS	97°30' GB.from B.1.c.73.92 F. to R.26 secs.	
	2 p.m.	4	77mm	T.13.b.		
	2.45pm	6	10.5cm	T.13.b.		
	3 p.m.	12	10.5cm	T.13.c.		
	3.12pm	10	77mm	B.10.	81°GB.from B.1.c.73.92 F. to R. 12 secs.	
	3.15pm	6	10.5cm	T.13.b.		
	4.30-5pm	Intermittent	15cm	T.13.d.		
	5 p.m.	12	15 cm	T.25.b.& c.		
	6 p.m.	6	10.5cm	T.13.b.		
	7 p.m.	30	10.5cm	T.19.d		
	8 p.m.	10	10.5cm	S.18.d.		
	9.50-10.15pm	200	10.5cm	B.3.	Area shoot. 89 & 96°GB.(S) from B.7.b.8.3.	
	10 p.m.	a few	77mmGas	T.25.c.		Blue cross.
	10.30pm	30	15 cm	T.13.c.		
7th.	4.15am	16	10.5cm	T.25.		H.E. and Smoke

FLASHES.   9.5am 15cm Gun 69° GB.from B.1.c.73.92 F.to R.21secs.
    9.30-10.30am 96° GB. from S.24.b.40.80.
    10.50am 82° GB. from S.29.b.40.80.
    11.15am-12.20pm A.A.84° & 85° GB. from B.1.c.73.92.
    3.20-3.40pm 15cm How.68°10' GB.from B.1.c.73.92
        F.to R. 23 secs.
    3.5pm 10 cm How. 88° GB. from B.1.c.73.92,F.to R.21 secs.

P.T.O.

Page 2.

(b) Work.   Work being done on trenches B.12.a. B.6.d.

(c) Movement. 4.10 p.m. men in U.26.c., C.2.b. and in quarry U.21.d.
From 6.45 p.m. to 7.45 p.m. parties of two or four men carrying white objects like sandbags along tracks in U.1.a. & b.   About 30 men in all.
7.20 p.m. two men carried from behind house T..5.d.45.30 on stretchers to a trench S.E. 18-pounders had hit this house at 7 p.m.
8.10 p.m. Single small trucks on Light Railway U.1.b. to O.32.a. at intervals of 5 minutes.

(d) Aerial.   E.A. high over our lines at 9.30 am. and 3.40 p.m. - 5 Observation balloons up.

3. GENERAL.   2.27 p.m white light went up from Road U.15.a., 66°30' GE. from B.1.c.73.92 - no action followed.
7.10 p.m. Enemy fired a few smoke shell making a screen from PEGGY Trench to VIMY in 200 yds. distances. The smoke did not last for any length of time.
Visibility - Good.

7th June 1918.

Lieutenant R.A.,
Reconnaissance Officer. 52nd D.A.

DAILY REPORT
52ND DIVISIONAL ARTILLERY
6.0.AM.7TH TO 6.AM.8TH JUNE 1918.

Appdx II.

1. OUR ACTIVITY.
   (a) Operations.   Movement was engaged by 18.Pdrs.during the day at U.20.c.8.8.(CHEZ BONTEMPS),B.6.c.6.6. and U.26.a.
   At 9.pm.18.Prs.and 4.5"Howrs fired in conjunction with T.Ms on T.M.emplacement at B.5.b.05.05.
   By night increased harassing fire was directed on C.a.a.45.00.,U.25.c.5.2.,U.8.a.8085. and on roads & tracks etc.in T.6,U.7,U.13,19,25 and 26.
   10.14pm.A TEST SOS was received and responded to by Left Group.
   Total Rounds fired :-
   18.Pounders   1672.   4.5"How. 546. 6"T.M. 10

2. HOSTILE ACTIVITY.
   (a) Artillery.   The period was quieter than previous 24 hours. The night was particularly quiet. THELUS and area to the South was heavily shelled during the morning.
   Some 100 rounds of BLUE CROSS Gas shell were fired into T.25 & B.1.at night

Date.	Time.	No.of Rds.	Calibre.	Area shelled.	Direction.	Remarks.
7th.	8-10am	15	10.5cm	T.19.c.		
	9.30-11.0am,	300	10.5,15cm & 8" How.	B.7.c.,A.12,18.		82°GB.(S)from B.7.b.8.3.
	10.0-11.0am.	100	10.5cm	FARBUS Area.		BOIS BERNARD.
	10.15am	5	do.	T.25.d.2585.		
		6	do.	B.9.a.		94°GB.(S)from B.7.b.8.3.
	1.20.pm		15cm	T.7.b.		
	5. 5pm.	30	10.5cm	T.7.& .8.		
	5.15pm.	25	10.5cm	T.8.a.		
	5.45pm.	15	do	COUNTS WOOD.(A.6.)		71°GB.from A.6.b.8.8. F.to R.26 secs.
	6.30-7.0pm.	15				
	9.10pm.	20	do.	T.19.d.		
	do.	20	15cm	T.25.c.& .d.		
	10.0pm.	10	10.5cm	T.13.c.		
	do.	25(Gas)	10.5cm	VIMY.		65°GB.(F)from B.8.a.3.2. Gas.
8th.	1.50am.	100	77mm	T.25.c.&.B.1.		
	2. 5am.	50	77mm	ditto		
	3.40am.	30	77mm	T.21.c.		

FLASHES-of H.V.Gun firing during afternoon 85°GB. & 93°30'from B.8.a.2.3. F/R. 25 & 23 secs.respectively.

   (b) Work.   Nil.
   (c) Movement.   A group with Maps at CHEZ BONTEMPS (U.20.c.) disappeared when fired on by 18.Pdr.
   Individual movement at U.26.a.&.B.6.c.6.6. was engaged by 18.Pdr.
   During the afternoon & evening individual movement was observed on tracks in U.21 & 22.
   7.30pm. 5 single trucks were seen on Light Railway in O.31 & 32.
   (d) Aerial.   One Rowland Scout high over B.13 in the morning.

3. GENERAL.   8.15pm. A Dump behind DROCOURT burnt for 15 minutes. Several explosions were observed.
   Visibility - Fair.

8th.May,1918.

A.F.Dufton
Lieut.RA
Reconnaissance Officer 52nd.D.A.

DAILY REPORT
52nd DIVISIONAL ARTILLERY
6.0AM 8th TO 6.0AM 9th JUNE 1918.

appx 2

1. OUR ACTIVITY
    (a) Operations. 5.0 pm LL Call N.28.b.90.40. - N.29.a.00.70.
    received by LEFT GROUP who fired 30 rounds
    18-pdr. and 20 rounds 4-5" How. in response.
      During the night harassing fire was directed
    on Roads Tracks etc. in T.6, U.7, 13, 19, 20,
    26A and C. and C.1.a.45.00 and U.8.a
      11.34 pm. a Test S.O.S. was received and respon-
    ded to by RIGHT GROUP.

    * Time of receipt is being investigated.
    Total Rounds fired :-
    18 pounders 1038. 4.5 Hows. 322.

2. HOSTILE ACTIVITY.
    (a) Artillery. Very quiet throughout the whole 24 hours.

Date.	Time.	No. of Rds.	Calibre.	Area Shelled.	Direction.	Remarks.
8th.	7 am.	9.	10.5 cm.	T.19.c.		
	9.am.	4.	10.5 cm.	T.8.		
	10.43-11 am.	20.	10.5 cm.	(3)B.1d.5.5	109° G(S)	from B.1d.2.3.
	12 noon.	4.	10.5 cm.	T.17.c.		
	2.20 pm.	5.	10.5 cm.	T.19.d.		
	3.30 pm.	10.	10 cm Gun.	VILLY.	69° G(F)	from B.1.c. 73.92 F. to R. 30 secs.
	2.45 pm.	40.	15 cm.	T.19.c.		
	3.30 pm.	15.	15 cm.	S.30.a.		
	3.15 pm.	5.	15 cm.	T.20.a.		
	3.35 pm.	20.	15 cm.	T.3.d.		
	3.50 pm.	4.	15 cm.	A.12.a.		
	10.20 - 10.45 pm.	60.	77 mm.	T.26.b., c. and B.2.a.		
9th.	5.30-7.15am.	50.	15 cm.	T.25.a.		

    FLASHES, 3.30 pm. Flash of H.V.G. 68°10" G.B. from B.1.d.2.3.
             10.30 pm. Flash seen 68° G.B. from A.6.b.80.70.

    (b) Work. Nil.

    (c) Movement. 8.15 pm. 10 men on road U.19.b.
                   8.25 pm. 1 horse and cart passed through U.27 and
                   28. North of East Copse.

    (d) Aerial. Nil.

3. GENERAL. From 9.30 pm. onwards heavy bombardment South of SCARPE.
    Visibility. Fair.

9th June 1918.

                               Lieut. RA.
                         for Reconnaissance Officer,
                             52nd D.A.

DAILY REPORT
52ND DIVISIONAL ARTILLERY.
6.0 a.m. 9th to 6.0 a.m. 10th June 1918.

app 13

1. **OUR ACTIVITY.**

   (a) **Operations.** During the day 4.5"Hows. fired 50 rounds on wire in front of MERIL trench, 30 rounds on MERINO trench and 150 rounds on MEGRIM trench.
   At night harassing fire was directed on Roads, tracks and centres of activity in T.6, 30, U.7, 13, 19 and 25.

   Total rounds fired :-
   18-pdrs. 735   4.5" Hows. 430.

   (b) **Aerial.** Our machines less active, probably on account of low visibility.

2. **HOSTILE ACTIVITY.**

   (a) **Artillery.** During the day the enemy was considerably more active particularly in the morning with 15 c.m. on the area N. of VIMY and with 15 c.m. and 21 c.m. on the area around THELUS. A heavy battery position S.W. of THELUS was heavily shelled.
   The night was quiet.

DATE.	TIME.	NO. ROUNDS.	CALIBRE.	AREA SHELLED.	DIRECTION. REMARKS.
9th.	6-11.30am.	400.	15 c.m.	T.13.c & T.19.a.	
	7-9.45am.	200.	15 c.m. & 8" How.	B.7.c.,A.6.c.,A.18 & A.17.a.0.0.	
	9-9.50.am.	25.	10.5 c.m.	S.30.a.	
	10-11.40am.	100.	77 mm & 10.5 c.m.	T.28.b &d. & b.4.	
	10.20-	12.	15 c.m.)	T.19.a.	
	10.45 am.	20.	10.5cm.)		
	10.55 am.	12.	77 mm.	T.17.	
	Intervals.	50.	77 mm.& 10.5 cm.	B.7.b.,& B.8.a.& c.)	66°, 87°30'.& 94°30! G.B.(S) from B.7.b.8.3.
	1.5-2.10pm.	30.	10.5 cm.	B.7a.	87°30' G.B.(S) from B.7.b.8.3.
	4.45-5.15 pm.	20.	77 mm.	B.4.& 10.	
	5.-5.30 pm.	12.	77 mm.	T.25.d.	
	During day.	(15.	77 mm.	T.20.c.2.8.	
		(20.	77 mm.	T.20.c.3.1.	
	10 pm.	10.Gas.	15 cm.	THELUS.	
		20.	15 cm.	B.2.b.0.5.	95° G.B. (F). from B.1.c.73.92.
10th.	4.0 am.	6.	10 cm.gun.	Back Areas.	74° G.B. from B.1.c.73.92. F to R.31$
	5.30 am.	20.	15 cm.	B.2.b. & T.26.c.	60° G.B (F) from B.1.c.73.92.

FLASHES. Flashes of H.V. Guns fired at 8.45 pm.:-
70° G.B. from A.3.b.8.8. Flash to report 25 secs.
86°30' G.B. from B.7.b.8.3. do. do. 27 secs.
70° G.B. from B.1.a.35.00.

   (b) **Work.** Nil.

   (c) **Movement.** Nil.

   (d) **Aerial.** 8.30 am. 3 E.A. over front line.
   8.11 pm. Captive balloon, 4,000 ft. up, observed drifting to Germany.

3. **GENERAL.**

   Visibility. Very poor.

10/6/18.

Lieut. R.A.
Reconnaissance Officer, 52nd D.A.

DAILY REPORT
52nd DIVISIONAL ARTILLERY.
6.am 10th to 6.am 11th June 18.

1. **OUR ACTIVITY.**
    (a) Operations. During the day 18-prs. fired 32 rounds on enemy working party in U.20.c and 20 rounds on movement in T.6. Movement in U.21.c. was also engaged.
    Harassing fire at night was directed on Roads, Tracks and Centres of activity.

    Total rounds fired :-
        18-prs. 860.   4.5" Hows. 200.

2. **HOSTILE ACTIVITY.**
    (a) Artillery. Enemy Artillery was less active than during the previous 24 hours.
    Throughout the morning a section of 10.5 cm Hows. fired on the area about the Railway embankment in T.26.c and B.2.b. This fire was probably intended for the forward guns in this area. The gun pit of the forward gun of A/52 was hit twice, no damage being done to the gun.
    FARBUS, VIMY and THELUS were fired on during the day.

Date.	Time.	No.of rds.	Calibre.	Area shelled.	Direction.	Remarks.
10th	7.0am-noon.	200.	10.5 cm. (?)	T.26.c.& B.2.b.	66°50' G.B.from B.1.c.73.92. F to R 20 secs.	Intermittent t' 10.0am. when a steady rate of fire was maintained.
	7.35 am. 9.10 -	7.	10.5 cm.	T.19.c.		
	9.15 am. 9.35 -	50.	15 cm.	T.17.a.		
	10.35 am.	20.	15 cm.& 10.5 cm.	T.22.a.		
	10.5 am.	30.	10.5 cm.	T.28.d.	72°30' GB from S.29.b.4.8. (F)	
	10.0- 11.12.am.		15 cm.	THELUS.	58°GB from B.1.d.2.3. F to R 23 secs.	
		4.	8"	do.	80°30' G.B. from B.8.a.3.2. F to R 35 secs.	
	10.0am-noon. 4.20-	40.	10.5 cm.	FARBUS.	?	
	8.0 pm.	50.	15 cm.	VIMY.	62° GB from B.1.d.2.3. F to R 24 secs.	
	9.50 pm.	25.	15 cm. or 8".	THELUS.	90° GB. from B.1.c. 73.92 (S).	
	10.0pm.	20.	10.5 cm.	T.13.c.		

FLASHES. During day 77 mm. 64° and 84° from B.1.d.2.3.
8.15 pm. 10 cm. gun 64° GB from B.1.c.73.92. F to R 29 secs.

P.T.O.

2.

- (b) <u>Work.</u>   NIL.

- (c) <u>Movement.</u>   8.30 am. 4 trains going South from BILLY MONTIGNY on line running through U.22.d.9.0.
    - 9.30 am. 3 trains travelling N.
    - 10.26 am. train going N towards BILLY MONTIGNY.
    - 10.55 am. 12 men went W. in U.13.d.
    - 11.0 am. working party at CHEZ BONTEMPS (U.20.c.) dispersed by 18-prs.
    - 11.10 am. 1 train going S.
    - 12 noon some movement around T.6.b.9.0. Train going S. from MONTIGNY.
    - 1.30 pm. 10 men going from ASHEVILLE towards BOIS BERNARD.
    - 2.15 pm. Train moving North.
    - 3.25 pm.   "   "   South.
    - 3.30 pm.   "   "   North.
        Movement about U.20.c & d and small parties about EAST COPSE (U.27.) all day.
    - 7.30 pm. Movement in U.21 engaged.
    - 7.55 pm. Horsed Transport in U.10.a. going to DAISY CORONS.

- (d) <u>Aerial.</u>   4 Observation Balloons up during the day.

3. <u>GENERAL.</u>   Much train movement throughout the day, see (C) above.

   <u>Visibility.</u> Good.

11th June 1918.   Reconnaissance Officer, 52nd Division.A.
                                    Lieut. R.A.

S E C R E T.   52nd.DA.No.53/A.

RIGHT GROUP
16TH BDE RGA

1. Bombardment as per Table below will take place on June 11th. 1918.

2. Bombardment will consist of 2 bursts of fire each of 3 Minutes duration, at 2 Hours interval. First burst to begin at ZERO.

3. Rates of Fire for both Field and Heavy Artillery – INTENSE.

4. ZERO will be at 9.PM.

5. Watches will be synchronised by a Staff Officer R.A. at Right Group HQ. at 7.pm.

6. Right Group & 16th.Bde RGA to ACKNOWLEDGE by wire.

UNIT.	NO.&.NATURE OF PIECES.	Objective.
16th.Bde RGA.	4-9.2"Hows.	Trench Junction T.24.d.40.13.
	4-6" Hows.	Trench T.24.d.40.30 – 40.13 – 60.10.
	4-6" Hows.	Trench T.24.d.25.20 to 50.00.
	2-6" Hows.	Trench Junction U.19.c.07.07.
	2-6" Hows.	Trench Junction U.25.a.17.81.
	6-60.Pdrs.	Trench T.24.d.40.13 to U.19.c.07.07.
	6-60.Pdrs.	Trench T.24.d.40.13 to T.30.b.70.68.
Right Group.	4-4.5"Howrs.	Trench Junction T.30.b.70.68.
	5-18.Pdrs.	Trench T.30.b.70.68 to U.25.a.17.81.

Major R.A.
Brigade Major R.A.,
52nd.Divisional Artillery.

10th.June,1918.

Copies to :- Left Group.)
            52nd.Divn.G.S.)
            155th.Inf.Bde.) For
            157th.Inf.Bde.) information.
            R.A.18th.Corps.)
            D.T.M.O.   )

War Diary

April 16

DAILY REPORT
52ND DIVISIONAL ARTILLERY.
6 A.M. 11th TO 6 A.M. 12th JUNE '16.

1. **OUR ACTIVITY.**

    (a) <u>Operations.</u> By day our fire was confined to checking registrations.

    At 8.22 p.m. T.K. T.13.a.2.2. was received. Three forward guns opened fire.

    During the night harassing fire was carried out on -

    TAMARISK TRENCH.
    T.M. at B.5.a.84.64.
    Roads and tracks
    and centres of activity } U.13. U.7. T.6.

    At 1.22 a.m. the Right Group answered a "Test" S.O.S..

    Total number of rounds fired :-
    <u>18-pounders</u> - 973.   <u>4.5" Hows.</u> - 268.

    (b) <u>Aerial.</u> Normal - Enemy A.A. specially active between 3 p.m. and 5 p.m.

2. <u>HOSTILE ACTIVITY.</u> Enemy's artillery still moderately quiet as on the 10th. No heavy shelling during the day. In the course of the night some 150 rounds of 15 cm. were fired into T.19.c. & d. 40 rounds 10.5 cm which fell in VIMY between 10 p.m. and 10.30 p.m. are suspected of being Gas.

Date.	Time.	No. of Rds.	Calibre.	Area shelled.	Direction.	Remarks.
11th.	7.20-10pm.	40	10.5cm	B.7.d.		
	10 a.m.	30	15 cm	FARBUS WOOD.		
	11.45-12noon	10	77mm	T.3.d.		
	-do-	15	10.5cm	T.10.c.		
	12.5 pm	3	77mm	T.16.b.		
	2.10pm	2	10.5cm	T.13.d.		
	10 pm.	40	10.5cm	VIMY		Gas ?
	10.30pm	20	77mm	B.1.a.		
during night		150	15 cm	T.19.c. & d.		

   FLASHES. Observed at 77 and 79° G.B. from B.7.b.8.8. at 9.30pm

   (b) <u>Work.</u> N I L

   (c) <u>Movement.</u> 6.30pm - Slight movement about OAK POST.
   8-8.30pm Movement of trucks on Light Railway in O.31. and O.32.

   (d) <u>Aerial.</u> Practically Nil. A few flights over our front trenches in the early morning by single machines.

3. <u>GENERAL.</u> Visibility - Good.

12th June, 1916.

Lieutenant R.A.,
Reconnaissance Officer, 52nd D.A.

SECRET.   COPY NO. 19

OPERATION ORDER NO.14
BY
BRIGADIER GENERAL E.HARDING NEWMAN., CMG., DSO.
COMMANDING 52ND DIVISIONAL ARTILLERY.

1. At 10.AM. June 18th. the composition of the Right Group will be re-adjusted as follows :-

   Commander - Lt.Colonel COTTER., CIE., DSO.

   (i) NORTH SUB-GROUP. - Commander - Lt.Col.MARRYAT., D.S.O.

   52nd.Army Brigade R.F.A.
   A/56. and C/56.

   (ii) SOUTH SUB-GROUP. - Commander - Lt.Colonel COTTER., CIE., DSO.

   9th.Brigade R.F.A.

2. By 10.AM. June 18th -

   (i) Lt.Col.COTTER will establish his H.Q. at H.Q. now used by Lt.Colonel MARRYAT at A.6.c.6.7.

   (ii) Lt.Col.MARRYAT will establish his HQ. at A.6.c.93.33 which will be vacated by D/242 before June 17th.

3. Lt.Colonel INGRAM and H.Q.56th.Bde RFA will take over command of North Sub-Group on June 25th.
   Lt.Colonel INGRAM and Adjutant will work under Lt.Colonel MARRYAT between June 18th.and 25th.

4. Right Group to ACKNOWLEDGE.

                                        Major RA
                                   Brigade Major R.A.
11th.June, 1918.   52nd.Divisional Artillery.
Issued at 1.15.PM.

           Copies 1/2 to Right Group.
                  3   " Left Group
                  4   " D.T.M.O.
                  5   " 16th.Bde RGA
                  6   " 16th.Squadron RAF
                  7   " RA.18th.Corps.
                  8   " 52nd.Divn.GS.
                  9   " 155th.Inf.Bde.
                 10   " 156th.Inf.Bde.
                 11   " 157th.Inf.Bde.
                 12   " 15th.D.A.
                 13   " O i/c RA Signals.
                 14   " S.C.R.A
                 15   " .RO.R.A.
                 16   " 56th.Bde RFA
                 17   " 52nd.D.A.C.
              18/19   " War Diary.
              20/21   " War Diary (14 DA)
                 22   " File.
                 23   " File (14 DA)
                 24   " B.M.R.A.
                 25   " 20th.Sec.No.1. Balloon Coy.

DAILY REPORT
52ND DIVISIONAL ARTILLERY
6.0 AM. 12TH TO 6.0 AM 13TH JUNE '18.

App 18

1. OUR ACTIVITY.
    (a) Operations.   No firing during the day.
        At 7.40 p.m. a working party at U.19.d.55.97 was scattered.
        Harassing fire during the night on the following:
    Suspected M.G's. - B.5.a.70.65. B.5.b.75.90.
    Roads, Tracks)
    and centres of) U.13., U.19., U.25., T.6., U.7.
    activity.)
        Total number of rounds fired :-
        18-pounder - 769.   4.5" How. - 200.

    (b) Aerial.   Usual activity of Corps Squadron.

2. HOSTILE ACTIVITY.
    (a) Artillery.   A very quiet day - shelling even less than on the 11th. and chiefly confined to small shoots on our "Forward Gun Area" from STATION WOOD to LA CHAUDIERE. No Gas reported. A 77mm Battery fired 3 rds from very close behind FRESNOY. B.2.a. & T.26.c. were intermittently shelled with 15 cm during the night. This shelling is reported as having increased in violence at 6.15 a.m. 13th.

Date.	Time.	No. of Rds.	Calibre.	Area Shelled.	Direction.	Remarks.
12th.	9 a.m.	30	10.5cm	T.13.c.		
	10.22am	20	77mm	T.25.c. B.1.a.	68° G.B.(S) from B.1.d.0.5.	
	11.20am	3	77mm	T.20.c.		
	11.30am	20	10.5cm & T.M's.)	B.4.a.		BOIS BERNARD.
	11.35am	4	10.5cm	T.23.c.		
	12.30pm	3	10.5cm	T.22.d.		
	1.40pm	10	15 cm	A.12.a.& c.		
	5.30pm	14	15cm	T.18.c.		
	5.45-8pm	45	15 cm	T.26.c. & B.2.c.	FRESNES & 61°from B.1.d.0.5.	)Sweeping)& searching.
	-do-	irregular bursts.	10.5cm	VIMY.	64°30'from B.1.c.75.92. F. to R. 25 secs.	
	6.10pm	10	15 cm	STATION WOOD.		
During night		50	15 cm	T.26.c. & B.2.a.		

    FLASHES.   8.45 p.m. - 2 flashes from Heavy Guns 82° from B.8.a.3.2.

    (b) Work.   Working party at U.19.d.55.98.(dispersed.)

    (c) Movement.   Usual movement around CHEZ BONTEMPS.

    (d) Aerial.   One E.A. over VIMY Ridge, from 10.30 a.m. -10.45am No enemy balloons up.

3. GENERAL.   Daylight Lamp seen working at U.6.b.9.9.(approx.)
    Visibility - only Fair.

Lieutenant, R.A.,
13th June, 1918.   Reconnaissance Officer 52nd D.A.

DAILY REPORT
52ND DIVISIONAL ARTILLERY
6.0.A.M. 13TH TO 6.0 A.M. 14TH JUNE '18.

1. **OUR ACTIVITY.**
   (a) <u>Operations</u>.   During the afternoon 4.5" Hows. fired 40 rds. on trench junction T.18.c.90.75. and 18-pdrs. fired on movement in T.6.c.

   At 6.15 p.m. and 8.15 p.m. the Right Group, and 16th Brigade RGA. carried out 3 mins.Bombardments as follows :-

Unit.	Objective.
16th Bde.R.G.A.	Trench Triangle T.24.b.55.02.
	Trench T.24.b.55.05.to 45.25.
	Trench T.24.b.60.00.to T.24.d.40.85.
	Trench T.24.b.60.00.to T.24.d.90.90.
	Trench T.24.b.60.00. to U.19.c.10.71.
	Road T.24.b.35.40.to 95.85.
Right Group.	Trench U.19.a.00.00.to T.24.b.80.50.

   At 11.18·5 p.m. the Left Group answered a 'Test' S.O.S.

   Night harassing fire on targets as under :-
   Roads and Tracks and) U.7., U.19., U.6., C.1.a.
   centres of activity.)   and U.13.d.
                              CHEZ BONTEMPS.
   Cross Roads   -   B.6.c.6.6.
   Total number of rounds fired :-
   18-Pounder - 930.   4.5"Howitzer - 340.

   (b) <u>Aerial</u>.   Fewer 'Planes over than usual.

2. **HOSTILE ACTIVITY.**
   (a) <u>Artillery</u>.   Enemy's guns still comparitively quiet. A destructive shoot was attempted on one of our forward guns without success; otherwise nature of fire chiefly harassing by 77mm and 10.5cm.

   T.13. was intermittently shelled throughout the 24 hours and in the evening bursts of harassing fire were opened on the FARBUS - WILLERVAL Road, THELUS - COMMANDANTS HOUSE Road and WILLERVAL. Both in the early evening and early morning GOULOT WOOD received bursts of 10.5cm. On the whole the night was quiet. No Gas reported.

   Details of destructive shoot.:-
   Time.   5.30 a.m. (13th) - 9.30 a.m.
   Bty.Shelled.   19th Battery Forward Gun T.26.c.70.15.
   Calibre.   10.5cm.
   No.of Rds.   250.
   Direction.   60° G.B. (S) from T.26.c.70.15.
   Method of Observation.   Unknown.
   Damage.   Pit caved in at back.

Date.	Time.	No.of Rds.	Calibre.	Area Shelled.	Direction.	Remarks.
13th.	5.30am -9.30am.	250	10.5cm	19th F.G.at T.26.c.70.15.	60° G.B.(S) from Gun Pit.	
	6.-7.0am	50	10.5cm	FARBUS-WILLERVAL ROAD B.8,5.		CPPY.
	9.55am	3	77mm	T.13.d.		
	10.0am	20	77mm	T.20.c.		
	10.20am	8	77mm	T.13.b.		
	10.30am	6	77mm	T.8.c.		
	3.0pm.	4	15cm	T.13.c.		
	3.20pm	3	10.5cm	T.13.d.		
	5.0pm	30	15cm	THELUS Rd.A.12.d., B.7.c.		

P.T.O.

- 2 -

Date.	Time.	No.of rds.	Calibre.	Area shelled.	Direction.	Remarks.
13th.	5.20pm	18	21 cm	B.2.c.		70°G.B.(S)from A.8.b.8.7.
	5.25-6.pm	30	10.5cm	B.1.a.8.3.(approx.)		69°30' G.B.(S) From A.6.b.8.8.F.to R.42secs
	7.45-10.30pm	18	10.5cm	T.19.a.		
	7.50pm	10	10.5cm	B.1.a.8.3.(approx.)		92°G.B.(S) from A.6.b.8.8. F.to R.35secs.
	8.0pm	8	15 cm	T.13.d.		
	9.-9.15pm	40	10.5cm	WILLERVAL & Vicinity.		79°G.B.(S) from B.7.b.7.3.
14th.	2.45am	27	77mm	T.13.b		
	2.45-2.15am	40	10.5cm	B.1.a.		
	3.50am	8	77mm	T.13.b.		
	5.0 am	10	77mm	T.13.b.		

(b) Work. NIL.

(c) Movement.
- 4.30pm — Movement in U.25.d. and BOIS BERNARD. Individuals on track U.21.c.8.8.-U.21.c.7.0.
- 6.0pm — Considerable movement on tracks in U.1.a. & b.
- 7.15-8.0pm — Trucks on Tramway in O.31. & O.32., all moving West.
- 7.45pm — 15 men in full kit in T.6.c.- dispersed.
- 6.45pm — Individual movement at U.1.b.7.1.

(d) Aerial. One E.A. over VIMY Ridge from 7.30am to 8am.

3. GENERAL. 10.30pm Two Red lights, repeated twice, sent up from behind MERICOURT. No apparent action.
Visibility - Good.

14th June, 1918.

Lieutenant R.A.,
Reconnaissance Officer 52nd D.A.

S E C R E T.   52nd.D.A.No.73/A.

RIGHT GROUP
18TH BDE RGA

1. Bombardment as per Table below will take place on June 13th. 1918.

2. Bombardment will consist of 2 bursts of fire each of 5 Minutes duration, at 2 Hours interval. First burst to begin at ZERO.

3. Rates of Fire for both Field and Heavy Artillery – INTENSE.

4. Zero will be at 6.15.PM.

5. Watches will be synchronised at Right Group H.Q. at 3.pm.

6. Right Group and 18th.Bde RGA to ACKNOWLEDGE by wire.

UNIT.	NO.& NATURE OF PIECES.	OBJECTIVE.
18th.Bde R.G.A.	4 –9.2" Hows))	Trench Triangle T.24.b.55.02.
	4 –6" Hows.	Trench T.24.b.55.05 to 45.25.
	4 –6" Hows.	Trench T.24.b.60.00 to T.24.d.10.85.
	4 –6" Hows.	Trench T.24.b.60.00 to T.24.d.90.90.
	6 –60.Pdrs.	Trench T.24.b.60.00 to U.19.c.10.71.
	6 –60.Pdrs.	Road T.24.b.35.40 to 95.85.
Right Group.	4 –4.5" Hows.) 5 –18.Pdrs.)	Trench U.19.a.00.00 to T.24.b.80.50.

Major R.A.
Brigade Major R.A.
52nd.Divisional Artillery.

13th.June,1918.

Copies to :- Left Group.   )
         52nd.Divn.G.S.   )
         156th.Inf.Bde.   ) For
         157th.Inf.Bde.   ) information.
         R.A.18th.Corps.   )
         D.T.M.O.   )

S E C R E T.   U R G E N T.

RIGHT GROUP
16TH BDE RGA
D.T.M.O.

52nd.D.A.No.78/A.

1. Following Bombardment will take place on June 14th. with the object of damaging enemy wire.

TIME.	UNIT.	NO. & NATURE OF PIECES.	AMMUNITION.	RATE OF FIRE.	OBJECTIVE.	REMARKS.
3.0.PM. to 5.5.PM.	16th.Brigade R.G.A.	12-6" Hows.	H.E. 106 Fuze.	INTENSE	Enemy wire in front of ANIMUX LOOP North from junction with TIRED ALLEY (B.5.c.55.95) to B.5.a.60.50.	A few rounds registration by F.A. and H.A. will be carried out before 12 noon.
		4-9.2"How.				
	Right Group	6-18.Pdrs.	ditto.	ditto.		
		4-4.5"How.				
	Medium T.Ms.	4 Mortars.		5 rounds per Mortar per minute.		

2. Addressees to ACKNOWLEDGE.

13th.June,1918.   Copies to :- 52nd.Divn.G.S.
157th.Inf.Bde.
158th.Inf.Bde.
R.A.XVIII Corps.
R.O.R.A.

Major R.A.
Brigade Major R.A.
52nd.Divisional Artillery.

DAILY REPORT
52ND DIVISIONAL ARTILLERY
8.0 AM 14TH JUNE TO 8.0 AM 15TH JUNE, 1918.

app 22

1. OUR ACTIVITY.
   (a) Operations.   At 3.PM the Right Group, 16th Bde RGA and
                     four 6" Newton Trench Mortars carried out a 5 mins.
                     bombardment of the enemy's wire from B.5.c.85.95
                     to B.5.a.80.50. M.P.I. reported well on wire.
                        During the afternoon 18-prs. fired 50 rds.
                     on Trench Junctions in T.13.
                        7.10 pm. a small party moving from U.19.b.3.3.
                     towards CHEZ BONTEMPS was dispersed.
                        Several registrations were checked during
                     the day.
                        From 12.25 am. - 12.55 am. the Right Group
                     swept from B.6.c.15.65. along ARLEUX Main Street
                     to CROSS ROADS B.5.b.60.65. with 270 rds. of 18-pr.
                     to assist an operation by the Division on our Right.
                        Harassing fire at night on following targets:-
                     Road, Tracks etc. T.6.
                                        U.7.
                                        U.13.
                                        U.25.
                        Total number of rounds fired :-
                     18-pdr.   = 1395.   4.5" (How.) - 267.

   (b) Aerial.   Normal.   One R.E. 8 forced to land near
                     NINE ELMS at 8.10 pm. owing to engine trouble.
                        At 6.10 pm. a Corps Machine fired S.O.S.
                     Smoke Rockets over T.4, and S.23" as a demonstration.

2. HOSTILE ACTIVITY.
   (a) Artillery.   Except for one attempted destructive shoot
                     on a forward 18-pdr. of C/52 in B.1. and 170 rds.
                     of 15 cm. on T.26.d. also probably meant for forward
                     guns in that subsquare, the enemy Artillery has been
                     extraordinarily quiet.

                        The intermittant shelling of T.13 reported in
                     yesterdays Summary is now reported as probable
                     registration.   Several single rounds of 77 mm. at
                     10.5 am. were fired into the same area yesterday,
                     possibly to check registration.
                        No gas reported.

                     DETAILS OF ATTEMPTED DESTRUCTIVE SHOOT.
                     Time.   8.15 am. - 10.30 am. and burst at 1.40 pm.
                     Bty. Shelled.   C/52 forward gun B.1.a.8.3.
                     Calibre.   10.5 cm. and 15 cm.
                     No. of Rds.   170.
                   n Direction.   78o G.B.(S) and 85°30' G.B.(S)
                                     respectively from B.1.d.0.5.
                     Method of Observation. Not known.
                     Damage.   Ammunition blown up.

Date.	Time.	No. of Rds.	Calibre.	Area shelled.	Direction.	Remarks.
14th.	8.15–10.30 am.	170.	15 cm.(4 Hows) 10.5 cm.	B.1.a. do.	85°30'. from B.1.d.0.5. 78° from B.1.a.4.0.	
	9.30 am.	2.	77 mm.	T.19.b.		
	11.40 am.	1.	77 mm.	T.14.c.		
	11.57 am.	1.	77 mm.	T.14.a.		
	12 noon.	2.	77 mm.	T.14.a.		
		1.	77 mm.	T.13.d.		
	12.35 pm.	1.	10.5 cm.	T.19.a.		
		1.	10.5 cm.	T.13.d.		
	12.39 pm.	1.	10.5 cm.	T.13.d.		
	12.43 pm.	1.	10.5 cm.	T.19.c.		

P.T.O.

2.

Date.	Time.	No. Rds.	Calibre.	Area Shelled.	Direction.	Remarks.
14th.	5.17-5.30 pm.	12.	10.5 cm.	T.10.d.		
	7.5 pm.	25.	10.5 cm.	MONT FORET QUARRY.	CREST WOOD.	
	7-9.0pm.	130.	15 cm.	T.26.a.	102° from A.6.b.8.7. 590 G.B.(S) from B.1.d.0.5.	Afterwards E.A. engaged Bty. Explosion caused.
	10 pm.	20.	15 cm.	T.26.	78° G.B. from B.8.a.3.2.(F)	

(b) <u>Work.</u>   NIL.

(c) <u>Movement.</u>

    8.30am. M.T. observed moving South on Track between EAST and WEST Copses.
    7.10 pm. Small party moving from U.19.b.3.6. towards CHEZ BONTEMPS — dispersed.

(d) One E.A. flew over our forward Trenches at 5. am. Otherwise Activity nil.
    No balloon up.

3. <u>GENERAL.</u>   <u>Visibility</u> Good.

signature: G.F.Peren

Lieut. R.A.
Reconnaissance-Officer, 52nd Div'l Artillery.

15th June 1918.

War Diary appx 23

SECRET.   COPY NO. 19

                              52nd.D.A.
                              No.O.O.14/1.

All Recipients 52nd.DA. O.O.No.14.
※=※=※=※=※=※=※=※=※=※=※=※=※=※=※

   52nd.D.A. O.O.No.14 is postponed until further orders.

                              S.F. Burne
                              for
                                      Major R.A.
                                      Brigade Major R.A.
14th.June,1918.   52nd.Divisional Artillery.

S E C R E T.   COPY NO. 25

OPERATION ORDER NO.15.
BY
BRIGADIER GENERAL E.HARDING NEWMAN., CMG., DSO.
COMMANDING 52ND DIVISIONAL ARTILLERY.

Reference - 1/20,000 Map - FOOTHILL Sheet &
1/10,000 Tracings attached.

1. Enemy defences in the ARLEUX Salient will be bombarded on a date to be notified later.

2. Procedure of Field Artillery supporting 52nd.Division and 16th.Bde RGA is shown in Tables A. & B. and tracings attached.
   (F.A.Tracings were issued to Groups and 52nd.Division G.S. under 52nd.DA.No.68/A. dated 12/6/18.)

3. The Left Battery of the Left Group and Right Battery of Right Group will fire 1 smoke shell in every 4 rounds throughout.

4. Rates of fire are shown in Tables A. and B. respectively.

5. ZERO Hour will be notified later.

6. Fire will cease at ZERO Plus 30 Minutes.

7. Groups and 16th.Bde RGA to ACKNOWLEDGE.

S.F.Burne
for Major RA
Brigade Major RA
52nd.Divisional Artillery.

14th.June,1918.
Issued at 8.PM.

	Tracings	
	F.A.	H.A.
Copies 1-12 to Right Group	-	1.
13-16 to Left Group	-	2.
17 to 16th.Bde RGA	1	1.
18 to D.T.M.O.	1	1.
19 to 52nd.Div.GS.	-	1.
20 to 155th.I.B.	1	1.
21 to 157th.I.B.	1	1.
22 to RA.18 Corps.	1	1.
23 to S.C.R.A.	-	-
24 to RO.R.A.	-	-
25/26 to War Diary.	1	1.
27 to File.	-	-
28/29 to War Diary 14 DA.	1	1.
30 to File 14 DA.	-	-
31 to B.M.R.A.	-	-

TABLE "A".

18 POUNDER.

Time.	Group.	Serial No.	No. & Nature of Guns.	Procedure.
Zero to Zero plus 5 mins.	Left.	1	12 - 18-pounders.	Barrage BLUE Line A - B.
	Right	2	48 - 18-pounders.	Barrage BLUE Line B - C.
Zero plus 5 minutes to Zero plus 30 minutes.	Left.	1	12 - 18-pounders.	Lift 100 yards every 3 mins. until final barrage line (Road T.29.d.95.90 to 90.20) is reached.
	Right.	2.	48 - 18-pounders.	Lift 100 yards every 3 mins. until final box barrage is reached. The box barrage between K - B1 - C1 will be formed as the barrage lifts back. Guns in ARLEUX LOOP South will lift off BLUE barrage line as the creeping barrage passes and take part in it.

4.5" HOWITZER.

Time.	Group.	Serial No.	No. & Nature of Guns.	Procedure.
Zero to Zero plus 5 mins.	Left.	5	6 - 4.5" Hows.	RED objective E - D - F.
Zero plus 5 mins. to Zero plus 30 mins.	"	3	6 - 4.5" Hows.	GREEN objective I.
Zero to Zero plus 11 mins.	Right.	4	6 - 4.5" Hows.	RED objective F - G - H.
" " " " " "	"	5	6 - 4.5" Hows.	RED objective E - G.
Zero plus 11 mins. to Zero plus 30 mins.	Right.	4	6 - 4.5" Hows.	4 Hows. GREEN objective J.
" " " " " "	"	5	6 - 4.5" Hows.	4 " " " K. 4 " " " L.

MEDIUM TRENCH MORTARS.

Time.	Group.	Serial No.	No. & Nature of Guns.	Procedure.
Zero to Zero plus 5 mins.	M.T.M's.	6	2 Mortars.	Trench B.5.b.15.00. to B.5.a.90.50.
		7	2 Mortars.	Trench T.29.c.90.20. to T.29.d.10.40.

RATES OF FIRE.

Zero to Zero plus 10 mins. - Rapid.
Zero plus 10 mins. to Zero plus 20 mins. - Normal.
Zero plus 20 mins. to Zero plus 30 mins. - Rapid.
M.T.M's.-Zero to Zero plus 5 mins. - 5 rounds per mortar per min.

TABLE "B".

Reference Tracing for Heavy Artillery.

TIME.	BRIGADE.	SERIAL No.	NO.& NATURE OF GUNS.	PROCEDURE.
Zero to Zero Plus 5 Minutes.	16th.Bde RGA.	1.	6-6" Hows.	Barrage h - f.
		2.	6-60.Pdrs.	
		3.	6-6" Hows.	Barrage i - g.
		4.	6-60.Pdrs.	
Zero Plus 5 Minutes to Zero plus 8 minutes.	do.	1.	3-6" Hows.	Barrage a - e.
			3-6" Hows.	Barrage e - f.
		2.	6-60.Pdrs.	Barrage a - e - f.
		3.	3-6" Hows.	Barrage f - k.
			3-6" Hows.	Barrage j - k.
		4.	6-60.Pdrs.	Barrage f - j.
Zero to Zero Plus 8 Minutes.	do.	5.	6-8" Hows.	Barrage a - e.
		6.	4-9.2" Hows.	Barrage j - k.
Zero Plus 8 Minutes to Zero Plus 30 Mins.	do.	1.	As above.	Barrage b - p.
		3.		Barrage p - n.
		5.		Barrage p - q.
		6.		Barrage d - p.
		2.		Barrage 3 Guns a - l ; 3 Guns c - d.
		4.		Barrage 3 Guns m - l ; 3 Guns o - n.

RATES OF FIRE.

Zero to Zero Plus 10 Minutes   - RAPID.
Zero Plus 10 Mins to Zero Plus 20 Mins -NORMAL.
Zero Plus 20 mins to Zero Plus 30 Mins -RAPID.

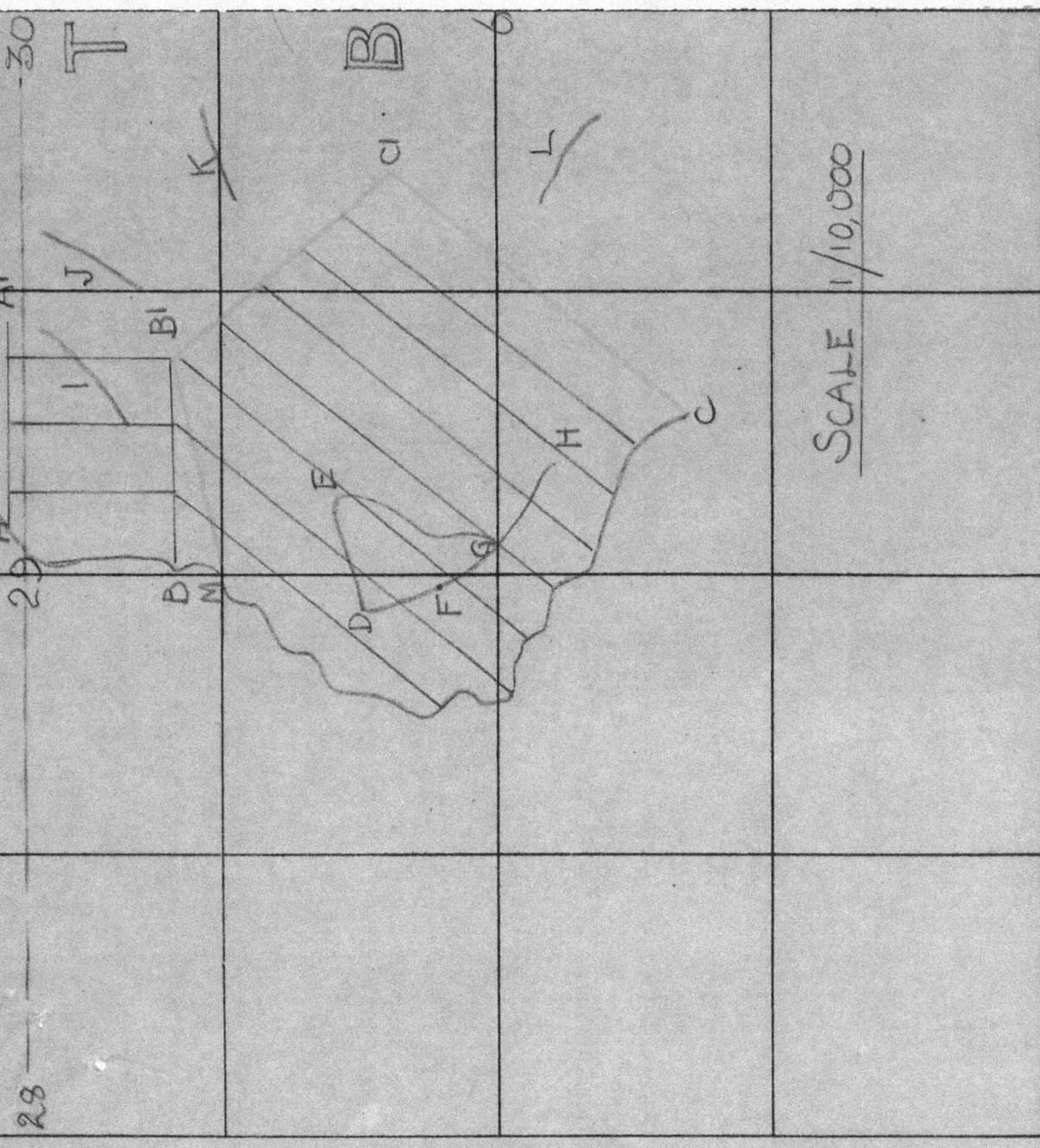

NOTE.—(1). These traces are intended to facilitate the communication of information as to the position of targets, which have map.
(2). The squares on this trace are 1,000 yards in length on the 1 20,000 scale, and 2,000 yards in length on the 1/40,0
(3). The squares on the trace are fitted to the squares of the map showing the targets, which are then drawn letters and numbers must also be added to enable the recipient to place the trace in the correct position on his c may also be traced, but this is not essential. The name and scale of the map to which the trace refers must be can be used for either the 1/20,000 or 1/40,000 scale.

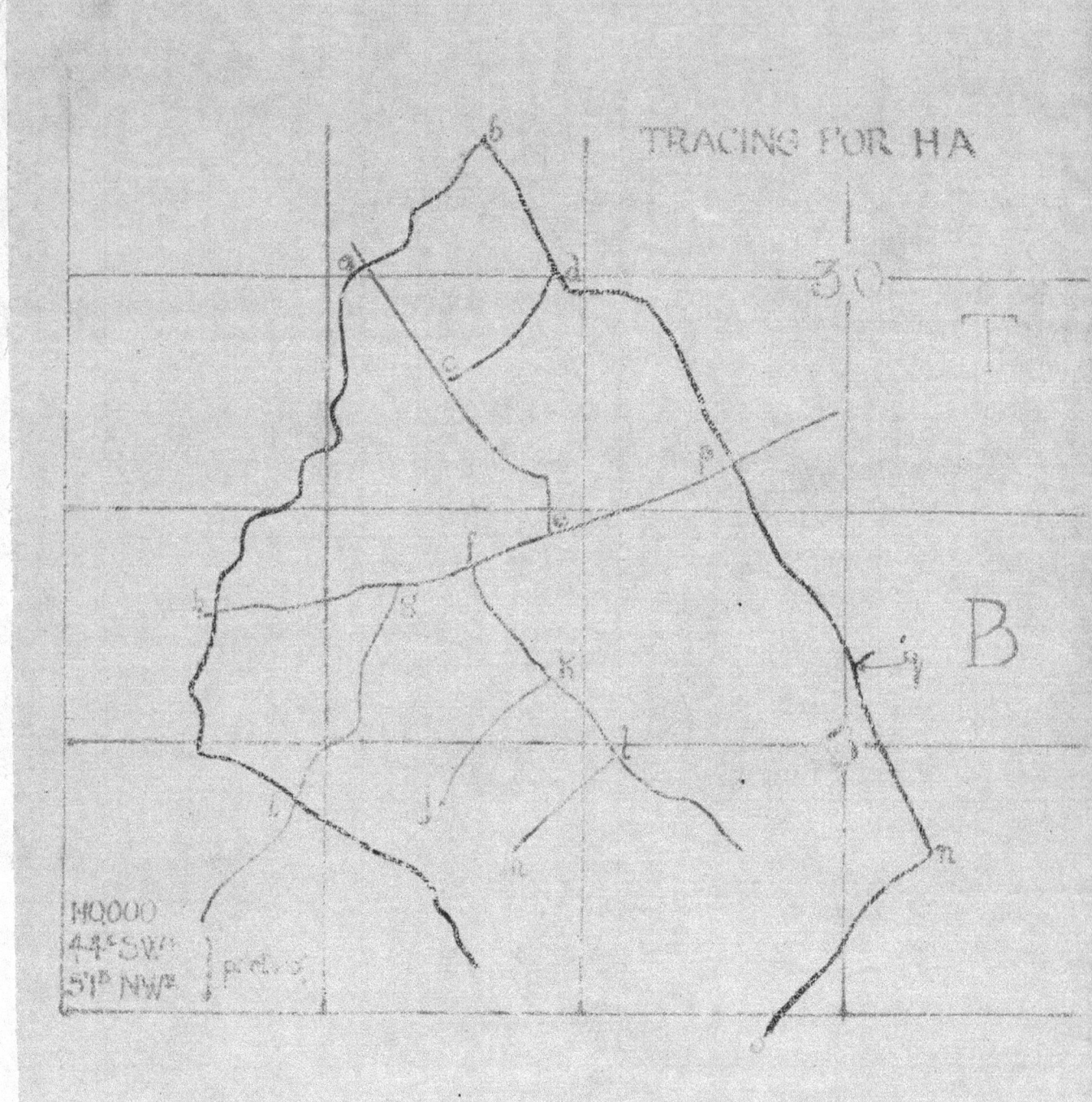

DAILY REPORT
52ND DIVISIONAL ARTILLERY
6.0.AM.15TH TO 6.0.AM.16TH JUNE'18

April 25'

1. OUR ACTIVITY.

(a) **Operations.** Movement in T.6.c.and U.1.a. was engaged by 18.Pdrs.in the afternoon and some rounds were fired for registration & instruction.

Harassing fire at night was directed on Roads, Tracks and trenches.

A TEST 'SOS' was received and responded to by Left Group at 12.11.am.

Total rounds fired :-
18.Pounders 800.   4.5"Howrs. 265.

(b) **Aerial.** Normal activity.

2. HOSTILE ACTIVITY.

(a) **Artillery.** 15cm and 10.5cm Hows. were active throughout the day on the area containing Forward Guns, near the Railway Embankment in T.26 & B.2.

T.20.c. and this area were shelled intermittently during the night.

The THELUS Area was particularly quiet.

Date.	Time.	No.of Rds.	Calibre.	Area shelled.	Direction.	Remarks.
15th.	5-7.am.	100	10.5cm	Approx.MPI.T.26.c.6064.		
	7.15-10.20am.	45	do.	B.1.		
	9-11.30am.	8	77mm	T.19.d.		
	10-10.30am.	75	15cm	T.26.c.,B.2.a.	65°GB.(F) from A.6.b.8.8 F. to R. 30 secs.	
	10.30am.	50	10.5cm	FARBUS WOOD (B.8.c.)		
	During Morning	35	77mm	T.15.b.		
	11.-11.30am.	10	10.5cm	B.1.		
	2.15-3.15.pm.	70	10.5cm	B.1.		
	3.20-4.0.p.m.	100	15cm	T.26.c.&.B.2.a.	53°GB from B.8.a.3.2. F. to R.20 secs.	
	9.40pm-11.pm.	20	10.5cm	T.19,20. Embankment.	67°GB.from B.1.d.0.5.(F	
	10.pm.-1.0am.	300	15cm	T.26.c.,T.20.c.		
16th.	1-3.30am.	30	15cm	T.20.c.		

(b) **Work.** See (c) below.

(c) **Movement.** 10.30am. Working party in trench in U.1.c.
Individuals digging in U.21,U.20 and U.26.d
During afternoon, Individual movement in T.6.d., and U.1.a.
6.45-7.30pm. Considerable movement between NEUVIREUIL and OPPY.
7.30pm. Unusual amount of movement on Light Rly. in O.31 and O.32. 15 Trucks and engine were seen.

(d) **Aerial.** 6 Observation Balloons up in morning.
2   "   "   " afternoon.
4   "   "   " 5.30am.16th.

3. GENERAL. Visibility - Good.

16th.June,1918.

Lieut.R.A.
Reconnaissance Officer 52nd.Div.Arty.

April 25'

DAILY REPORT
52ND DIVISIONAL ARTILLERY
6.0.AM.15TH TO 6.0.AM.16TH JUNE'18

1. OUR ACTIVITY.
    (a) Operations.   Movement in T.6.c.and U.1.a. was engaged by
                          18.Pdrs.in the afternoon and some rounds were
                          fired for registration & instruction.
                          Harassing fire at night was directed on
                          Roads, Tracks and trenches.
                          A TEST'SOS'was received and responded to by
                          Loft Group at 12.11.am.
                          Total rounds fired :-
                          18.Pounders 800.   4.5"Hows. 265.

    (b) Aerial.   Normal activity.

2. HOSTILE ACTIVITY.
    (a) Artillery.   15cm and 10.5cm Hows.were active throughout
                          the day on the area containing Forward Guns,
                          near the Railway Embankment in T.26 & B.2.
                          T.20.c.and this area were shelled inter-
                          mittently during the night.
                          The THELUS Area was particularly quiet.

Date. Time.	No.of Rds.	Calibre.	Area shelled.	Direction. Remarks.
15th.5-7.am.	100	10.5cm	Approx.MPI.T.26.c.6084.	
7.15-10.20am.	45	do.	B.1.	
9-11.30am.	8	77mm	T.19.d.	
10-10.30am.	75	15cm	T.26.c.,B.2.a.	65°GB.(F)from A.6.b.8.8 F. to R. 30 secs.
10.30am.	50	10.5cm	FARBUS WOOD (B.8.c.)	
During Morning	35	77mm	T.15.b.	
11.-11.30am.	10	10.5cm	B.1.	
2.15-3.15.pm.	70	10.5cm	B.1.	
3.20-4.0.p.m.	100	15cm	T.26.c.&.B.2.a.	53°GB from B.8.a.3.2. F. to R.20 secs.
9.40pm-11.pm.	20	10.5cm	T.19,20. Embankment.	67°GB.from B.1.d.0.5.(F
10.pm.-1.0am.	300	15cm	T.26.c.,T.20.c.	
16th.1-3.30am.	30	15cm	T.20.c.	

    (b) Work.   See (c) below.

    (c) Movement. 10.30am.Working party in trench in U.1.c.
                    Individuals digging in U.21,U.20 and U.26.d
             During afternoon, Individual movement in T.6.d.,
                 and U.1.a.
             6.45-7.30pm. Considerable movement between
                NEUVIREUIL and OPPY.
             7.30pm. Unusual amount of movement on Light Rly.
                in O.31 and O.32. 15 Trucks and engine
                were seen.

    (d) Aerial.   6 Observation Balloons up in morning.
                    2   "   "   " afternoon.
                  4   "   "   " 5.30am.16th.

3. GENERAL. Visibility - Good.

                                                        Lieut.R.A.
16th.June,1918.   Reconnaissance Officer 52nd.Div.Arty.

DAILY REPORT.
52ND DIVISIONAL ARTILLERY
6.0 AM 16th to 6.0 AM. 17th JUNE 1918.

1. OUR ACTIVITY.
   (a) Operations.   Movement around dug-out at T.6.d.25.78 and in
                      U.1.b. was engaged and dispersed.
                         50 rounds were spent in checking registrations,
                      and Zero lines.
                         Night harassing fire as follows :-

                              Roads and Tracks (T.6., U.19., U.26.,
                                                (T.7., U.20., T.8.
                                                (U.13., U.25.
                              Total number of rounds fired :-
                                 18-pr.   810.   4.5" How.   200.

   (b) Aerial.   Our machines very active - A.A. fire less than
                      usual.

2. HOSTILE ACTIVITY.
   (a) Artillery.   Hostile Artillery very quiet during the day.
                         T.16.c. and T.22.a., MONT FORET QUARRIES, came
                      in for several small shoots, possibly registration,
                      and VIMY Station was shelled with 50 rounds of 77 mm
                      during the afternoon. A H.V. gun intermittently shell-
                      ed A.17 during the morning was eventually silenced by
                      our H.V. guns.
                         At night some 100 rds. of 77 mm harassing fire
                      fell in T.19.d. and T.25.b. and from 3.25 am - 4.30 am
                      50 rds. of 10.5 cm. in T.20.a. and c.   Between 12.15
                      am and 12.45 am. a 10.5 cm. gun fired 8 rds. into
                      NEUVILLE ST. VAAST.

Date.	Time.	No. of Rds.	Calibre.	Area shelled.	Direction.	Remarks.
16th	8-8.30am.	6.	10.5 cm.	T.16.c.		
	8.10-8.50 am.	2.	77 mm.	T.15.b.		
	9.16 am.	40.	15 cm.	T.9.c.		
	10.0am.	12.	10.5 cm.	MONT FORET QUARRIES.	ACHEVILLE.	
	10.27 am.	10.	15 cm.	?		52°20' from B.1.c.75.92.
	10.30 am.	30.	10.5 cm.	B.8.b.		
	1.45 pm.	2.	10.5 cm.	T.16.d.2.5.		
	1.55 pm.	15.	10.5 cm.	T.16.c.		
	Afternoon.	50.	77 mm.	T.20.c.		
	Night.	100.	77 mm.	T.19.d.&T.25.b.		
	10.30 pm.	20.	77 mm.	B.7.b.		Gas - BLUE CROSS.
17th	3.25 am.	50.	10.5 cm.	T.20.a.&c.		
	5.30-6am.	20.	15 cm.	T.8.c.		

           Flashes.   10.55-11.5 am.   Heavy Gun- G.B. 78° from S.29.b.4.8.
                       11.0- 2.5 pm.   H.V. Gun - G.B. 64°30' from S.29.b.4.8.
                       11.47 am.   H.V. Gun - G.B. 68°30' from B.1.c.75.92.
                                        (verified by another O.P.) F. to R. guns
                                        probably firing on A.17, stopped when
                                        engaged by our H.V. Guns.
                       Also flashes 75 and 56 degrees from B.8.c.35.95.
   (b) Work.   Nil.

   (c) Movement. Individual movement in MERICOURT and U.1.b. during
                      morning. Dug- out at T.6.d.25.78 possibly H.Q. as much
                      movement seen round here, mostly in pairs. During afternoon
                      2 cyclists came up.
                         12.45 pm. - train at HENIN LIETARD moving West (2 engines

                                                                    P.T.O.

2.

Movement (contd.)
    4.55 pm. - train going N.   51° from B.1.c.83.92.
    6.35 pm. -   "   "   S.W. 91° from B.1.d.01.54.
    7.5 pm. - truck working at slag heap - 70° from
                     B.1.c.73.92.
    7.0-9.30pm. Small movement about CHEZ BONTEMPS and
               trenches in U.20., 21., 25., 26. (rations?)

5. GENERAL.   Helio working at U.19.b.4.3.
                    A large number of lights were dropped by
                    Aeroplanes last night.

                                         Lieut. R.A.

17th June 1918.   Reconnaissance Officer, 52nd D.A.

DAILY REPORT.
52ND DIVISIONAL ARTILLERY.
6.0AM 17th to 6.0AM 18th JUNE 1918.

1. **OUR ACTIVITY.**
   (a) <u>Operations</u>. 4.5" Hows fired 250 rounds during the day on Wire T.12.c.10.00 and T.4.d.9.1. in order to cut lanes for Infantry Patrols, and on T.11.c.8020 & T.18.c.7080 as a 'blind'.
   At 11.23pm. the Right Group responded to a 'TEST' S.O.S.
   Usual night harassing fire carried out.
   Total number of rounds fired :-
   18.Pounders - 800.   4.5"Howr. 501.

   (b) <u>Aerial</u>. Usual activity. AA.very active on front of Corps on our right.

2. **HOSTILE ACTIVITY.**
   (a) <u>Artillery</u>. Quiet except for the shelling of THELUS from 6am. to 8.30am. with 100 rds of 15cm and T.16.c., the Northern part of MONT FORET Quarries,with some 150 rounds of 77mm during the afternoon.
   Several small shoots were carried out on VIMY and vicinity occupied by our Forward Guns and one small shoot on FARBUS - Sum Total of rounds reported slightly larger than that of the 16th.
   Night quiet.

Date.	Time.	No.of Rds.	Calibre.	Area shelled.	Direction. Remarks.
17th.	6-8.30am.	100	15cm	THELUS.	53°GB.from B.8.a.2.1. F. to R. 20 secs.
	9am.	30	do.	B.7.b.&.B.8.	
	10-11.30am.	85	do.	THELUS.	53°GB.from B.8.a.2.1. F. to R. 20 secs.
	10am.-Noon.	70	10.5cm	T.25(near CEMETERY).	64½°GB.from A.6.b.8.6. F. to R. 32 secs.
	10.35am.	2	do.	T.10.	
	2.30pm.) to 5. 0pm.)	150	77mm	T.16.c.	
	Afternoon.	40	77mm	T.20.c.	
	do.	30	15cm	T.25.b.	
	8-8.15p.m.	25	15 & 10.5cm(?)	THELUS.	(89°GB.from B.1.a.4.0. F. to R. 18 secs. (95°GB.from B.1.d.0.5. Time of Flight 20 secs.
	11pm-1.am.	60	10.5cm	T.19.a.	
18th.	1.30-1.45am	20	do.	T.19.a.	
	6.am.	20	15cm	T.25.c.	

FLASHES. 8.45pm. Flashes 80½°,73°,70° GB.from B.8.a.3.2.

   (b) <u>Work</u>. Nil.

   (c) <u>Movement</u>. Usual individual movement around CHEZ BONTEMPS.
   Two men looking over parapet of trench at U.19.d.55.97.
   Individual movement in U.1.a.&.b. during the afternoon.

   (d) <u>Aerial</u>. One E.A. over the Ridge from 10am. to 10.15am. It eventually flew back as far as VILLERS AU BOIS and then disappeared Northwards.

3. **GENERAL.** Visibility - Fair whilst fine.

19th.June,1918.
Lieut.R.A.
Reconnaissance Officer 52nd.Div.Arty.

DAILY REPORT.
52ND DIVISIONAL ARTILLERY.
6.0AM. 18TH TO 6.0AM 19TH JUNE, 1918.

1. OUR ACTIVITY.
    (a) Operations.   18-Pounders fired on movement at T.6.d.25.72.
              and at U.25.c.80.50. FRESNOY PARK was also fired on.
                     4.5" Hows. registered with balloon observation
    on Brick Stacks T.11.a.80.08.
                     At night harassing was directed on Roads,
    tracks etc. in T.6. and U.7., on suspected M.G.emplacements
    from T.23.d.70. to T.29.b.65.70., and on trench B.5.a.55.47
    - B.5.c.55.92.
                     Total number of rounds fired :-
              18-Pounder -- 1,002.   4.5" Hows. - 440.

    (b) Aerial.   Our machines were active all day.
                     Hostile A.A. was active on 'planes which
    crossed the line especially to the North.

2. HOSTILE ACTIVITY.
    (a) Artillery.   Quiet all day   A few rounds of gas shell were
              fired.

Date.	Time.	No.of Rds.	Calibre.	Area shelled.	Direction.	Remarks.
18th.	6 am.	30	15 cm.	TIRED ALLEY.B.4.& B.3.		
	11.30-11.35am	12	10.5cm	B.1.d.	64°10'GB. from B.1.c.73.92 F. to R. 20 secs.	
	12.27-12.51pm	60	10.5cm or T.M.	T.17.	65° GB. from B.1.a.4.0.	
	1 pm.	10	10.5 or 15cm	B.13.		Blue & Yellow cross.
	1.10pm - 1.30	18	10.5cm	T.16.d.	73°30'GB. (F) from S.20.b 40.80.	
	1.15-1.30pm	10	77mm	T.8.c.		
	3 pm	12	10.5cm	T.13.c. & d.		
	4.10-5.15pm	17	10.5cm	T.19.c.		
	4.30pm	30	15 cm	TIRED ALLEY B.4.		
	5.15pm	10	77mm	B.3.		BOIS-EN-T.
	5.30pm	20	10.5cm or 15cm.	B.13.		Blue & Yellow cross.
	11 pm	8				
19th.	1 am	8	77mm	A.6.c.		-----do-----
"	3 am	8				
	3.45am	200	10.5cm	B.3.a.1.1.		

    (b) Work.   NIL.

    (c) Movement.   Individual movement on U.1.b., around T.6.d.
              25.78., and throughout the day about U.20., 21., 25 and
              26.
                     Parties at U.25.c.8.3. and North of FRESNOY
    PARK (U.25.a.) were dispersed by 18-pounders.

    (d) Aerial.   Two observation balloons were up.

3. GENERAL.   10.10am. large fire 94°GB. from B.1.a.4.0.
                     5.13pm. Dump exploded 79°GB. from B.1.a.4.0.,
              estimated 12 miles distant.
                     10.10pm. Gas alarms, probably sounded by
              enemy, heard South.
                     12.25am. Fire 65°GB. from B.1.a.4.0., burnt
              strongly for 5 minutes.
                     Visibility - GOOD.

                                        A.F.Dufton
                                        Lieutenant, R.A.,
19th June, 1918.   Reconnaissance Officer 52nd D.A.

DAILY REPORT
52ND DIVISIONAL ARTILLERY.
6.0.AM.19TH TO 6.0.AM.20TH JUNE,1918.

1. OUR ACTIVITY.
    (a) Operations. During the day 18.Pdrs. fired 100 rounds on Movement in T.6.c. and some instructional shoots were carried out.
        At 11.15.pm.a TEST SOS was received and responded to by LEFT GROUP.
        At Night Roads, Tracks and centres of activity were harassed particularly in T.C. and at U.13.b. 3.7, U.19.d.9.5. and B.6.a.5.2. Bursts of fire were directed on the Gaps in wire at T.12.c. 10.00 and T.4.d.90.10.
        Harassing fire was also directed on the Railway in N.27.c.&.d. (20th.Divn.Front).
        Total rounds fired –
        18.Pounders 1000   4.5"Hows. 300.

    (b) Aerial. Our machines were active particularly in the afternoon.

2. HOSTILE ACTIVITY.
    (a) Artillery. Abnormally quiet throughout the period.
        At 7.35pm. 40 rds 77mm were fired at intense rate at Movement on the Ridge about B.1.a. and S.30.d.

Date. Time.	No.of Rds.	Calibre.	Area shelled.	Direction. Remarks.
19th.8–9am.	20	15cm	A.18.	
11.15–1.30pm.	30	10.5cm	T.13.	
1.15pm.	12	77mm	T.19.d.8.6.	
2.15pm.	10	77mm	T.13.c.7.3.	
2.55 & 3.20pm.	12	77mm	T.13.d.	
3.15–4.0.pm.	8	10.5cm	T.13.b.	
6.30pm.	20	10.5cm	T.25.d.	MERICOURT.
7.55pm.	40	77mm	B.1.a.&.S.30.d.	FRESNOY.

    FLASHES. Flash of HV.Gun, possibly firing on A.14., 69°GB. from B.1.a.4.0. F. to R. 25 secs.
    3.20a.m. Flash 101°GB. from B.8.a.20.15. F. to R.30 secs.

    (b) Work. Small parties working on shell holes in C.1.d., C.2.a. C.7.a.&.b.

    (c) Movement. 12 noon.Train going ESE.from HARNES.
        3.20pm. Train going N.E. from HARNES,apparently a goods Train of 30 Trucks.
        Twelve men left Rly in T.6.d. and walked towards LONDON COPSE in great hurry.
        4.45pm.Helio working 60°GB.from B.1.a.40.10.
        5.45pm.Train of about 30 Trucks going N.from HARNES.
        7 men seen pushing truck on Light Rly in C.31.b.
        6.35pm.Two men walked from trench U.19.b.4.3. to BOIS VILAIN.
        Slight movement in FRESNES-ROUVROY Line U.21.a. 1.0.

    (d) Aerial. Three balloons up until 4.30pm.
        One balloon up till 6.30.pm.
        Hostile bombing planes were over the line during the night and bombs were dropped in the vicinity of LES TILLEULS X Roads.

3. GENERAL. Visibility – Good.

Lieut.R.A.
20th.June,1918.   Reconnaissance Officer 52nd.D.A.

SECRET.   COPY NO. 18.

                                        52nd. D.A.
                                        No. O.O. 14/2.

All Recipients 52nd D.A. O.O. No. 14.
※=※=※=※=※=※=※=※=※=※=※=※=※=※=※=※=※=※

52nd D.A. O.O. No. 14 is cancelled.

                                        S. F. Burus
                                              Maj
                                        Captain R.A.
                                        for Brigade Major, R.A.
19th June 1918.   52nd Divisional Artillery.

DAILY REPORT
52ND DIVISIONAL ARTILLERY.
6.0 am 20th to 3.0 am 21st JUNE 1918.

1. **OUR ACTIVITY.**
   (a) <u>OPERATIONS</u>. During the day 4.5" Howitzers fired 50 rounds on wire at T.12.c.10.00, T.4.d.90.10, T.11.c.80.20 and T.18.c.70.80 and bursts of fire were directed on these points until 10.30 pm. 18 pdrs. fired 50 rounds on movement and some instructional shoots were carried out.

   Harrassing fire on Roads, Tracks, and Centres of activity was carried out during the night and also, by 18 pdrs. of the Right Group, during the day.

   At night 18 pdrs. of the Left Group fired 50 rds. on Track parallel to MEMBER TRENCH in N.34.c. (20th DIV: Front).

   At 8.30 pm. 6" T.M. fired on T.M. at B.5.Central, and on ARLEUX LOOP S (B.5.d.1.6), obtaining several direct hits in trenches.

   Total rounds fired:-
   18 pounders - 960.   4.5" How: - 260.   6" TM - 24.

   (b) <u>Aerial</u>.   Few machines were up during the day.

2. <u>HOSTILE ACTIVITY</u>.
   (a) <u>Artillery</u>.   As on the previous day, the enemy guns were very quiet.

Date.	Time.	No.of Rds.	Calibre.	Area shelled.	Direction.	Remarks.
20th.	8-9am.	12	15cm.	S.18.d.		
	8-9.30am.	50	77mm.	U.13.c.		
	8.30-9.30am.	50	15cm.	T.9.b.		
	9.45am.	12	77mm.	B.8.a. & B.9.	ROUVROY.	
	10-10.20am.	12	15cm.	A.13.b.	80°B.B.(s) from B.1.c.73.92.	
	12.50-2pm.	30	77mm.	BROWN LINE. B.2.d.	85°G.B.(s) from B.1.c.73.92.	
	3.0pm.	20	77mm.	B.8.a.		
	3.30pm.	40	77mm.	B.9.d.		
	11.0pm.	6	10.5cm.	B.2.d.	65°G.B.(s) from B.7.b.7.3.	
	11.30pm.	8	10.5cm.	B.8.a.	-do-	
21st.	3.0am.	12	10.5cm.	S.29.c.		
	4.0am.	10.	77mm.	B.7.d.	99°G.B.(s) from B.7.b.7.3.	

   FLASHES.   7.0pm.   66°G.B. from S.22.b.65.50.
             10.5pm.   69°G.B. from S.22.b.65.50.
             11.15pm. 71°B.B. from S.22.b.65.50.

   (b) <u>Work</u>. Small parties were working in U.26.a.6.4 and C.9.a. and at 3.30pm. in C.2.b.

   (c) <u>Movement</u>. See (b) above.
   Individual movement in T.6 & U.1 during the afternoon.

   (d) <u>Aerial</u>. Nil.

3. <u>GENERAL</u>. 5.20pm. Large amount of black smoke in DROCOURT, 51°G.B. from B.1.d.0.5.

   <u>Visibility</u>. Poor.

21st June 1918.

Lieut: R.A.
Reconnaissance Officer, 52nd Divnl; Arty.

APPENDIX A.
================

Distribution of guns.

Section.	Right Group.	Left Group.
V.	19th Bty., 122nd Bty. & 3 hows. D/52.	
W.	20th Bty., C/52 Bty. & 3 hows. D/52.	B/242 Bty.
X.	A/52 and 2 hows. D/69.	C/242 & ? Btys. 527 Bty.
Y.	A/56, 3 guns 28th Bty. & 2 hows. D/69.	A/242 Bty. & 4 hows. D/242.
Z.	C/56, 3 guns 28th Bty. & 2 hows. D/69.	B/56 Bty. & 2 hows. D/242.

SECRET.   52ND DIVISIONAL ARTILLERY ORDER NO. 16.   COPY NO 36.

Ref. Maps 1/20,000 - 44 A. S.W.
              51 B. N.W.

1.   Counter preparation is the Artillery action to be taken during an intense hostile bombardment, which is evidently the prelude to an attack.

Its object will include the destruction of the enemy's trench system, from which the attack will be launched, including machine guns and trench mortars, and the killing of his troops whilst assembling.

On the Left Group front, owing to the lie of the VIMY Ridge and the consequent siting of the batteries, the Role of Field Artillery during counter preparation is mainly restricted to preventing the enemy sending forward patrols and M.G. parties to establish themselves well forward in "NO MAN'S LAND".

2.   Field Artillery counter preparation will consist of :-
(a) Frequent rolling barrages by 18-pounders fired at irregular intervals backwards and forwards over the zones allotted to Groups.
(b) 4.5" Hows. firing on selected targets in the Sections allotted to them.

For this purpose lifts for 18-pounders will be parallel to the S.O.S. Line which will be lettered A, and each successive lift B, C, D, E, F, G, H.

The Group zones are divided into Sections, which are again sub-divided into lanes, vide attached map. The broadth of these Sections and lanes vary according to their tactical importance.

The allotment of guns to these Sections is given in Appendix A.

3.   When counter preparation is ordered, each 18-pounder Bty. will open fire on any one of these lanes in its own Section, and after covering it once, will switch to another lane. The above will be carried out in bursts of fire at irregular intervals so timed that the whole of the lanes are covered at least once in the period, or periods, for which counter preparation has been ordered.

The order in which the lanes will be treated and the barrage lines on which the guns will open will be decided by the Group Commander, as the tactical situation demands, but the principle that the barrage will search backwards as well as forwards will be adhered to.

In the Left Group each forward gun still in action will fire on the point, marked with the same number as the lane, in the Section in which the battery is firing.

These points are marked O = 18-pounder and △ = 4.5"How. on the map. 18-pounders without air recuperators will not fire at ranges over 7,000 yards.

4.   The number and intensity of bursts cannot be laid down previously, these depend on the duration of the enemy bombardment, having regard to the necessity for keeping detachments as fresh as possible for the S.O.S. barrage to be fired at the time of the assault, and for the subsequent battle.

The necessity for keeping in hand sufficient ammunition to deal with the successive assaults has also to be considered.

Where possible the amount of ammunition to be fired during counter preparation will be controlled by C.R.A. Should communication be cut however, Brigade and Battery Commanders must use their own discretion in this matter.

At no time during counter preparation will ammunition at guns be allowed to fall below 400 rounds per 18-pounder and 300 rounds per 4.5"How.

All 18-pounders firing under 5,500 yards will fire shrapnel only and those above, H.E. only, as far as possible.

The proportion of ammunition on hand with batteries will be reallotted within Groups to meet the above requirements.

P.T.O.

- 2 -

5. Counter preparation will be ordered from D.A.,H.Q. If communications are cut Brigade Commanders must act upon their own initiative.

It will be ordered in the following code :-

The word "COUNTER" wired from this office will be the signal that counter preparation is to be carried out. 12 noon will be Zero hour. The hour for opening fire will be so many hours plus or minus. The date will be given.

Example - "Counter 12th minus 6½ hours" - denotes that counter preparation will be fired on 12th inst. commencing 5.30 a.m.

Where it is considered advisable, duration of fire will also be ordered from this office.

6. ACKNOWLEDGE on attached slip.

[signature]
Captain R.A.,
Brigade Major R.A.,
52nd (Lowland) Division.

21st January, 1918.

Right Group 19
Left Group 20
66th Brigade RFA 21
2nd C.G.A. 22
T.A.C.G.A. 23
D.T.M.O. 24
52nd Div. 25
R.A. XVIIth Corps 26
XVIIth Corps H.A. 27
20th D.A. 28
51st D.A. 29
155 Inf. Bde. 30
156 " 31
157 " 32
B.M.,R.A. 33
S.C.R.A. 34
R.O.R.A. .... 35 & 36
War Diary 37
File 38
Spare

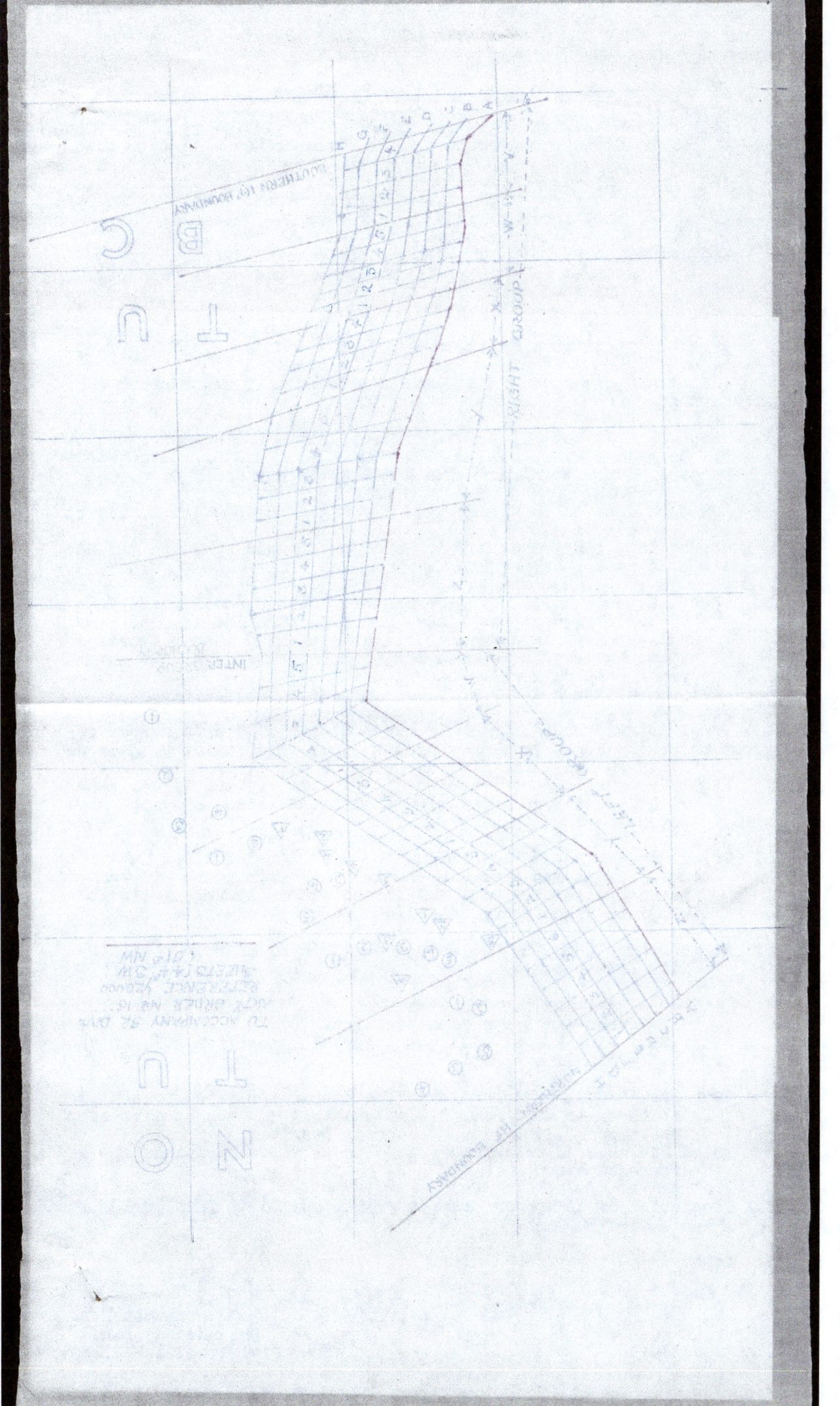

SECRET. 52ND DIVISIONAL ARTILLERY ORDER NO. 17.   COPY NO....

Reference 1/20,000 Sheets 44.b. S.W. & 51.b. N.W.

1. With a view to giving greater depth to the Artillery dispositions on the Divisional front, the following moves will take place:-

    (a) On night 24/25th June one Section 122nd Bty. will withdraw to position "B.2", A.4.c.75.10, and one Section C/52 Bty. to position "B.3", A.10.a.70.90.

    (b) On night 25/26th June the remainder of the two above mentioned batteries, including forward guns, will withdraw to the same positions.

    (c) At a date to be notified later, A/52 and D/52 will withdraw to positions "B.1", A.5.a.00.10, and "B.4", A.4.d.60.90.

    All the above moves to take place after dark, under group arrangements and to be complete by dawn.

2. Lt.Col. H.J. Cotter, O.I.E., D.S.O., R.A., and Headquarters 9th Brigade R.F.A. will relieve 52nd. Bde. R.F.A. Headquarters and assume command of the Right Artillery Group at noon June 26th.
    Further details to be arranged by Brigade Commanders in direct communication.
    On relief, 52nd. Bde. R.F.A. Headquarters will move to "B" Bde. Headquarters at AU RIETZ.

3. 52nd. Brigade R.F.A. will arrange to leave a small guard in each of their present positions, and all communications to them will be kept intact. Map boards etc. will also be kept, so that they can be re-occupied at short notice, should our raiding operations require it.
    All ammunition however will be removed to new positions.

4. 52nd. Brigade R.F.A. in their new position will remain as a sub group under the Right Artillery Group. They will register their SOS lines and will not fire except on SOS.
    Right Group will report the re-distribution of SOS lines, which will keep the same junction points on flanks and gaps, as before.

5. To ensure a turn-over of ammunition in 52nd Bde. R.F.A. after the move, Right Group will replenish all expenditure from ammunition in hand with 52nd Bde. R.F.A. and all fresh ammunition to complete Right Group establishment will be sent to 52nd Bde.

6. At noon June 26th the following re-allotment of rear positions will take place:-

    (i) 9th Bde. R.F.A. will take over Bde. position "A" as their green and brown line position.
    (ii) 52nd Bde. R.F.A. will take over Bde. position "G", as their green line position.

    9th Bde. R.F.A. will hand over the labour party, at present lent to them, to 52nd Bde. R.F.A. and they will be used to complete positions B.1. & B.4. as soon as possible.
    52nd Bde. R.F.A. will report as soon as these positions are ready for occupation.

7. Completion of all moves ordered will be wired to this office, using code word "HOGIA".

8. Acknowledge on attached slip.

W.G. Harris
Captain R.A.
Brigade Major R.A.
52nd Divisional Artillery.

21st June 1918.

For distribution see over leaf

SECRET.   52ND DIVISIONAL ARTILLERY ORDER NO. 17.   COPY NO......

Reference 1/20,000 trench 44.l, S.W., A Sldt. L.M.

Copy No. 1-12 to Right Group.
"   "   13   to Left Group.
"   "   14   to 56th Bde RFA.
"   "   15   to 52nd D.A.C.
"   "   16   to D.T.M.B.
"   "   17   to 155th Infantry Bde.
"   "   18   to 156th Infantry Bde.
"   "   19   to 157th Infantry Bde.
"   "   20   to 20th Div'l Artillery.
"   "   21   to 51st Div'l Artillery.
"   "   22   to 52nd Division 'G'.
"   "   23   to D.A. Gro., 52nd Division.
"   "   24   to R.A., XVlll Corps.
"   "   25   to H.A., XVlll Corps.
"   "   26   to C.B., S.O., XVlll Corps.
"   "   27   to S.O.R.A.
"   "   28   to R.O., R.A.
"   "   29   to R.A. Signal Officer.
"   "   30   to No. 20 Scottish Balloon Coy.
"   "   31   to B.M., R.A.
"   "   32   to File.
"   "   33/34 to War Diary.
"   "   35   Spare.

1. With a view to giving greater depth to our dispositions on the Divisional front, the following will take place:-

(a) On night 24/25th June one 52nd D.A.C. will withdraw to position "3-G", A.6.C.75.80. One Section "/52 Bde. to position "4".

(b) On night 25/26th June 52nd D.A.C. will withdraw to the same positions mentioned above.

(c) As a case of emergency 52nd D.A.C. will withdraw to positions "3", A.6.C.75.80.

All the above moves will be completed by dawn on the 26th.

2. Lt.Col. H.L. Cotton., commanding, will establish Brigade H.Q. at [...] and assume Command of the Right Group at 12 noon 26th.

Further details to be arranged during 25th to effect [...] organisation.

On Relief, 22nd. Bde. R.H.A. Headquarters will move to "B" Bde. Headquarters at AUBIGNY.

3. 80th. Brigade R.F.A. will arrange to leave a small party in each of their present positions, and all communications to them will be kept intact. Map boards etc. will also be kept, so that they can be reoccupied at short notice, should our raiding operations require it.

All ammunition however will be removed to new positions.

4. 52nd. Brigade R.F.A. in their new position, will remain as a mid group under the Right Artillery Group. They will register their lines and will not fire except on S.O.S.

Right Group will report the re-distribution of SOS lines, what will keep the same junction points on flanks and rear, as before.

5. To ensure a turn-over of ammunition in 52nd Bde. R.F.A. after the move, Right Group will replenish all expenditure from ammunition in hand with 22nd Bde. R.H.A. and all fresh ammunition to complete Right Group establishment will be sent to 52nd Bde.

6. At noon June 26th the following readjustment of gun positions will take place:

(i) 6th Bde. R.F.A. will take over Bde. position "A" as their own, and throw line positions.

(ii) 22nd Bde. R.H.A. will take over Bde. position "B" as their gun line position.

6th Bde. R.F.A. will hand over the latter party at present left to them, to 52nd Bde. R.F.A., and they will be used to complete position B.L.A R.A. as soon as possible.

52nd Bde. R.F.A. will report as soon as these positions are ready for occupation.

7. Completion of all moves ordered will be sent to this Office, using code word "NORA".

8. Acknowledge on attached slip.

(signed)
Captain A.
Brigade Major R.A.
52nd Divisional Artillery.

21st June 1918.

DAILY REPORT
52ND DIVISIONAL ARTILLERY.
6.0 am. 21st to 6.0 am 22nd JUNE 1918.

1. **OUR ACTIVITY.**
   (a) *Operations.* 18-pdrs. fired 70 rounds on movement during the day and some rounds were fired for registration and instruction.
   Harassing fire was carried out at night on various points including the Railway in N.27.c. and d. (20th Div: front).
   Total rounds fired:-
   18-pdrs. - 920.   4.5" How: - 303.   6" T.M. Nil.

   (b) *Aerial.* Less activity on account of poor visibility.

2. **HOSTILE ACTIVITY.**
   (a) *Artillery.* After two exceptionally quiet days activity has become normal. 77 m have been very active, the chief objective being the embankment in T.26.a. and c.

Date.	Time.	No. of rds.	Calibre.	Area shelled.	Direction.	Remarks.
21st.	9.45am	10	15cm	STATION WOOD.	83°G.B. from B.8.a.30.15. F to R 20 secs.	
	9.55 am	30	77mm	EMBANKMENT. T.26.c.	59°G.B.(s) from B.1.a.40.01.	
	10.35-11am	10	15cm	T.13.d.		
	10.45 am	20	77mm	B.9.d.4.6.		
	11.0 am.	20	77mm	Embankment.	MERICOURT.	
	11.30 am.	12	10.5cm	T.26.a. & c. B.8.a.8.6.	81°G.B. from B.8.a.25.20 F to R 20 secs.	
	12.15 pm	28	77mm	T.16.b.		
	Day.	50	10.5cm	T.19.d.		
	1.25) 3.35) pm. 6.35) 6.55)	150 approx.	77mm	Embankment. T.26.a. & c.		
	9.35 pm.	50	77mm	B.1.c. & B.7.c	81°G.B.(s) from B.1.a. 4.0.	4 rds. per minute.
	8-9.30 pm.	20	10.5cm	VIMY.		Slow rate of fire.
	10.30 pm	12	15cm Gun.	Back areas.	67°20' GB/from B.1.a.4.0. F to R 25secs.	4 rounds per min.
22nd.	2.45am	50	77mm	B.1.c. & B.7.c.	81°G.B(s) from B.1.a.4.0.	
	Night.	100	10.5cm	T.19.c.		
	Night.	100	15cm	T.13.c. & d.		

   (b) *Work.* NIL

   (c) *Movement.* Individual movement in T.6. and U.1.
   Slight movement in U.20.c.1.6, C.1.b. and U.25.a.
   2 men seen pushing truck along tramway from U.27.b.3.5 - U.22.b.00.15.
   11.45 am smoke of train moving N. from DOUAI.

   (d) *Aerial.* 6.0pm. 1 E.A. which crossed our lines at about 4,000 feet was driven off by A.A.

3. **GENERAL.**
   Visibility. Poor.

22nd June 1918.

R. Sutton
Lieut: R.A.
Reconnaissance Officer, 52nd D.A.

DAILY REPORT
52ND DIVISIONAL ARTILLERY.
6.0 am. 22nd to 6.0 am. 23rd JUNE 1918.

1. OUR ACTIVITY.
   (a) Operations.   18-pdrs. fired on movement during the day and
   4.5" Hows. fired 30 rounds in response to an N.F. call on
   U.20.d.1.6.
   Harassing fire was carried out at night and 46 rounds
   were fired before 11.0 pm. on N.34.c.(20th Div: front).
   At 5.10 pm. SOS signal was observed by a battery of Left
   Group who responded, 145 rounds 4.5" How. and 150 rounds
   18-pdr. being fired.
   The SOS was not sent up by the Infantry. Many coloured
   rockets were sent up by the enemy at this time.
   Total rounds fired:-
   18-pdr. - 950.   4.5" How: - 375.   6" T.M. - Nil.

   (b) Aerial.   Slight activity.

2. HOSTILE ACTIVITY.
   (a) Artillery.   As yesterday, the total number of rounds fired
   by the enemy was normal. Only 10 rounds of 15cm. were
   reported, however, the bulk of the shelling being 77mm which
   is unusual. The area containing forward guns, by the
   Embankment, continues to be the principal target.

Date.	Time.	No. of Rds.	Calibre.	Area shelled.	Direction.	Remarks.
22nd.	9am - 3pm	200	77mm) 10.5cm)	T.13.c.	75°G.B.(s)	from S.22.b. 65,50.
	10.30 am.	10	10.5cm	S.18.b.		
	10.30 am.	20	10.5cm	B.8.b.8.9		
	11.0 am.	10	15 cm	B.8.central.		
	11.50 am.	40	77 mm	B.8.c.		
	1.26-2.20) 5.25-5.50) 8.10-8.20)	275	77 mm	T.26.a. & c.	65°G.B.(s)	from B.1.a.4.0.
23rd.	1-2 am.	20	10.5 cm	B.1.a.		

   (b) Work.   Nil.

   (c) Movement.   During morning a certain amount of individual movement around U.1.c.3.3.
   3.0 pm.   Motor lorry moving East behind LONDON COPSE,
   U.1.b.7.7.
   6.30 pm.   Considerable movement at U.21.a.65.75 and
   usual movement at T.30.c. and d, C.2.b. and d.
   7.30 pm.   Small parties in U.3.b.
   8.0 pm.   Light Railway engine and 2 trucks went
   behind LONDON COPSE (U.1.b.)

   (d) Aerial.   1.am. 2 aeroplane bombs were dropped GOULOT WOOD (B.1.a)
   (From 1.am. to 2 am. 20 rounds of 10.5 cm. were fired
   into GOULOT WOOD).

3. GENERAL.   3.10 am. - Enemy sent up numerous coloured rockets on the
   Left front.
   3.45 pm.   Heavy firing heard from ROUVROY going in N.W.
   direction.

   Visibility.   Fair.

                                                    A.F. Drifton
                                                    Lieut: R.A.
23rd June 1918.   Reconnaissance Officer, 52nd Divisional Arty.

SECRET.

RIGHT GROUP.
LEFT GROUP.

WARNING ORDER.

There will be a Gas Shell bombardment of area T.5. on night 24th/25th probably about dusk.
All 4.5" How. Batteries will move up into forward positions to reach these areas to-night.
ZERO hour will be about dusk.
Targets will be as under:-

No. 9. T.5.b.50.00.)
No.10. T.5.b.20.30.) 527 and D/242 Batteries.

No.12. T.5.d.10.35.   D/69 and D/52 Batteries.

Time table will be :-

ZERO to ZERO plus 5 minutes. Targets 9 & 12. Lethal-Rate 4 rds per min.
ZERO plus 5 to ZERO plus 10 mins. Target 10. Lethal-Rate 4 rds per min.
ZERO plus 10 to ZERO plus 20 mins. Target 9 (6 Hows.))
                                   Target 10 (6 Hows)) Lachrymatory
                                   Target 12   ) Rate rapid.

Zero plus 20 to Zero plus 50 mins. Target 9 (6 Hows.))
                                   Target 10 (6 Hows)) Lachrymatory.
                                   Target 12   ) Rate slow.

Zero plus 2 hrs 10 mins to) Target 9 (12 Hows) Lethal. Rate 4 rds
Zero plus 2 hrs 15 mins.   ) Target 12   per min.

Zero plus 2 hrs.15 mins. to) Target 10 (12 Hows) Lethal. Rate 4 rds.
Zero plus 2 hrs 20 mins.   )   per min.

Forward 18-pounders will be required to shoot on targets in this area with H.E. during concentration.

Targets will be notified later.

After shoot batteries will withdraw.

                                        Captain R.A.,
                                     Brigade Major R.A.,
23rd June, 1918.   52nd (Lowland) Division.

DAILY REPORT
52ND DIVISIONAL ARTILLERY.
6.0 am 23rd to 6.0 am 24th JUNE 1918.

1. OUR ACTIVITY.
   (a) Operations.   18-pdrs. fired on movement in T.6 at U.25.b.
       85.15, U.27.a.7.8, U.25.c.9.5, C.1.a.70.80 and in U.20.c.
       causing men to scatter.
           7pm. 4.5" Hows. fired 100 rounds on wire at T.11.a.85.30,
       T.11.a.20.65 and T.10.b.90.90.
           Harassing fire was carried out by night on selected
       targets, the Railway in N.27.c. & d. (20th Div: front) being
       included.
       10.9pm. Right Group received and responded to a Test S.O.S.
       2.53am. Left Group received and responded to a Test S.O.S.
       6" T.M. fired at 5pm. on suspected T.M. emplacement, B.5.
       central, and on front line, B.5.a.5.0, obtaining several
       direct hits.
           Total rounds fired:-
       18-pdrs. - 900.   4.5" How: - 400.   6" T.M. - 21.

           Correction.   In report of 23rd June, line 10, for 3.10pm.
       read 3.10 am.

   (b) Aerial.   Normal.

2. HOSTILE ACTIVITY.
   (a) Artillery.   As yesterday the enemy fired chiefly 77mm: 15cm
       Hows. were particularly quiet. The 'forward gun' areas in
       T.26.a., T.20.c. and T.13 again received the bulk of the
       shelling.

Date.	Time.	No. of rds.	Calibre.	Area shelled.	Direction. Remarks.
23rd.	7-11.30am	100	77mm	T.19. VIMY STA.	79°G.B.(s) from B.1.a.4.0
	9.50 am.	12	77mm	WILLERVAL RD. B.8 and 9.	
	8.15-10.15am.	20	77mm	T.13.c.	
	10.40 am.	15	10.5cm.	B.4.b., T.28.d.	
	11.15-11.40am	200	77mm	T.13.c.	75°G.B.(s) from S.22.b.6.4.
	11am-1pm.	150	10.5cm	T.20.c., U.26.a.	
	11pm-midnight.	70	10.5cm	S.24.a & c.	
24th.	3am-7am.	20	?	S.30.d.	

   (b) Work.   Nil.

   (c) Movement.   More movement than usual was observed East of FRESNOY.
           Parties were seen and engaged in T.6., at U.25.b.85.15,
       U.27.a.7.8, U.25.c.9.5, C.1.a.70.80, and in U.20.c.

   (d) Aerial.   E.A. crossed our lines at 11.56 pm. and at 12.18 am.

3. GENERAL.
       Visibility.   Fair.

                                                A.F. Lufton
                                                Lieut: R.A.
24th June 1918.   Reconnaissance Officer, 52nd Divnl:Arty.

SECRET.   COPY NO. 21
                                              52nd R.A.No.O.O.18/1.

To all recipients of O.O. 18.
----

1. Zero hour will be 9.50 pm.

2. Watches will be synchronised 7.45 pm. from this Office and forecast of wind given.

3. A wire will be sent 7.0 pm. as to whether bombardment will take place or not.

    Bombardment will take place = ON.
    "   " "NOT" "   = OFF.

4. ACKNOWLEDGE.

                                              W.H. Harriott
                                              Captain R.A.
                                   Brigade-Major R.A., 52nd DA.

24th June 1918.

52ND DIVISIONAL ARTILLERY ORDER NO. 18.

SECRET.   COPY NO. 21.

Reference map 1/20,000. Sheets 44.a.S.W. & 51.b.N.W.

1. There will be a gas shell bombardment of the enemy's trench system on the night 24/25th June.

2. The area to be shelled is that immediately N.W. of HERICOURT. Attached tracing shows targets to be engaged.

3. 4.5" How. of 52nd Divisional Artillery will engage targets as under:—

UNIT.	Target No.	Time.	Nature of ammunition.	Rate of fire.
LEFT GROUP.	9	Zero to zero plus 5 mins.	LETHAL.	4 rounds per gun per minute.
RIGHT GROUP.	12	Zero to Zero plus 5 mins.	LETHAL.	4 rounds per gun per minute.
LEFT GROUP.	10	Zero plus 10 mins. to zero plus 15 mins.	LETHAL.	4 rounds per gun per minute.
6 HOWS. LEFT GROUP.	9	Zero plus 15 mins. to zero plus 55 mins.	LACHRYMATORY.	Zero plus 15 mins. to zero plus 25 mins — RAPID. Zero plus 25 mins. to zero plus 55 mins — SLOW.
6 HOWS. LEFT GROUP.	10	Zero plus 15 mins. to zero plus 55 mins.	LACHRYMATORY.	Zero plus 15 mins. to zero plus 25 mins. — RAPID. Zero plus 25 mins. to zero plus 55 mins — SLOW.
RIGHT GROUP.	12	Zero plus 15 mins. to zero 55 mins.	LACHRYMATORY.	Zero plus 15 mins. to zero plus 25 mins — RAPID. Zero plus 25 mins. to zero plus 55 mins — SLOW.

4. In addition, each of the targets mentioned below will be engaged by one 18-pdr., firing H.E.
    Left Group:— Targets No. 3, 4, 5, & 6.
    Right Group:— Targets No. 7, 9, 10 & 12.
    Rates of fire — during lethal bombardment of the target INTENSE.
        During lachrymatory bombardment as for 4.5" Hows.

5. Batteries will withdraw to normal positions as soon after bombardment as possible.

6. ACKNOWLEDGE on attached slip.

7. Zero will be notified later.

                                                       Captain, R.A.
                                                       Brigade Major, R.A.
    24th June 1918.   52nd Divisional Artillery.

    For distribution see over-leaf.

52ND DIVISIONAL ARTILLERY ORDER NO. 12.

SECRET.   COPY NO. _____

Reference map 1/20,000. Shoots 44,S.W, & 51,N.W.

1. There will be a raw shell bombardment of the enemy's trench system on the night of/26th June.

2. The area to be shelled is that immediately N.E. of LARICOURT. Attached tracing shows targets to be engaged.

3. A.T" Bdo. CF 52nd Division Artillery will engage targets as under:-

Unit.	Task.	Time.	Nature.
RIGHT GROUP.	8	Zero to zero plus 5 mins.	4 rds per gun per min.
		plus 5 mins.	
CENTRE GP.	12	Zero to zero plus 5 mins.	4 rds per gun per min.
		plus 5 mins.	
LEFT GROUP.	10	Zero plus 10 LAUDELLE plus 15 mins.	4 rds per gun per min.
		plus 15 mins.	
" HOWR.	8	Zero plus 15 mins plus 15 mins, to zero plus 20 mins - BAPT.	
HEVY HOWR.		zero to zero plus 25 mins	zero plus 25 mins to zero plus 35 mins - TROY.
2 HOWR.	10	Zero plus 15 LAGHNICOURT, plus 15 mins, to zero plus 30 mins - BAPT. plus 35 mins.	
		zero plus 25 mins.	zero plus 25 mins - BAPT.
HEVY HOWR.	15	Zero plus 15 - LAGHNICOURT, zero plus 15 mins, to zero plus 25 mins. mins to zero - BAPT.	
		Zero plus 25 mins, to zero plus 35 mins - TROY.	

Copy No. 1/3 to Right Group.
"   "   4/7 to Left Group.
"   "   8. to 56th Bde RFA.
"   "   9. to 52nd D.A.C.
"   "   10 to 2nd C.G.A.
"   "   11 to 20th D.A.
"   "   12 to 51st D.A.
"   "   13. to D.T.M.O.
"   "   14. to D.G.O.
"   "   15. to D.A.,G.O.
"   "   16. to S.O.,R.A.
"   "   17. to R.O.,R.A.
"   "   18. to 156th Infantry Bde.
"   "   19. to B.M.,R.A.
"   "   20/21 War Diary.
"   "   22. to File.

4. In addition, 75% of the targets mentioned below be engaged by otherfield guns.

Left Group: Targets No. 3, 4, 5, & 6.
Right Group: Targets No. 9, 10, 12, & 13.

Rate of Fire - During lethal bombardment of the target INTENSE. During Leaping/Wrecking bombardment as for A.T"Bdo.

5. Infantry will withdraw to normal positions as soon after shoot as possible.

6. ACKNOWLEDGE on Attached slip.

7. Zero will be notified later.

(signed) W.J.Hamm.

Captain, R.A.
Signed "for"D.
52nd Divisional Artillery.

Date, June 1916.

Non-distributing R.A. of R.A. of.

Identification Trace for use with Artillery Maps.

1/20000

44 NSW

DAILY REPORT
52ND DIVISIONAL ARTILLERY.
6.0 am. 24th to 6.0 am 25th June 1918.

1. OUR ACTIVITY.
   (a) Operations. By day 4.5" Hows. fired 24 rounds on Hostile Battery at U.14.a.70.55 and 18-pdrs. fired on a 77mm gun firing from T.18.d.80.05.
   In the afternoon movement in U.26.a. was engaged by 18-pdr.
   At 9.30 pm. 4.5" Hows. in conjunction with 20th D.A. and Heavy Artillery carried out a Gas Shell bombardment NW of MERICOURT. 18-pdrs. co-operating with H.E. on the same targets.
   At night harassing fire was carried out as usual, tracks in N.34.c. (20th Div: front) being included.
   Total rounds fired:-
   18-pdrs. - 1108.   4.5" Hows. 1482.   6" TM - Nil.

   (b) Aerial. Our machines were active.

2. HOSTILE ACTIVITY.
   (a) Artillery. Activity of 77mm guns continues, T.13.c., by the embankment, receiving some 500 rounds during the day.
   25 rounds YELLOW CROSS gas shell were fired on A.18.c. during the morning. From fragments, the calibre appeared to be 15cm or possibly 21cm.
   Apart from these rounds the enemy heavy guns remain inactive.
   There was practically no retaliation for the gas bombardment.

Date.	Time.	No.of rds.	Calibre.	Area shelled.	Direction.	Remarks.
24th.	9.25am	40	77mm	T.13.c.		
	10.20am	20	10.5cm	LA CHAUDIERE (S.18.d.)	66°G.B. from B.1.a. 4.0	Position U. 19.b.1.9 - flash & smoke ring.
	10.25 - 11.20am	400	77mm	T.13.c.		
	11.40 am	30	10.5cm	VIMY STA. (T.19.d.)	65°20" from B.1.c.73.92	F to R 30 secs. - Gun fire.
	10.40 - noon	15) 10)	15cm?	A.18.c.		Gas (Yellow Cross).
	12 - 12.30 pm.	60	77mm	T.13.c.	72°30' G.B. (s) from S.23.a.3.2	
	1 pm.	40	77mm	?		Gun at T.18 d.80.05 - ceased when 18pdrs started.
	4.45 - 5.30 pm	40	10.5cm	T.13.d.		
	10.15 pm.	20	77mm or 10.5cm	B.2.c., B.8.d.		

   (b) Work. Nil.

   (c) Movement. Enemy continues to show himself in small parties and individually.
   10.9 am. 1 mounted man went to U.16.c. 2.2
   10.31 am - G.S. wagon went to BOIS BERNARD (U.15.c.)

P.T.O.

During the morning, movement was seen from DICK HOUSE (U.22.d.) to EAST COPSE (U.27.b.) and CHEZ BONTEMPS (U.20.c.), also in C.2.

In the afternoon movement in U.26.a. was engaged.

During the day individual movement was observed around T.6.d.

(d) Aerial. None reported.

3. GENERAL.

11.10 am. - Smoke and flame W. of BEAUMONT CHURCH (V.13.b.)
11.50 am -) White smoke up from 2 places, 39°30' and 40°40' from
1.35 pm.) B.].c.73.92. This did not appear to be used as a screen.

Visibility. Poor.

A. J. Drufton
Lieut: R.A.
25th June 1918. Reconnaissance Officer, 52nd Divisional Ar

SECRET.   52ND DIVISIONAL ARTILLERY ORDER NO. 19.   COPY NO. 39

Reference Maps 1/20,000, Sheets 44.a. S.W. & 51.b. N.W.

1.   One Section from A/242 and C/56 Brigades R.F.A. will relieve each other on night 27/28th June.
   Remainder of main positions and forward guns will relieve each other on night 28th/29th June.
   Guns stripped, Aiming Posts, map boards, etc., will be taken over in situ.
   After completion of relief A/242 will move into C/56 Brigades present alternative position, the old position becoming the alternative.

2.   On night 27th/28th June one Section A/56 Brigade R.F.A. will move into C/242 Brigade's alternative position, and one Section C/242 Brigade R.F.A. into A/56 Brigade's alternative position.
   On night 28th/29th June guns of A/56 and C/242 Brigade's main positions will join their above-mentioned Sections.
   On night 29th/30th June forward guns of these two batteries will exchange positions.
   All map boards etc. will be handed over.
   On completion of these moves A/56 and C/242 Brigades present positions will become the alternative positions of C/242 and A/56 Brigades R.F.A. respectively.

3.   On completion of moves on night 28th/29th, A & C Batteries 56th Brigade will come under Left Group and A & C Batteries 242 Bde. under Right Group.
   56th Brigade and 242 Brigade will also exchange all rear line positions.

4.   At a date to be notified later, 56th Brigade Headquarters will relieve 242 Brigade Headquarters at Left Group and 242 Brigade Headquarters will withdraw to its own W.L. Headquarters

5.   ACKNOWLEDGE.

                                        Captain R.A.
                                        Brigade Major R.A.
                                        52nd Division.
24th June 1918.

Distribution:-
   Copy No. 1/12 to Right Group.   Copy No. 29 to 20th D.A.
         13/20 to Left Group.   30 to 51st D.A.
            21 to 56th Brigade.   31 to R.A. 18th Corps.
            22 to 52nd D.A.C.   32 to H.A. 18th Corps.
            23 to 2nd C.G.A.   33 to 52nd Div: G.
            24 to DAG.O.   34 to B.M.R.A.
            25 to D.T.M.O.   35 to S.C.R.A.
            26 to 155 Infy: Bde.   36 to R.O.R.A.
            27 to 156 Infy: Bde.   37 to R.A. Sig: Officer.
            28 to 157 Infy: Bde.   38/39 to War Diary.
                                               40   File.

DAILY REPORT
52ND DIVISIONAL ARTILLERY.
6.0 am. 25th to 6.0 am. 26th JUNE 1918.

1. **OUR ACTIVITY.**
    (a) Operations. 18-pdrs. fired on movement at U.26.a.3.9 and in T.6.c & d., and some series were fired for registration and instruction.
    Harassing fire at night was carried out as usual.
    Total rounds fired:-
    18-pdrs. - 1,100.   4.5" Hows. - 200.   6" T.M. - Nil.

    (b) Aerial. Considerable activity all day.

2. **HOSTILE ACTIVITY.**
    (a) Artillery. Very quiet. Heavy artillery remains inactive, and the activity of field guns has dropped to normal.

Date.	Time.	No. of rds.	Calibre.	Area shelled.	Direction.	Remarks.
25th.	10-10.4am.	10	77mm	FARBUS WOOD. (B.8.c.)		?
	10.30 am.	10	10.5cm	B.2.c.		
	12.50 pm.	10	15 cm	T.25.a.		
	2-3 pm.	50	10.5cm	T.20.c.		
	2.30-4.30pm	30	10.5cm	VIMY (T.19.c.)		Slow rate of fire.
	3.40-5 pm	30	10.5cm & 15cm.	T.16.c.		
	4.0 pm.	5	10 cm	FARBUS WOOD. (B.8.c.)		
	6.30 pm	8	10.5 cm	T.26.c.6.6.		
	10 pm to 2 am.	60	10.5 cm	S.30.		
26th	2.am	20	10 cm gun.	VIMY (T.19.c.)		
	3.50 am	20	77mm	LONE TREE T.27.c.0.7)	60° G.B.(s) from B.1.d.0.5.	
	4.40 am	20	10.5cm	VIMY.(T.19.c.)		Intense.
	5.40 - 7.am.	200	77mm & 10.5cm	T.15.c.		

    (b) Work. Nil.

    (c) Movement. A party at U.26.a.3.9 was sniped by 18-pdrs. and individual movement was observed in T.6.c and d., U.27.a., C.1.c., C.2.b and d., and C.7.

    (d) Aerial. 11.30am, 3 E.A. very high over our lines.

3. **GENERAL.**

    An ammunition dump in AVION was burning all night.

    Visibility. Fair.

A. F. Drayton
Lieut: R.A.
Reconnaissance Officer, 52nd Div. Arty.

26th June 1918.

DAILY REPORT
52ND DIVISIONAL ARTILLERY.
6.0 am. 26th to 6.0 am 27th June 1918.

1. **OUR ACTIVITY.**

    (a) Operations.   During morning 4.5" Hows. fired on T.5.d.8.4. and T.30.d.1.5. and 18-pdrs. fired on targets in T.6.
    At 8.50 p.m. 4.5" Hows. dispersed a party of 50 men in file moving towards MERICOURT.
    The usual harassing fire was carried out at night.   At 6 p.m. 6" T.M's fired on trench junction at B.5.c.55.90 and on earthwork B.5.cent.
    Total rounds fired :-
    18-pounders -- 950   4.5" Hows. - 250.   6"T.M. 12.

    (b) Aerial.   Our Aeroplanes were active especially in the evening.

2. **HOSTILE ACTIVITY.**

    (a) Artillery.   All calibres continue to be very quiet.

Date.	Time.	No. of Rds.	Calibre.	Area Shelled.	Direction.	Remarks.
26th.	6.30am	9	10 cm.	FARBUS WOOD (B.8.c.)		
	6-7am	10	15cm	S.18.b.		
	10.30-11am	40	10.5cm	T.26.a.		
	12.5pm	30	10 cm	A.18.c.		
	2.15-2.40pm	25	10.5cm	T.13.c.		70°GB.(S) from S.23.d.5.2.
	2.30pm	10	15 cm	T.19.b.		
27th.	3.30am	5	77mm	FARBUS WOOD (B.8.c.)		
	3.30-5am	30	77mm	VIMY area.		

    (b) Work.   N I L.

    (c) Movement.   11 am. Groups of 2 or 3 men at C.3.a.
    11.15am Smoke of engine in C.16.
    During afternoon individual movement on HALIFAX Road (T.6.).
    Groups of men seen near trees, C.2.b.1.7. and walking from U.26.c.3.3. to U.26.c.7.4.
    5.30pm. Smoke of engine in C.16.
    8.50pm. Party of 50 in file moving towards MERICOURT, dispersed by 4.5" How.

    (d) Aerial.   Below normal.

3. **GENERAL.**   Visibility - Poor early, improving towards midday.

A. F. Dufton
Lieutenant R.A.,
Reconnaissance Officer 52nd D.A.

27/6/18.

DAILY REPORT
52ND DIVISIONAL ARTILLERY.
6 am 27th to 6 am 28th JUNE 1918.

appx "D"
appx 43

1. **OUR ACTIVITY.**
   (a) <u>Operations</u>. During the day, 18-pdrs. fired on movement in T.6.c & d. CHEZ BONTEMPS (U.20.c.), Road junctions and trench junction in U.25 a and c. were also fired on. From 5.30 to 6.30 pm. 6" T.M. fired on earthwork B.5.central, on ARLEUX LOOP South (B.5.c.9.8), on WILLERVAL - ARLEUX ROAD and on trench B.5.b.1.8.
   At 1.5 am. a Test S.O.S. was received and responded to by Right Group.
   Total rounds fired:-
   18-pdrs. - 1025.   4.5" Hows. 270.   6"T.M. 25.

   (b) <u>Aerial</u>. Considerable activity.

2. **HOSTILE ACTIVITY.**
   (a) <u>Artillery</u>. Hostile artillery was quiet all day and practically all the shelling was directed on the area by the Embankment from T.13.c. to T.26.c.
   10.5cm Howitzers were slightly more active than during the previous days.

Date.	Time.	No.of rds.	Calibre.	Area shelled.	Direction.	Remarks.
27th.	9.17 am & throughout day.	200	10.5cm	T.26.a.	83°G.B.(s) from S.22.b.6.4.	
	9.30-10 am.	50	77mm	T.26.c.55.45.		
	11 am.	20	77mm	T.26.c.55.45.		
	1.15 pm.	7	10.5cm	T.13.d.		
	5.15 pm.	70	77mm	T.13.c.		
	5.20 pm - 5.50	60	10.5cm	T.13.c.		
	9-12 pm.	100	10.5cm	T.20.c.		
	10.20-11pm	20	77mm	FARBUS WOOD (B.8.c.)		

FLASHES.	10.0am.	From A.6.b.84.64.	64°G.B.		
	12.50pm.	92°G.B. from	B.8.a.25.20.	A.A. Guns.	
	1.0 pm.	69°30'GB "	B.8.a.25.20.		
	1.10 pm.	69°30'GB "	B.8.a.25.20.		
	1.15 pm	91°GB "	A.6.b.84.64.	A.A. Guns.	
	1.30 pm	74°30'GB "	A.6.b.84.64.		
	3.13 pm.	82°G.B. "	S.22.b.6.4.		
	9.15 pm.	74°30'GB "	A.6.b.84.64.		
	9.45 pm.	Large calibre gun was spotted at U.14.d.30.40.			

   (b) <u>Work</u>. Nil.

   (c) <u>Movement</u>. Individual movement in T.6.c and d.

   (d) <u>Aerial</u>. Below normal. E.A. were over our lines about noon, at 5 pm. and 7 pm.

3. **GENERAL.**

   <u>Visibility</u>. Poor in the early morning, improving at 11am.

   A.F.Dufton
   Lieut: R.A.
   Reconnaissance Officer 52nd Div: Arty.

28/6/1918.

53ND DIVISIONAL ARTILLERY INSTRUCTIONS NO. 1.

Reference sheets 44.a. S.W. and 51.b. N.W.

1. The BLACK line has now become the main line of resistance on the Divisional front.
It is covered by an outpost line of observation and an outpost support line.

2. There will be 2 S.O.S. Barrages to be known as:-
    The OUTPOST Barrage.
    The BLACK Barrage.
The details of these barrages are shown in the attached tracing.
Previous barrage orders are cancelled.

3. There will be 2 different procedures in replying to an S.O.S. signal or message -
(a) <u>In normal times.</u>
    The outpost barrage will be fired as follows:-
        5 minutes INTENSE.
        5 minutes RAPID.
        5 minutes NORMAL.
after which fire will depend upon the situation, to ascertain which, the Artillery Commanders must make the most strenuous efforts.
(b) <u>After the order "MAN BATTLE STATIONS" has been issued.</u>
    The outpost barrage will be fired as follows:-
        10 minutes INTENSE,
        10 minutes RAPID, during which, barrage will roll forward 500 yards at the rate of 100 yards per 2 minutes and then jump back to original line for 2 minutes INTENSE followed by 8 minutes normal.
After this, fire will be controlled according to the situation.
On the barrage coming back to the BLACK line, a similar 30 minutes burst will be fired.
The BLACK barrage will not be fired till a definite S.O.S. call from the BLACK line is received. On this call being received, the BLACK barrage will be fired on the whole Divisional front. Pending the introduction of a distinctive signal, this will be a message "S.O.S. BLACK".
    Group Commanders must consequently inform each other immediately this call is received
    In order to ensure continuity of fire along the whole front, the following procedure will be adopted until it is known that the fire of the flank divisions has also been brought back.
    2 of the guns superimposed on the right and left flanks will be used to connect the right and left points of the BLACK barrage with the Right and Left points of the Outpost barrage.

4. The barrage will not be brought back from the BLACK line to the BROWN line except by order of the Divisional Commander and will then come back along the whole Divisional front. This does not refer to the fire of superimposed 18-pdrs.

5. 18-pdr. spring guns will not fire at ranges above 7,000 yards.

6. The following table gives the Trench Mortar dispositions which will come into force at once:-

P.T.O.

-2-

Battery.	Position to be occupied at present.	How numbered.	New position.	Number of new position.	S.O.S. point from new position.	Remarks
X/52.	T.3.d.05.20.	X.3 X.4	T.2.d. central.	X.9 & X.10.	Able to engage WIL-LERVAL and cover BROWN Line.	Move back when complete.
	T.23.d.40.25.	X.5.	--		T.28.c.20.30.	No move.
	T.28.a.40.15.	X.2.	T.27.c.0.4.	X.11.	T.28.c.20.20.	
	B.2.a.80.60.	X.6.			B.3.b.60.00.	No move. Can also cover BROWN Line.
	T.28.a.40.08.	X.1.	T.28.c.80.00.	X.12.	Cover BROWN Line.	
Y/52.	T.20.c.20.10.	Y.5.	--		)	) No move. Can
	T.20.c.15.30.	Y.6.	--		) On line) cover BROWN	
	T.13.b.48.35.	Y.7.	--		) T.8.d.0.0 -) line.	
	T.15.b.85.70.	Y.8.			) T.14 central-	
	T.22.a.71.60.	Y.1.)	About	Y.12	) T.15.c.0.0.	) Y.1 to move
	T.22.a.73.80.	Y.2.)	T.19.b.30.50.	Y.13	)	) back when ready. Can cover BROWN Line.

The Mortars at X.1, X.2 and Y.2 will keep beds at X7, Y.11 and Y10 for offensive work.
These mortars will withdraw to their rear positions on the order "prepare for action". Beds will be prepared in those positions for them.

7. ACKNOWLEDGE.

W.G. Harris
Captain, R.A.
Brigade Major, R.A.
52nd Divisional Artillery.

28th June 1918.

Distribution.

Nos. 1/12 - Right Group.   28 - 20th Div.
     13/20 - Left Group.   29 - 51st Div.
     21 - 53th Bde. R.F.A.   30 - R.A. 13th Corps.
     22 - 52nd D.A.C.   31 - D.A. "
     23 - D.T.M.O.   32 - C.B.S.O. "
     24 - 2nd C.G.A.   33 - R.A. Sig.Officer.
     25 - 155th Inf: Bde.   34 - S. " A.
     26 - 156th Inf: Bde.   35 - T.O.R.A.
     27 - 157th Inf: Bde.   36 - Staff Captain.
                                  37/38 - War diary.
                                  39 - File.
                                  40 - Retain.

F.T.O.

FIELD ARTILLERY - OUTPOST & BLACK BARRAGES
REF. MAP 44 A.S.W & 51 B.NW

DAILY REPORT
52nd DIVISIONAL ARTILLERY.
6.0 am 28th to 6.0 am 29th June 1918.

1. OUR ACTIVITY.
   (a) <u>Operations</u>. During the day, movement in T.6 and at B.6.c.80.90 was fired on and a small party at B.5.c.7.7 was engaged and dispersed. Fire was also directed on roads in U.25.b, U.19.d and B.6.d.
   At night the enemy's Tracks, Roads etc. were harassed.
   At 4.30 pm. 6" T.M. fired on WILLERVAL-ARLEUX Road (B.5.b.05.05) and on M.G. at B.5.a.05.25.
   Total rounds fired:-
   18-pdrs. - 1,000.   4.5" Hows. - 200.   6" T.M. - 16.

   (b) <u>Aerial</u>. Our machines were active all day, particularly in the evening.

2. HOSTILE ACTIVITY.
   (a) <u>Artillery</u>. Heavy artillery quiet; Field guns normal.
   A few rounds of Blue Cross gas were fired on A.6.c.

Date.	Time.	No. of rds.	Calibre.	Area shelled.	Direction.	Remarks.
28th.	8 am.	10.	15cm.	FARBUS WOOD (B.8.c).		
	7.45-11am.	140.	10.5cm.	B.7.b.		
	9.15 am.	20.	15cm.	B.7.b.central.		
	12 noon.	30.	10cm.	THELUS.		
	12 noon.	20.	77mm.	FARBUS WOOD (B.8.c).		
	1 pm.	7.	10.5cm.	T.13.d.		
	1.10pm.	20.	10.5cm.	T.13.c.		
	1.30 pm.	24.	10cm.	B.7. central.		
	7 pm.	50.	77mm.	A.6.c.central.		Some Blue Cross gas.

FLASHES. 7.45am.   81°45' G.B. from B.8.a.25.20.
         9.15 am. 65°30' G.B. from B.8.a.25.20. F/R 13 secs.
         1.30 am. 71°45' G.B. from B.8.a.25.20.

(b) <u>Work</u>. Nil.

(c) <u>Movement</u>. Individual movement in T.6.
    6 pm. A small party at B.5.c.7.7.

(d) <u>Aerial</u>. Below normal during the daytime.
    Machines were over our lines at night from 11 pm. to 3 am.

3. GENERAL. <u>Visibility</u>. Poor. Fair at intervals.

A. F. D[signature]

Lieut: R.A.
Reconnaissance Officer, 52nd Div:Arty

29th June 1918.

52nd DA. No. 197/A2.

To all recipients of 52nd Divisional Artillery Order No.1.

The following will be the points for the attached Heavy Arty. BLACK barrage.

<u>2nd C.G.A. Bde.</u>
Heavy Howitzers. B.4.d.45.40.   B.4.b.30.05.
                  T.28.b.40.40. T.28.d.80.90.
                  T.28.b.80.60. T.23.c.30.05.
                  T.22.b.50.70. T.16.c.60.05.
                  T.15.d.50.80. T.15.a.98.70.

4 – 60 Pounders. T.28.c.98.10. to B.4.a.70.30.
8 – 60 Pounders. T.15.c.70.80. T.9.c.20.40.

MEDIUM HOWZRS.   B.4.d.05.15.   B.4.a.80.40.
                  T.28.d.05.40. T.28.b.10.05.
                  T.28.b.40.50. T.22.d.98.20.
                  T.22.d.98.50. T.22.d.70.90.
                  T.22.b.05.50. T.22.a.90.05.
                  T.22.a.65.70. T.16.c.05.05.

<u>Reinforcing Heavy Artillery.</u>
Heavy Howitzers. T.8.b.98.70.
                  T.8.b.70.98.

MEDIUM HOWRS.   T.15.d.60.30. T.15.d.20.60.
                  T.15.c.80.80. T.9.c.20.40.
                  T.9.c.05.70.   T.8b.98.05.

(signed)

Captain RA.
<u>Brigade Major RA.</u> <s>52nd Division.</s>

29th June 1918.

SECRET.   52ND DIVISIONAL ARTILLERY ORDER NO. 20.   COPY NO. 34

Reference Maps 1/20,000, Sheets 44.a. S.W. and 51.b.N.W.

1. A gas projection will be carried out on ARLEUX-EN-GOHELLE on night 1st/2nd JULY.

2. Projectors will be sited at B.10.a.50.70 and target will be B.5.d.60.60 to B.5.b.20.35.

3. Projectors will be fired in winds S. to NN.W.

4. (a) At 6 pm on July 1st (and daily afterwards if necessary) one of the following code words will be wired:-
   STRAFFE = GAS will be projected.
   BOSCHE = GAS will NOT be projected.

   (b) NIX will be wired if the operation has been ordered and is then cancelled.

   (c) This operation will be known as G.F.11.

5. Area between line B.10.a.50.70 – B.4.d.35.35 and line B.10.a.50.70 – B.10.b.45.70 will be cleared of troops and all troops remaining within area T.29.a.00.70 – B.10.a.50.70 – B.10.b.45.20 will wear S.B.R's from zero till orders for removal are given by Brigade Gas Officer.

6. Zero hour will be 11 pm.
   Artillery will co-operate by firing from zero to zero plus 6 minutes.
   Projectors will be fired at zero plus one.
   Tasks for artillery are shown below.

7. Each group & O.C. 2nd. Bde. C.G.A. will send an Officer (with two watches with second hands) to Right Infantry Bde. Hd.Qrs. A.6.c.60.50 to synchronise watches, at 6 pm. July 1st. (or on such day as the operation is postponed to).

8. Groups and 2nd Bde. C.G.A. to Acknowledge.

ARTILLERY TASKS.

Unit.	Serial No.	Number of guns.	Tasks.	Rate of fire.
Left Group.	1.	1 – 4.5" How.	B.5.b.45.85.	INTENSE.
	2.	2 – 18-pdrs.	B.5.c.50.95 to B.5.d.30.55.	-do-
	3.	2 – 18-pdrs.	B.5.a.90.30 to B.5.d.40.80.	-do-
Right Group.	4.	1 – 4.5" How.	B.6.a.15.00.	INTENSE.
	5.	4 – 18-pdrs.	B.5.c.50.95 to B.5.a.70.70.	-do-
2nd Bde. C.G.A.	6.	6 – 6" Hows.	T.30.c.40.75 to B.6.b.05.25.	NORMAL.

W.G. Harris
Captain R.A.
Brigade Major, R.A.
52nd Divisional Artillery.

30th June 1918.

Distribution.
1/12 Right Group.   13/20 Left Gp.   21 60th Bde.   22 – 52nd D.A.C.
2nd C.G.A.   24 D.T.M.O.   26 – 20th D.A.
51st D.A.   28 R.A. 18th   30 – C.B.S.O. 18 C
?? Div:G.   34 – D.H.R.A.
                     R.A. 37/38   File.

DAILY REPORT, 52ND DIVISIONAL ARTILLERY.
6.0am 29th to 6.0am 30th JUNE 1918.

1. OUR ACTIVITY.
    (a) Operations. At night harassing fire was increased, 2,400 rounds of 18-pdr. and 420 rounds 4.5" How., including 240 gas shell, being fired, and directed on the trenches & approaches N. of ACHEVILLE to catch the suspected relief.

        12.39 am. Right Group received and responded to a test S.O.S.

        6" T.M. did not fire during the period.

    (b) Aerial. Normal.

2. HOSTILE ACTIVITY.
    (a) Artillery. 77mm were rather more active than usual on the Embankment area.

        10.5 cm Hows. and 15 cm Hows. were inactive.

Date.	Time.	No. of rds.	Calibre.	Area shelled.	Direction.	Remarks.
29th.						
	12.50 pm.	30.	77mm.	B.8.a.		
	1.40 pm.	5.	15cm	STATION WOOD (B.2.c.)		
	During afternoon.	200.	77mm	T.13.c.	G.B.(s)55° from S.22.b.6.4.	
	3 pm.	40.	77mm	S.24.b. & d.		
	7-7.30pm.	30.	10.5cm	T.19.c.		
	10.50-11.30pm.	100.	77mm	T.13.c., T.19.d.		
	12.45 am - 4. am	20.	15cm.	C.18.d.		
	1.30 - 1.45 am.	40.	77mm	T.20.c.		

    FLASHES. 11.55 pm. G.B. 71°, 52° and 58° from SS.23.c.7.8.

    (b) Work. Nil.

    (c) Movement. Little movement observed owing to mist. Parties were seen around CHEZ BONTEMPS (U.20.c.), FRESNOY PARK (T.30.d.) and U.21.d.

    (d) Aerial. Below normal.

3. GENERAL.
    Visibility. Was poor during the morning owing to mist, but improved during the afternoon.

A.F.Dufton

30th June 1918.

Lieut: R.A.,
Reconnaissance Officer, 52nd Div: Arty.

DAILY REPORT.
52nd DIVISIONAL ARTILLERY
6 am 30th June to 6 am 1st July, 1918.

1. **OUR ACTIVITY.**

    (a) <u>Operations</u>. At 5.14 pm. movement in U.20.a. was fired on by 18-pdrs.
    At 7.15 pm. 6" T.M. fired on M.G. at B.5.a.4.4 and on front line trench B.5.a.6.4.
    Between 1am and 2am 18-pdrs. fired 50 rounds on B.5.central where the enemy was reported to be working on his wire.
    Harassing fire was directed at night on the enemy's Roads, Tracks and Centres of Activity.
    Total rounds fired:-
    18-pdrs. - 910.   4.5" Hows. - 200.   6" T.M - 20.

    (b) <u>Aerial</u>. Active all day. Our aeroplanes brought down an observation balloon in flames.

2. **HOSTILE ACTIVITY.**

    (a) <u>Artillery</u>. At 9.30 am. 10.5cm hows. fired about 500 rounds at the rate of about 30 rounds per minute on the Embankment area. No damage is reported.
    15cm Hows. have become active again, LES TILLEULS Cross Roads being shelled in the morning and 100 rounds being fired during the night on the THELUS area.
    77mm guns were inactive.

Date.	Time.	No. of rds.	Calibre.	Area shelled.	Direction.
30th June	9.5 am.	50.	10cm.	B.8.a.	
	9.30-9.45am	500.	10.5cm.	T.26.a & c, & T.19.b.	
	11.40 am.	4.	15cm.	THELUS Wood. (A.8.d.)	C.15.c.45.35.
	11.45 am.	12.	15cm.	LES TILLEULS X Roads (A.11)	
	5.10 pm.	9.	10cm.	B.8.b.	
	At intervals, 9pm-4am.	100.	15cm.	A.11.b.	

    FLASHES.   9.47 am.   92° from B.14.a.60.75.
               11.10 am. 71°   ,,   ,,
               11.40 am. 96°   ,,   ,,
               11.45 am. 99°   ,,   ,,

    (b) <u>Work</u>. Nil.

    (c) <u>Movement</u>. 5.5 pm. Lamp Signalling from Slag Heap in O.33.c.
    Following groups were sent - URD VIN 5AAE UAV break SAE SAE UST UAV DSA break TVR A-R.
    5.14pm. Movement in U.20.a. - engaged by 18-pdrs.
    6.50 pm. Men walking in U.25.d.
    9.45 pm. Lamp Signalling 74°G.B. from S.25.c.70.60

    (b) <u>Aerial</u>. Below normal. One or two machines active over back areas.

3. **GENERAL.**
    Visibility good.

A.F. Drufton

1st July 1918.   Lieut: R.A.
                        Reconnaissance Officer, 52nd Div: Arty:

CONFIDENTIAL.

APPENDICES.
to
WAR DIARY of 52ND DIVISIONAL ARTILLERY.
for
JULY 1918.

CONFIDENTIAL.
==*=*=*=*=*

ORIGINAL.
==*=*=*

War Diary.

OF

HEADQUARTERS 52ND DIVISIONAL ARTILLERY.

VOLUME - IV.
PART - VII.

FROM -
1st JULY 1918.

TO -
31st JULY 1918.

Army Form C. 2118.

WAR DIARY

JULY. 1918.
****

OR

INTELLIGENCE SUMMARY.

(Erase heading not required.)

Instructions regarding War Diaries and Intelligence Summaries are contained in F. S. Regs., Part II, and the Staff Manual, respectively. Title pages will be prepared in manuscript.

Hour. Date. Place.	Summary of Events and Information.	Remarks and references to Appendices
VILLERS AU BOIS.		
1st July.	Very quiet. 4.5" How. fired on CHEZ BONTEMPS with balloon observation, vide Daily Report.	Appendix 1.
2nd July.	52nd D.A. No. 218/M, re alteration of BLACK Line barrage issued, vide Daily Report. — Quiet, vide Daily Report. — Amendment to 52nd D.A. No. 218/M issued, vide —	Appendix 2. Appendix 3. Appendix 4.
3rd July.	52nd D.A. Order No. 21, bombardment programme issued, vide —	Appendix 5.
4th July.	Quiet, vide Daily Report — At 11 am a five minute intense bombardment of H.Q. etc. in T.24.b. & d., was carried out in conjunction with 2nd Bde CGA and repeated at 11.15a.m. 15 cm Hows. were slightly more active, 100 rounds being fired in vicinity of PETIT VIMY and LA CHAUDIERE. 77 mm gun fired 3 shoots of 100 rounds each on T.19.c. - vide Daily Report —	Appendix 6. Appendix 7.
5th July.	Quiet. At 3pm 2nd Bde CGA fired a five minute bombardment on Bn. HQ., U.22.b. & d. This was repeated at 3.30pm. At 11 pm ARLEUX was bombarded in conjunction with a gas projection - vide Daily Report - (App.8) 52nd DA.No.237/A issued - vide 56th Bde RFA took over command of Left Group at noon.	Appendix 8. App.8-A.
6th July.	Very quiet. For Daily Report vide –	Appendix 9.
7th July.	At 7 am a 5 minute bombardment of Headquarters etc. in T.18.b. was carried out in conjunction with 2nd Bde CGA and repeated at 7.10 am. Quiet. 15 cm. Hows. were somewhat more active in front of Left Bde, for Daily Report vide –	
8th July.	Very quiet. Right Group fired in support of raid by 152nd Inf. Bde., 51st Division. For Daily Report vide –	Appendix 10.
9th July.	At 11 am a 5 minute bombardment of S.P., trench and dugout in U.13.a. was carried out in conjunction with 2nd Bde CGA and repeated at 11.15 am.	Appendix 11.
~~10th July.~~	Our aeroplanes brought down an E.A. near FARBUS. 15 cm showed more activity. For Daily Report vide –	Appendix 12.

Army Form C. 2118.

WAR DIARY
OR
INTELLIGENCE SUMMARY.
****

(Erase heading not required.)

Instructions regarding War Diaries and Intelligence
Summaries are contained in F. S. Regs., Part II,
and the Staff Manual, respectively. Title pages
will be prepared in manuscript.

Hour. Date. Place.	Summary of Events and Information.	Remarks and references to Appendices
VILLERS AU BOIS.		
10th July.	52nd D.A. Defence Scheme issued vide -	Appendix 13.
11th July.	Quiet. For Daily Report vide -	Appendix 14.
	52nd D.A. Order No. 22, re short bombardment issued vide -	Appendix 15.
	Quiet, except for shelling of VIMY by 15 cm Hows. between 3 pm and 5 pm and of PETIT VIMY at 11 am and 3 pm. For Daily Report vide -	
12th July.	Orders for relief of 52nd Army Bde RFA by 8th Army Bde CFA issued, vide -	Appendix 16.
	At 11 am a hurricane bombardment of Headquarters in U.25.d.40.90 was carried out in conjunction with 2nd Bde CGA.	Appendix 17.
	In connection with a gas beam discharge harassing fire was increased. Very quiet during the day. Vimy and B.4.e. & c. were shelled during the night. For Daily Report vide -	
13th July.	Amendment to 52nd D.A. Order No. 22 re short bombardments issued, vide-	Appendix 18.
	At 9 am a bombardment of H.Q. in C.1.a.40.60 to C.1.a.30.75 was carried out in conjunction with 2nd Bde CGA.	Appendix 19.
	Increased harassing fire was maintained in connection with gas beam discharge of previous night./ For Daily Report vide -	Appendix 20.
	Quiet-	
14th July.	52nd D.A. Order No. 24 re re-organisation consequent on change of Southern Divisional Boundary issued vide -	Appendix 21.
	52nd D.A. Order No. 25 re withdrawal of H.Q. and 2 batteries of 242nd Army Bde RFA to ESTREE CAUCHIE issued vide -	Appendix 22.
	52nd D.A. No. M/302 re Appendix 'G' of Defence Scheme issued vide -	Appendix 23.
	At 3 pm and 3.85 pm a bombardment of living trench and of road track and light railway junction in C.1.b. was carried out in conjunction with 2nd Bde CGA.	
	Quiet day. For Daily Report vide -	Appendix 24.

Army Form C. 2118.

WAR DIARY
OR
INTELLIGENCE SUMMARY.
JULY 1918.

(Erase heading not required.)

Instructions regarding War Diaries and Intelligence Summaries are contained in F. S. Regs., Part II, and the Staff Manual, respectively. Title pages will be prepared in manuscript.

Hour. Date. Place.	Summary of Events and Information.	Remarks and references to Appendices
VILLERS AU BOIS.		
15th July.	52nd D.A. No. R/306 amending Order No. 24 issued vide -	Appendix 25.
	52nd D.A. No. M/309 amendments to Defence Scheme consequent on change of Divisional Boundary issued vide -	Appendix 26.
	At 7 pm and at 7.30 pm a short bombardment of Headquarters in C.I.C. was carried out by 2nd Bde CGA - field guns engaging the trenches leading to it.	
	Enemy Artillery was more active than in previous day. For Daily Report vide -	Appendix 27.
16th July.	4.5" Hows. fired with balloon observation.	Appendix 28.
	Quiet day. For Daily Report vide Appendix 28.	
17th July.	Quiet day. For Daily Report vide -	Appendix 29.
	52nd D.A. No. M/321. Appendices 'A', 'C' & 'G' to Defence Scheme issued vide -	Appendix 30.
18th July.	Enemy Artillery was more active than during previous 24 hours. For Daily Report vide -	Appendix 31.
19th July.	52nd D.A. No. R/344, warning order re relief of 52nd Division by 8th Division and transfer of 52nd Division to XVII Corps in GHQ Reserve issued vide -	Appendix 32.
	52nd D.A. Order No. 26 and R/350 re relief of 52nd D.A. issued.Vide -	Appendix 34 & Appendix 35.
20th July.	Amendments to 52nd D.A. Defence Scheme issued. Vide -	Appendix 36.
	Hostile activity rather above normal. Gas shell were fired on B.13 during the night and VIMY was shelled by 15 cm Hows. at intervals throughout the day. For Daily Report vide -	
	52nd D.A. Order No. 27 re move of 52nd D.A. to reserve area vide -	Appendix 37.
21st July.	Quiet day. For Daily Report vide -	Appendix 38.
	D.A.C. moved to OURTON.	Appendix 39.
CUVIGNY.		
22nd July.	Relief of 8th D.A. complete. HQRA moved to CUVIGNY.	
23rd July.	52nd D.A. Order No. 28 re entraining stations in the event of a move issued vide -	Appendix 40.

Army Form C. 2118.

WAR DIARY
or
INTELLIGENCE SUMMARY.

JULY

(Erase heading not required.)

Instructions regarding War Diaries and Intelligence Summaries are contained in F. S. Regs., Part II, and the Staff Manual, respectively. Title pages will be prepared in manuscript.

Hour. Date. Place.	Summary of Events and Information.	Remarks and references to Appendices.
CUVIGNY.		
July 24th -27th.	Nothing to report.	
July 28th	Orders to relieve the 5th Canadian D.A.M in action received.	
ETRUN.		
July 29th	52nd D.A. Order No. 29 re move to 5th CDA area issued - vide	Appendix 41.
	Units move to MADAGASCAR Camp. HQ 52nd D. A. move to ETRUN.	
	52nd D.A. Orders for relief issued vide	Appendix 42.
	Relief of 2 guns per battery completed.	
July 30th	Relief completed - quiet day.	
July 31st.	Quiet day. 52nd D.A. No. A/392 re 10 minutes concentration on	
	GAVRELLE issued vide	Appendix 43

[signature]
Brigadier General R.A.
Commanding R.A., 52nd (Lowland) Division.

DAILY REPORT, 52ND DIVISIONAL ARTILLERY.
6 am. 1st to 6 am 2nd July 1918.

1. OUR ACTIVITY.

(a) <u>Operations</u>. 4.5" Hows. carried out a shoot on CHEZ BONTEMPS with balloon observation.

At 11.10 pm. a Test S.O.S. was received and responded to by the Loft Group.

Normal harassing fire was carried out at night.
Total rounds fired:-
18-pdrs. - 850.   4.5" Hows. - 250.   6" T.M. - Nil.

(b) <u>Aerial</u>. Active all day particularly in the evening.

2. HOSTILE ACTIVITY.

(a) <u>Artillery</u>. Very quiet during the whole period, less than 100 rounds being reported.

Date.	Time.	No. of rds.	Calibre.	Area shelled.	Direction.	Remarks.
1st July.	8.10am	6.	77mm	T.13.c.		
	9.50 - 10.20 am.	15.	77mm	FARBUS WOOD (B.8.c.)	FRESNOY WOOD.	Neutralised by heavies.
	10.30 am.	30.	10.5cm.	B.14.a.60.75.		
	11.0 am.	10.	15cm.	(T.19.c. (T.19.d. SW.		
	11-11.15 am.	20.	10.5cm.	FARBUS WOOD (B.8.c.)	U.26.d.10.47.	
	12.55pm.	2.	10.5cm.	T.10.c.		
	2.45 pm.	15.	10.5 cm.	THELUS ROAD.	C.9.c.10.40.	Neutralised by heavies.

(b) <u>Work</u>. Nil.

(c) <u>Movement</u>. None observed.

(d) <u>Aerial</u>. Below normal during the day, but machines were over our lines during the night.

3. GENERAL.

<u>Visibility</u> poor.

A. F. Dufton

2nd July 1918.

Lieut: R.A.,
Reconnaissance Officer, 52nd Div: Arty.

SECRET

To all recipients of 52nd D.A. Instructions No. 1.

It has now been decided that CANADA POST will not be held as a portion of the BLACK Line.

In consequence of this the Field Artillery BLACK barrage on Right Group front will be altered as follows:-

19th Bty. RFA.	B.10.b.10.90 - B.4.c.30.30 - B.4.a.00.10.
122 Bty. RFA.	B.10.b.10.90 - B.4.c.30.30.
A/52 Bde. RFA.	B.4.c.30.30 - B.4.a.00.10.
D/52 Bde. RFA.	B.4.c.70.25, B.4.c.50.80, B.4.b.37.25.
	B.4.a.27.75, B.4.a.70.75, T.28.c.70.30.
20th Bty. RFA.	T.28.c.20.50 - T.27.b.97.85.
C/52 Bde. RFA.	T.28.c.20.50 - T.28.b.00.45.
C/242 Bde. RFA.	T.28.b.00.45 - T.27.b.97.85 - T.22.c.40.30.
A/242 Bde. RFA.	T.22.c.40.30 - T.22.a.05.25
28th Bty. RFA.	T.27.b.97.85 - T.22.c.40.30 - T.22.a.05.25.
D/69 Bde. RFA.	T.28.a.61.35, T.28.a.80.60, T.28.a.58.78.
	T.22.c.74.30, T.22.c.60.55, T.22.c.47.73.

The Heavy Artillery BLACK S.O.S. Points will be:-

2nd Bde. C.G.A.

Heavy Hows.	B.4.d.50.40,	B.4.b.40.10.
	T.28.d.30.20,	T.28.d.80.80.
	T.28.b.80.60,	T.28.b.40.80.
	T.22.b.50.65,	T.16.c.60.05.
	T.15.d.50.80.	T.15.a.98.70.
Medium hows.	B.4.d.05.15,	B.4.a.70.40.
	T.28.d.05.35,	T.28.a.70.20.
	T.28.a.95.60,	T.22.d.50.25.
	T.22.d.20.65.	T.22.b.05.10.
	T.22.a.90.40,	T.22.a.80.60.
	T.22.a.60.80.	T.16.c.05.05.
4 - 60-pdrs.	B.4.a.60.35 - T.28.d.00.40.	
3 - 60-pdrs.	T.15.c.70.80 - T.9.c.20.40.	

Reinforcing Heavy Artillery.

Heavy Hows.	T.8.b.98.70.	
	T.8.b.70.98.	
Medium Hows.	T.15.d.80.30,	T.15.d.20.60.
	T.15.c.80.80,	T.9.c.20.40.
	T.9.c.05.70,	T.8.b.98.05.

Captain R.A.
Brigade Major, R.A.
52nd Divisional Artillery

1st July 1918.

DAILY REPORT
52ND DIVISIONAL ARTILLERY
6 am 2nd to 6 am 3rd July 1918.

1. OUR ACTIVITY.
   (a) Operations. At 12.30pm 6" T.M. fired on suspected T.M. about T.18.d.1.3 and on trench junction T.18.c.35.05.
   Harassing fire was directed at night on Roads, Tracks and centres of activity.
   Total rounds fired:-
   18-pdrs. - 800.   4.5" Hows. - 200.   6" T.M. - 19.

   (b) Aerial. Our machines were active throughout the day.

2. HOSTILE ACTIVITY.
   (a) Artillery. 15cm Howitzers and 10.5cm Howitzers were inactive during the period. The activity of 77mm guns was normal.

Date.	Time.	No.of rds.	Calibre.	Area shelled.	Direction.
2/8/18	7.45 - 8.45am.	10	10.5cm ?	B.2.d.	? U.14.d.
	9.15-10.5am.	15	77mm	T.13.c.	
	9.45-10.5am.	5	77mm	T.13.d.	
	10.30 am.	4	10.5cm ?	B.7.d.3.4.	? U.14.d.
	10-10.5am.	25	77mm.	T.21.b.	
	10.30 am.	10	77mm	T.8.b.	
	10.50 am.	6	77mm	T.21.b.	
	11-11.30am.	30	77mm	FARBUS WOOD B.8.c.	U.20.b.90.49.
	3.15 pm.	10	15cm	STATION WOOD B.2.c.	
	3.30 pm.	15	77mm	T.26.c.	
	7.30 pm.	20	10.5cm.	T.26.a.	
	7.40-8.30pm.	10	77mm	O.T's.	
	8.30 pm.	6	77mm	FARBUS WOOD B.8.c.	
	11.30 pm.	20	77mm	STATION WOOD B.2.c.	ROUVROY.
3/7/18.	5.30am.	100	77mm	Trenches T.22 and T.27.	

   FLASHES. 3.15pm. 53°G.B. from B.8.a.25.20.

   (b) Work. Nil.

   (c) Movement. 11 am. Slight movement in U.26.a, c and d.

   (d) Aerial. Below normal.

3. GENERAL.
   Visibility poor.

                                        A.J. Drufton
                                        Lieut: R.A.
3rd July 1918.   Reconnaissance Officer, 52nd Div; Arty.

Appx H. W.D

To all recipients of 218/M dated 1st July 1918.

Please amend my 218/M as follows:-

D/52nd Brigade R.F.A. - For B.4.b.3725 read B.4.a.37.25.

C/52nd Brigade R.F.A. - For T.28.b.00.45 read T.28.a.20.45.

C/242nd Brigade R.F.A. - For T.28.b.00.45 read T.28.a.20.45.

(signed)

Captain R.A.,
Brigade Major R.A.,
52nd Divisional Artillery.

2nd July 1918.

SECRET. 52ND DIVISIONAL ARTILLERY ORDER NO. 21. COPY NO. 31

Reference Maps 44.a. S.W. & 51.b. N.W.

1. Short bombardments will take place on dates as specified in the attached bombardment Table.

2. Fire in each case will consist of two bursts, fired as under:-

    July 4th.   11 am   - 11.5 am.
                    11.15 am - 11.20 am.

    July 5th.   5 pm   - 5.5 pm.
                    5.30 pm - 5.35 pm.

    July 7th.   7 am   - 7.5 am.
                    7.10 am - 7.15 am.

    July 9th.   11 am   - 11.5 am
                    11.15 am - 11.20 am.

3. Rates of fire will be:-

    8" Howitzers   - RAPID.
    6" Howitzers)   - INTENSE.
    4.5" Howitzers)
    18-Pounders.   - INTENSE for first 2 minutes
                          then RAPID.

4. Watches will be synchronised on each of the above days with this Office one hour before shoot, by telephone.

5. F.A. Groups and 2nd Brigade C.G.A. please ACKNOWLEDGE.

[signature]
Captain R.A.,
Brigade Major, R.A.,
52nd Divisional Artillery.

2 July 1918.

Distribution.

Copy No. 1/6 to Right Group.
       7/12 to Left Group.
       13/15 to 2nd C.G.A.
       16 to D.T.M.O.
       17 to 53th Brigade.
       18 to 52nd D.A.C.
       19 to 155th Infantry Brigade.
       20 to 156th   ,,   ,,
       21 to 157th   ,,   ,,
       22 to 20th D.A.
       23 to 51st D.A.
       24 to R.A. 18th Corps.
       25 to H.A. 18th Corps.
       26 to C.B.S.O., 18th Corps.
       27 to 52nd Division 'G'.
       28 to B.A. Signalling Officer.
       29 to B.G.R.A.
       30 to R.O.R.A.
       31/32 to War Diary.
       33 to File.

Date.	Unit.	Number & nature of guns.	Tasks.
July 4th.	2nd Bde. C.G.A.	1 - 8" How. 2 - 6" Hows.	Headquarters. T.24.d.80.98.
		1 - 8" How. 2 - 6" Hows.	Headquarters & M.G. T.24.b.66.12.
		1 - 8" How. 2 - 6" Hows.	Headquarters & T.M. T.24.b.60.14.
	Left Group.	2 - 18-pdrs. 1 - 4.5" How.	Headquarters & T.M. T.24.b.60.14.
	Right Group.	1 - 18-pdr. 1 - 4.5" How.	Headquarters & M.G. T.24.b.66.12.
		2 - 18-pdrs.	Headquarters T.24.d.80.93.
July 5th.	2nd Bde. C.G.A.	4 - 8" Hows. 8 - 6" Hows.	Battn: Headquarters. U.26.d.04.35 - U.2.b.05.17.
July 7th.	2nd Bde. C.G.A.	1 - 8" How. 2 - 6" Hows.	Headquarters. T.18.b.18.05.
		1 - 8" How. 2 - 6" Hows.	T.M. T.18.b.08.10.
		2 - 8" Hows. 4 - 6" Hows.	Trench T.18.d.00.89 - T.18.b.08.10.
	Left Group.	2 - 18-pdrs.	Headquarters T.18.b.18.05.
		1 - 4.5" How. 1 - 18-pdr.	T.M. T.18.b.82.10.
	Right Group.	3 - 18-pdrs. 1 - 4.5" How.	Trench T.18.d.00.89.- T.18.b.08.10.
July 9th.	2nd Bde. C.G.A.	1 - 8" How. 2 - 6" Hows.	S.P. U.13.a.06.23.
		1 - 8" How. 2 - 6" Hows.	Trench and dugouts - U.13.a.17.56 - U.13.a.25.25.
		2 - 8" Hows. 4 - 6" Hows.	Trench U.13.a.39.26 - U.13.a.30.41.
	Right Group.	3 - 18-pdrs. 1 - 4.5" How.	U.13.a.25.25 - U.13.a.39.26.

DAILY REPORT 52ND DIVISIONAL ARTILLERY
6 am 3rd to 6 am 4th July 1918.

1. OUR ACTIVITY.
   (a) Operations. During the day movement in U.28.b. was
       engaged by 18-pounders. Cross Roads U.25.a.25.20,
       FRESNOI and ULSTER Trench were also fired on.
       At 5 pm 6" T.M. fired on M.G. at B.5.a.00.25
      and on trench junction B.5.c.55.95.
       Harassing fire was carried out at night.
       Total rounds fired:-
       18-pdrs. - 830.   4.5" Hows. - 200.   6" T.M. - 20.

   (b) Aerial. Normal.

2. HOSTILE ACTIVITY.
   (a) Artillery. Very quiet except for shelling by Field guns
       during morning on Railway Embankment in T.13.c. and B.2.d.

Date.	Time.	No. of rds.	Calibre.	Area shelled.	Direction.	Remarks.
3rd July	8.30-10am	85	10.5cm	Railway embkt. B.2.d.	56° G.B.(s) from B.7.b.70.80	
	8-9am.	150	77mm	T.13.c.		
	9-9.30am.	8	77mm	FARBUS WOOD. B.8.c.		
	10-11am.	8	15cm	T.22.d.	47° G.B.(s) from B.14.a.60.75.	
	11.30am.	6	77mm	B.11.a.	88°30' G.B.(s) from B.14.a.30.75.	
	12 noon.	4	10.5cm	B.11.a.		
	1.30pm.	10	77mm	B.8.b.50.80.		
4th July	6 am.	6	15cm	FARBUS.		

   (b) Work. Nil.

   (c) Movement. 9 am and 12 noon. Small parties in U.27.a.,
      U.27.b., U.21.a., U.20.c., U.25.d., U.23.c., C.1.b.,
      C.2.a.
      During the afternoon individual movement in C.2.a.
      and U.27.d.
      8 - 10 pm. Wagon   at U.28.d.3.8.

   (d) Aerial. No activity reported.

3. GENERAL.
   Visibility fair.

4th July 1918.

Lieut: R.A.
Reconnaissance Officer, 52nd Div: Arty.

SECRET.

52nd D.A. No. 257/A.

appx 8-A

Right Group,
Left Group,
2nd C.A.A.
R.C., R.A.
S.C.R.A.

W.D

Reference 52nd Division Order No. 118.

1. The following will be the procedure as regards harassing fire, after the discharge of the Gas Beam.

2. The objectives will be considered under two headings:-
   Case i. When the wind is between S.W. & W.
   Case ii. When the wind is between W. & W.N.W.

3. (a) In case (i). The right flank of the beam will be taken as on line T.17.c.00.80 – T.18.c.00.80.
   (b) In Case (ii) The Right flank will be taken as T.17.d.00.00 – T.24.b.00.00

4. From zero plus one hour to zero plus 3 hours, 52nd Divisional Artillery and 2nd C.A.A. will, within their zones, harass communications on the flanks of the Beam, paying particular attention to the following:-
   In Case (i).
   HENIN-LIEVARD road running N.E. from U.19.d.5020
   BOIS BERNARD road in U.13 and U.14.

5. From zero plus 3 hours to zero plus 5 hours, all Tracks and Roads within the limit of the Beam as laid down in para 3 will be vigorously harassed.
   Should visibility be bad at zero plus 5 hours, harassing fire at NORMAL rates will be continued till it is possible to see movement in the German lines.
   This will be repeated during the night following the discharge.

6. There will be no increase in harassing fire till zero plus one hour.
   Ammunition allotment:-
   Per Group.   Zero night.   18-pdr. 1125 rounds.
                               4.5" How. 300 rounds.
                Night after   18-pdr. 750 rounds.
                discharge.   4.5" How. 200 rounds.
         H.A.   Zero night.   Treble normal allotment.
                Night after   Double normal allotment.
                zero

7. Dividing line between Groups will be:-
   Case i. Zero plus one hour,) Line T.17.c.00.40 to T.18.c.00.40.
           to zero plus 3 hours)

           Zero plus 3 hours   ) T.11.d.00.00 to T.12.central.
           to zero plus 5 hours)

   Case ii. Zero plus one hour to) Line T.23.b.00.60 – T.24.d.00.60.
            zero plus 3 hours   )

            Zero plus 3 hours   ) Line T.12.c.00.00 – U.7.c.00.00.
            to zero plus 5 hours)
   On following night, as from zero plus 3 hours to zero plus 5 hours.

8. ACKNOWLEDGE.

5th July 1918.

Brigade Major, 52nd Div: Artillery.
Captain R.A.

DAILY REPORT, 52ND DIVISIONAL ARTILLERY.
6.am 6th to 6 am 7th July 1918.

OUR ACTIVITY.

(a) <u>Operations</u>. Movement around CHEZ BONTEMPS (U.30c) was engaged
by a forward 18-pr. and some registration was carried
out.
Harassing fire was directed at night on enemy roads,
tracks and centres of activity.
TOTAL ROUNDS FIRED
18-pr. 900. 4.5" How. 330. 6" F.H. 18

(b) <u>Aerial</u>. Normal.

3. HOSTILE ACTIVITY.

(a) <u>Artillery</u>. Very quiet throughout the period.

Date	Time	No. of Rounds	Calibre	Area Shelled
6th.	6.30am.	10.	10.5 cm.	WILLERVAL ROAD.(B.4)
	8.30am.	15.	10.5 cm.	B13a.
	5.pm.	15.	77 mm.	WILLERVAL.
	11 pm.	50.	15 cm.	T30a.

FLASHES. 7.0 pm. 80° G. from B1.a.6075. F/R 21 secs.

(b) <u>Work</u>. Nil.

(c) <u>Movement</u>. During afternoon movement around CHEZ BONTEMPS was
engaged by a forward 18-pr.
Movement in B18c. between OPPY and ARLEUX - probably
runners - and individual movement in C13 during P.M.

(d) <u>Aerial</u>. Below normal.

4. GENERAL. Visibility poor all day owing to mist. Very misty during
early morning 7th.

7th July 1918 - Reconnaissance Officer, 52nd D.A.

Lieut. R.A.

DAILY REPORT 52nd DIVISIONAL ARTILLERY.
6 am 5th to 6 am 6th JULY 1918.

1. OUR ACTIVITY.
   (a) Operations. At 10.30 am. 6" H. fired on M.G. at
       W13d1803 and at 5.0pm. on Earthwork B8c ntral and on
       trench B5d1066.
       At 3 pm. 2nd Bde. C.F.A. carried out a five minute
       bombardment of Battalion H.Q. U26d0465 - U26b0517.
       This was repeated at 5.30pm.
       At 11pm. ARLEUX was bombarded in conjunction with
       a gas projection.
       Harassing fire was directed at night on enemy
       approaches and Centres of Activity.
       Total rounds fired:-
       18-Pdr. - 1000.   4.5" Hows. 250.   6" H. - 45.

   (b) Aerial. Active during the morning and from 4pm. to dusk.

2. HOSTILE ACTIVITY.
   (a) Artillery. Very quiet.

Date.	Time.	No. of rds.	Calibre.	Area shelled.	Direction.
5th	12.30pm.	6	15cm.	B7a.	
	1.30pm.	3	10cm.	B8b58.	
	11.30pm.	12	15cm.	B7b.	
	12 mid: to	8	15cm.	A.central.	
6th	12.30am.				

   FLASHES. 10.30am. 95°G from B.14a6075.
            10.45am. 92°G   ,,   ,,   F/R 20 secs.
            1 pm.   77°G   ,,   ,,
            1 pm.   79°30' G from B8a3015.
            3 pm.   98°G from B14a6075.

   (b) Work. Nil.

   (c) Movement. Movement at U20c9080 was ...... engaged by
                 18-pdrs.

   (d) Aerial. Inactive. 1 E.A. seen at 12.10pm. 4 Observation
               Balloons were up during the morning.

3. GENERAL.

   Visibility good.

6th July 1918.   Lieut: R.A.
                        Reconnaissance Officer 52nd Div: Artillery.

DAILY REPORT 52ND DIVISIONAL ARTILLERY.
9 a.m. 4th to 9 a.m. 5th July 1918.

1. OUR ACTIVITY.
   (a) Operations. At 11 am. a five minutes intense bombardment of H.Q. at T24d8098, H.Q. and M.G. at T24b3612 and H.Q. and T.M. at T24b3014 was carried out in conjunction with 2nd Brigade C.G.A. and repeated at 11.15 am.
   Harassing fire was directed at night on enemy Roads, Tracks and centres of activity.
   Total rounds fired:-
   18-pdr. - 1010.   4.5" How. - 280.   6" T.M. - Nil.

   (b) Aerial. Normal.

2. HOSTILE ACTIVITY.
   (a) Artillery. 15cm Hows. have been slightly more active, some 100 rounds being fired in the vicinity of LA CHAUDIERE and PETIT VIMY. 77mm guns were active; 5 shoots of 100 rounds each on T.19c being reported.

Date.	Time.	No. of rds.	Calibre.	Area shelled.	Direction.
4th.	9am.	20	10.5cm.	T22 & 27.	
	9-9.55am.	100	77mm.	T19c.	92°G from S22b8040 (A)
	9.30am.	60	15cm.	S18c & d.	
	10.55-11am.	100	77mm.	T19c.	
	11am.	15	10.5cm.	B13c.	
	11.25am.	6	15cm.	B13c.	C2b1585.
	12-12.30pm.	6	15cm.	WILLERVAL B3d.	
	12.15pm.	?	15cm.	T26.	72°G from B14a8075(F).
	12.20pm.	20	10.5cm.	S24d.	
	12.25-12.30pm.	100	77mm.	T19c.	
	12.30pm.	20	15cm.	S23b & d.	
	4.30pm.	20	T.M.	T9b.	
	5pm.	10	10.5cm.	B7d, B13b.	NEUVIREUIL.
	9-9.15pm.	10	10cm gun.	A17.	U15d3040.
5th.	1am.	20	10.5cm.	B8c.	
	2.30-3am.	40	10.5cm.	T25d.	
	4.30am.	6	77mm.	T19c.	

   FLASHES:- 7.40am. 91°30' G. from B14a6075.
              9 am.   52°30' G.   ,,   ,,
              11 am.   72° G.   ,,   ,,
              11.25am. 72° G.   ,,   ,,
              3.15 pm. 95°30' G.   ,,   ,,
              3.30pm. 75° G.   ,,   ,,
              4 pm.   81° G.   ,,   B8a2025.
              5 pm.   62° G.   ,,   ,,   F.R 19 secs.

   (b) Work. Nil.

   (c) Movement. Individuals seen in U26d, U27c, C2b, C3a and O4a.

   (d) Aerial. 7.15 pm, E.A. attempted to approach our observation balloons but were repulsed by A.A. fire.
   At night some machines were over our lines.

3. GENERAL. 1.40pm. Helio in Church Tower, HENIN-LIETARD, O29b8065.
   4 pm. Large column of smoke from series of explosions in BEAUMONT, (also reported 77°10' G. from S22b6550 and as a large fire 76°30' G. from S23c7080).

   Visibility good.

                                                A.J. Drufton
5th July 1918.   Lieut: R.A.
                                   Reconnaissance Officer, 52nd Div:Arty.

DAILY REPORT, 52ND DIVISIONAL ARTILLERY.
3 am 7th to 3 am 8th JULY 1918.

OUR ACTIVITY.
(a) **Operations.** At 7 am a 5 minute intense bombardment of Headquarters, T.13.b.18.05, T.4., T.18.b.38.10 and Trench, T.18.d.00.89 to T.18.b.08.10, was carried out in conjunction with 2nd C.F.A. and repeated at 7.10 am.
  10.55 pm. Right Group received and responded to a Test S.O.S.
  At night, harassing fire was carried out as usual.
  Total rounds fired -
    18-pdr. 950.   4.5" How. 250.   6" T.M. Nil.

(b) **Aerial.**   Our machines were active.

2. **HOSTILE ACTIVITY.**
(a) **Artillery.** The enemy guns were fairly quiet, although 15 cm How. were somewhat more active, on the front of Left Brigade.

Date.	Time	No. of rds.	Calibre.	Area Shelled.	Direction.
7th.	8 - 9.10 am.	28.	15 cm.	T.13.c.	
	8.30 - 9 am.	20.	10.5 cm.	T.22.a.40.75.	
	9.30 am.	6.	T.M.	B.9.b.9.8.	
	12 noon - 12.30 pm.	64.	15 cm.	T.20.	
	12.55 - 1.30 pm.	47.	15 cm.	T.8.a.	
	1.5 pm.	30.	10.5 cm.	B.8.c.	
	1.45 pm.	6.	10.5 cm.	T.16.c.	
	2.55 pm.	10.	77 mm.	T.21.	
	3.15 pm.	15.	15 cm.	B.7.a.	
	7.30 pm.	6.	21 cm. H.V.	B.7.c.&.5.	
		5.	15 cm.	B.7.d.2.4.	
	7.40 pm.	10.	10 cm. gun.	B.8.a.	
	10.30 pm - 12.30 am.	30.	10 cm. gun.	A.6. cont.	
	10.30 pm - 12.30 am.	100.	10.5 cm.	B.1.b. & d.	
	11 pm - midnight.	50.	10.5 cm.	T.20.c.	

  Flashes. 1 pm. 85°30' G. from B.14.a.80.75.
    1 pm. 79° G.   "   B.8.a.30.15.
    1.40 pm. 79°30' J.   "   B.8.a.30.15.
    6.15 pm. 65°30' G.   "   B.14.a.80.75. F/R 25 secs.
    6.15 pm. 75° G.   "   B.14.a.80.75.

(b) **Work.**   Nil.

(c) **Movement.** Individual movement observed in T.8. and at 12.45 pm at U.20.c.85.90.

(d) **Aerial.** 10 am - one E.A. over enemy lines.
  E.A. crossed our lines at night.

3. **GENERAL.** 5.0 pm dense column of smoke from behind DOROTHY COPSE 72° G. from S.22.b.65.50.
  Visibility fair.

Lieut RA.
Reconnaissance Officer, 52nd D.A.

8th July 1918.

DAILY REPORT, 52ND DIVISIONAL ARTILLERY.
6 am 8th to 6 am 9th JULY 1918.

OUR ACTIVITY.
(a) Operations. At 11 am 6" T.M. fired on T.M. at T.18.d.1.8.
From 12 noon to 12.30pm 18-prs fired on ACACIA trench and ROUVROY Road to harass enemy ration parties.
At night harassing fire was directed on enemy approaches and 4.5" Hows of Right Group fired on M.G. emplacements B.5.a.4.4. and T.29.b.9.4.
Total rounds fired -
18-pdr. 850.   4.5"How. 200   6" T.M. 14.

(b) Aerial.   Normal. Considerable A.A. fire on our returning aeroplanes.

2. HOSTILE ACTIVITY.
(a) Artillery. Very quiet in the morning and less than 100 rounds reported during the whole period.

Date.	Time.	No. of Rds.	Calibre.	Area shelled.
8th.	12 noon- 3 pm.	20.	15 cm.	B.7.c. & B.8.b.
	2 pm - 3.50 pm	30.	15 cm.	THELUS WOOD.(A.6.d.)
	4.30 pm- 5.30 pm.	10.	10 cm gun.	B.7.c.
	3 pm.	5.	10.5 cm.	BILLIE BURKE. T.9.b.
9th.	3.30 am	20.	15 cm.	T.20.c.

(b) Work.   Nil.

(c) Movement. 4.40 pm movement along PORTAGE Road U.7.c. & d.
5. 0 pm movement along MONTREAL Road. T.12.d.

(d) Aerial.   E.A. were over the lines at 10 am., 1.0 pm, 5.0 pm and 8.0 pm.
No balloons observed.

3. GENERAL. Visibility poor.

Lieut. RA.
Reconnaissance Officer, 52nd DA.

9th July 1918.

Appx 12

DAILY REPORT, 52ND DIVISIONAL ARTILLERY.
6. am 9th to 6 am 10th July 1918.
****

1. OUR ACTIVITY.
   (a) Operations. At 11 am. a 3 minute bombardment of enemy S.P. trench and dug-outs in U.13.a. was carried out in conjunction with 2nd Bde R.G.A. and repeated at 11.15 am.
   At noon enemy ration parties in ACACIA trench were harassed.
   During the night harassing fire was directed on enemy approaches and centres of activity.
   Total rounds fired –
   18-pdr.   900.   4.5" How.   360.   6" T.M. Nil.

   (b) Aerial. Our aeroplanes were active all day and brought down an E.A. which fell near FARBUS at 11.10 am.

2. HOSTILE ACTIVITY.
   (a) Artillery. 15 cm. howitzers have shown more activity, some 300 rounds being reported.
   S.34., B.2.b., B.7.d. and T.25 were the principal targets.

Date.	Time.	No. of rds.	Calibre.	Area shelled.	Direction.	Remarks.
9th.	9am – 12.30 pm.	30.	15 cm.	B.7.d.2.3.	OPPY.	
	10.15 am.	15.	10.5 cm.	FARBUS WOODS.	B.8.c.	
	11.30 am.	50.	15 cm.	B.2.b.		
	1.30 pm.	12.	10.5 cm.	S.29.c.		
	2.0 pm.	30.	10.5 cm.	B.2.d.5.7.		
	2.30 pm.	50.	10.5 cm.	S.29.c.		
	3.0 pm.	30.	15 cm.	S.23.		79°G from S.23.c.70.80.
	3.50 pm.	10.	10.5 cm.	T.13.c.		
	3.50 pm.	10.	10.5 cm.	S.25.		
	5.0 pm.	21.	15 cm.	T.25.		
	5.0 pm.	40.	15 cm.	T.25.		80°G from S.23.c.70.80.
	10.30 – 11.0 pm.	?	15 cm.	Cross Roads, A.11.		Included some Gas.
	10.55 pm.	20.	77 mm.	FARBUS,B.2.c.		
10th.	4.0 am.	100.	15 cm.	S.34.		

Flashes. 2.45 pm. 88°G from A.3.b.84.88.

   (b) Work   Nil.

   (c) Movement. None reported.

   (d) Aerial. An E.A. which crossed our lines 3 times during the morning was brought down by our machines and fell near FARBUS at 11.10 am.

3. GENERAL   1.0 pm dense cloud of smoke issuing from behind DOROTHY COPSE 72°30' CB from S.22.b.65.50.
   Visibility good throughout the day, poor on morning of 10th.

   Addendum to yesterdays report.
   1.(a) Operations.
   Right Group fired 1,200 rounds 18- pounder and 300 rounds 4.5" How. on night 8th/9th in support of raid by 152nd Inf. Bde., 51st Division.

10th July 1918.

A. J. Drifton
Lieut. RA.
Reconnaissance Officer, 52nd DA.

App. 13

52ND DIVISIONAL ARTILLERY DEFENCE SCHEME.

Table of Contents.

SECTION.	APPENDIX.
1. Divisional frontage and flank divisions.	A. Disposition Statement.
2. Distribution, Boundaries and Headquarters of Infantry.	B. Field Artillery S.O.S. lines.
3. Systems of Defence.	C. Mutual Support.
4. General principles of Defence.	D. Reserve positions.
5. Grouping and dispositions of Field Artillery.	E. Observation Posts.
	F. Orders for Anti-Tank Guns.
6. Artillery instructions for the defence	G. Heavy Artillery S.O.S. & Counter Preparation.
(a) Artillery policy.	
(b) Harassing fire boundaries.	H. Gas Shell bombardments.
(c) Counter preparation.	J. Ecurie Switch.
(d) S.O.S.	
(e) Mutual Support.	
(f) Observation Posts and repeating stations.	
(g) Liaison.	
(h) Artillery defence against Tanks.	MAPS.
(i) Artillery defence of Reserve Lines.	
(j) "PREPARE FOR ACTION" and "MAN BATTLE STATIONS".	A. Systems of defence.
7. Signal Communications.	B. Counter preparation.
8. Co-operation of Field Artillery with Royal Air Force.	C. Signal communications.
9. Heavy Artillery.	
10. Gas.	
11. Ammunition.	

This document will NOT be taken beyond Battery Headquarters.

If there is any danger of it falling into enemy hands, it will be destroyed.

52ND DIVISIONAL ARTILLERY DEFENCE SCHEME.

1. **DIVISIONAL FRONTAGE AND FLANK DIVISIONS.**
   The 52nd (Lowland) Division front extends from B.10.b.50.80 to the junction of BILLIE BURKE trench and BETTY trench (latter inclusive). The 51st (Highland) Division is on the right and the 20th (Light) Division on the left.

2. **DISTRIBUTION, BOUNDARIES AND HEADQUARTERS OF INFANTRY.**
   (a) The front is divided into two Infantry Brigade Sections, that on the right is known as the WILLERVAL Section and that on the left as the LA CHAUDIERE Section.
   The Right Section is held by 3 Battalions in the line, and the Left Section by 2 Battalions in the line with 1 in defended localities in their rear. One Infantry Brigade is in Divisional Reserve.
   (b) Boundaries are:-
   Divisional Southern Boundary.
   B.10.b.50.80 - B.10.a.70.50 thence along TIRED ALLEY (inclusive) to B.15.b.80.20 - B.17.c.50.80, BORDER POST (inclusive) - A.13.c.00.00 thence westwards along grid between squares A.11 and A.17.
   Divisional Northern Boundary.
   Junction of BILLIE BURKE and BETTY trenches - T2c.30.00 - T.1.d.70.50 - Junction of RED trench and LENS-ARRAS Road, thence along Red trench and CYRIL trench (both exclusive) to S.11.c.00.40 - S.13.c.00.00-S.19.b.00.00 - X.22 central - X.15.c.00.00 - X.14.c.00.00 - W.28.b.00.00 - W.27.b.00.00.
   Inter Infantry Brigade Boundary.
   ACHEVILLE - NEW BRUNSWICK road as far as the railway embankment in T.20.c.90.10 (exclusive to Right Section) - thence to Cemetery - T.25.d.60.90 (inclusive to Right Section, thence to BOIS DU GOULOT at T.25.c.00.00 and thence due west along grid line.
   (c) Headquarters.
   52nd (Lowland) Division - CHATEAU D'ACQ.
   WILLERVAL Section. Infantry Brigade Headquarters, A.6.c.60.70.
   LA CHAUDIERE Section Infantry Brigade Headquarters, S.27.b.00.60.
   Reserve Infantry Brigade Headquarters, F.8.d.30.10.

3. **SYSTEMS OF DEFENCE.**
   The Divisional Sector is divided into two zones:-
   The OUTPOST Zone.
   The BATTLE Zone.
   (a) The outpost zone consists of:- from
   (i) The outpost line of observation running/PLUMER extension - PLUMER - MONTREAL - QUEBEC - LILIE ELSIE - BILLIE BURKE.
   (ii) The outpost line of supports running from YUKON - NOME - OTTAWA - HUDSON - NEW BRUNSWICK - TEDDY GERARD.

   (b) The Battle zone. The main line of resistance of the outpost zone coincides with the forward line of the Battle Zone, and is known as the BLACK line. It runs along the post line - BEEHIVE trench - GRAND TRUNK trench from T.21.d.5.2 to T.21.d.90.30, thence along Canada - GERTIE - JULIA JAMES - HAYTER - GLADYS - DARTMOUTH - BEAVER.
   In front of the main line of resistance is the defended locality of WILLERVAL.
   In rear of the main line of resistance is the BROWN line, behind that certain defended localities and the GREEN Line.
   Details of the above lines are shown in Map 'A'.

4. **GENERAL PRINCIPLES OF DEFENCE.**
   The outpost zone is lightly held, the disposition being such that our greatest strength is available for the defence of the BLACK line. Raids and minor operations of the enemy are met in the outpost zone, if necessary by counter attack. In the event of our having several hours warning of an intended attack in force, the G.O.C. will issue

-2-

issue the order "Prepare for Action" on which the outpost zone will be still further thinned out, leaving only a small nucleus to watch the enemy's movements and give the S.O.S. warning.

If the attack comes as a complete surprise no order "Prepare for action" will be given, but "MAN BATTLE STATIONS" will be ordered. In this case no withdrawals from the outpost zone take place. Once the enemy attack is launched all lines and defended localities are to be fought to the last.

5. GROUPING AND DISPOSITIONS OF THE FIELD ARTILLERY.

(a) The Field Artillery covering the 52nd (Lowland) Division consists of its own Divisional Artillery with the 52nd and 242nd Army Field Artillery Brigades attached.

This Artillery is allotted as under:-

WILLERVAL Section.
Right Artillery Group Commander - Lt.Col.H.J.COTTER, C.I.E., DSO., RA.
        9th Brigade R.F.A.
        52nd Brigade R.F.A.
        A/242nd Brigade R.F.A.
        C/242nd Brigade R.F.A.

LA CHAUDIERE Section.
Left Artillery Group Commander - Lt.Col. J.A.INGHAM, R.F.A.
        58th Brigade R.F.A.
        B/242nd Brigade R.F.A.
        D/242nd Brigade R.F.A.

(b) X/52 and Y/52 Medium Trench Mortar Batteries are allotted to the WILLERVAL and LA CHAUDIERE Sections respectively.

A disposition statement of the above Artillery is given in Appendix A.

6. ARTILLERY INSTRUCTIONS FOR THE DEFENCE.

(a) Artillery Policy.

While we are holding the line, under normal conditions, an aggressive artillery policy is maintained by the sniping of all movement and work seen by day, and by vigorous harassing fire at night.

The Group Commander ascertains daily from the Infantry Brigadier what his requirements in this respect are and arranges his harassing fire programme accordingly. Special targets to be engaged are also ordered from this office as occasion demands.

Each Group maintains 3 18-Pounders and 1 4.5" Howitzer in forward emplacements, from which all harassing and sniping fire is carried out, the main battery positions being kept silent, as far as possible. In addition each Group sends up 1 roving 18-Pounder by night to assist those guns.

To economise Officers, these forward guns may be grouped into Sections under an Officer, if desired; and as the bulk of the firing falls on them, the detachments must be relieved at least once a week.

These forward guns do not withdraw in the event of hostile attack. They will have specially selected positions ready from which they can fire at close targets over the open sights, and will move into these positions upon the order "Prepare for action", XXXXXXXXXXXXX XXXXXXX", and must be in action ready for counter p/reparation.

Three Trench Mortars are situated in the outpost zone with forward emplacements for offensive work. The remainder are disposed to cover the BLACK and BROWN lines. On the order "prepare for action" or "man battle stations" these three guns will withdraw to their rear positions if possible. If they cannot do this, they will fight where they stand and be destroyed before falling into enemy hands.

Normally half the personnel of a Trench Mortar Battery man the guns, with the remainder in rest.

The Officer in charge of the trench mortars in the line must keep close touch with the Infantry on his front and Battery Commanders and D.T.M.O. must in addition visit Infantry Brigade Headquarters regularly to ascertain what their requirements are.

(b)

(b) Harassing fire, boundaries etc.
Boundaries for harassing fire are as follows:-
(i) Between Field Artillery and Heavy Artillery T.27.d.05.00 - U.21.a.00.00 - U.14 central - N.35 central.
(ii) Between 51st Divisional Artillery and Right Group. B.10.b.50.80 to C.3.c.10.10.
(iii) Between Right Group and Left Group. ACHEVILLE Road to T.18.c.80.60 and thence to U.14.d.20.50.
(iv) Between 20th Divisional Artillery and Left Group. Junction of BILLIE BURKE and BETTY Trenches to N.35 central.

The normal allotment of ammunition for night firing is:-

	18-pounder.	4.5" Howitzer.
Right Group.	375 rounds.	100 rounds.
Left Group.	375 rounds.	100 rounds.

During the day (5am to 8.30pm) the C.B.S.O. has a call upon the two forward Howitzers except under the following conditions:-
(i) During counter preparation.
(ii) In the event of an S.O.S.
In addition forward guns are also prepared to engage active batteries within range with neutralising fire.
Harassing fire by night on enemy batteries engaged for destruction during the day is also carried out, when asked for by C.B.S.O.

(c) Counter preparation.
(i) Counter preparation is the Artillery action to be taken during an intense hostile bombardment, which is evidently the prelude to an attack.
Its object will include the destruction of the enemy's trench system, from which the attack will be launched, including machine guns and trench mortars, and the killing of his troops whilst assembling.
On the Left Group front, owing to the lie of the VIMY RIDGE and the consequent siting of the batteries, the role of Field Artillery during counter preparation is mainly restricted to preventing the enemy sending forward patrols and M.G. parties to establish themselves well forward in "NO MAN'S LAND".

(ii) Field Artillery counter preparation will consist of:-
(a) Frequent rolling barrages by 18-Pounders fired at irregular intervals backwards and forwards over the zones allotted to Groups.
(b) 4.5" Howitzers firing on selected targets in the Sections allotted to them.

For this purpose lifts for 18-Pounders will be parallel to the S.O.S. line which will be lettered 'A', and each successive lift B, C, D, E, F, G and H.
The Group Zones are divided into sections, which are again subdivided into lanes, vide Map B. The breadth of these sections and lanes vary according to their tactical importance.
The allotment of guns to these sections is:-

	Right Group.	Left Group.
V Section.	19th Bty. & 3 Howitzers D/52 Brigade and 3 guns C/52 Brigade (recuperator guns)	
W Section.	20th Bty. & 3 Howitzers D/52 Brigade and 3 guns C/52 Brigade (Recuperator guns).	B/242 Brigade.
X Section.	28th Bty. & 2 Howitzers D/69 Brigade.	A/56 Bde. & 527 Bty.
Y Section.	C/242 Brigade and 2 Howitzers D/69th Brigade.	C/56 Bde. and 4 Hows. D/242 Brigade.
Z Section.	A/242 Brigade and 2 Howitzers D/69th Brigade.	B/56 Brigade & 2 Hows. D/242 Brigade.

(iii) When counter preparation is ordered each 18-Pounder Battery will open fire on any one of these lanes in its own section, and after covering it once, will switch to another lane. The above will be carried out in bursts of fire at irregular intervals so timed that the whole of the lanes are covered at least in a period, or periods, for which counter preparation has been ordered.
The order in which the lanes will be treated and the barrage lines on which the guns will open will be decided by the Group Commander, as the tactical situation demands, but the principle that the barrage will search backwards as well as forwards will be adhered to.

In the Left Group each forward gun still in action will fire on the point, marked with the same number as the lane, in the section in which the Battery is firing.

These points are marked O = 18-Pounder and △ = 4.5" Howitzer on the map. 18-Pounders without air Recuperators will not fire at ranges over 7,000 yards.

(iv) The number and intensity of bursts cannot be laid down previously, these depend on the duration of the enemy bombardment, having regard to the necessity for keeping the detachments as fresh as possible for the S.O.S. barrage to be fired at the time of the assault, and for the subsequent battle.

The necessity for keeping in hand sufficient ammunition to deal with the successive assaults has also to be considered.

Where possible the amount of ammunition to be fired during counter preparation will be controlled by C.R.A. Should communication be cut however, Brigade and Battery Commanders must use their own discretion in this matter.

At no time during counter preparation will ammunition at guns be allowed to fall below 400 rounds per 18-Pounder and 300 rounds per 4.5" Howitzer.

All 18-Pounders firing under 3,500 yards will fire shrapnel only and those above, H.E. only, as far as possible.

The proportion of ammunition on hand with batteries will be re-allotted within Groups to meet the above requirements.

(v) Counter preparation will be ordered from S.A., H.Q. If communications are cut Brigade Commanders must act upon their own initiative.

It will be ordered in the following code:-

The word "COUNTER" wired from this office will be the signal that counter preparation is to be carried out.

12 noon will be zero hour. The hour for opening fire will be so many hours plus or minus. The date will be given.

Example:- "Counter 12th minus 6½ hours) - denotes that counter preparation will be fired on 12th instant commencing 5.30am.

Where it is considered advisable, duration of fire will also be ordered from this office.

(d) S.O.S.

There are two procedures in answering the S.O.S. signal or message:-

(1) (a) In normal times.

The outpost barrage will be fired as follows:-
5 minutes INTENSE.
5 minutes RAPID.
5 minutes NORMAL.

after which fire will depend upon the situation, to ascertain which, the Artillery Commanders must make the most strenuous efforts.

(b) After the order "MAN BATTLE STATIONS" has been issued.

The outpost barrage will be fired as follows:-
10 minutes INTENSE
10 minutes RAPID, during which, barrage will roll forward 500 yards at the rate of 100 yards per 2 minutes and then jump back to original line for 2 minutes INTENSE followed by 8 minutes NORMAL. After this, fire will be controlled according to the situation. On the barrage coming back to the BLACK line, a similar 30 minutes burst will be fired.

The BLACK barrage will not be fired till a definite S.O.S. call from the BLACK line is received. On this call being received, the BLACK barrage will be fired on the whole Divisional Front. Pending the introduction of a distinctive signal, this will be a message "S.O.S. BLACK".

Group Commanders must consequently inform each other immediately this call is received.

In order to ensure continuity of fire along the whole front, the following procedure will be adopted until it is known that the fire of the flank divisions has also been brought back.

2 of the guns superimposed on the right and left flanks will be used to connect the right and left points of the BLACK barrage with the right and left points of the outpost barrage.

(2) The barrage will not be brought back from the BLACK line to the BROWN line except by order of the Divisional Commander and will then come back along the whole Divisional Front. This does not refer to the fire of superimposed 18-Pounders.

-5-

(3) 18-Pounder spring guns will not fire at ranges above 7,000 yards.
(4) 18-pounders firing at over 3,000 will fire H.E.106 fuze.
(5) Details of these barrages are shown in Appendix 'B'.
(6) On receipt of a Cloud GAS message or signal, all guns will open a slow rate of fire on the trenches from which the gas is being emitted. In the case of a cloud gas attack accompanied by Infantry action, the Infantry in the front line will eventually send the S.O.S. message or signal, on receipt of which the procedure as detailed above will be carried out.

(e) Mutual Support.
Groups are connected by telephone with flanking Groups. The arrangements for mutual support are shown in Appendix 'C'.

(f) Observation Posts and Repeating Stations.
(i) A list of Observation Posts and the periods during which they are manned is given in Appendix 'E'.

In addition each Group Commander will construct an Observation Post as near his Headquarters as possible, from which a good general view of the country can be obtained, and from which, if necessary, he can see what is going on on his immediate front.

(ii) Repeating stations for S.O.S. Signals. The Artillery are responsible for getting the S.O.S. Signal back from the Observation Posts to the guns - forward of Observation Posts the responsibility rests with the Infantry.

Every Observation Post that is manned by night will be provided with a complete outfit of S.O.S. light signals and these light signals will invariably be used in addition to, or instead of, - if the wires are cut - any telephone message that may be sent.

The rapid transmission of S.O.S. Signals and messages to the guns requires the utmost care and forethought during the present defensive phase in order to ensure efficiency.

The only sure test of a really efficient system is when messages can get back to the guns even though the weather is foggy and the telephone is broken down.

For this purpose alternative methods of communication will be established in every Battery between the Observation Post and the position of employment of visual signalling, runners, mounted orderlies, or Cyclists, or a combination of them.

These alternative methods must be frequently practised, so that when the emergency arises every man knows exactly what is expected of him. In every Battery an "Alarm" sentry will be permanently posted. He should be provided with a pointer on a board by means of which he can obtain the direction of the Observation Post or repeating station and also the frontage that his battery is covering.

(iii) On misty mornings, Officers patrols must be sent forward of Observation Posts to ascertain the situation - under certain circumstances, a light telephone wire, say enamel wire, may be laid out and prove useful-. It is essential that some means of determining when and where the S.O.S. signal has been sent up should be provided to meet all conditions.

(g) Liaison.
R.A. Group Headquarters are situated alongside the Headquarters of the Infantry Brigade they are supporting.

In addition Right Group finds two liaison Officers with the three Battalions in the line in the Right Section; and Left Group 1 with each Infantry Battalion in the line in the Left Section.
The tour of duty of these Liaison Officers is arranged mutually between Groups and Infantry Brigadiers concerned.

(h) Artillery Defence against Tanks.
(1) The main principle of Anti-Tank Defence will be organisation in depth. This will be given effect to as follows:-
(a) By defensive barrage fire from normally placed guns and howitzers.
(b) By specially placed forward guns laying direct over the open sights.
(c) By direct fire from selected guns from all 18-Pounder Batteries in action.

(2) Under the above subheads the following special points occur.
(a) This is the normal S.O.S. barrage - If tanks form part of the attack, 25% of 18-Pounders should fire H.E.
Note:- It has been found that 4.5" Howitzers with 106 fuze are more effective against Tanks than with 101 fuze, (with or without delay). With 18-Pounders however it is preferable to use 101 fuze.

(b)

-6-

(b) There are 8 15-pounder B.L.C. Guns on the Divisional front located as detailed in Appendix 'A' and manned by Batteries as shewn. A detachment of 1 Sergeant or senior Corporal and 2 men will live permanently at each gun. This detachment will be changed at least every 10 days. In those cases where a detachment comes to relieve another, the N.C.O. in charge of the detachment relieved will remain behind 24 hours to give instruction in gun drill and also in ranges to prominent points etc.

In addition each Group will detail an Officer to supervise the Tank guns manned by them to ensure that the training of the detachments is carried out in accordance with G.H.Q. Artillery Circular No.12, as far as feasible.

Each gun will have 200 complete rounds of High Explosive at or near its position with 10% surplus tubes.

One round High Explosive with 106 fuze will be kept for the purpose of destroying the gun should such a course be necessary. A copy of G.H.Q. "Instructions for the disablement of Guns" O.B.851 should be hung up in each pit. It is pointed out that a short length of trench in which the men detailed to fire the gun with lanyard can take cover, is also necessary.

Ranges and bearings to prominent points both in our own and the enemy's lines must be known and recorded on a board in each pit.

(c) In each 18-pounder battery one or two guns (the flank ones are most easily handled) must be told off to run out, in the event of a Tank attack, to positions in the open close to their Batteries.

Such positions must have a good view to their front, and flanks, so as to be able to bring direct fire to bear on advancing tanks. Regardless of the position of our own troops, these guns must fire at all surviving tanks till they are definitely put out of action. The remaining guns of Batteries will continue to engage the hostile Infantry either by Barrage fire or individual action as the situation may demand. A sharp lookout must be kept at all batteries to give immediate warning of the approach of tanks to the selected guns.

(3) In dealing with Tanks, shrapnel which is practically non-effective, and smoke shell, which only increases the Tanks power of Manoeuvre, will not be used.

(4) Experience shows that if Tanks are advancing straight towards the gun the aim should be low - a burst under a Tank being nearly as effective as a direct hit.

Fire must be maintained on any stationary Tank until its extrication is an impossibility.

(5) As it is not so much the Tank itself, as the facilities it affords to hostile Infantry to advance that constitutes the real danger, it is most important that only those guns, which have been specially detailed, engage them and that the remainder maintain their fire on the hostile Infantry.

Special Instructions for Officers or Non-commissioned-officers in charge of Anti-Tank Guns are hung up in each pit. A copy of these Instructions are laid down in Appendix 'F'.

(i) Artillery Defence of Reserve lines and alternative positions.

Positions have been chosen, and are in course of construction, and Observation Posts have been reconnoitred, to cover the various reserve systems.

In addition there is an alternative position for every Battery in the line ready for immediate occupation. These may be used as positions for reinforcing Brigades in case of necessity.

There are also two spare positions for both the BROWN and GREEN lines and 3 positions chosen to cover the ECURIE switch.

The details of the above are given in Appendix 'D'.

Artillery routes to these positions, as used by Brigades, are given in the above mentioned Appendix.

These routes which are clearly marked with notice boards lettered "Artillery Track" are shewn on the Track Map already issued.

On withdrawal to BROWN line, the present grouping will break up and Batteries revert to their own Brigades.

In the absence of special orders, 52nd Brigade R.F.A. will work under 9th Brigade R.F.A. in support of Right Infantry Brigade and 242nd Brigade R.F.A. under 53rd Brigade R.F.A. in support of Left Infantry Brigade.

Action for ECURIE switch is shewn in Appendix J. (j)

(j) Prepare for action and Man Battle Stations.
On the order "PREPARE FOR ACTION".
The three forward Trench Mortars will move back to their rear positions.
All Trench Mortar personnel will move up and man the guns. Forward guns will be moved into their Battle positions. Headquarters 242nd Brigade R.F.A. will move up to its BROWN line Headquarters.
On the order "MAN BATTLE STATIONS".
Gun teams and limbers will move up to previously reconnoitred forward positions.
T.M. personnel and Headquarters 242nd Brigade R.F.A. will move up, if order "Prepare for action" has not been received.

7. SIGNAL COMMUNICATIONS.
Telegraph and Telephone.
The lines are mainly in the buried system which extends from MONT ST. ELOI and BERTHONVAL FARM towards the front line. Two pairs are allotted to each Group Headquarters - one for speaking and one for telegraph - a telephone pair is in use to sub Group. There is also a telephone pair to Divisional Advanced Exchange which has telephone communications to Right and Left Groups.
Other lines on Divisional Exchange are:- Infantry Division, Right Divisional Artillery, Heavy Artillery and Corps Heavy Artillery.
A pair of lines have been led into Division Emergency Signal Office which would be manned in event of Divisional Headquarters being shelled and a line is apportioned from there to "G" Dugout for use of Brigade Major.
Forward of Brigade, lines are in all cases apportioned in the buried system except for short lengths from Test Boxes which are in some cases "ditched". These provide for communications from Groups to Batteries and from Batteries to Forward Guns and Observation Posts. From Groups to Flanking Groups, and from Groups to Liaison Officers with Right and Left Infantry Battalions.
Wireless. Wireless stations are established at each Infantry Brigade Headquarters working back to Divisional Headquarters. These are available for Artillery purposes. Coding and decoding is done by the Signal personnel using the Signal Service Code word.
Visual. Groups are in communication with Batteries by Visual. There are two Central Visual Stations at A.3.b.90.90 and S.23.d.30.20 for forward working, from these points messages are sent back by Telegraph or Runner. In the event of communications being cut between Divisional Artillery Headquarters and Brigades, a Visual Station would be established at LA MOTTE FARM (F.2.d.60.70).
Despatch Rider, Mounted Orderly, Runner. Two Despatch Riders and four Mounted Orderlies are with Divisional Artillery Headquarters for forward work, a relay of four Mounted Orderlies is stationed at X.V. Test Box (X.28.b.30.20), four runners at Left and Right Groups and a runner relay at Left Group Exchange (S.29.c.20.97).
Pigeons. Two pairs of birds are sent daily to each Group Headquarters for use as decided by Groups. These are usually liberated from Observation Posts. The loft which is situated near CAMBLAIN L'ABBE is in telephonic communication through Divisional Headquarters.
Rockets. Rocket sending Stations have been established at:-
B/56 Observation Post (S.22.b.6.0) working to Left Group.
Left Group Exchange (S.29.c.20.97)   ,,   ,, Left & Right Group.
28th Battery Observation Post. (B.7.b.80.80) working to Right Group.
Right Group Headquarters (A.6.c.60.70) working to Left Group Exchange.
19th Battery Observation Post (B.14.a.60.75) working to 19th Battery position (B.13.c.33.88).
10 rockets are in possession at all these stations.
Alternative means of communication are tested weekly.
BROWN LINE. For the defence of the BROWN LINE, wires have been allotted in the buried system as follows:-
  1 pair from Divisional Artillery Headquarters to each Brigade Headquarters (6 in all).
  1 pair from each Brigade Headquarters to A.D. Test Box (OOBLEY Exchange A.3.d.70.80).
  1 pair from A.D. Test Box to 1 selected Observation Post per Brigade.
  1 pair from Brigade to each Battery.
  1 pair to Flanking Brigades.

The

The exchange at A.D. will be manned by 4 Telephonists (two from each Group).

Alternative means of communication will be as at present.
Plans and diagrams. A large number of changes are being made in the Routing of lines at present by Area Signals with a view to straightening out lines but Signal Officers are responsible for keeping their diagrams and Routing Lists to date.

Details of these communications are shown in Map 'G'.

8. COOPERATION OF FIELD ARTILLERY WITH ROYAL AIR FORCE.

Aerial observation on the Divisional Front is carried out by 16th Squadron Royal Air Force and No. 20 Section, 1st Balloon Co.

(1) When indications point to the possibility of a hostile attack an S.O.S. aeroplane stands by ready to leave the ground at very short notice in the event of a hostile bombardment.

This aeroplane is ordered out by Corps Headquarters.
It has a double duty to perform:-
  (a) Primarily it is required to give the earliest possible notice of an attack.
  (b) It is further required to keep Commanders informed of the movement of the enemy masses and to direct fire, by means of Zone and LL Calls, on favourable targets both before and after the attack has taken place.

With regard to (a), if a general lifting of the hostile fire from our front line is seen and the Infantry assault noticed, a smoke signal will be dropped by the airman and S.O.S. sent by wireless. The signal, a red smoke bomb, will be dropped as nearly as possible over the scene of the attack and also over the Field Artillery positions.

With regard to (b), it should be realised that Zone and LL Calls afford a means of appreciating the strength of the attack, movement of reserves etc., and therefore such information as is received by this means by the Artillery must be passed to the General Staff without delay.

(2) Calls from the Air.
  (a) LL Calls. LL Calls will not be answered during counter preparation and after S.O.S., by Field Artillery.
At all other times by all forward guns and howitzers, in addition if a hostile attack has been launched, by 1 Section from all Batteries that can be brought to bear.
  (b) GF Calls. GF Calls will be answered by Field Artillery during counter preparation, by one Section forward 18-Pounders to be detailed by Right Group.
At all other times by all forward 18-Pounders and 4.5" Howitzers, or, if a hostile attack has been launched, by the equivalent of one 18-pounder Battery to be detailed by Left Group, and 1 18-pounder Battery and 1 4.5" Howitzer Battery to be detailed by Right Group.
  (3) Rates of fire for LL and GF Calls:-
INTENSE for 3 minutes.

9. HEAVY ARTILLERY.
  (a) The 2nd Brigade C.G.A. (4 9.2" Howitzers, 6 8" Howitzers, 12 6" Howitzers, 12 60-pounders) is affiliated to the Division for bombardment and S.O.S. purposes.

S.O.S. lines and points for bombardment during counter preparation are attached Appendix 'G'.

These barrages are reinforced by reinforcing Brigades under the orders of the G.O.C. Heavy Artillery, 8th Corps.
  (b) In the event of a retirement, the G.O.C., 52nd Division will be responsible for the withdrawal of all 60-pounders and 6" Howitzers to reserve positions.

He will also be responsible for the issue of bombardment orders to them.

9.2" and 8" Howitzers will be withdrawn from the 2nd Brigade C.G.A.

10. GAS.
  (1) Gas zones are as follows:-
Alert. East of a line A.22.d.20.00 - A.10.a.40.00 - A.4.c.40.50 - A.4.a.00.00 (East of NEUVILLE ST. VAAST) - S.6.central (East of SOUCHEZ).

Ready.

Ready. Westwards from above line to a line drawn through F.9.b.00.20 (VILLERS AU BOIS) to X.19.b.80.00 (MONT ST. ELOI).
Precautionary. Westwards of ready line to a line drawn through CAMBLAIN L'ABBE) to CAMBLIGNEUL (both inclusive).
2. Alarm will be raised as follows:-
   (a) <u>Cloud Gas</u>. (i) "Cloud gas alert" will be sent by priority wire or special despatch rider, where there is no telephone. Small box respirators will then be worn in the alert position. Each unit as it receives warning, will transmit to:-
Flank Units, Next higher formation, all units under them. Attached Brigade R.G.A. will also warn Area Commandant BERTHONVAL FARM.
      (ii) "Strombos Horns" will be sounded on the approach of gas or when other horns are sounded. Small box respirators will then be adjusted.
   (b) <u>Gas Shell and Projectors</u>.
      By Gongs, Rattles and Telephone. In the case of projectors the flash and explosion of discharge is the best warning but these may not be recognised during a bombardment.
3. Special precautions against Yellow Cross Shells.
   (a) Batteries not firing will arrange for their personnel being placed in an Area free from gas, communication being kept between them and the guns so that the latter can be manned at once, when necessary by men wearing small box respirators.
   (b) Each Battery keeps 30 suits of clothes at Battery position for men whose clothes are splashed with gas liquid.
     In addition:-
     100 sets of clothes kept at A.D.S. AUX RIETZ.
     200 sets at the Divisional Baths, NEUVILLE ST. VAAST.
   (c) Clothes taken from gassed cases are sent to the Baths at BERTHONVAL FARM.
   (d) Battery positions and Brigade Headquarters must keep ample supplies of chloride of Lime for sprinkling in shell holes.
4. Divisional Gas Centre - Divisional Baths, NEUVILLE ST. VAAST.
   <u>Anti-Gas Depot</u> - LA TARGETTE.
   <u>Gas Chambers</u> - LA TARGETTE; MONT ST. ELOI, F.14.b.10.80; VILLERS AU BOIS, X.19.a.20.00.
At Divisional Gas Centre, arrangements will be made for bathing cases in special baths containing sodium carbonate solution and arranging shelter of patients pending their disposal.
5. Men suffering from the effects of gas should be sent to M.D.S. of 2nd Lowland Field Ambulance at AUX RIETZ, A.8.c.50.50.
6. For special orders re Yellow Cross bombardments see Appendix H.

11. AMMUNITION.
   (a) The distribution of ammunition will be as follows:-

	Main positions.	Forward guns.	Echelons.	Dump.
18-pdr. per gun.	600	700	276	200
4.5" How. per How.	550	550	222	100

When the ranges of Barrages admit, each Group will keep 25% H.E. and 75% shrapnel of its 18-pdr. ammunition establishment. In the Left Group, the actual amounts of H.E. and shrapnel with each Battery may be varied to meet local conditions of range etc.
The 4.5" How. establishment includes 30 rounds Lethal and 30 rounds Lachrymatory per gun.
Each Battery will also keep 100 rounds per gun or Howitzer at its BROWN line position.
   (b) Establishments per Group, at guns.
     Right Group. 18-pdr. - 3 forward guns .... 2100.
                            45 guns main positions .... 27000.
                            BROWN line positions .... 4800.
                                                33900.

            4.5" Hows. 1 forward Howitzer .... 550.
                      11 Hows. main positions. .... 6050.
                      BROWN line positions .... 1200.
                                                7800.

                                                          Left Group.

Left Group.	18-pdrs.	3 forward guns	2100.
		21 18-pdrs. main positions .	12600.
		36 18-pdrs. BROWN LINE	3600.
			18300.

	4.5" How.	1 forward Howitzer	550.
		11 Howitzers main position..	6050.
		12 Howitzers BROWN line positions	1200.
			7800.

The following Batteries whose S.O.S. ranges are over 6000 yards will keep 200 rounds AX fuze 106 per gun for use during S.O.S. only and to be included in the establishment shown above.

Left Group.	B/242 Battery.	Right Group.	A/52 Battery.
	A/56 Battery.		122 Battery.
	B/56 Battery.		C/52 Battery.
	C/56 Battery.		A/242 Battery.

(c) TRENCH MORTARS:

　　At Mortars .... 100 rounds per mortar.
　　At Dump .... 100 rounds per mortar.

(d) Refilling point.

　　TARGETTE DUMP - A.8.a.30.70, or if anything happens to prevent this, BRANDON DUMP - F.10.c.00.50.

APPENDIX 'A'.
DISPOSITION STATEMENT.
Reference 1/40,000 Map. Sheets 44 A & B, 51 B & C.

Unit		Position.	Wagon Lines.
2nd D.A.	H.Q.	W.30.a.4.3.	
D.T.M.O. }		A.3.d.3.5.	
D.A.G.O. }			

RIGHT GROUP.

Unit		Position.	Wagon Lines.
9th Brigade RFA.	H.Q.	A.3.c.3.7.	F.9.b.
19th Battery RFA.	5 18-pdrs.	B.13.c.35.83.	F.9.a.
	1	T.26.c.30.30.	
20th Battery RFA.	5	B.13.a.14.76.	F.9.a.8.5.
	1	T.26.c.15.98.	
28th Battery RFA.	5	B.7.c.29.20.	F.5 central.
	1	T.25.b.85.32.	
D/69 Brigade RFA.	5 Hows.	A.13.d.90.77.	F.9.b.
	1	B.2.c.05.55.	
A/242 Brigade RFA.	5 18-pdrs.	A.3.c.23.80.	X.23.d.
	1	A.5.d.50.90.	
C/242 Brigade RFA.	6	A.6.c.83.85.	X.28.b.8.1.
52nd A. Brigade RFA.	H.Q.	A.8.c.7.8.	
A/52 Brigade RFA.	6 18-pdrs.	A.4.b.73.13.	A.7.b.2.4
122nd Battery RFA.	3	A.4.c.79.09.	A.7.d.1.3.
C/52nd Brigade RFA.	6	A.10.b.30.98.	F.5.d.5.3.
D/52nd Brigade RFA.	6 Hows.	A.4.d.40.75.	F.12.a.8.4.
Anti-Tank.	1 15-pdr.	B.8.d.10.40.	
	1	B.1.b.1.7.	
	1	B.8.a.5.4.	

LEFT GROUP.

Unit		Position.	Wagon Lines.
53th Brigade RFA.	H.Q.	S.27.b.00.30.	S.23.c.1.8.
A/53th Brigade RFA.	6 18-pdrs.	S.29.c.57.85.	F.12.a & c.
B/58th Brigade RFA.	5	S.22.c.80.14.	S.25.b.2.0.
	1	T.13.c.20.75.	
C/53th Brigade RFA.	5	S.28.b.80.25.	F.12.a & c.
	1	T.13.c.94.75.	
527th Battery RFA.	6 Hows.	S.28.b.50.95.	A.2.c.0.1.
D/242 Brigade RFA.	5 18-pdrs.	S.29.c.84.27.	F.5.b.5.0.
	1	T.19.a.35.80.	
D/242 Brigade RFA.	5 Hows.	S.22.d.25.83.	S.25.d.1.8.
	1	T.20.c.17.52.	
Anti Tank.	1 15-pdr.	T.21.a.58.15.	
	1	T.19.b.77.75.	
	1	T.19.c.75.95.	

Unit		Position.	
242nd A.Brigade RFA.	H.Q.	F.3.c.0.5.	
52nd B.A.C.		S.26.c.0.5.	
242nd B.A.C.		A.2.c.3.2.	
52nd D.A.C.		F.8.b.5.5.	
S.A.A. Section.		F.9.c.9.8.	

Ammunition refilling points.

La Targotte Dump.	A.8.a.3.7.	
Brandon Dump.	F.10.c.0.5.	

Unit		Position.	
D.T.M.O.	H.Q.	A.2.d.3.3.	
X/52.	H.Q.	T.26.d.4.3.	
		B.2.d.50.10 *	
		B.2.d.50.30 *	
		B.2.a.75.50 *	
		B.2.a.80.30	
		T.26.d.40.25	
		T.27.c.00.40 *	
Y/52.	H.Q.	T.19.a.7.3.	
		T.20.c.00.20	
		T.20.c.15.30	
		T.19.b.20.20 *	
		T.19.b.20.20 *	
		T.13.b.50.40	
		T.13.b.30.70.	

* In forward position pending completion of emplacement.

APPENDIX "D".

Field Artillery S.O.S. Lines.

Unit.	OUTPOST BARRAGE	BLACK BARRAGE.	BROWN BARRAGE From BROWN LINE POSITIONS.
19th Battery.	B.5.c.05.00 - B.4.b.50.55.	B.10.b.10.90 - B.4.c.30.30 - B.4.a.00.10.	B.9.c.55.45 - B.3.c.10.30.
20th Battery.	2 guns B.4.b.50.55 - B.4.b.80.100. 4 guns T.29.a.55.10 - T.23.c.90.00.	T.28.c.20.50 - T.27.b.97.85.	B.3.c.10.50 - T.26.d.65.30.
28th Battery.	T.25.c.90.00 - T.23.d.40.80 - T.17.c.85.15.	T.27.b.97.85 - T.23.c.40.30 - T.22.a.05.25.	T.23.d.65.30 - T.20.d.15.10.
D/39th Brigade.	T.29.c.20.70 - T.25.d.75.87 - T.17.d.50.15 (sweeping).	T.28.a.31.55 - T.28.a.80.60. T.28.a.56.78. T.22.c.74.50. T.22.c.30.55. T.22.c.47.73.	B.9.d.00.45 - T.20.d.55.20. (sweeping).
A/52nd Brigade.	B.4.b.70.00 - B.4.b.50.55 - B.4.b.80.100.	B.4.c.30.30 - B.4.a.00.10.	T.23.d.65.30 - T.20.d.15.10.
122nd Battery.	B.5.c.05.00 - B.4.b.70.00.	B.10.b.10.90 - B.4.c.50.30.	B.9.c.55.45 - B.3.c.10.30.
C/52nd Brigade.	T.29.a.35.10 - T.23.c.90.00.	T.29.c.20.50 - T.28.a.00.45.	B.3.c.10.50 - T.26.d.65.30.
D/52nd Brigade.	B.5.c.25.30. B.5.c.15.35. B.5.a.08.10. B.4.b.95.45. B.5.a.15.80. T.29.a.80.15. (sweeping).	B.4.c.70.25. B.4.c.50.80. B.4.a.57.25. B.4.a.27.75. B.4.a.70.75. T.28.c.70.30.	B.9.d.00.45 - T.20.d.55.20. (sweeping).
A/242nd Brigade.	T.23.b.26.10 - T.17.c.85.15.	T.23.c.40.50 - T.29.c.05.25.	Superimposed on C & B 242 Bde.
C/242nd Brigade.	T.23.c.90.00 - T.23.d.40.80 - T.23.b.23.10.	T.23.a.00.45 - T.27.b.97.85 - T.22.c.40.30.	T.19.b.20.40 - S.24.a.70.85.
D/242nd Brigade.	4 guns T.17.c.85.15 - T.17.c.65.65. 2 guns T.10.c.50.80 - T.10.a.35.25.	T.22.a.05.25 - T.15.c.73.05.	T.20.d.15.10 - T.20.a.20.50. T.10.b.20.40.

D/242nd Bde.

APPENDIX "B". (Continued).

Unit.	OUTPOST BARRAGE.	BLACK BARRAGE.	BROWN BARRAGE. FROM BROWN LINE POSITIONS.
D/242nd Brigade.	T.16.b.55.70 - T.10.c.90.35.	T.22.a.35.45. - T.21.b.80.80. T.21.b.70.65. - T.15.c.90.45. T.15.c.50.40. - T.15.c.50.65.	Sweeping 200 yards beyond C & B 242nd Brigade.
A/56th Brigade.	T.13.b.20.55 - T.10.c.40.20 - T.10.c.52.80.	3 guns T.15.d.73.05 - T.15.c.05.50. 3 guns T.8.d.50.00 - T.8.d.30.60.	Superimposed on barrages B & C 56th Brigade.
B/56th Brigade.	m.5.d.90.30 - T.3.d.60.80.	T.8.d.30.60 - T.2.c.85.00.	S.24.a.70.85 - S.17.b.80.00.
C/56th Battery.	T.13.b.20.55 - T.10.c.40.20 - T.10.c.52.80 - T.10.a.35.25.	3 guns T.22.a.05.25 - T.15.c.05.50. 3 guns T.8.d.50.00 - T.2.c.85.00.	S.17.b.80.00 - S.11.c.40.75.
527th Battery.	T.10.c.90.35 - T.10.a.80.50.	T.15.a.30.85. - T.9.c.10.20 T.8.d.56.55. - T.8.b.65.20. T.8.b.30.50. - T.8.b.85.60.	Sweeping 200 yards beyond barrages B & C 56th Brigade.
X/52 Battery. 3" Newtons.	T.17.c.80.90 * T.16.b.45.40.	T.28.c.20.60 - T.28.c.20.20. B.3.b.60.00.	
Y/52 Battery. 3" Newtons.	T.29.c.55.45. T.29.c.65.30.	T.8.d.0.0 - T.14 central - T.15.c.0.0 (sweeping).	

* temporarily, pending construction of new emplacement.

NOTE:- S.O.S. is tested at least twice a week on each Group front. The code words "TEST WILL" on Right Group front and "TEST CHAD" on Left Group front are sent by the infantry on receipt of which each Battery fires one round on S.O.S. lines.
Times are taken and reported to this Office.

APPENDIX "C".

MUTUAL SUPPORT.

Sector.	Call sent or received.	Assisting Artillery.	Number and nature of guns.	Zone of assistance.
Division on our left.	HELP AVION.	Left Group.	10 - 18-pounders.	T.4.a.55.65 - M.35.d.45.55.
Left Infantry Brigade, 52nd Division.	HELP MERICOURT.	Division on our left.	6 - 18-pounders. 2 - 4.5" Howitzers.	T.3.d.80.58 - T.4.a.00.00. T.4.d.00.90 - T.4.a.50.30.
		Right Group.	6 - 18-pounders.	T.17.d.00.90 - T.4.a.50.30
Right Infantry Brigade, 52nd Division.	ASSIST PEUMER.	Left Group.	6 - 18-pounders. 3 - 4.5" Howitzers.	T.23.d.30.00 - T.17.d.0.2. T.29.b.00.50. T.29.b.70.85. T.23.d.85.00.
		Division on our right.	12 - 18-pounders. 3 - 4.5" Howitzers.	B.5.c.30.65 - B.5.a.30.70. B.5.c.55.90. B.5.a.55.15. B.5.a.60.50.
Division on our Right.	ASSIST OPPY.	Right Group.	12 - 18-pounders. 3 - 4.5" Howitzers.	B.17.a.35.60 - B.17.d.35.60. B.17.b.10.50 - B.17.b.50.00.
Division on our Right.	ASSIST ARLEUX.	Right Group.	12 - 18-pounders. 3 - 4.5" Howitzers.	B.11.a.60.65 - B.5.c.20.75. B.5.c.50.20 - B.11.a.80.80.

The above assistance only to be given if the tactical situation permits.

APPENDIX "D".

Unit.	Present main position.		Maximum Arcs T.B.	Alternative positions.	Maximum arcs. T.B.	Observation Post.	How marked.
9th Brigade RFA							
Headquarters.	A.4.c.60.70.						
19th Battery.	B.13.c.35.88		30 - 95	A.12.b.65.53	30 - 110	VANE.	FA1
20th Battery.	B.13.a.14.76		27 - 87	B.13.c.02.44	28 - 88	JANE.	FA2
29th Battery.	B.7.c.30.30		32 - 92	A.6.d.50.30	58 - 79	ZEAL.	FA3
D/69th Bde.	A.18.d.96.77		30 - 90	B.7.c.58.15	37 - 97	KAPE.	FA4
52nd Bde. RFA.	ANY BIETE.						
Headquarters.							
A Battery.	A.4.b.73.16	FA21	46 - 104	A.3.d.70.20	53 - 78	OCCULIST.	FA5
122nd Battery.	A.4.c.79.09	FA22	53 - 102	B.15.d.10.80	29 - 95	OLDHAM.	FA6
C Battery.	A.10.b.30.98	FA23	48 - 110	B.13.b.40.40	27 - 96	LAKE.	FA7
D Battery.	A.4.d.40.75	FA24	52 - 107	B.13.a.70.10	30 - 93	OGRE.	FA8
242nd Bde. RFA.	.6.c.00.30.						
Headquarters.							
A Battery.	A.3.c.24.87		40 - 96	A.4.d.51.34	40 - 90	VAPE.	FA9
B Battery.	S.29.c.84.27		25 - 90	S.26.b.71.98	35 - 100	PEANE.	FA10
C Battery.	A.3.c.86.85		44½ - 91½	A.3.d.27.83	35 - 70	SASH.	FA11
D Battery.	S.22.d.23.86		33 - 120	S.22.d.35.19	29 - 109	GRAHAM.	FA12
56th Bde. RFA.	S.27.b.00.30						
Headquarters.							
A Battery.	S.29.c.37.85		28 - 98	S.22.d.37.07	30 - 90	PILL.	FA13
B Battery.	S.22.c.88.14		57 - 98	S.22.c.70.30	25 - 105	GRAHAM.	FA14
C Battery.	S.28.b.60.26		31 - 95	S.28.b.27.52	23 - 82	COVENTRY.	FA15
527th Battery.	S.29.b.50.95		34 - 98	S.29.a.12.33	73 - 122	BIRDSEYE.	FA16

BROWN LINE.

Unit.	Position.	How marked.	Centre line of fire (Grid).	C.P.	Wagon lines.	Route from present positions.	Brigade Zone.
9th Brigade R.F.A. Headquarters.	A.9.c.50.70.						
19th Battery.	A.9.d.51.33.	FA17	92	B.14.a.70.70.	} Fwd.	Track to 9 Elms, Artillery Track D, Rod Mill Track. Artillery Track D through 9 Elms.	B.8.c.75.55 to B.20.d.25.10.
20th Battery.	A.9.d.25.50.	FA18	81	B.8.c.35.95.			
29th Battery.	A.9.c.80.75.	FA19	77	B.7.b.80.80.		Track to 9 Elms, D Track, branching off about A.16.a.	
D/59th Bde. R.F.A.	A.9.d.81.81.	FA20	83	B.8.a.20.12.		Plank track to 9 Elms, D Artillery Track A Rod Mill Track to A.9.d.	
53rd Brigade R.F.A. Headquarters.	S.23.b.						
A Battery.				PRESENT POSITIONS			B.8.c.75.55 to T.20.a.00.20.
122nd Battery.							
C Battery.							
D Battery.							
242nd Bde. R.F.A. Headquarters.	S.23.b.						
A Battery.	S.27.c.50.40.	FA25	68	S.29.b.40.80.	} Fob.	Q track, BRUVILLE ST. VAAST, Sunken road A.3.a, S.27.c. FOLIE TAMY road to track A.3.c.9.7.	B.20.d.12.10 to S.24.c.70.95.
B Battery.	A.2.b.18.72.	FA26	63	S.25.c.37.53.			
C Battery.	S.27.d.18.28.	FA27	71	S.27.c.55.62.		Q track, BRUVILLE ST. VAAST, Sunken Road A.3.a, S.27.c. FOLIE track to track S.27.b.8.3.	
D Battery.	S.27.c.73.83.	FA28	75	S.23.b.30.40.			
59th Brigade R.F.A. Headquarters.	S.27.b.00.30.			S.23.b.10.40.	} Wood.	FOLIE track, CAMPBELL Road.	S.24.c.70.85 to S.11.c.40.75.
A Battery.	T.3.a.31.72.	FA29	37			-do-	
B Battery.	R29.b.92.20.	FA30	37			-do-	
C Battery.	X.36.a.93.79.	FA31	60			-do-	
527th Battery.	X.30.c.72.49.	FA32	62			-do-	

BROWN LINE (continued).

Unit.	Position.	How marked.	Centre line of fire (Grid).	O.P.	Wagon lines.	Route from present positions.	Brigade Zone.
Spare Headquarters.	A.8.c.50.70.			B.7.b.80.80.			
A.	A.15.b.85.25.	FA 45.	79		⎫		B.9.c.25.35
B.	A.16.a.20.35.	FA 40.	66	B.8.d.00.35.	⎬ F.14.c.		to
C.	A.15.b.90.80.	FA 47.	56	and	⎬		
D.	A.16.c.50.95.	FA 48.	62	B.1.c.05.35.	⎭		T.20.a.00.20.
Headquarters.	X.27.b.5.1.						
A.	X.29./.20.70.	FA 41.	79		⎫		T.20.a.00.20
B.	X.29.d.60.70.	FA 42.	75		⎬ X.25.d.		to
C.	X.29.d.40.45.	FA 43.	31		⎬		
D.	F.5.b.40.52.	FA 44.	71		⎭		S.11.c.15.50.

GREEN LINE.

Unit.	Position.	How marked	Centre line of fire (grid)	O.P.	Wagon Lines.	Route from present positions.	Brigade zone.
9th Brigade RFA							
Headquarters.							B.13.b.70.10
19th Battery.		FA17		SAME AS			to
20th Battery.		FA18	BROWN	LINE POSITIONS			B.7.a.10.78.
25th Battery.		FA19					
D/69th Bde.RFA.		FA20					
52nd Brigade RFA.							
Headquarters.	F.12.a.00.00			F.18.a.30.50			B.7.a.10.78
A Battery.	A.7.b.00.00	FA33	85	& front line.		Q & BONVAL Tracks.	to
122nd Battery.	F.13.c.90.80	FA34	80		F14.b.	G & RED HILL Tracks.	A.5.b.80.45.
C Battery.	A.7.d.20.77	FA35	76			-do-	
D Battery.	A.7.d.15.25	FA36	78			Q & BONVAL Tracks.	
242nd Bde. R.F.A.							
A Battery.	F.12.a.00.10.	sp=.				BONVAL track to F.6.b.3.3,	
	A.7.b.00.15.	FA37	73			track to road F.12.b.5.3,	
						RED MILL Track.	
B Battery.	F.5.d.82.58.	FA38	73	F.6.c.50.50.	F.8.a.	Track to BONVAL track &	A.5.b.80.45
						BONVAL Track.	
C Battery.	A.7.d.50.15.	FA39	52			Track to BONVAL track,	
						Bonval track to F.6.b.3.3,	
						track to road F.12.b.5.3,	
						RED HILL Track.	
D Battery.	A.8.c.05.80.	FA40	60			Track through S.27.c.8.2	S.23.c.00.00.
						to Souchez Road, track to	
						F.6.b.3.6, track to road	
						F.12.b.5.3, RED HILL Track	
53th Brigade RFA							
A Battery.	S.27.b.00.50.	FA29	72	S.27.b.60.30.		FOLIE track, JAMPBELL ROAD.	S.23.c.00.00
B Battery.	F.3.a.65.72.	FA30	77	S.28.a.30.70.	W.30.d.	-do-	to
C Battery.	X.29.b.92.90.	FA31	71	S.19.b.60.50.		-do-	S.16.c.00.00.
527th Battery.	X.30.a.93.79.	FA32	68	S.22.a.40.60.		-do-	
	X.30.c.74.48.						

GREEN LINE. (Continued).

Unit.	Position.	How armed.	Centre line of fire (Grid).	O.P.	Wagon lines.	Routs from present position.	Brigade Zone.
Brigade Headquarters.				P.18.a.30.50.			
A Battery.		HH.FA45	83				B.13.b.70.10 to A.5.b.80.45.
B Battery.		HH.FA46	70				
C Battery.		HH.FA47	58				
D Battery.		HH.FA48	62				
Headquarters.							
A Battery.		HH.FA41	91	S.29.b.80.30 and S.19.b.30.50.	X.25.d.		A.5.b.80.45 to S.18.c.40.00.
B Battery.		HH.FA42	81				
C Battery.		HH.BA43	67				
D Battery.		HH.FA44	75				

ECURIE SWITCH.

Brigade.	Battery.	Position.	No.	Grid bearing Centre line of fire.	O.P.	Wagon line.	Route.	Brigade Zone.
H.Bde. H.Q. S.20.c.56.81.	18-pdr.	S.20.d.90.57.	FA49	125°	B.14 crater.	BOIS DES ALLEUX F.2.c & d.	Track leading E. from Road about S.19.d.6.4 runs along line of positions.	B.7.a.5.2 to Angle of trees Angle of A.17.a.
	do.	S.20.d.30.55.	FA50	132	A.4.a.5.8 (approx.)			
	do.	S.20.d.05.51.	FA51	138	or a point in A.5.d.			
	4.5" How	S.20.c.70.50.	FA52	128				
J.Bde. H.Q. A.30.a.40.38.	18-pdr.	S.25.d.65.35.	FA53	140	A.4.a.5.8 or S.26.b.4.5 or Ridge A.1.b.5.5 to F.6.c.8.8 or A.5.d.	ditto.	Main line of communication the track from BERTHONVAL FARM to S.25.b.9.1 (CAMPBELL ROAD). There are side tracks to each position.	Angle of trees A.17.a.3.1 t A.23.a.0.3
	do.	S.25.d.05.15.	FA54	143				
	do.	F.5.a.50.42.	FA55	140				
	4.5" How	F.5.c.05.42.	FA56	132				
K.Bde. H.Q. F.5.a.00.75.	18-pdr.	F.5.d.61.52.	FA57	144	F.15.a.7.2 or F.29.a. or F.18.a.5.3.	ditto.		A.23.a.0.5 t G.1.d.1.5.
	do.	F.5.d.20.20.	FA58	151				
	do.	F.5.a.52.10.	FA59	161				
	4.5" How	F.11.a.70.92.	FA60	147				

APPENDIX "E".

List of Observation posts and how manned.

Code Name.	Location.	Arc G.B.	Battery.	How manned.
OCCULIST.	D.1.c.73.92.	25 - 95	A/52.	
ODDMENT.	B.7.b.80.30.	50 - 92.	122nd.	
LAKE.	B.1.a.35.00.	50 - 100	C/52.	
OGRE.	B.1.a.35.01.	50 - 100	D/52.	By Right Group.
SASH.	B.1.d.20.30.	25 - 90	C/242.	3 from 9.30 pm to
WART.	A.6.b.80.80.	15 - 92.	A/242.	9.30 pm on a Roster
VANE.	B.14.a.50.75.	45 - 135.	19th.	& 3 more during
JANE.	B.8.c.38.98.	38 - 98.	20th.	daylight.
ZEAL.	B.8.c.80.80.	45 - 145.	28th.	
NAPE.	B.8.a.30.20.	50 - 105.	D/69.	
WINDY.	T.22.d.70.40.	330 - 40.		
COVENTRY.	S.29.b.40.80.	30 - 100.	C/58.	By Left Group.
PEACH.	S.23.d.30.20.	45 - 90.	B/242.	2 are manned day
PLUM.	S.23.c.70.30.	45 - 90.	A/56.	and night on a
GRAHAM.	S.22.b.30.40.	20 - 110.	D/242 & B/56.	roster and the
BIRDSEYE.	S.22.b.65.50.	60 - 120.	527th.	remainder during daylight.

~~The Left Group front can also be observed from GREEN line trench in S.22.b. and d. and Hill 145.~~

APPENDIX "F".

Orders for Anti-Tank Guns.

1. Enemy Tanks will be engaged whenever they are seen, irrespective of the position of our Infantry. Although the primary object of these guns is the destruction of Tanks, the gun Commander must be prepared to engage any favourable targets such as massing of enemy Infantry, which present themselves.

2. Open sights only will be used.

3. 200 High explosive shells, 200 Cartridges and 220 Tubes, friction T push per gun will be kept at each gun - a small portion will be kept in weather proof racks ready for use. The remainder will be kept boxed with the lids unscrewed, ready for immediate action.

4. Fighting Maps will be kept at each position showing all principal points in view, with names and range marked against each point.

   Each man in the detachments must know these points and the ranges to them.

5. In exposed positions, no movement will take place in daylight.

6. A supply of water, 48-hours emergency rations and a spare box respirator per 4 men will be kept at each gun.

7. Each detachment will "stand to" from half an hour before dawn till one hour after dawn.

8. There will always be a sentry on duty at each gun position.

9. Detachments will be put through a special course of training in Gun Drill at moving targets over the open sights at Battery position, before being sent up to man Anti-Tank Guns.

10. Anti-Tank guns must be prepared to fire in any direction running out of the pit if necessary.

11. A copy of these orders will be hung up in each pit.

APPENDIX "G".

Heavy Artillery Counter preparation and S.O.S. points.

Unit.	Outpost Barrage.	Black Barrage.	TABLE 'A'. NORMAL POINTS.	Counter preparation. TABLE 'B'. Bursts of Fire.
1st C.H.B.	T.10.c.15.50. T.24.a.15.15. T.9.c.20.20. T.9.c.50.05. T.24.c.00.60. T.24.c.40.50. T.15.c.55.90. T.15.a.45.70. T.24.a.17.90. T.50.a.50.90. T.15.a.50.50. T.15.a.57.20.	T.12.c.55.60 – U.7.b.80.30. T.12.c.80.10 – U.7 central. T.13.d.80.85 – U.13.b.80.80. B.5.b.80.90. B.25.c.25.15. B.5.b.90.30. B.6.c.30.00.)One B.3.c.70.40. B.3.d.85.00.)Gun B.6.cont: – U.25.c.20.10.	U.27.c.20.30 – U.27.c.70.50. 0.3.a.20.75. U.27.c.50.75 – U.27.b.00.90. U.27.a.70.55 – U.27.b.63.30. U.14.b.00.25 – U.14.a.45.80. U.20.b.85.20 – U.20.b.90.55.
2nd C.H.B.	T.17.b.15.85. T.17.b.40.60. T.28.d.00.40. T.28.c.90.15. T.17.b.60.55. T.17.b.90.05. T.28.c.85.00. B.4.a.80.80. T.4.c.95.70. T.4.a.40.20. T.15.a.64.18. T.15.a.70.00.	T.5.a.40.15. T.3.a.70.98. T.5.a.55.50. T.3.d.90.10.)One T.5.d.70.00. T.3.c.50.40)gun T.12.a.45.50. T.5.d.75.50. U.13.c.40.25. U.13.d.98.50. U.19.c.15.70. U.19.b.98.98. U.25.d.20.70. U.19.d.65.65.	U.8.c.75.75 – U.8.c.85.15. U.8.a.75.75 – U.8.b.40.35. U.14.d.50.10 – U.15.a.90.55. U.8.c.20.35 – U.8.b.20.55.
2nd C.S.B.	T.4.c.80.00. B.11.c.00.80. B.23.b.50.30. B.23.b.05.80. T.18.c.50.00. B.23.b.50.50. B.23.a.80.20. T.28.d.05.20. B.5.b.90.30. B.11.b.70.50. B.4.a.38.40. B.4.d.07.18.	T.11.d.98.40. T.18.b.60.98. T.18.b.20.00. T.18.d.80.90. T.18.c.90.25. T.18.d.50.75. T.24.b.55.85. T.18.d.75.15. T.24.a.10.90. T.24.c.60.70. B.5.a.70.70. T.29.d.05.30.	U.21.c.00.00 U.21.c.10.98. U.27.c.55.80.
5th C.S.B.	T.11.a.60.10. T.18.a.70.50. B.5.d.50.55. T.4.d.80.70.	T.18.d.70.30. T.18.d.90.00. T.24.d.40.15. T.30.b.75.00. B.5.b.60.30. B.5.b.90.25.	U.27.c.25.25 – U.27.c.75.30. U.27.c.50.10 – U.27.a.70.65. U.14.c.95.70 – U.14.d.25.00.
4th C.S.B.	T.4.a.50.20. T.10.b.50.50. T.19.c.15.15. T.22.a.60.80. T.18.c.80.70. T.29.c.70.00. T.15.d.70.59. T.22.a.95.40. B.5.c.90.80. T.11.c.90.20. T.22.b.10.10. T.22.d.50.35.	T.11.b.25.35. T.11.b.80.10. T.12.a.20.00. T.12.c.75.50. T.24.b.65.10. T.30.b.75.25. B.5.c.95.25. T.29.d.95.90.	T.8.a.00.50. T.8.b.10.30. U.8.a.95.20. U.7.b.90.75. U.14.d.10.65. U.27.a.35.75.
5th S.B.	T.4.d.60.00. T.18.c.90.30. T.15.d.45.80. T.22.b.50.88. T.29.d.90.90. T.29.d.50.30. T.26.b.55.80. T.28.d.85.75.	T.18.c.95.90. T.12.c.50.50. T.18.d.30.98. T.18.b.20.00. T.24.b.05.85. T.24.b.25.20. T.24.b.05.50. T.24.c.65.85.	U.20.b.35.20 – U.20.b.55.20. U.14.a.55.98 – U.14.b.00.85.
224th S.B.	B.5.a.30.50. B.5.d.80.05.	T.29.d.55.20. B.4.b.35.18. T.29.d.25.85.	U.21.c.60.00 – U.21.c.10.93.

Reinforcing Arty:

APPENDIX "G". (Continued).

Unit.	Outpost Barrage.	Black Barrage.	TABLE 'A'. NORMAL POINTS. Counter preparation.	TABLE 'B'. BURSTS OF FIRE.
Reinforcing Arty. / HEAVY HOUR.	T.4.b.50.10. T.11.c.00.25. T.2.d.70.00. T.8.b.95.38.		T.5.c.00.25. T.5.d.20.90.	T.55.c.98.30.
	T.4.c.85.05. T.11.c.55.60. T.9.a.00.03. T.6.c.00.80.		T.5.d.00.30. T.5.d.70.00.	
	T.4.d.65.95. T.4.d.80.65. T.9.c.10.20. T.15.d.45.95.		T.5.b.70.00. T.5.c.05.45.	N.55.d.25.30
			T.5.c.20.75 - 25.98.	— 10.93.
			T.5.c.10.25. T.11.a.60.75.	T.6.a.65.50.
			T.11.a.70.50. T.5.d.10.10.	
Medium Hours.	T.15.b.80.50. T.11.c.75.80. T.15.d.10.55. T.15.c.85.82.		T.5.b.05.50. N.34.d.05.10.	N.35.d.10.90.
			T.5.b.05.82. T.4.b.50.45. N.54.d.50.10.	T.5.b.55.90.
				T.5.d.10.85.

In addition, arrangements have been made to concentrate all fire on the front of either Infantry Brigade, in the event of a local attack.

APPENDIX "H".

ANTI GAS INSTRUCTIONS.   (To be read in conjunction with SS212.)

---oOo---

YELLOW CROSS GAS SHELL BOMBARDMENTS.

1. Serious concentrations of gas shell, especially of yellow Cross, may be anticipated in all Battery areas.

2. Men are better off in the open than in cellars and dugouts which are not properly gas proof. The work of gas proofing all dugouts must therefore be pressed on.

3. The use of protected dugouts will be controlled as far as possible on the following lines:-

   (a) Protected dugouts will be apportioned as follows – A certain number will be allotted as traffic dugouts i.e. dugouts in and out of which traffic during a gas bombardment is allowed: the remainder will be dugouts in which troops will stay throughout the bombardment or as long as necessary before relieving the personnel who occupy the traffic dugouts, or are engaged in manning the guns (see (b)).

   (b) Only sufficient personnel necessary to man the guns for 8 hours will be kept in the traffic dugouts. The residue will be lodged in the remaining protected dugouts and all traffic in and out of these will be forbidden.

   (c) Signal dugouts and Command Posts cannot be duplicated, hence the following procedure will be adopted. A special orderly, wearing his box respirator, will stand between the inner and outer curtains; messages can then be handed through the outer curtain and then passed on by this orderly through the inner curtain as soon as the outer one has been readjusted.

4. All batteries will arrange to have as many Drivers as possible trained as Gunners, so that in the event of a prolonged gas bombardment, men who have been exposed to gas for a long time may to some extent be withdrawn to wagon lines and their places taken by Drivers.

APPENDIX "J".

Action for ECURIE SWITCH.

1. In the event of a hostile attack on a large scale from ARLEUX Southwards, with a view to turning the VIMY RIDGE from the South, the enemy may either make his flank rest on the high ground North of WILLERVAL and include FARBUS and the high ground to the West of it in his initial attack or he may make his flank on the high ground South of WILLERVAL, excluding FARBUS in his initial attack. In either case it may be assumed that he will endeavour to turn North West up the VIMY RIDGE and to the West of it.

2. Taking the first situation.
    In the event of the enemy penetrating our defences and capturing FARBUS and the high ground to the West of it, a Division will in the first instance occupy the PADDOCK switch from A.9.1. to S.20.1. and from there be prepared to deliver a deliberate counter attack and drive the enemy off the VIMY RIDGE.
    The first objective will be the ECURIE switch from LIME redoubt, A.16.d., (inclusive) to its junction with the GREEN line in S.7.a.
    Taking the second situation.
    In the event of the enemy penetrating the defences of the Corps on our right, a Division will concentrate under cover of the PADDOCK switch, occupy the ECURIE switch from A.16.d. to GREEN line and be prepared to deliver an immediate counter attack in conjunction with the Corps on our right.
    The first objective for this attack will be the ST. CATHERINE SWITCH from A.30.c and d to B.20.c.

3. In either case it will be necessary for the Artillery covering the 52nd Division to give as much support as possible, bearing in mind the vital importance of this flank to the possession of the VIMY RIDGE.
    The amount of support will naturally be entirely dependent on the amount of frontal pressure we are experiencing and the necessity for safeguarding the Left Flank of the counter stroke.

4. Taking the first situation.
    We shall by then be holding the GREEN line, at any rate on the South. It may be possible to withdraw a Brigade R.F.A. from the Left Group and put them in to support the counter attack.
    The three ECURIE SWITCH positions shown in Appendix 'D' will be available for this, but two may be occupied by guns of the counter attacking Division.
    As large a proportion as possible of the attached H.A. Brigade will also have to support them.
    It is doubtful whether the Right Group will be able to assist at all, as their front will almost certainly be subjected to heavy containing pressure and on them will devolve the covering of the troops guarding the left flank of the counter stroke.
    It may however be possible to superimpose the fire of some of their Batteries on the Left front of the attack, from which they could be taken away, if necessary.
    Taking the second situation.
    The pressure on our front would not be so great as in the first situation, and might be very little on Left Group front.
    We should probably be holding the BROWN line with our right flank refused.
    In view of this, it will be possible to switch the fire of our Brigade from the Left Group front to the Right Group front and so free a Brigade of the Right Group to support the attack.
    It may also be possible to superimpose the fire of further Right Group Batteries. This could be done from present BROWN LINE position, by running out of pits.
    The attached H.A. Brigade will also have to support this attack fully.
    In order to conform to the above general principles all F.A. Brigades will reconnoitre the three ECURIE SWITCH positions and O.P's with a view to occupation.
    The attached H.A. Brigade will also carry out reconnaissances with a view to supporting these attacks to the fullest possible extent.
    Both F.A. and H.A. Brigade and Battery Commanders will reconnoitre the various switches and ground over which these counter attacks will be delivered, making special note of all localities from which observation on them can be obtained and ensure that all Officers understand the broad principles of our action in these eventualities.

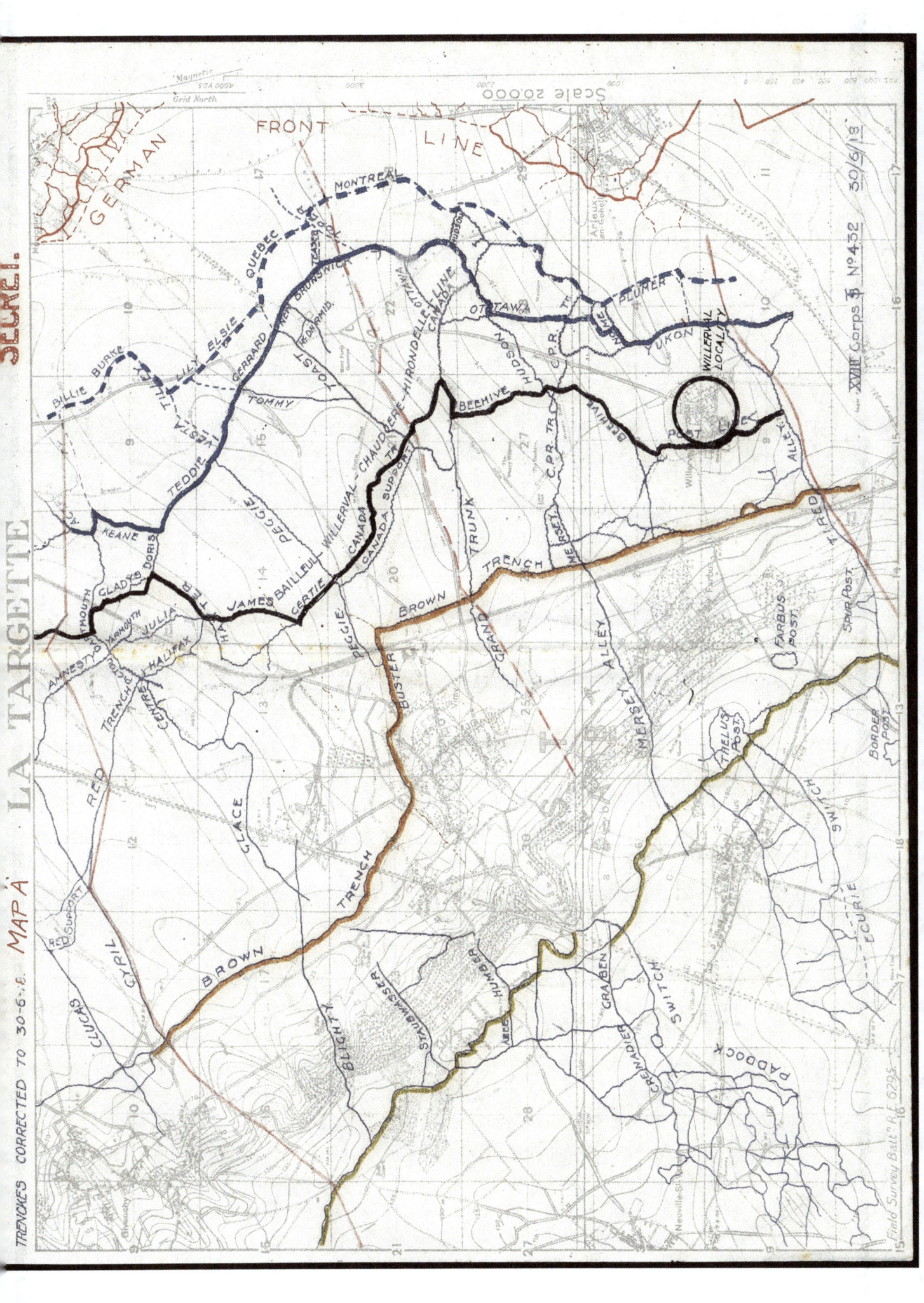

DAILY REPORT.
52nd DIVISIONAL ARTILLERY.
3.0am 10th to 3.0am 11th JULY 1918

appx 14
W D

1. OUR ACTIVITY.
   (a) Operations. During the day movement around CHEZ BONTEMPS (U.
       was engaged by 18-pdrs. and in the afternoon/East of BERIDO
                                                        movement
       by 4.5" How.
                At 3.0 pm. 9" ... fired on AVILUX LOOP.
                During the night harassing fire was directed on
       tracks, roads and centres of activity.
                10.9 pm. a test S.O.S. was received and responded
       by Right Group.
                Total rounds fired :-
                18-pdr.   900.   4.5" How.   250.   6" T.M.

   (b) Aerial.   Our machines were active throughout the day.

2. HOSTILE ACTIVITY.
   (a) Artillery. The period was quieter than the preceeding 24 hr
       TIRED ALLEY and the O.Ps in B.14.a. were shelled with 30 r
       15 cm. How. in the morning and with a further 20 rounds in
       afternoon.

Date.	Time.	No. of rds.	Calibre.	Area shelled.
10th.	7.30- 8.15am.	30.	15 cm.	TIRED ALLEY & B.14.a.
	8.15-10.30am.	50.	10.5 cm.	A.3.a.
	11.30am.	12.	10.5 cm.	A.3.a.
	11.45am.	1.	10.5 cm.	B.3.
	3.45 pm.	14.	10.5cm.	A.3.
	3.30- 4.30pm.	30.	15 cm.	NINE ELMS. A.17.
	3.30- 4.0pm.	30.	15 cm.	TIRED ALLEY & B.14.a.
	11pm-midnight.	30.	10 cm.gun	STATION WOOD B.8.c.

(2)

   (b) Work.   Nil.

   (c) Movement. Individual movement was observed around CHEZ BO
       and individual and massed movement was observed continuou
       between 5.0pm and 6.0pm. in N.36.b., N.36.c., U.1.a., U.1.
       N.36.c. and U.3.c.

   (b) Aerial. Enemy machines were active all day.   Pamphlets
       dropped at the foot of VIMY.
                12.45pm a hostile observation balloon which had
       broken loose was seen going in the direction of AVION.

3. GENERAL.   A helio observed in U.3.a. - letters M.H.M.L.
   3.10pm Dump on fire 94° from S.28.b.55.80.
   3.5pm large fire at U.29.c. probably caused by H.A.
   Visibility fair.

11th July 1918.

                                    Lieut.
                        Reconnaissance Officer, 52n

SECRET.

52nd D.A. No. A/379.

To all recipients of 52nd D.A. Order No. 22.

In task for 12th July - for T.25.d.40.90 read U.35.d.40.90.

[signature]
Captain R.A.
11th July 1918.   Brigade Major R.A., 52nd D.A.

SECRET.   Copy No. 20

52ND DIVISIONAL ARTILLERY ORDER NO. 22.

Reference VIII Corps log map No. 6.B.

1. The following short bombardments will take place, as detailed below, with a view to killing personnel.

2. Bombardments will take place at dates and times as under:- Tasks are given in the attached Table.

    July 12th.   11am - 11.5 am.
    July 13th.   9am - 9.5 am.
    July 14th.   3 pm - 3.5 pm.
                    5.35pm - 5.40pm.
    July 15th   7pm - 7.5 pm.
                    7.50pm - 7.55pm.

3. Rates of fire during each 5 minutes burst will be:-

    Heavy Hows:- RAPID.
    Medium Hows:- First two minutes INTENSE then three minutes NORMAL.
    60-pdrs and
    Field Artillery:- First two minutes INTENSE then cease fire.
    60-pdrs. and 18-pdrs. will fire shrapnel.

4. Watches will be synchronised by telephone with this Headquarters one hour before shoot.

5. Groups and 2nd Brigade C.G.A. please ACKNOWLEDGE.

                                           Captain R.A.
                                           Brigade Major R.A.
11th July 1918.   52nd Divisional Artillery.

DISTRIBUTION.

    Copy No. 1 to R.A. 8th Corps.
            2 to H.A. 8th Corps.
            3 to 2nd Bde. C.G.A.
            4 to C.B.S.O. 8th Corps.
            5 to 52nd Div: 'G'.
         6/10 to Right Group.
           11 to Left Group.
           12 to D.T.M.O.
           13 to 155th Inf: Bde.
           14 to 156th Inf: Bde.
           15 to 157th Inf: Bde.
           16 to 51st Div: Arty.
           17 R.A. Signal Officer.
           18 to E.M., R.A.
           19 to R.O., R.A.
        20/21 to War Diary.
           22 File.
           23 Retain.

T A S K S.

Date.	Unit.	No. & nature of guns.	Tasks.
12th July.	2nd Bde. C.G.A.	4 heavy hows. 6 medium hows. 2 60-pounders.	Headquarters - T.25.d.40.90.
	Right Group.	3 18-pounders. 1 4.5" How.	- ditto -
13th July.	2nd Bde. C.G.A.	4 heavy hows. 6 medium hows. 2 60-pounders.	Headquarters C.1.a.40.60 - C.1.a.30.75
	Right Group.	3 18-pounders. 1 4.5" How.	- ditto -
14th July.	2nd Bde. C.G.A.	4 heavy hows. 6 medium hows. 2 60-pounders.	Living trench C.1.b.54.60 - C.1.b.33.85, Road & track junction C.1.b.55.55.
	Right Group.	3 18-pounders. 1 4.5" How.	Trench & track C.1.b.54.60 - C.1.b.33.85 Road and track junction C.1.b.55.55.
15th July.	2nd Bde. C.G.A.	4 heavy hows. 6 medium hows. 2 60-pounders.	Headquarters C.1.c.55.80 - C.1.a.45.00.
	Right Group.	3 18-pounders. 1 4.5" How.	Tracks leading into the above.

DAILY REPORT, 52:DIVISIONAL ARTILLERY.
3 am 11th to 3 am 12th JULY 1918.

1. OUR ACTIVITY.
   (a) Operations. At 10 am 60 pounders fired a burst of fire on
       ALBERT Road (U.7.d.- U.13.b.) to catch enemy ration
       parties.
           At 4 pm a working party at U.26.a.3.9. was engaged
       by a forward 18-pdr.
       At night harassing fire was directed on enemy roads,
       tracks etc.
           Total rounds fired -
           18-pdr.   850.   4.5" Hows.   250.   6" T.M. Nil.

   (b) Aerial.   R.E.8 machines were active.

2. HOSTILE ACTIVITY.
   (a) Artillery.   Very quiet except for shelling of VIMY by 15 cm.
       Hows. between 3 pm and 5 pm., and of PETIT VIMY at 11am
       and 3 pm.

Date.	Time.	No. of Rds.	Calibre.	Area shelled.
11th.	9 am- 10am.	10.	77 mm.	FARBUS WOOD, (B.8.c.)
	10.30am.	5.	77 mm.	T.20.b.5.0.
	11. am.	40.	15 cm.	PETIT VIMY (S.24.c.)
	3.0 pm.	37.	10.5 cm.	" " "
	3pm - 5 pm.	200.	15 cm.	T.19.d.

   Flashes. 9 pm H.V. gun 61°45' from E.8.a.20.25.

   (b) Work.   4 pm digging observed at U.26.a.3.9 - engaged by
       18-pr.

   (c) Movement.   12.15 pm. small parties on roads in O.35.d., U.4.a.
       U.3.b. and U.4.c.
           1.45 pm. mounted men and cart with occupants seen
       on road in O.33.d. and U.3.b.

   (d) Aerial.   Inactive. One E.A. crossed our lines at 11 am
       but was driven back by A.A. and M.G.

3. GENERAL.   Visibility good during fine intervals.

                                    A.F. Drifton
                                    Lieut RA.
                                    Reconnaissance Officer, 52nd D.A.

12th July 1918.

SECRET.   52ND DIVISIONAL ARTILLERY ORDER NO. 25.   Copy No. 18

Reference maps 1/20,000 sheets 44.A S.W. & 51.B. N.W.

1. 52nd Army Brigade R.F.A. and 8th Army Brigade C.F.A. will exchange battery positions as under.

2. On night 13th/14th July 1 section A/52, 122, C/52 and D/52 Batteries will exchange with 1 section 24th, 30th, 32 and 43 Batteries C.F.A. respectively.

3. On night 14th/15th July the remainder of the Batteries will exchange positions, Command of batteries and Brigade Headquarters will also be changed. B.A.C's will exchange camps on the evening July 14th under arrangements between Brigade Commanders concerned. Incoming Units will take over wagon lines of outgoing units.

4. Batteries will retain their own guns but all position stores, such as Map boards, Defence schemes, Maps and gas clothing will be exchanged.
Receipts will be taken and forwarded to this office on completion of reliefs.

5. Battery Captains and Adjutants will remain behind till incoming Battery and Brigade Commanders have arrived and taken over.

6. Completion of moves on each night will be reported to this office by Right Group, using code word RUDLI.

7. 52nd Army Brigade to ACKNOWLEDGE.

Captain R.A.
Brigade Major, R.A.
52nd Divisional Artillery.

12th July 1918.

DISTRIBUTION.

Copy No. 1 to Right Group.
2 to Left Group.
3 to D.T.M.O.
4/8 to 52nd Brigade.
9 to 242nd Brigade.
10 to S.C., R.A.
11 to 155th Inf: Brigade.
12 to 156th Inf: Brigade.
13 to 157th Inf: Bde.
14 to 52nd Div: "G".
15 to D.A.G.O.
16 to R.A., Signal Officer.
17 to R.O., R.A.
18/19 to War Diary.
20 File.
21 Retain.
22 to 52nd D.A.C.

DAILY REPORT, 52ND DIVISIONAL ARTILLERY.
6 am. 12th to 6 am 13th JULY 1918.

1. OUR ACTIVITY.
   (a) Operations. At 11 am a hurricane bombardment of Headquarters
       U.25.3.40.90 was carried out in conjunction with 2nd Bde CGA.
       At 11.31 pm and at 11.35 pm test S.O.S. were
       received and responded to by Night Group.
       Harassing fire was carried out during the night
       and was increased after the Gas Beam discharge, and directed
       on communications on the flanks of the Beam, special atten-
       tion being paid to the HENIN LIETARD road running N.E. from
       U.13.c.50.20 and the BOIS BERNARD in U.13 and U.14.
       All tracks and roads within the limit of the Beam were
       vigourously harassed from 5 hours after the discharge until
       daylight.
       Total rounds fired -
           18-pr. 2,500.   4.5" H.W.   550.   6" H.   Nil.

   (b) Aerial.   Our machines were active particularly from 9 am.
       to 2 pm and from 5 pm to 9 pm.

2. HOSTILE ACTIVITY.
   (a) Artillery. Very quiet during the day. At 12.45 am, after
       the gas discharge, enemy fired 200 rounds on R.1.a & c, and
       at 5.30 am fired about 300 rounds of 15 cm. on VIMY.

Time.	No. of rds.	Calibre.	Area shelled.	Direction.
12 noon.	3.	10 cm. gun.	B.7.a.	C.I. 90.
12 noon.	12.	10 cm. gun.	R.1.c.	
9.45 pm.	6.	15 cm.	T.23.c.	
10.10 pm.	10.	77 mm.	B.S.b.	FRIENDLY.
10.15 pm.	20.	15 cm.	T.19.d.	
12.15 am.	6.	10.5 cm.	B.8.c.	
12.45 am.	200.	10.5cm.	R.1.a & c.	
5.30 am.	300.	15 cm.	VIMY, T.12.c & 6.	

   (b) Tank.   Nil.

   (c) Movement.   Individual movement in T.5.b., U.5.b., U.7.d., R.1.a.,
       and in LONDON COPSE, U.1.b.
       5 pm. small groups of men in U.27.
       A signal station was observed at CINQ CHEMINS.

   (d) Aerial.   5 pm - 5 observation balloons up.
       H.A. active from 8 am. to 9 am.   Bombing 'planes
       were over our lines from 11.30 pm. to midnight.

3. GENERAL. Visibility fair during the day and good in the evening,
   poor on morning of 13th.

                                            Lieut. RA.
                                Reconnaissance Officer, 52nd DA.

13th July 1918.

appx 19   WD

SECRET.   52nd D.A. A/291.

To all recipients of D.A. Order No. 22.

    In the bombardments for the 14th and 15th the bursts of fire will be for the first 2 minutes of INTENSE fire only, in each case.

    Heavy Howitzers will not be used.

    Groups and 2nd Brigade C.G.A. please ACKNOWLEDGE.

                                                          Captain R.A.
                                                       Brigade Major R.A.
13th July 1918.   52nd Divisional Artillery.

DAILY REPORT 52ND DIVISIONAL ARTILLERY.
6 am 13th to 6 am 14th July 1918.

1. OUR ACTIVITY.
    (a) Operations. At 3am. 6" T.M. fired on MANITOBA ROAD and on dugout and trench T.29.d. central.
    At 9am a bombardment of H.Q., C.1.a.40.60 to C.1.a.30.75 was carried out in conjunction with 2nd Brigade C.G.A.
    At 9.45am. 60-pdrs. fired a synchronised burst on ROUVROY ROAD U.7.d. and U.13.b. for the benefit of enemy ration parties.
    During the afternoon 6" Hows. fired on T.M. at T.18.d.98.22, T.18.d.10.67, T.18.d.4.1, T.18.d.67.22, T.18.d.58.65 and on M.G. at T.18.d.50.86 and T.18.d.67.51.
    18-pdrs. fired on movement in T.11.a, B.6.c.central, B.6.b central, in U.25.d. and around CHEZ BONTEMPS.
    At 3.30 pm and 8pm 9.2" Hows. carried out a destructive shoot on houses in ROUVROY U.8.a.6.1.
    Increased harassing fire was directed on all tracks and roads within the limit of the beam of the gas discharge of the previous night and maintained until dawn.
    Total rounds fired:-
    18-pdr. 2640.   4.5" How. 500.   6" T.M. 20.

    (b) Aerial. Our aeroplanes were active from 7 to 11am, from 4 to 8 pm, from 9 to 11 pm. and at dawn.

2. HOSTILE ACTIVITY.
    (a) Artillery. Quiet. At 1pm 15cm and 10.5cm Hows. fired about 100 rounds on LA CHAUDIERE. At 7pm. 12 rounds were fired near LA TARGETTE.

Date.	Time.	No. of rds.	Calibre.	Area shelled.	Direction.
13th.	11am.	9	10.5cm.	S.18.b.	
	1-1.30pm.	100	15cm & 10.5cm.	LA CHAUDIERE & S.18.b.	Includes 4 Gas, nature not reported.
	1.30pm.	8	77mm.	VIMY.	
	7pm.	12	10.5cm.	A.7.b.9.8.	
14th.	1.30am	20	10.5cm.	VIMY.	
	3am.	9	77mm.	S.23	

    (b) Work. None reported.

    (c) Movement. Individual movement was observed in HERICOURT. 4 men walking from behind brickstack in T.11.a. were fired on and disappeared into trench at T.5.c.5.4.
    Movement was also engaged in B.6.c.central, B.6.b. con: in U.25.d. and around CHEZ BONTEMPS.

    (d) Aerial. One E.A. over our lines at 6.30am.
    One Observation balloon up for half an hour at 4.30pm.

3. GENERAL. Visibility fair, improving in the evening, good on morning of 14th.

14th July 1918.

Lieut: R.A.
Reconnaissance Officer 52nd Div: Arty.

SECRET.   April 21   Copy No ......

52ND DIVISIONAL ARTILLERY ORDER NO. 24.

Reference maps 1/20,000 - sheets 44-A S.W. and 51-B N.W.

1. The boundary between the 52nd Division and the 4th Canadian Division will be amended as shown in the attached tracing.
The 10th Canadian Infantry Brigade are relieving troops of 52nd Division in the area to be handed over on night 15/16th July.

2. On completion of above relief, the 52nd Divisional front will be reorganised as follows :-
The Right Infantry Brigade Section will be organised into a 2 Battalion front and the Left Infantry Brigade Section into a 1 Battalion front.

3. At 6.0 am. July 16th the S.O.S. lines for Batteries will be readjusted as in the attached tracing and the Grouping will be altered to.
RIGHT GROUP.
   Commander, Lieut. Colonel H.J. COOPER, C.M.G., D.S.O., R.A.
                        9th Brigade RFA.
        Sub-group.   242nd Brigade RFA.

LEFT GROUP.
   Commander, Lieut. Colonel J. INGRAM, RFA.
                        58th Brigade RFA.

C/56th Brigade RFA is superimposed on the barrage of the Right Group but will be at the disposal of the Left Group Commander to meet any special requirements of the G.O.C., Left Infantry Brigade Section.

4. At 6.0 am. July 16th, the 8th Army Brigade C.F.A. will pass under the orders of the C.R.A., 4th Canadian Division.

5. 8th Brigade C.F.A. will, on July 15th, take over the 2 anti-tank guns at B.8.a.30.40 and B.8.d.10.40. These 2 guns will pass under control of 4th C.D.A. at 6.0 am July 16th.
From July 13th onwards, the 4 remaining tank guns will be manned as under :-
   by Right Group - guns at O.1.b.10.70 and T.26.a.53.45.
   by Left Group   - guns at T.19.b.77.95 and T.19.c.75.15.
Arrangements for relief of detachments in accordance with the above will be made by Group Commanders concerned.

6. Groups will find liaison Officers with the Headquarters of each Battalion in the front line of the section they are covering.

7. Harassing fire boundaries from 6.0 am July 15th will be as under :-
   between 52nd Division and Division on our right will be :-
   line T.28.d.80.80 - U.19.c.00.00 - U.29.c.00.00 and thence due East.

   between Right Group and Left Group :-
   line T.10.c.00.75 to U.14 central.

   between 52nd Division and Division on left :-
   junction of BILLY BURKE and BETTY to N.35 central.

   between F.A. and H.A. :-
   N.35. central - U.14 central - U.21.c.00.00 - U.21.c.00.00.

8. Heavy Artillery S.O.S. lines, arrangements for counter-preparation and new dispositions of Trench Mortars will issue later.

9. ACKNOWLEDGE on attached slip.

                                                  [signature]
                                                  Captain R.A.
14th July 1918.   Brigade Major R.A., 52nd D.A.
For distribution please see overleaf.

Distribution.

```
Copy No.  1.   to  R.A. 8th Corps.
 "    "   2    "   20th D.A.
 "    "   3    "   4th Canadian D.A.
 "    "   4    "   H.A. 8th Corps.
 "    "   5    "   C.B.S.O. 8th Corps.
 "    "   6    "   2nd C.G.A.
 "    "  7/18  "   Right Group.
 "    " 19/26  "   Left Group.
 "    "  27    "   D.T.,M.O.
 "    "  28    "  242nd Bde RFA.
 "    "  29    "   52nd D.A.C.
 "    "  30    "   S.C.,R.A.
 "    "  31    "   R.O.,R.A.
 "    "  32    "   R.A. Signal Officer.
 "    "  33    "   D.A.,C.O.
 "    "  34    "  52nd Division 'G'.
 "    "  35    "   155th Inf. Bde.
 "    "  36    "   156th Inf. Bde.
 "    "  37    "   157th Inf. Bde.
 "    "  38    :   D.C.,R.A.
 "    " 39/40  "   War Diary.
 "    "  41    "   File.
```

MAP TO ACCOMPANY 62ND DIV. ARTY. ORDER Nº 24
REF. MAPS 1/20000 SHEETS 44 A.S.W. 57B.N.W.
OUTPOST BARRAGE — RED
BLACK " — BLACK

SECRET.　　　52ND DIVISIONAL ARTILLERY ORDER NO. 25.　　　COPY NO. 14

app.22

1. Headquarters and "A" and "B" of 242nd Army Brigade R.F.A. will be withdrawn from the line on the night of 16th/17th July; and on the morning of the 17th instant, will march to ESTREE CAUCHIE.

2. Route:- VILLERS AU BOIS - GRAND SERVINS.
   Time:- No restrictions.
   Billets from S.C., R.A. 8th Corps.

3. While at ESTREE CAUCHIE these Units will be at 4 hours notice to move back into present positions.

4. O.C., 242nd Brigade will arrange with his 2 Batteries remaining in the line to safeguard all positions, O.P's, and communications and Wagon Lines while they are out.

5. All labour lent to dig R.A. positions, not required for special work on Command Posts etc., will be concentrated on 242nd Brigade BROWN line and alternative positions. O.C., 242nd Brigade will detail an Officer to supervise this work and will leave complete instructions with him.
   He should get into touch with R.E. Officer in charge of attached labour.
   The Officer detailed by 242nd Brigade will render weekly work report on the Brigade's BROWN line and alternative positions direct to this office.

6. In view of this move, Headquarters 242nd Brigade will not move up to take over its Brigade as a Sub-Group and "A" and "B" Batteries will remain under their present Group till they move out but will cover the new S.O.S. line.
   "C" and "D" Batteries will temporarily come directly under Right Group.
   All arrangements will however be made so that on 242nd Brigade H. being ordered back into action, the Headquarters can go straight into their new positions and take over the whole of their Brigade as a Sub-Group under the Right Group.

7. All Defence Schemes, Maps etc., must be carefully kept so as to be immediately available.

8. Group Commanders will arrange to thicken barrage on the front covered by "A" and "B" Batteries 242nd Brigade, during their absence, by switching the fire of a portion of the superimposed guns on to them.

9. Groups and 242nd Brigade to ACKNOWLEDGE.

　　　　　　　　　　　　　　　　　　　　　　　　Captain R.A.
　　　　　　　　　　　　　　　　　　　　　　　　Brigade Major R.A.
14th July 1918.　　　　　　　　　　　　　　　　　52nd Divisional Artillery.

Distribution:-
No. 1 - R.A. 8th Corps.　　　No. 2 - Right Group.　　　No. 3 Left Group.
　　4 - D.T.M.O.　　　　　　5/10 - 242nd Bde.　　　　　11 52nd D.A.C.
　 12 S.C.R.A.　　　　　　　13 R.O.R.A.　　　　　　　　14 Sig. Officer.
　 15 - D.A.G.O.　　　　　　16 - 52nd Div:'G'.　　　　 17 52nd Div:'Q'.
　 18 - B.M.R.A.　　　　　　19/20 War Diary.　　　　　 21 File.
　 22 - 52nd Div: C.R.E.

SECRET.   52nd D.A. No. M/302.

                                                          appx 23   L.D

To all recipients of 52nd D.A. Defence Scheme.
Please substitute attached for first page of Appendix G.
This will come into effect from 6 am July 16th.

                                                          Captain R.A.

APPENDIX "G"

Heavy Artillery Counter Preparation and S.O.S. points.

TABLE 'A'. Counter preparation. TABLE 'B'. Bursts of fire.

Unit.	Outpost Barrage.	Black Barrage.	Normal Points.		Bursts of fire.
1st C.H.B.	T.18.c.15.50. T.24.a.15.75.	T.9.c.80.20. T.9.c.30.05.	T.12.c.55.50. — U.7.a.80.50.		U.14.b.00.25. — U.14.b.45.60.
	T.24.c.00.30. T.24.c.40.30.	T.15.c.35.90. T.15.a.43.70.	T.12.d.80.10. — U.7 central.		
			T.15.d.80.85. — U.15.b.80.20.		U.20.b.65.20. — U.20.b.90.65.
	T.24.c.17.90. T.30.c.50.90.	T.15.c.50.50. T.15.a.57.20.	U.25.d.25.15. — U.20.c.20.70.		
			T.6.c.40.50. — T.6.b.80.60.		T.6.d.20.30. — U.1.c.50.60.
			U.7.c.40.20. — U.8.c.20.50.		
2nd C.H.B.	T.17.b.15.85. T.17.b.40.60.	T.15.c.35.90. T.15.c.43.70.	T.5.a.40.15. — T.3.c.70.98.		U.8.a.75.75. — U.2.c.85.15.
			T.5.d.55.50. T.6.d.90.10.)one		U.8.a.75.75. — U.3.b.40.35.
	T.17.b.60.35. T.17.b.90.05.	T.15.c.50.50. T.15.c.57.20.	T.5.d.70.00. T.6.c.50.40.)Gun.		U.14.d.30.10. — U.15.c.90.55.
			T.12.d.45.30. U.6.d.75.50.		
	T.4.c.95.70. T.4.d.40.20.	T.15.c.64.15. T.15.c.70.00.	U.13.c.40.25. U.13.d.98.30.		U.8.c.20.65. — U.8.b.20.55.
			U.19.b.15.70. U.19.b.98.98.		
			U.19.d.65.85.		
2nd C.S.B.	T.4.c.80.00. T.11.c.00.80.	T.22.d.30.50. T.28.b.05.60.	T.11.b.65.40. T.11.b.80.98.		
			T.18.d.20.00. T.18.d.60.90.		
	T.18.c.50.00. T.29.b.60.50.	T.28.a.80.20. T.28.c.90.80.	T.18.c.90.25. T.18.d.50.75.		U.8.c.10.00. — U.8.c.30.00.
			T.24.b.35.85. T.18.c.75.15.		
	T.29.b.20.10. T.29.b.70.80.	T.15.d.central.T.15.d.85.20.	T.24.c.10.90. T.24.c.60.70.		
			T.29.b.70.50. T.29.b.20.20.		
5th C.S.B.	T.11.c.60.10.	T.15.b.00.70.	T.18.d.70.60. T.18.d.90.00.		U.14.c.95.70. — U.14.d.25.00.
	T.18.a.70.50.	T.18.c.60.10.	T.24.d.40.15. T.30.b.75.00.		U.8.a.10.00. — U.8.a.30.70.
	T.23.d.80.50.	T.28.b.90.55.	T.13.c.30.40.		
	T.4.d.80.70.	T.13.c.40.30.	T.18.c.85.80.		
6th C.S.B.	T.4.c.50.20. T.10.b.50.50.	T.18.c.15.15. T.22.d.60.80.	T.11.b.40.35. T.11.b.80.10.		T.5.c.60.50.
			T.12.c.20.00. T.12.c.75.30.		T.6.b.10.30.
	T.18.c.80.70. T.29.c.78.00.	T.15.d.70.59. T.15.d.95.40.	T.24.b.65.10. T.12.c.00.40.		T.6.c.95.20.
			T.12.c.25.00. T.12.c.80.70.		U.7.b.98.78.
	T.23.b.85.40. T.11.c.90.40.	T.22.b.10.10. T.22.d.30.35.	T.25.d.60.30. T.11.c.60.70.		U.14.d.10.85.
			T.11.c.20.85.		U.20.
8th C.S.B.	T.4.d.30.00. T.18.c.90.30.	T.15.d.45.80. T.23.b.50.68.	T.12.c.05.30. T.12.c.50.50.		U.14.d.25.00. — U.20.b.65.20.
			T.18.c.60.98. T.18.b.20.00.		
	T.29.d.90.90. T.29.d.50.60.	T.28.b.55.80. T.28.d.86.75.	T.24.b.85.20. T.24.d.05.50.		U.14.c.55.98. — U.14.b.00.25.
	T.11.d.98.50. T.12.c.30.05.	T.22.d.98.20. T.22.d.70.80.	T.24.d.05.50. T.30.c.65.65.		
253rd S.B.			T.19.c.05.80.		U.21.c.60.00. — U.21.c.10.98.

Reinforcing Artillery.

DAILY REPORT 52ND DIVISIONAL ARTILLERY.
8am 14th to 8am 15th July 1918.

1. OUR ACTIVITY.
    (a) Operations. At 3.0pm and again at 8.35pm a bombardment of
        living trench C.1.b.54.60 - C.1.b.53.85 and of Road,
        track and light railway junction C.1.b.55.55 was carried
        out in conjuction with 2nd Bde. C.G.A.
            Movement t U.20.c.9.7 and at C.4.a.9.0 was engaged
        by 18-pdrs. and M.G. at B.5.b.80.14 was fired on.
            At 8.30 p. 6" T.M. fired on trench junction
        T.30.c.3.7 and on OAK ALLEY.
            Harassing fire was directed at night on enemy roads,
        tracks and centres of activity.
            Total rounds fired:-
        18-pdrs. 950.   4.5" Hows. 340.   6" T.M. 20.

    (b) Aerial. Active during the day and from 8pm to 11pm

2. HOSTILE ACTIVITY.
    (a) Artillery. Very quiet throughout the day. During the
        night 10.5cm Hows. fired 150 rounds on the area N. of
        VIMY. 15cm Hows. were inactive.

Date.	Time.	No. of rds.	Calibre.	Area shelled.	Direction.
14th.	9am.	12	10.5cm.	T.26.d.	
	11pm.	2	10cm gun.	Back areas.	BOIS BERNARD.
	1am.	5	15cm.	T.8.a.	
	1am-3.30am.	100	10.5cm.	T.19.a.	
	2am.	12	77mm.	T.26.a.	U.26 & 4.5.
	4am-4.30am.	50.	10.5cm.	T.19.b.	

    (b) Work. Nil.

    (c) Movement. Continual movement was observed in U.7.c & d and
        U.13.a. & b. The men wore no equipment   appeared to
        be ration parties and mostly went along ROUVROY ROAD to
        ACONITE and along PORTAGE ROAD to ABUSE trench.
            Movement at U.20.c.9.7 and C.4.a.9.0 was engaged by
        18-pdrs.
            Movement was also observed during the afternoon at
        C.7.b.5.5 and on track U.20.c.7.9.

    (d) Aerial. 2 E.A. over our lines at 7am were driven back by
        A.A. One E.A. was over our lines from 10am to noon
        being driven back several times by A.A.
            Six balloons were up about midday.
            One E.A. was over our lines at 5am on 15th.

3. GENERAL.
        Visibility during the morning was good, becoming poor during
        the evening owing to rain and mist.

                                        A. F. Buxton
                                        Lieut: R.A.
15th July 1918.   Reconnaissance Officer, 52nd Div: Arty.

Appx 25

52nd D.A. No. R/306.

To all recipients of 52nd Divisional Artillery Order No.24.

Para. 4. For "6am" read "9am".

Para. 7. For "U.29.c.00.00" read "U.21.c.00.00", and delete "due East".

                                          Captain R.A.
                                      Brigade Major R.A.

15th July 1918.   52nd Divisional Artillery.

SECRET. Appx 26 War Diary

52nd D.A. No. M/309.

All recipients of 52nd Divisional Artillery Defence Scheme.

1. Herewith new pages 3 and 4 and new Map '5' which please substitute for originals.

2. Amendment.

In Section (h) sub-section 2 (b) - for "6 15-pounder B.L.C." read "4 15-pounder B.L.C."

15th July 1918.

Captain R.A.
Brigade Major R.A.
52nd Divisional Artillery.

MAP B

REF. MAP 1/20.000
44 A SW SQUARE T

(b) **Harassing fire boundaries etc.**
Boundaries for harassing fire are as follows:-
(i) Between Field Artillery and Heavy Artillery, U.21.d.00.00 U.21.a.00.00 - U.14 central - N.35 central.
(ii) Between Divisional Artillery on our right and Right Group. T.23.d.80.80 - U.19.c.00.00 - U.21.c.00.00.
(iii) Between Right and Left Group. T.10.c.00.75 - U.14 central.
(iv) Between Divisional Artillery on our Left & Left Group. Junction of BILLIE BURKE and BETTY trenches to N.35 central.

The normal allotment of ammunition per Group for night firing is:-
18-pdr. 375 rounds, 4.5" How. 150 rounds.

During the day (5am - 8.30pm) the C.B.S.O. has a call upon the two forward Howitzers except under the following conditions:-
(1) During Counter Preparation.
(2) In the event of an S.O.S.

In addition forward guns are also prepared to engage active batteries within range with neutralising fire.

Harassing fire by night on enemy batteries engaged for destruction during the day is also carried out, when asked for by C.B.S.O.

(c) **Counter Preparation.**
(i) Counter preparation is the Artillery action to be taken during an intense hostile bombardment which is evidently the prelude to an attack.

Its object will include the destruction of the enemys trench system, from which the attack will be launched, including M.G's and T.M's and the killing of his troops whilst assembling

On the Divisional front, owing to the lie of the VIMY RIDGE and the consequent siting of the Batteries, the role of Field Artillery during counter preparation is mainly restricted to preventing the enemy sending out patrols and M.G. parties to establish themselves well forward in NO MANS LAND.

(ii) Field Artillery Counter preparation will consist of
(a) Frequent rolling barrages by 18-pounders backwards and forwards over the zones allotted to Groups.
(b) 4.5" Howitzers searching communication trenches, and destroying trench junctions, Machine Gun and Trench Mortar emplacements and likely assembling places, on their Group front.

For this purpose lifts for 18-pounders will be parallel to the Red line lettered 'A' on Map 'B', each successive lift is lettered B, C, D, E, F, G and H.

The Divisional front is divided into nine sections each allotted to an 18-pounder Battery, as shown in Map 'B'. These sections are sub-divided into lanes.

(iii) When counter preparation is ordered each 18-pounder Battery will open fire on any one of the lanes in its own section, and after covering it once, will switch to another lane.

The above will be carried out in bursts of fire at irregular intervals so timed that the whole of the lanes are covered at least once in the period, or periods, for which counter preparation has been ordered, the principle that the barrage searches backwards as well as forwards being adhered to.

The barrage lines on which the guns will open will be decided by the Group Commander.

In the Left Group forward 18-pounders will not join in the barrage but will search communication trenches and trench junctions.

18-pounders without air recuperators will not fire at ranges over 7,000 yards.

(iv) The number and intensity of bursts cannot be laid down previously, these depend on the duration of the enemy bombardment, having regard to the necessity for keeping the detachments as fresh as possible for the S.O.S. barrage to be fired at the time of the assault, and for the subsequent battle.

The necessity for keeping in hand sufficient ammunition to deal with the successive assaults has also to be considered.

Where possible the amount of ammunition to be fired during Counter Preparation will be controlled by C.R.A. Should communication be cut however, Brigade and Battery Commanders must use their own discretion in this matter.

At no time during Counter Preparation will ammunition at guns be allowed to fall below 400 rounds per 18-pounder and 300 rounds per 4.5" Howitzer.

All 18-pounders firing under 5,500 yards will fire shrapnel only and those above, H.E. only, as far as possible.

The proportion of ammunition on hand with Batteries will be reallotted within Groups to meet the above requirements.

(v) Counter preparation will be ordered from D.A., H.Q. If communications are cut Brigade Commanders must act upon their own initiative.

It will be ordered in the following code:-

The word "COUNTER" wired from this office will be the signal that counter preparation is to be carried out.

12 noon will be zero hour. The hour for opening fire will be so many hours plus or minus. The date will be given.

Example:- "Counter 12th minus 6½ hours" - denotes that counter preparation will be fired on the 12th instant commencing 5.30 am.

Where it is considered advisable, duration of fire will also be ordered from this office.

(d) S.O.S.

There are two procedures in answering the S.O.S. signal or message:-

(1) (a) In normal times.
The outpost barrage will be fired as follows:-
5 minutes INTENSE.
5 minutes RAPID.
5 minutes NORMAL.

after which fire will depend upon the situation, to ascertain which, the Artillery Commanders must make the most strenuous efforts.

(b) After the order "MAN BATTLE STATIONS" has been issued.
The outpost barrage will be fired as follows:-
10 minutes INTENSE.
10 minutes RAPID, during which, barrage will roll forward 500 yards at the rate of 100 yards per 2 minutes and then jump back to original line for 2 minutes INTENSE followed by 8 minutes normal. After this fire will be controlled according to the situation. On the barrage coming back to the BLACK line, a similar 30 minutes burst will be fired.

The BLACK barrage will not be fired till a definite S.O.S. call from the BLACK line is received. On this call being received, the BLACK barrage will be fired on the whole Divisional front.

Pending the introduction of a distinctive signal, this will be a message "S.O.S. BLACK".

Group Commanders must consequently inform each other immediately this call is received.

In order to ensure continuity of fire along the whole front, the following procedure will be adopted until it is known that the fire of the Flank Divisions has also been brought back.

Two of the guns superimposed on the Right and Left flanks will be used to connect the right and left points of the BLACK barrage with the right and left points of the outpose barrage.

(2) The barrage will not be brought back from the Black line to the BROWN line except by order of the Divisional Commander and will then come back along the whole Divisional front. This does not refer to the fire of superimposed 18-pounders.

appx 27. WD

DAILY REPORT 52ND DIVISIONAL ARTILLERY.
6 am 15 to 6 am 16th July 1918.

1. **OUR ACTIVITY.**
   (a) *Operations.* During the afternoon 4.5" Hows. fired on road track and light railway junction C.1.b.55.55, on ULSTER trench, and on junction of NOVA SCOTIA trench and ALBERT Road in T.24.d.
   At 7 pm. and again at 7.50 pm. a short bombardment of Headquarters C.1.c.55.80 - C.1.a.45.00 was carried out by 2nd Brigade C.G.A., field guns engaging the tracks leading into the Headquarters at the same time.
   Harassing fire was carried out at night and at 10 pm, 11 pm, and 12.20 am. bursts of fire were directed on suspected M.G's at T.29.d.20.99.
   6" T.M. fired at 7 am. on trench junction T.18.c.9.2 and at 9 pm on ARLEUX LOOP NORTH in T.29.d.
   Total rounds fired:-
   18-pdr. 1150.   4.5" HOW. 400.   6" T.M. 23.
   (b) *Aerial.* Normal activity.

2. **HOSTILE ACTIVITY.**
   (a) *Artillery.* More active than during previous 24 hours. 15cm Hows. fired 100 rounds on trenches of left Brigade and 100 rounds on THELUS in the morning. FARBUS WOOD was shelled by 10.5cm. and 15cm. Hows. and VIMY by 10.5cm.Hows.
   During the night the enemy fired gas shell in the VIMY area and near LA FOLIE FARM. The nature of this is being investigated.

Date.	Time.	No.of rds.	Calibre.	Area shelled.	Direction.
15th	9am-noon.	50	10.5cm.	FARBUS WOOD (B8c)	82°30' G from B.8.c.30.08. F/R 20 secs.
	-do-	28	15cm.	-do-	
	9-11.15am.	100	15cm.	TEDDIE GERRARD. VESTA TILLEY. (T.9,15 & 16).	
	10.30-11am.	20	10.5cm.	VIMY (T.19.c.)	
	8.45-9.15am.	25)			
	10.30-11am.	15)	15cm.	THELUS. A.12.	C.A.20.
	12-12.10pm.	30)			
	2.15-2.45pm.	50)			
	2.15pm.	28	10.5cm.	FARBUS WOOD (B8c) and B.7.c.	82°30' G from B.8.c.30.08. F/R 20 secs.
	11-1145pm.	50	10.5cm.	VIMY (T.19.c.)	
16th	11-11.25pm.	30	Gas shell.	S.29.a.55.50.	Nature not reported
	3.37-5.47am.	about 400	Gas shell.	T.25.b.0.5 T.19.d.55.50.	-do-
	4-4.30am.	50	10.5cm.	T.19.a.	

   (b) *Work.* None reported.

   (c) *Movement.* Continual movement in T.12.d., U.7, and U.8.c., small parties went along PORTAGE ROAD and large parties along RUPERT road into BERNARD trench.
   Movement was also seen at T.6.c.1.7, at T.6.d.8.4 where 2 men were climbing telegraph poles and at BOIS VILAIN.
   At 11.15am. and at 12.5pm. a man parachuted from observation balloon in U.28.a.

   (d) *Aerial.* During the night enemy bombing planes were over our lines. Some bombs were dropped near PETIT VIMY.

3. GENERAL. Visibility fair improving towards evening, bad on early morning of 16th.

16th July 1918.

Lieut: R.A.
Reconnaissance Officer, 52nd Div: Arty.

app. 28

WD

DAILY REPORT, 52ND DIVISIONAL ARTILLERY.
6am 16th to 6 am 17th July 1918.
****

1. OWN ACTIVITY.
   (a) Operations. During the day 4.5" Howitzers fired on Cross
       Roads U.15.a.40.05 with Balloon observation and on M.G.
       emplacements in T.11.b., and T.18.d.
           Movement in LONDON COPSE (U.1.b.) was fired on at
       6.0pm.
           6" Hows. fired on new work, apparently an O.P., at
       U.20.a.35.00 with satisfactory results.
           Harassing fire at night was directed on Roads,
       Tracks, Centres of activity, on hostile battery U.W.94
       and on suspected M.G. emplacements.
           At 10.54 pm. a Test S.O.S. was received and responded
       to by Right Group.
           Total rounds fired:-
           18-pr. 1540.   4.5" Hows. 475.   6" T.M. Nil.
   (b) ACTION. Active throughout the day, from 9pm to 11pm and
       from 3am to 5am.

2. HOSTILE ACTIVITY.
   (a) Artillery. Quiet during the day except for Area shoots
       at 9.38.   10.5cm Hows. fired 130 rounds into
       VIMY at night.

Date.	Time.	No.of rds.	Calibre.	Area shelled.	Direction.	Remarks.
16th.	9am.	40	10.5cm.	S.28.b.6.3.		Area shoot.
	10-10.30am.	6	7.7cm.	RAILWAY in T.13.		
	12.50pm.	20	7.7cm.	B.1.d.	BOIS BERNARD.	
	1-3pm.	50	15cm.	S.28.		Area shoot.
	12midnight.	130	10.5cm.	VIMY.		Includes 30 gas.

   (b) Work. Some new work near CHEZ BONTEMPS about U.20.a.65.00
       was successfully fired on by 6" Hows.

   (c) Movement. During morning movement was observed in U.20.d.
       and at U.20.c.9.3. Movement was fired on in LONDON COPSE
       at 6pm. Individuals were seen in MERICOURT during the day.

   (d) Aerial. An E.A. attempted to cross the lines at 2.30pm but
       was driven back by A.A.
           6 balloons were up during the day.

3. GENERAL. At 11.10am. a smoke screen was created behind ROUVROY.
       Visibility good, poor on early morning of 17th.

                                              Lieut: R.A.
                               Reconnaissance Officer 52nd Div: Arty.

appx 29.

DAILY REPORT, 52ND DIVISIONAL ARTILLERY.
6 am 17th to 6 am 18th July 1918.

OUR ACTIVITY.
  (a) <u>Operations</u>.   During the day 4.5" Hows engaged movement at
      N.35.c.75.70 and some instructional series were fired.
          Harassing fire was directed on enemy roads,
    tracks and centres of activity.
        Total rounds fired -
      18-pr. 1050   4.5" Hows. 470   6" M. Nil.

  (b) <u>Aerial</u>.   Our machines were active all day.

2. HOSTILE ACTIVITY.
  (a) <u>Artillery</u>. Quiet. At 10 am 50 rounds of 77 mm were fired
    on trenches in T.16.c & d and during the night 10.5 cm.
    Hows fired 200 rounds near the embankment in T.13.d.

Date.	Time.	No. of rds.	Calibre.	Direction.
17th.	9.45 am.	40.	10.5 cm.	VIMY.
	10.0 am.	50.	77 mm.	Trenches T.16.c. & d.
	11.0 am.	30.	?	T.20.
	10.0 pm.	10.	77 mm.	VIMY.
	12 midnight.	200.	10.5 cm.	T.13.d.
18th.	to 5 am.			

  (b) <u>Work</u>.   None reported.

  (c) <u>Movement</u>. 4.5" Hows. engaged movement at N.35.c.75.70.

  (d) <u>Aerial</u>.   7 E.A. were over our lines during the
    morning and some machines were over during the night.
      5 balloons were up during the day.

3. <u>GENERAL</u>. Visibility fair improving towards evening.

                                            Lieut. RA.
                            Reconnaissance Officer, 52nd DA.

18th July 1918.

App. 30   WO

52nd D.A. No. M/321.

To all recipients of 52nd Divisional Artillery Defence Scheme.

Herewith Appendices 'A', 'C' and 'G' which please substitute for those already issued.

N Beresford Peirse
Major R.F.A.
for Brigade Major R.A.
52nd Divisional Artillery.

17th July 1918.

APPENDIX 'A'.
DISPOSITION STATEMENT.
Reference 1/40,000 map. Sheets 44-a & b, 51- b & c.

Unit.			Position.	Wagon Lines.
52nd D.A.		H.Q.	W.30.a.4.6.	
D.T.M.O.)				
D.A.,G.O.)			A.2.d.3.5.	

RIGHT GROUP.

Unit.			Position.	Wagon Lines.
9th Bde RFA.		H.Q.	A.6.c.6.7.	F.9.b.
19th Bty RFA.	5	18-prs.	B.13.c.33.86.	F.9.a.
	1		T.26.c.60.60	
20th Bty RFA.	5		B.13.a.14.76.	F.12.a.5.1.
	1		T.26.c.13.98.	
28th Bty RFA.	5		B.7.c.29.20.	F.5 central.
	1		T.25.b.63.62.	
D/69 Bty RFA.	5	Hows.	A.10.d.96.77.	F.9.b.
	1		B.3.c.05.85.	
242nd Army Bde RFA*		H.Q.	S.27.c.50.40.	F.6.c.0.3.
A/242 Bty.RFA*	3	18-prs.	A.6.c.25.85.	X.28.d.
B/242 Bty.RFA*	3		S.29.c.84.27.	F.5.b.5.0.
C/242 Bty RFA.	3		A.3.c.80.85.	X.28.b.8.1.
D/242 Bty RFA.	3	Hows.	S.22.d.25.85.	S.25.d.1.8.
Anti-tank.	1	18-pr.	B.1.b.1.7.	
	1		T.26.a.58.15.	

* Withdrawn to ESTREE CAUCHIE for training.

LEFT GROUP.

Unit.			Position.	Wagon Lines.
56th Bde RFA.		H.Q.	S.27.b.00.60.	S.26.c.1.8.
A/56 Bty RFA	5	18-prs.	S.29.c.57.85.	F.12.a & c.
	1		T.15.c.24.75.	
B/56 Bty RFA.	5		S.22.c.86.14.	S.25.b.2.0.
	1		T.15.c.20.75.	
C/56 Bty RFA.	5		S.26.b.60.25.	F.12.a. & c.
	1		S.29.c.84.87.	
527 Bty RFA.c	5	Hows.	S.28.b.50.95.	A.2.a.0.1.
	1		T.19.a.55.80.	
Anti-tank.	1	18-pr.	T.19.b.77.75.	
	1		T.19.c.75.95.	

Unit		Position.	
242nd B.A.C.		A.2.c.5.2.	
52nd D.A.C.		F.8.b.5.5.	
S.A.A.Section.		F.9.c.9.8.	

Ammunition refilling points.

		Position.
La Targette Dump.		A.8.a.3.7.
Brandon Dump.		F.10.c.0.5.

TRENCH MORTARS.

Unit.			Position.
D.T.M.O.		H.Q.	A.3.d.5.5.
X/52 Bty.		H.Q.	B.1.d.10.95
	1 gun		B.2.a.85.55.
	1		T.26.d.45.15.
	1		T.27.c.00.35.
	1		T.20.c.20.15.
	1		T.20.c.20.30.
	1		T.22.c.78.35.
Y/52 Bty.		H.Q.	T.19.a.70.50.
	2 guns		T.19.c.70.50.
	1 gun		T.13.b.45.50.
	1		T.13.b.60.70
	1		T.7.d.75.00.
	1		T.22.a.75.75.

APPENDIX 'C'.

MUTUAL SUPPORT.

Sector.	Call sent or Received.	Assisting Artillery.	Number and nature of guns.	Tasks.
Division on our Left.	HELP AVION.	Left Group.	10 - 18-Pounders.	T.4.a.55.65 - N.33.d.45.55.
Left Infantry Bde. 52nd Div:	HELP MERICOURT.	Divisional Artillery on our Left.	8 - 18-Pounders. 2 - 4.5" Howitzers.	T.3.d.80.58 - T.4.a.00.00. T.4.d.00.90 - T.4.a.30.60.
Right Infantry Bde. 52nd Div:	HELP ACHEVILLE.	Divisional Artillery on our Right.	12 - 18-Pounders. 3 - 4.5" Howitzers.	T.29.c.00.30 - T.29.a.20.00. T.29.c.20.25 - T.29.c.45.60. T.29.c.40.90.
Division on our Right.	HELP WILLERVAL.	Right Group.	6 - 18-Pounders.	T.29.b.00.60 - B.4.b.52.53. B.4.b.52.53 - B.4.b.61.19.

The above assistance only to be given if the tactical situation permits.

APPENDIX "G".

Heavy Artillery Counter Preparation and S.O.S. points.

Unit.	Outpost Barrage.	Black Barrage.	TABLE 'A'. Normal points. Counter preparation.	TABLE 'B'. Bursts of fire.
1st C.H.B.	T.18.c.15.30.	T.9.c.20.20. T.9.c.30.05.	T.12.c.55.60 - U.7.a.80.60.	U.14.b.00.25. - U.14.b.45.60.
2nd C.H.B.	T.24.c.00.60.	T.24.c.40.30. T.15.a.35.90. T.15.a.43.70.	T.12.c.80.10 - U.7 central. T.18.d.80.85 - U.13.b.80.80. U.25.a.25.15 - U.20.c.20.70.	U.20.b.65.20 - U.20.b.90.55.
2nd C.S.B.	T.24.a.17.90.	T.30.a.50.90. T.15.a.50.50. T.15.a.57.20.	T.6.c.40.50 - T.6.b.80.60. U.7.c.40.20 - U.8.c.20.50.	T.6.d.20.60 - U.1.a.50.60.
3rd C.S.B.	T.17.b.15.85. T.17.b.60.35. T.4.c.95.70.	T.17.b.40.60. T.22.a.70.60. T.22.a.95.40. T.17.b.90.05. T.22.a.75.55. T.22.a.85.50. T.4.d.40.20. T.15.a.64.18. T.15.e.70.00.	T.5.a.40.15 - T.6.a.70.98. T.5.d.55.50 - T.6.d.90.10)One T.5.d.70.00 - T.6.c.50.40)Gun. T.12.a.45.30 - T.6.d.75.30. U.13.c.40.25 - U.13.d.98.30. U.19.c.15.70 - U.19.b.98.98. U.25.a.20.70 - U.19.d.65.85.	U.8.a.75.75 - U.2.c.85.15. U.8.a.75.75 - U.8.b.40.65. U.14.d.30.10 - U.15.a.90.55. U.8.c.20.65 - U.8.b.20.55.
4th C.S.B.	T.4.a.80.00. T.18.c.50.00. T.29.b.20.10.	T.11.c.00.80. T.22.d.30.30. T.28.b.05.60. T.29.b.60.50. T.28.a.80.20. T.28.c.90.80. T.15.d.50.50. T.15.d.85.20.	T.11.a.98.40 - T.11.b.60.98. T.18.b.20.00 - T.18.d.30.90. T.18.c.90.25 - T.18.d.50.75. T.24.b.35.85 - T.18.c.75.15. T.24.a.10.90 - T.24.c.60.70. T.29.b.70.50 - T.29.b.90.20.	U.8.a.10.00 - U.8.c.30.00.
5th C.S.B.	T.25.b.85.40. T.11.a.60.10. T.18.a.70.30. T.11.d.98.50. T.4.d.80.70.	T.15.b.00.70. T.16.c.60.10. T.28.b.90.55. T.16.c.40.50. T.16.c.85.80.	T.18.d.70.60. T.24.d.40.15. T.12.a.30.40. T.18.c.85.80.	U.14.c.95.70 - U.14.d.25.00. U.8.a.10.00 - U.8.a.30.70.
	T.11.c.20.40.	T.29.b.70.80. T.22.a.60.80.	T.11.b.40.35 - T.11.b.80.10. T.12.c.20.00 - T.12.c.75.30.	T.5.a.00.50. T.5.b.10.60.
	T.4.a.50.20.	T.10.b.50.50. T.22.a.95.40.	T.24.b.65.10 - T.12.c.00.40.	T.6.a.95.20. U.7.b.98.78.
	T.18.c.80.70.	T.29.c.78.00. T.22.b.10.10. T.22.d.30.35.	T.12.c.25.00 - T.12.c.00.40. T.23.d.80.30 - T.23.d.80.70. T.11.a.30.85 - T.11.a.60.50.	U.14.d.10.85 - U.14.d.25.00. U.20.b.65.20 - U.21.c.10.98.
	T.25.d.80.30.	T.12.c.30.05. T.15.d.45.80. T.22.b.50.68.	T.12.c.05.50 - T.12.c.50.30. T.18.a.50.98 - T.18.b.20.00.	U.14.d.25.00 - U.20.b.65.20.
	T.4.d.60.00.	T.18.c.90.30. T.28.b.35.80. T.28.d.86.75.	T.24.b.95.85 - T.24.d.05.50. T.24.b.25.20 - T.24.d.05.50.	U.14.a.35.98 - U.14.b.00.25.
225th SB.	T.29.d.98.50.	T.12.c.30.05. T.22.d.98.20. T.22.d.70.80.	T.30.a.65.50 - T.30.e.65.65. U.19.c.05.80 -	U.21.c.60.00 - U.21.c.10.98.

Reinforcing Artillery.

DAILY REPORT, 52ND DIVISIONAL ARTILLERY.
6 am 18th to 6 am 19th July 1918.

OUR ACTIVITY.

(a) <u>Operations</u>.   At 9 am 4.5" Hows fired 30 rounds on M.G. and T.M. emplacements at T.13.d.20.70.

Harassing fire at night was directed on centres of activity.

Total rounds fired
18- pr.   1050   4.5" Hows   385.   6" T.M. Nil.

(b) <u>Aerial</u>.   Our aeroplanes were active day and night.

2 HOSTILE ACTIVITY.

(a) <u>Artillery</u>.   More active than previous 24 hours.

During the morning 15 cm Hows fired 50 rounds on T.26.a. where the Railway Embankment crosses the NEW BRUNSWICK Road.

During the afternoon 15 cm Hows fired 120 rds. on T.13.c. and T.19.d., the forward gun of A/56 being neutralised. No damage was done to the gun.

At night 15 cm Hows fired 200 rounds on T.25.d.

Date	Time	No. of rds.	Calibre.	Area shelled.
18th	9.30 - 11am	23.	77 mm	T.13.d.
	10.5 - Noon.	50.	15 cm	T.26.a.3.9.
	10.30 - Noon.	55.	10.5cm	T.25.a.
	5.0 - 6 pm.	120.	15 cm	T.19.d.,T.13.c.
	4.0 pm	20.	10.5cm	S.18.c.
	11.45 - 2.15am	200.	15 cm	T.25.d.
	12.50 - 1.20a.	24.	10.5 cm	E.13.c.

(b) <u>Work</u>.   Nil.

(c) <u>Movement</u>.   At 5.30 pm parties of men on road O.32.c. to U.1.b and a.

(d) <u>Aerial</u>.   E.A. were inactive during the day but at 8 pm 5 machines crossed our lines and were driven back by A.A. and M.G.

From 10 pm to 2 am. E.A. were over our lines and bombs were dropped.

3. <u>GENERAL</u>.   Visibility good, fair on morning of 19th.

A.F. Dufton
Lieut: R.A.
Reconnaissance Officer, 52nd Div:Arty.

19th July 1918.

52nd D.A.No.R/344.

VERY SECRET.

9th Brigade R.F.A.,   242nd Army Bde R.F.A.
56th Brigade R.F.A.
52nd Div'l Ammunition Column.
52nd D.T.M.O.

WARNING ORDER.

      52nd Division will be relieved in VIII Corps by 8th Division
      On relief, 52nd Division will be transferred to XVII Corps in G.H.Q. reserve, and located in areas adjoining First and Fifth Armies.
      Infantry Relief will probably commence night 19th/20th July.
      Orders re relief of Divisional Artillery will be issued later.

                                              Major R.F.A.
                               a/ Brigade Major R.A., 52nd D.A.

19th July 1918.

SECRET.

242nd Brigade.

1. The 52nd D.A. will be relieved in action by the 8th D.A. on nights of 20th/21st and 21st/22nd July.

2. The 242nd Brigade R.F.A. will pass under 8th D.A. on completion of relief.

Major R.F.A.
A/Brigade Major, R.A.
52nd Divisional Artillery.

20th July 1918.

SECRET.   52ND DIVISIONAL ARTILLERY ORDER NO.25.   COPY NO. 27

appx 35

1. 52nd Divisional Artillery will be relieved by 8th Divisional Artillery in action on nights of July 20th/21st and 21st/22nd.

2. On 20th 3 guns per battery - detachments for 1 Section per battery and Battery Staffs 8th D.A. will march to Wagon lines in 52nd D.A. Area.
   Guides will be provided by Units of 52nd D.A. as shewn in attached Table 'A' (1).
   On 21st remainder of 8th D.A. will march to Wagon lines. Guides to be provided by 52nd D.A. Units as shewn in attached Table 'A'(11).

3. Reliefs will be carried out as shewn in attached Table 'B' Field Artillery Units retaining their own equipments.

4. Two guns per Battery will be relieved on night 20th/21st, one of those guns will be a forward gun, in cases where batteries have forward gun. Teams to be provided by 52nd D.A. Units.
   The remaining guns will be relieved on night 21st/22nd, teams being provided by 8th D.A. Units.
   Details of wagons for kits to be settled between Units concerned.

5. On 20th advanced parties - 52nd D.A. - will proceed by Lorry to take over Camps of their relieving Units as shewn in attached Table 'C'.
   On morning 22nd 52nd D.A. will march to 17th Corps Area. March orders will be issued later.

6. During the relief wagon line accommodation must be shared with incoming Units as necessary.

7. D.T.M.O., 52nd D.A., will hand over stripped guns and beds in situ.

8. Relief of Dumps will be completed by 12 noon 21st inst.
   Relief of Trench Mortar personnel will be completed by 4pm 21st instant.
   D.A.C.O. will join D.A.C. Headquarters on 21st.

9. During reliefs no horses will approach Battery positions during daylight.

10. Reliefs will be notified to this Office on completion by F.A. Brigades, D.A.C. and D.T.M.O., by use of code word FINIS.

11. Commands will pass on completion of reliefs.

12. Brigades, D.A.C., D.T.M.O. D.A.C.O. to acknowledge.

                                                    Major R.A.
20th July 1918.   A/Brigade Major, 52nd D.A.

Distribution.
1/5 5th Brigade.   6/10 to 56th Brigade.   11/13 to D.A.C.
14/16 D.T.M.O.   17 to   13th RGA.   16 to D.A.C.O.
  19 to 52nd Div:G.   20 52nd Div:Q.   21
  22 to 242nd Bde.   23 to R.A. 8th Corps.
  25 to R.O., R.A.   26   27/28 to War Diary.
  29 File.   30 Retain.

T A B L E 'A' - Reliefs.

9th Brigade (19th, 20th, 23rd, D/69 Batteries) will be relieved by 33rd Bde. (32nd, 33rd, 36th 55th Batteries) respectively

53rd Bde. (A/53, B/53, C/53, 527 Btys.) will be relieved by 45th Bde. (1st, 3rd, 5th, 57th Btys) respectively.

52nd D.A.C. will be relieved by 8th D.A.C.

Trench Mortar personnel 52nd D.A. will be relieved by T.M. Personnel, 8th D.A.

R.A. Train wagons 52nd Div: will be relieved by No. 1 Transport Coy. 8th Div: Train.

T A B L E 'B' - Advanced parties 52nd D.A. July 20th.

9th Bde. relieving 33rd Bde. H.Q. located at Billet No.7 HERMIN (1 Lorry at TARGETTE Cross Roads 12 noon July 20th.
19th Battery. relieving 32nd Bty. located at TARBARLE. (9th Bde. parties will be met by guides at GAUCHIN
20th Battery. relieving 33rd Bty. located at GAUCHIN LEGAL. LEGAL at 2pm.
23th Battery. relieving 36th Fty. located at HERMIN.
D/69th Bty. relieving 55th Battery located at HERMIN.
52nd D.A.C. relieving 8th D.A.C. located at OURTON. D.A.C. will be met by guide at OUREC Church at 3.30 pm.

_____

55th Brigade & Batteries relieving 45th Bde. & Batteries located at N.E. end of BOIS DE HAZECIS.(One lorry at CAMPBELL
(Road corner S.25.a.0.1)
at 12 noon.
guides meet 52nd Bde. parties at
HOUDAIN Level Crossing 3pm).
T.M. Personnel, 52nd D.A. relieving T.M. personnel 8th D.A. located at OURTON
Guides meet T.M. personnel at OURTON
Church at 3.30 pm.

TABLE 'A' (1).

Guides to meet advance parties of 8th D.A. July 20th.

Unit.	Guide from.	Time.	Place of meeting.	Destination.
33rd Bde. HQ.	9th Bde. HQ.			9th Bde. HQ. lines at A.8.c.5.5.
52nd Bty.	19th Bty.		) Cross Roads at	Empty wagon lines at F.12.a.8.4.
53rd Bty.	20th Bty.	11.30am.	) MONT ST. ELOI.	20th Bty. wagon lines at F.12.a.7.2.
56th Bty.	28th Bty.		)	28th Bty. Wagon lines at F.5 central.
55th Bty.	D/69 Bty.		) F.15.a.0.6.	Empty wagon line at A.7.b.2.6.
45th Bde. HQ.	56th Bde. HQ.		)	56th HQ. wagon line at S.26.c.5.8.
1st Bty.	A/56 Bty.		)	A/56 Bty. ,, ,, T.12.a.5.0.
3rd Bty.	B/56 Bty.	12 noon.	) F.15.a.0.6.	B/56th Bty. ,, ,, S.25.b.7.0.
5th Bty.	C/56 Bty.		)	C/56 Bty. ,, ,, S.25.d.8.8.
57th Bty.	D/56 Bty.		)	527th Bty. ,, ,, A.2.a.0.2.
8th D.A.C.	52nd D.A.C.	12.30pm.	F.15.a.0.6.	D.A.C. lines F.9.b.8.8. and F.9.a.7.9.
Trench Mortars.	D.T.M.O.	12 noon.	TARGETTE DUMP	T.M., H.Q. A.2.d.3.5.
No.1 Coy.	56th Bde.HQ.	1.0pm.	TARGETTE X Roads.	52nd Div: Train lines H.Q. section.

TABLE 'A' (11).

Guides to meet main bodies of 8th D.A. on July 21st.

Unit.	Guides from.	Time.	Place of Meeting.	Destination.
33rd Bde. HQ.	9th Bde. HQ.		)	
52nd Bty.	19th Bty.		)	
53rd Bty.	20th Bty.	11.30am.	) F.15.a.0.6.	As for advance parties in Table 'A' (1),
56th Bty.	28th Bty.		)	
55th Bty.	D/69 Bty.		)	
45th Bde.HQ.	56th Bde. HQ.		)	
1st Bty.	A/56 Bty.		)	
3rd Bty.	B/56 Bty.	12.30pm.	) F.15.a.0.6.	As for advance parties in Table A (1).
5th Bty.	C/56 Bty.		)	
57th Bty.	527th Bty.		)	
8th D.A.C.	52nd D.A.C.	1.15pm	F.15.a.0.6.	As for advance parties in Table 'A' (1).
Trench Mortars.	D.T.M.O.	11 am.	TARGETTE DUMP.	,, ,, ,,
No.1 Coy.	55th Bde. HQ.	3.0 pm.	TARGETTE X Roads.	,, ,, ,,

appx 86

52ND DIVISIONAL ARTILLERY DEFENCE SCHEME.

1. DIVISIONAL FRONTAGE AND FLANK DIVISIONS.

The 52nd (Lowland) Division front extends from WESTERN ROAD (T.28.d.55.75) to the junction of BILLIE BURKE trench and BETTY trench (latter inclusive) and is holding the Right Sector of the VIIIth Corps front.

The 4th Canadian Division is on the right and 20th (Light) Division on the left.

2. DISTRIBUTION, BOUNDARIES AND HEADQUARTERS OF INFANTRY.

The front is divided into two Infantry Brigade Sections, that on the right is known as the ACHEVILLE Section and that on the left as the MERICOURT Section.

The right section is held by 2 Battalions in the line and the left section by 1 Battalion in the line each with 1 Battalion in defended localities in their rear.

One Infantry Brigade is in Corps Reserve at MONT ST. ELOY.
(b) Boundaries are:-

  Divisional Southern Boundary.
T.28.d.5.8 – along N. side of WESTERN Road to B.2.b.80.70 – B.2.a.80.70 – B.1.d.65.80 – A.12.a.70.60 – A.10.a.30.55 – A.9.d.1.9 – A.8.d.8.0, thence Westwards along grid line between Squares A.8 and A.14.

  Divisional Northern Boundary.
Line at Junction of BILLIE BURKE and BETTY Trenches (inclusive to Right Sector), Westwards along grid line to T.2.c.3.0 – Junction of RED Trench and LENS – ARRAS Road (road inclusive to Right Sector), thence RED Trench and CYRIL (both inclusive to Center Sector) to S.11.c.0.4 – S.16.c.0.0 – S.19.b.0.0 – X.22 central – X.15.c.0.0 – X.14.c.0.0 – W.28.b.0.0 – W.27.b.0.0.

  Inter Infantry Brigade Boundary.
The Section boundary is from T.10.c.0.2 – Junction of VESTA TILLEY and TEDDIE GERARD, T.15.a.9.7 – T.14.c.25.65 – T.13.d.5.4 – S.24 central – S.24.c.1.8 – S.38.c.4.0, thence Westwards along grid line between Square S.27 and Square A.3.

  Headquarters.
52nd (Lowland) Division – CHATEAU D'ACQ.
Right Section – Infantry Brigade Headquarters, A.6.c.60.70.
Left Section – Infantry Brigade Headquarters – S.27.b.00.60.

3. SYSTEMS OF DEFENCE.

The Divisional Sector is divided into two zones:-
  The OUTPOST Zone.
  The BATTLE Zone.

(a) The Outpost zone consists of:-
  (i) The outpost line of observation running from MONTREAL – QUEBEC – LILLIE ELSIE – BILLIE BURKE.
  (ii) The outpost line of supports running from OTTAWA – HUDSON – NEW BRUNSWICK – TEDDY GERARD.
(b) The Battle Zone. The main line of resistance of the outpost zone coincides with the forward line of the Battle zone, and is known as the BLACK line. It runs from BEEHIVE trench – GRAND TRUNK trench from T.21.d.5.2 to T.21.d.90.50, thence along CANADA – GERTIE – JULIA JAMES – HAYTER – GLADYS – DARTMOUTH – BEAVER.

In rear of the main line of resistance is the BROWN line, behind that certain defended localities and the GREEN line.
Details of the above lines are shown in Map 'A'.

4. GENERAL PRINCIPLES OF DEFENCE.

The outpost zone is lightly held, the disposition being such that our greatest strength is available for the defence of the BLACK line. Raids and minor operations of the enemy are met in the outpost zone, if necessary by Counter attack. In the event of our having several hours warning of an intended attack in force, the G.O.C. will

issue

issue the order "Prepare for Action" on which the outpost zone will be still further thinned out, leaving only a small nucleus to watch the enemy's movements and give the S.O.S. warning.

If the attack comes as a complete surprise no order "Prepare for Action" will be given, but "MAN BATTLE STATIONS" will be ordered. In this case no withdrawals from the outpost zone will take place. Once the enemy attack is launched all lines and defended localities are to be fought to the last.

5. GROUPING AND DISPOSITIONS OF THE FIELD ARTILLERY.
(a) The Field Artillery covering the 52nd (Lowland) Division consists of its own Divisional Artillery with the 242nd Army Field Artillery Brigade attached.

This Artillery is allotted as under:-

ACHEVILLE Section.
Right Artillery Group Commander - Lt.Col.H.J.COTTER, C.I.E., DSO., RA.
          9th Brigade R.F.A.
          242nd Brigade R.F.A.

MERICOURT Section.
Left Artillery Group Commander - Lt.Col. J.M.INGRAM, R.F.A.
          56th Brigade R.F.A.

(b) X/52 and Y/52 Medium Trench Mortar Batteries are allotted to the Left Section.

A disposition statement of the above Artillery is given in Appendix A.

6. ARTILLERY INSTRUCTIONS FOR THE DEFENCE.
(a) Artillery Policy.

While we are holding the line, under normal conditions, an aggressive artillery policy is maintained by the sniping of all movement and work seen by day, and by vigorous harassing fire at night.

The Group Commander ascertains daily from the Infantry Brigadier what his requirements in this respect are and arranges his harassing fire programme accordingly. Special targets to be engaged are also ordered from this Office as occasion demands.

Each Group maintains 3 18-pounders and 1 4.5" Howitzer in forward emplacements, from which all harassing and sniping fire is carried out, the main battery positions being kept silent, as far as possible. In addition each Group sends up 1 roving 18-Pounder by night to assist these guns.

To economise Officers, these forward guns may be grouped into Sections under an Officer if desired; and as the bulk of the firing falls on them, the detachments must be relieved at least once a week.

These forward guns do not withdraw in the event of a hostile attack. They will have specially selected positions ready from which they can fire at close targets over the open sights, and will move into these positions upon the order "Prepare for Action", and must be in action ready for Counter Preparation.

Two Trench Mortars are situated in the outpost zone with forward emplacements for offensive work. The remainder are disposed to cover the BLACK and BROWN lines. On the order "Prepare for action" or "man battle stations" these two guns will withdraw to their rear positions if possible. If they cannot do this, they will fight where they stand and be destroyed before falling into enemy hands.

Normally half the personnel of a Trench Mortar Battery man the guns, with the remainder in rest.

The Officer in charge of the trench mortars in the line must keep close touch with the Infantry on his front and Battery Commanders and D.T.M.O. must in addition visit Infantry Brigade Headquarters regularly to ascertain what their requirements are.

(b)

11. **AMMUNITION.**
   (a) The distribution of ammunition will be as follows :-

	Main Positions.	Forward guns.	Echelons.	Dump.
18-pdr. per gun	600.	700.	273.	200.
4.5" How. per gun	550.	550.	322.	100.

When the ranges of barrages admit each Group will keep 25% H.E. and 75% shrapnol of its 18-pdr. establishment.
The 4.5" How. establishment includes 30 rounds LETHAL and 30 rounds LACHRIMATORY per How. including forward Hows.
Each battery will also keep 100 rounds per gun or Howitzer in its BROWN Line position.

(b) **Establishment per Group at Guns.**

			Rounds.
Right Group.	18-pdr.	3 forward guns.	2,100.
		33 Guns main positions.	19,800.
		BROWN Line positions.	3,300.
			25,200.
	4.5" Hows.	1 forward How.	550.
		11 Hows Main positions.	6,050.
		BROWN Line positions.	1,200.
			7,800.

2 15 pounder B.L.C. Anti-tank guns (200 rds ea.)   400.

Left Group.	18-pdr.	3 forward guns.	2,100.
		15 guns main positions.	9,000.
		BROWN Line positions.	1,800.
			12,900.
	4.5" Hows.	1 forward How.	550.
		5 Hows main positions.	2,750.
		BROWN Line positions.	600.
			3,750.

2 15 pounder B.L.C. Anti-tank guns (200 rds ea.)   400.

The following batteries whose S.O.S. ranges are over 6,000 yards will keep 200 rounds AX fuze 106 per gun for use during S.O.S. only at Main Positions, to be included in establishment shown above :-

Left Group. A/56th Bde RFA.   Right Group. B/245 Bde RFA.
18 guns.   B/56 Bde RFA.   A/242 Bde RFA.
            C/56 Bde RFA.

(c). **Trench Mortars.**
   At Mortars. 100 rounds per Mortar.
   At Dump. 100 Rounds per Mortar.

(d) **Refilling Point.**
GAZETTE Dump. A.8.a.30.70 or if anything happens to prevent this BRANDON Dump F.10.c.00.50.

APPENDIX 'B'.

Unit.	Outpost Barrage.	Black Barrage.	Brown Barrage. From Brown line position.
19th Battery.	T.29.c.00.65 - T.23.c.88.00.	T.28.a.01.55 - T.28.c.15.60.	B.2.b.45.55 - T.26.b.40.55 - T.26.b.25.90.
20th Battery.	T.29.c.00.65 - T.23.c.88.00.	T.27.b.96.85 - T.28.c.15.60.	T.26.b.25.90 - T.26.b.40.75.
28th Battery.	T.23.c.88.00 - T.23.d.44.80 T.17.c.69.57.	T.22.a.02.23 - T.23.c.38.26 T.27.b.96.85.	B.2.b.65.55 - T.26.b.40.55 T.20.a.40.75.
D/89 Brigade.	T.23.d.71.86 - T.17.d.06.30.	T.22.c.75.30 - T.28.a.52.15	T.26.d.95.55 - T.26.b.8.9. T.26.b.95.05 - T.20.d.65.40. T.26.b.85.55 - T.20.d.3.8.
A/242 Brigade.	T.17.c.69.57 - T.23.b.25.27.	T.21.b.65.45 - T.22.a.02.25 T.22.c.38.26.	T.20.a.40.75 - T.16.a.9.4 S.24.b.55.35.
B/242 Brigade.	T.10.c.45.30 - T.16.b.19.63.	T.15.c.06.50 - T.22.a.02.23.	1 sec: S.24.b.4.3 to S.18.c.15.35. 1 sec: S.18.c.15.35 to S.17.b.35.65 1 sec: S.17.b.35.65 to S.11.c.5.8.
C/242 Brigade.	T.23.b.25.27 - T.23.c.88.00.	T.22.c.38.26 - T.27.b.96.85 T.28.a.01.55.	T.20.a.40.75 - T.19.a.9.4 S.24.b.50.15.
D/242 Brigade.	T.29.c.55.77 - T.23.d.71.86.	T.15.c.39.90 - T.22.c.88.70.	T.19.a.4.6 - T.20.a.75.75. T.19.b.35.95 - T.20.a.9.2. T.19.b.30.75 - T.20.b.2.5.
A/56th Brigade.	T.10.c.45.30 - T.10.c.55.85 T.10.a.40.23.	T.8.b.15.00 - T.8.d.50.00.	S.24.b.50.15 - S.18.c.15.35.
B/56 Brigade.	T.3.d.95.30 - T.3.d.65.83.	T.2.c.80.03 - T.8.b.15.00.	S.18.c.15.35 - S.17.b.35.65.
C/56 Brigade.	T.10.a.40.23 - T.10.c.55.85 T.10.c.45.30 - T.16.b.19.63.	T.15.c.09.50 - T.22.a.02.23.	S.17.b.35.65 - S.11.c.5.8.
527th Battery.	T.10.a.85.32 - T.16.b.30.70.	T.9.a.00.74 - T.15.a.30.55.	T.13.c.05.55 - T.18.d.5.2. T.13.c.67.28 - T.18.d.45.67. T.13.c.12.20 - T.18.b.12.00.
X/52 6"Newton.	T.29.b.50.10.	T.28.a.58.10. T.28.a.30.60. T.21.b.75.50. T.15.c.38.18. T.15.c.00.55.	
Y/52.	T.17.d.10.95.	T.14.d.55.90. T.14.b.40.15. T.14.b.40.65. T.8.d.40.20. T.8.d.70.77. T.8.b.45.60.	

APPENDIX 'E'.
LIST OF OBSERVATION POSTS AND HOW MANNED.

Name of O.P	Map co-ordinates	Maximum Arcs of view (grid bearing)	Unit by which maintained.	System on which O.Ps are manned in Groups.
VAIN.	B.1.a.39.02.	340-105.	19th Bty.	RIGHT GROUP.
JANE.	B.8.a.30.08.	35-98.	20th Bty.	
ZEAL.	B.7.b.85.80.	0-102.	28th Bty.	Two manned
NAPE.	B.8.a.25.20.	25-100.	D/69 Bty.	daily for
WART.	A.6.b.84.86.	15-92.	A/242 Bty.	24 hours.
SASH.	B.1.d.1.4.	9-175.	C/242 Bty.	9 pm to 9pm
GRAHAM.	S.22.b.60.40.	33-100.	D/242 Bty.	
PEACH.	S.23.d.67.53.	45-90.	B/242 Bty.	
HAWK	S.23.d.10.30.	33-106.	A/56 Bty.	LEFT GROUP.
GRAHAM.	S.22.b.60.40.	33-100.	B/56 Bty.	Two manned
COVENTRY.	S.29.b.4.7.	28-114.	C/56 Bty.	daily for 24 hours
BIRDSEYE.	S.22.b.65.80.	45-110.	527 Bty.	8 am to 8 am.
	B.7.b.70.30.	30-92.	20th Bty.	ALTERNATIVE O.Ps.
	B.1.c.73.92.	29-61.	28th Bty.	
	B.1.a.43.01.	15-100.	D/69 Bty.	
PLUM.	S.23.c.70.75.	85-91.	A/56 Bty.	

app 37

DAILY REPORT.
52ND DIVISIONAL ARTILLERY.
6 am 19th to 6 am 20th July 1918.

OUR ACTIVITY.
(a) <u>Operations.</u> Dug out
4.5" Hows fired 60 rounds on H.Q./ at N.35.c.
A test S.O.S. was received and responded to by the
Right Group at 11.22 pm.
Harassing fire by night and day on centres of activi
Total rounds fired –
18-pr. 1224   4.5" How. 565.   3" T.M. Ni

(b) <u>Aerial.</u> Our aeroplanes were active day and night.

2. HOSTILE ACTIVITY.
(a) <u>Artillery.</u> Quiet during the night 77 mm fired 60 rounds
B.8.b. and 100 rounds on T.26.c.

Date.	Time.	No. of rds.	Calibre.	Area shelled.
19th.	7.30-8.0 pm.	30.	15 cm.	T.26.a.6.2.
	11.0 pm.	10.	77 mm.	T.13.d.
	11.15 pm.	30.	10.5 cm.	T.19.b.
20th.	12.15 am.	30.	15 cm.	T.19.d.
	1.0 am.	50.	77 mm.	B.8.b.
	1.5 am.	100.	77 mm	T.26.c.
	1.50 am.	20.	77 mm.	PARBUS.
	4.0 am.	4.	10.5 cm.	T.13.b.
	5.0 am.	15.	10.5 cm.	T.13.d.

(b) <u>Work.</u> Nil.

(c) <u>Movement.</u> Movement at U.26.b. of small party, fired on and
dispersed. Movement and men seen pushing trucks in N.35.b.
and U.1.a.

(d) <u>Aerial.</u> 4 Observation balloons up by day.
Aeroplane activity normal. Two E.A. were over
our lines during the night.

3. GENERAL.
Visibility – Good.
Two dumps in enemy lines seen to be burning at 11.15 pm.

for Lieut R.A.
Reconnaissance Officer, 52nd D.A.

20th July 1918.

SECRET.   52ND DIVISIONAL ARTILLERY ORDER No. 27.   COPY NO. 23

appx 38

Reference Maps 1/40,000 - Sheets 44.B. - 51.C.

1. On completion of relief F.A. Brigades will withdraw to their wagon lines.

2. Units will march on July (21st & 22nd) to billeting areas vacated by 8th Divisional Artillery - shown in Table 'C' issued with 52nd D.A. Order No. 26.

3. F.A. Brigades and D.A.C. will march independently. No restrictions as to route from MONT ST. ELOY.

Times and order of march as under:-

52nd D.A.C. will be clear of Cross Roads at F.15.a.66. by 8pm July 21st
56th F.A. Bde.   ,,   ,,   ,,   9am ,, 22nd
9th F.A. Bde.   ,,   ,,   ,,   10am ,, 22nd.

4. T.M. personnel will move in the motor transport bringing incoming personnel of 8th D.A. T.M. on afternoon of July 21st.

5. Staff Captain will arrange:-

 (1) Distribution of mechanical Transport to D.A. Units;
 (2) That supply and baggage wagons march and remain with Div: Arty: Bdes. and D.A.C.

6. 52nd D.A.H.Q. will open at CUVIGNY (P.15.c.0.2) at 10am. July 22nd - (S.C., R.A's Office).

                                    Beresford Peirse
                                    Major, R.F.A.
                                    A/Brigade Major, R.A.
20th July 1918.   52nd Divisional Artillery.

                    Distribution.
        Copy Nos. 1/5 - 9th Brigade R.F.A.
                  6/10 - 56th Brigade R.F.A.
                  11/13 - D.T.M.O.
                  14/16 - 52nd D.A.C.
                    17 - 52nd Div: 'G'.
                    18 - 52nd Div: 'Q'.
                    19 - R.A. 8th Corps.
                    20 - D.A.C.O.
                    21 - S.C., R.A.
                    22 - R.O., R.A.
                  23/24 - War Diary.
                    25 - File.
                    26 - Retain.

DAILY REPORT RIGHT DIVISIONAL ARTILLERY, VIII CORPS.
6am 20th to 6am 21st July 1918.

1. OUR ACTIVITY.
    (a) Operations. 4.5" Hows. fired 50 rounds on T.M.
        emplacements in T.18.d.20.10 between 3 and 5pm.
        6" T.M's fired 51 rounds wire cutting at
        T.24.a.0.7 at 11am and 45 rounds searching OAK ALLEY
        and ARLEUX LOOP NORTH at 6.30pm.
        Harassing fire was carried out bu night on Tracks
        and centres of activity.
        Total Rounds fired:-
        18-pdr. - 1100.   4.5" How. - 380.   6". T.M. 96.
    (b) Aerial. Our aeroplanes were active day and night.
        At 4pm the balloon at NEUVILLE ST. VAAST broke loose
        and was seen drifting towards GIVENCHY - there was no
        car attached and balloon was rapidly deflating.

2. HOSTILE ACTIVITY.
    (a) Artillery. Activity rather above normal. Gas shell fired
        on B.13 during the night. VIMY shelled by 15cm Hows.
        at intervals throughout the day. T.M's very active
        between 3.30 and 4.0pm.

Date.	Time.	No. of rds.	Calibre.	Area shelled.	Direction.	Remarks.
20th.	10am.	50	77mm	Trenches in B.4.c. to B.10.a.		Apparently registration.
	10-11am.	100	15cm.	VIMY.		
	12.15pm.	20	10cm. gun.	T.26.a.	G.B. 87° from B.14.a.60.75. F/R 22 secs.	
	12 noon - 3.0pm.	47	15cm.	VIMY.	0.25 central.	
	1pm.	11	15cm.	S.28.c.7.0.		
	4pm.	20	77mm.	B.8.a.		
	7pm.	20	15cm.	VIMY.		
	8.30-9pm.	15	15cm.	VIMY.		
21st.	Midnight -	(100	10.5cm.	VIMY.		
	2am.	(50	15cm.	A.6.c.		
		(100	77mm	B.13.c.3.6.		GAS.
	2.45am.	60	77mm	}B.13.a.10.60.		}GAS.
	5.0am.	10	77mm			

   (b) Work. Nil.

   (c) Movement. Considerable movement about U.26 central to
       U.26.b.8.7 at 10am anf 6pm.
       Slight movement in MERICOURT and O.25.

   (d) Aerial. Normal activity.
       An E.A. patrolling our lines at 9.30am was met by 12
       of our machines and driven down out of control,
       landing at approximately U.1.a.
       7 E.A. over our lines during the afternoon.

3. GENERAL. Visibility fair in morning, improving during the day,
       but bad in the evening owing to rain.

                                       (Sd) H.J. ESCREET.
                                            for Lieut: R.A.
                                  Reconnaissance Officer, Right Divnl:
                                       Artillery, VIIIth Corps.

21st July 1918.

SECRET.   52ND DIVISIONAL ARTILLERY ORDER NO. 28.   COPY NO.

Reference LENS, Sheet 11 - 1/100,000.

1. From 12 noon July 23rd the 52nd Division is in G.H.Q. Reserve ready to move at 12 hours notice.

2. The 52nd Division Infantry are in three Groups:-

		Entraining Station.
(i) 157th Infantry Brigade - AUCHY Brigade.		PERNES.
(ii) 154th Infantry Brigade - BOIS DES CLARCS - BRACQUENCOURT Brigade.		CALONNE-RICOUART.
(iii) 155th Infantry Brigade - CAMBLAIN L'ABBE - VERDREL Brigade.		ACQ.

3. In the event of a tactical move the Divisional Artillery will move by Road.

4. In the event of a strategical move - the complete Division will move by Rail - a Brigade Group and a portion of the Divisional Artillery will entrain at each station.

5. Divisional Artillery entraining stations:-

Entraining Station.	52nd D.A. Units.
PERNES.	52nd D.A. Headquarters. 56th Brigade (less 1 18-pdr.Battery) D.A.C. - 1 Sec: less 6 amn: wagons. 1 Sec: S.A.A. Section.
CALONNE-RICOUART.	1 18-pdr. Battery, 9th Brigade, with 6 amn: wagons attached from D.A.C. 1 18-pdr. Battery, 56th Brigade, with six amn: wagons attached from D.A.C. Headquarters and 2 Batteries 52nd D.A. Trench Mortars. D.A.C. - 1 Section, S.A.A. Section.
ACQ.	9th Brigade (less 1 18-pdr.Battery) D.A.C. - Hd.Qrs. & 1 Section less 6 18-pdr. ammunition wagons. 1 Sec: S.A.A. Section.

6. Supply and Baggage wagons will move with Units.

7. Reconnaissance of their entraining stations and routes by Officers Commanding Units of the 52nd Divisional Artillery will be carried out forthwith.

[signature]
Major R.F.A.
A/Brigade Major, R.A.
52nd Divisional Artillery.

23rd July 1918.

Distribution.
Copy Nos. 1 - 52nd Div: 'G'.   2 - 52nd Div: 'Q'.
           3 - S.O., R.A.   4 - R.O., R.A.
           5/9 - 9th Brigade.   10/14 - 56th Brigade.
           15/22 - 52nd D.A.C.   23/25 - D.T.M.O.
           26/27 - War Diary.   28 - File.

SECRET.   COPY NO......

52ND DIVISIONAL ARTILLERY ORDER NO. 29.

Reference Maps 1/40,000 Sheets 44-B, 51-B - 51-C.

1. The 52nd Divisional Artillery will relieve the 5th Canadian Artillery in action on the nights of July 29/30 and July 30/31.

2. Units will march by route - GAUCHIN LEGAL - ESTREE CAUCHIE - CAMBLAIN L'ABBE - F.15.a.0.7 (Map 51-C.) - CHAUSSEE BRUNE HAUT - G.1.d.6.0 (Map 51-B) - G.2.b.0.2, - A.26.c.6.2, - MADAGASCAR CAMP.

    9th Bde RFA will be clear of Cross Roads at P.30.d.6.4. (Map 44-B) by 8.30 am.

    56th Bde RFA will be clear of Cross Roads at P.30.d.6.4. (Map 44-B) by 9.15 am.

    D.A.C. will be clear " " " " " " " by 10 am.

    Units to be at MADAGASCAR CAMP by 2.0 pm.

3. Staff Captain will arrange lorries to move 52nd D.A. Trench Mortar Headquarters and Batteries and Advance Parties from Units.

4. 52nd D.A. Units to ACKNOWLEDGE.

                                                                     N. Beresford-Peirse
                                                                          Major RFA.
                              A/ Brigade Major R.A., 52nd D.A.

Issued by Special D.R. at 1.0 pm.

Distribution.

Copies No.	1	52nd Division 'G'.
"	" 2.	R.O.R.A.
"	" 3/7.	9th Bde RFA.
"	" 8/12	56th Bde RFA.
"	" 13/16	D.A.C.
"	" 17/19	D.T.M.O.
"	" 20	S.C.R.A.
"	" 21	5th C.F.A.
"	" 22/23	War Diary.
"	" 24	File.
"	" 25	Retain.

SECRET.   COPY NO...............

52ND. D.A. RELIEF ORDER.   July 29th 1918.

1. Reliefs will be as shown on Table "A" attached.

2. Two guns per battery — including any forward gun or guns — and one anti-tank gun (9th Brigade RFA) will be relieved on the night of 29th/30th July.
   Four guns per battery will be relieved on night July 30th/31st.
   Maps, Orders, etc., and Aiming Posts will be taken over.
   Units will retain their own equipment.
   Liaison and Observing Officers will assume responsibility at 12 Noon, July 30th, but should join the 5th CDA O.O's. and L.O's on the night of July 29th/30th.
   Gun Teams will be provided by 5th CDA on night of July 29th/30th, and by 52nd D.A. on night July 30th/31st.
   Guides will be provided at MADAGASCAR CAMP on each night, by 5th CDA — details to be arranged between Units concerned.
   All reliefs will be completed by Midnight July 30th/31st.

3. TRENCH MORTARS.
   D.T.M.O., 52nd D.A. will arrange with D.T.M.O. 5th CDA, as follows:—

   (a) Take over and relieve Rear Control Station.
   (b) On Centre Group front. To relieve personnel only, taking over nine 6" Newton T.Ms. in action. Nine 6" Newton T.Ms. to be handed over to the 5th CDA.
   To relieve personnel only, taking over one 9.45" T.M. in action. to relieve forward control station.
   (c) On Right Group front. Relief of personnel only — manning four 6" Newton T.Ms. of the Right Battery, Right Group.
   Relief of A/D.T.M.O. Right Group by an Officer to be detailed by D.T.M.O. 52nd D.A.
   Infantry attached to 5th CDA will be attached to 52nd D.A. T.Ms.
   Trench Mortar reliefs will be completed by 2 p.m. July 30th.
   Relief of personnel should overlap as far as possible.

4. D.A.C's and Dump reliefs will be complete by 12 Noon, July 30th.

5. 52nd D.A. will function as a group under the 4th C.D.A. the command passing at 6.00 p.m. July 30th from 5th CDA to 52nd D.A.

6. Commands will pass on completion of reliefs.

7. Completion of reliefs will be notified by wire to this Office by use of code word ARRAS up to 12 Noon July 30th and code word RHEIMS from that hour until completion of relief.

8. F.A. Brigade Wagon Lines and D.A.C. Sections will temporarily occupy MADAGASCAR CAMP Area.

9. All Wagon Lines will move early on July 31st into Wagon Lines vacated by 5th CDA Units.

10. 52nd D.A. will be responsible for accounting for ammunition from 12 Noon July 30th.

11. ACKNOWLEDGE.

                                                N. Beresford Peirse
                                                Major R.F.A.
                                                c/ Brigade Major RA.
                                                52nd Division.

Distribution Overleaf.

- 2 -

DISTRIBUTION.

1. Staff Capt. R.A.
2-5. R.O., R.A.
6-10. 9th Brigade RFA.
11-15. 56th Brigade RFA.
16-18. 52nd D.A.C.
19-22. 52nd D.T.M.O.
23. 52nd Div. "G".
24. 4th C.D.A.
25. 5th C.D.A.

PART 'A'.
==========

	Code Name.	Code Name.	No. of Guns.	O.Ps & Code Names.	Wagon Lines (not to be taken over yet).
52nd D.A.	BEJA.				
52nd.A.H.Q.	BEJA.	5th GDA.HQ. NEZO. L.8.b.95.50.			L.8.b.95.50.
9th Bde RFA Anti-Tank Bty.	BEZA.	15th Bde OPA. KUNI. Dispecker. H.7.a.10.20. H.3.b.70.45.	1.	RUSH. H.3.d.40.85.	F.28.d.20.40
19th Bty.	BERA.	52nd Bty. KUGU. H.2.c.25.85. H.1.d.27.34.	5.	MARITIME. H.10.b.01.79.	F.29.a.30.20.
20th Bty.	BEKA.	53rd Bty. KULU. H.7.d.05.83. H.7.b.70.20.	5. 1.	BLAZING. H.3.b.70.28.	F.28.b.80.90.
28th Bty.	BESA.	55th Bty. KUHU. H.1.d.30.75. H.2.a.25.35.	4. 2.	MARITIME. H.10.b.01.79.	F.29.c.40.95.
B/89th Bty.	BEMA.	51st How. Bty. KUPI. G.12.a.40.40. H.3.c.96.17.	4. 2.	SPOT. H.3.b.70.50.	F.24.c.40.60.
53rd Bde HQ.	BEWA.	14th Bde OPA. KUVU. G.5.b.30.15.			L.6.c.50.90.
A/78th Bty.	BEFA.	60th Bty. KUZU. A.30.c.50.00. B.26.d.24.90.	5. 1.	TAURUS. H.3.d.70.99.	L.10.b.20.80.
B/78th Bty.	BEPA.	61st Bty. KURU. A.30.c.29.89. B.25.d.55.55. B.25.d.95.53.	4. 1. 1.	HAWK. B.27.b.50.90.	F.25.d.80.50.
C/78th Bty.	BEGA.	9th Bty. KUKU. A.30.c.11.84. B.26.b.00.00. B.25.b.70.30.	4. 1. 1.	BLOOD. B.27.b.20.70.	F.29.c.90.30.
82nd Bty.	BEDA.	56th How. Bty. KUCU. A.29.c.41.70. B.1.b.39.15.	4. 2.	BOXES. B.27.d.95.75.	B.8.a.40.30.
22nd BAC.	BELA.	7th B.de.A.C. HEDO. K.8.c.75.65.			K.8.c.90.25.
		5th Bdo Assist Bdo. H.2.d.97.85. B.21.c.38.20.		H.11.c.10.98.	

SECRET.   52nd D.A. No. A/392.

9th Brigade RFA   (10)   R.O.R.A. (1)
56th Brigade RFA (10)

CONCENTRATION.

1.   A 10 minutes concentration will be fired on GAVRELLE - Zero hour
2.0 am , night of 31st/1st.

2.   9th Brigade RFA 18 pdrs :-
0-0.2   Road from B.30.b.10.35 - C.25.a.4.7.   All A. Rate INTENSE.
0.2-0.8. Search area C.25.a. West of CHICO Trench. 50% A and 50% AX.
                                                       Rate NORMAL.
0.8-0.10 B.30.central - C.25 central.   75% A. Rate INTENSE.
                 How. Batteries :-
0-0.3.   Road C.25.a.25.60 - 25.10.
0.3-0.10. Area from CHICO Trench from C.25.a.65.85 - C.25.a.70.00 to
          200 yards Westwards.
                 Howitzer Ammunition. 75% BCBR or BVN.
                                       25% BX.

        56th Brigade RFA 18 pdrs :-
0-0.2   Road B.30.a.50.80 - B.30.b.15.40
         300 yards of FOXY ALLEY East of B.30.a.80.75. Rate of fire INTENSE
                                                              100% A.
0.2-0.8. Area C.25.b. East of line C.25.b.5.0.-5.5. and south of line
         C.25.b.5.5 - 95.50. Rate of fire NORMAL 50% A and AX.
0.8-0.10. 300 yards of FOXY ALLEY east of line between B.30 and C.25.
                       Rate of fire INTENSE 75% A.
                 How. Batteries :-
         Same area as for 18prs second period.
0-0.10. 75% BCBR or BVN.
         25% BX.   Rate of fire rapid.

                                              Major RFA.
                                    A/ Brigade Major R.A., 52nd D.A.

31st July 1918.

Ho RA 52D
vol 5
apts

CONFIDENTIAL

On His Majesty's Service.

D.A.G.
G.H.Q.
3rd Echelon.

CONFIDENTIAL.
****

ORIGINAL.
****

WAR DIARY OF 52ND DIVISIONAL ARTILLERY. H.Q.
===*===*===*===*===*===*===*===*===*===*===*===*===*===*===*===*===*

VOLUME - V,
PART - VIII.

FROM - 1st AUGUST 1918.   TO - 31st AUGUST 1918.

Army Form C. 2118.

WAR DIARY
or
INTELLIGENCE SUMMARY.   AUGUST 1918.

(Erase heading not required.)

Instructions regarding War Diaries and Intelligence Summaries are contained in F. S. Regs., Part II. and the Staff Manual respectively. Title pages will be prepared in manuscript.

Place	Date	Hour	Summary of Events and Information	Remarks and references to Appendices
ETRUN.	1st		Normal day vide Daily Report.	Appx.1.
			52nd Div: Arty. Instrns. No*s*. 2 - re liaison arrangements issued vide -	" 2
			" " " " 3.- Arrangements to come into force on 52nd D.A. taking over from 5th C.D.A. vide -	" 3.
MAROEUIL.	2nd.		52nd D.A. took over from 5th C.D.A. at MAROEUIL at 10.0am. vide -	" 4.
			Normal day, vide daily report -	" 5.
			Amendment to 52nd D.A. instructions No. 2 issued, vide -	" 6.
	3rd.		Hostile Artillery activity was above normal, there being considerable harassing fire throughout the day, vide Daily Report	" 7.
	4th.		Southern Divisional Boundary changed vide -	" 8.
			Normal day, vide Daily report -	" 9.
			52nd D.A. No. Q/435, re change of Divisional & Inter-Brigade boundaries & adjustment of dispositions, vide -	" 10.
	5th.		Quiet day, vide Daily Report -	" 11.
			52nd D.A. No. A/423, re Artillery action in conjunction with gas beam attack, vide -	" 12.
			52nd D.A. No. X/427/2, re move of A/277, D/277, 19th & D/69 Batteries, vide -	" 13.
			52nd D.A. No. Q/433/1, re further adjustments of inter-Brigade boundaries, vide -	" 14.
			52nd D.A. No. A/438 re retaliation "MARO", vide -	" 15.
			52nd D.A. No. M/440 re grouping of Batteries into, Left, Centre & Right Groups from 10.0am August 8th, vide -	" 16.
	6th.		Normal day, vide Daily Report. 230 rounds 10.5cm. were fired on forward guns without causing any damage, vide -	" 17.
			Amendment to 52nd D.A. No. M/440 issued vide -	" 18.
	7th.		Quiet day, vide Daily Report -	" 19.
	8th.		Quiet day, vide Daily Report -	" 20.
			52nd D.A. No. F/470, re new S.O.S. Barrage & rates of fire issued vide -	" 21.
			52nd D.A. No. M/471, re Mutual Support between Groups & Flan1 Divisions, vide -	" 22.
			Amendment to M/471 issued vide -	" 23.
			52nd D.A. No. A/478, Orders re Gas Shell bombardment to be carried out by all 4.5" Howitzers on first favourable night after the 10th.	" 24.

Army Form C. 2118.

WAR DIARY
or
INTELLIGENCE SUMMARY.
(Erase heading not required.)

Instructions regarding War Diaries and Intelligence Summaries are contained in F. S. Regs., Part II. and the Staff Manual respectively. Title pages will be prepared in manuscript.

Place	Date	Hour	Summary of Events and Information	Remarks and references to Appendices
MAROEUIL.	9th.		Normal day, vide Daily Report.- 52nd D.A. No. M/481 - Provisional Defence Scheme issued vide -	Appendix 25
	10th.		Quiet day, but intense bombardment of our trenches on the right of the Sector at 3.0am 10th, we fired S.O.S. at 3.9am. vide Daily Report.-	,, 26.
	11th.		Quiet day except for destructive shoot on forward guns of B/56 from 2 to 5pm, followed by heavy gas shelling of the same area. Gun pit and gun damaged & some casualties in the detachment, vide Daily Report.-	,, 27.
	12th.		Quiet day. B/56 forward guns again shelled with Gas Shell & H.E. mixed, vide daily report -	,, 28.
	13th.		Quiet day, vide Daily Report.-	,, 29.
			Warning Order re relief of 52nd D.A. by 51st D.A. - 52nd D.A. Order No. 30, vide -	,, 30.
	14th.		Normal day, vide Daily Report -	,, 31.
			Fresh Instructions issued re relief of 52nd D.A., only 56th Brigade to be relieved by 51st D.A. 9th Brigade being relieved by 45th Brigade, 8th D.A. & 277th & 311th Brigades passing under Command of 8th D.A. Both reliefs nights 14th/15th & 15th/16th - 52nd D.A. Operation Order No. 31, vide -	,, 32.
			Orders for concentration of 52nd D.A. in ACQ - FREVIN CAPELLE area issued, 52nd D.A. Order No. 32, vide -	,, 33.
	15th.		52nd D.A. No. Z/528 issued re move of B & C/277 on coming under 8th D.A. vide -	,, 34.
			52nd D.A.C. marched from MAROEUIL to FREVIN CAPELLE on being relieved by 51st D.A.C., 52nd D.A.Order No. S.C. 1140, vide -	,, 35.
			9th & 56th Brigades being relieved withdrew to their Wagon Lines on night 15th/16th.	
	16th.		52nd D.A. Headquarters moved to AUBIGNY on being relieved by 51st D.A., 56th Brigade moved to ACQ, 9th Brigade remained in their Wagon lines.	,, 36.
AUBIGNY.	17th. 18th) to) 20th) 21st.		9th Brigade moved to ACQ, reaching there about 7.0pm, 52nd D.A.Order No. 33, vide - At AUBIGNY, nothing occurred of note.	,, 37.
BEAUMETZ- les-LOGES.	22nd.		The whole 52nd D.A. moved to BEAUMETZ area in the evening. Headquarters, 9th & 56th Brigades were billeted in BEAUMETZ-les-LOGES, 52nd D.A.C. at MONCHIET. Some casualties from bombing whilst moving. 52nd D.A. Order No. 34 & Amendment to same 52nd D.A. No. A/549, vide - 52nd D.A. Came under Command of 40th D.A. 9th & 56th Brigades & D.A.C. moving forward into action, under their orders. Battle Headquarters of 52nd D.A. moved to BRETENCOURT at 5pm.	,, 38.

Army Form C. 2118.

WAR DIARY
August 1918.

OR

INTELLIGENCE SUMMARY.

(Erase heading not required.)

Instructions regarding War Diaries and Intelligence Summaries are contained in F. S. Regs., Part II, and the Staff Manual, respectively. Title pages will be prepared in manuscript.

Place.	Date.	Hour.	Summary of Events and Information.	Remarks and references to Appendices
BEAUMETZ-les-LOGES.	23rd.		52nd Div: Infantry attacked through 59th Div: at 5am. All objectives were gained by 6.45am. Approximate line running East of BOYELLES & BOIRY BECQUERELLE. Batteries moved forward in support of Infantry during the night.	
BLAIRVILLE.	24th.		Rear Headquarters moved up to BRETENCOURT at 5.0am & thence whole of 52nd Div: Artillery Headquarters moved up to BLAIRVILLE. At 7.0am our Infantry advanced & by 11am were established on a line from NEUVILLE VITASSE in front of HENIN & St.MARTIN SUR COJEUL.	
	25th. 26th.		Quiet, situation unchanged. 52nd Div: attacked at 3.0am in conjunction with Canadian Corps on the Left & 56th Division on the right. By 8.0am Canadians had captured MONCHY LE PREUX & GUEMAPPE and surrounded NEUVILLE VITASSE & 52nd Div: had captured HENINEL and attained their objective in the HINDENBURG LINE. At 3.0pm the attack was pressed in a S.E. direction in order to take a portion of the HINDENBURG LINE in rear. Batteries again advanced during the night.	
	27th.		At 10.0am further attacks were made by the Canadian Corps & 52nd Division resulting in the capture of CHERISY & FONTAINE-les-CROISILLES; the final line being approximately that of the SENSEE RIVER. 52nd Div: Infantry were relieved by 57th Division at night, our Artillery remaining in action under the 57th Divisional Artillery. HENDECOURT & CROISILLES taken during the day, Batteries again advanced. RIENCOURT & BULLECOURT captured.	
	28th. 29th. 30th		As a result of Hun counterattack, HENDECOURT, RIENCOURT, and BULLECOURT were lost. BULLECOURT was subsequently retaken by us.	
FONTAIN-LEZ-CROISILLES.	31st		52nd D.A. moved up to Headquarters in the HINDENBURG line about 2,000 yards West of FONTAINE LEZ CROISILLES, and at 11 am took over command of 9th Bde and 56th Bde RFA, forming the Left Group of 57th D.A. Orders for Artillery Support of an Operation for the recapture of HENDECOURT and the CROWS NEST by the 57th Division in conjunction with the Canadians at 4.50 am September 1st issued at	

Army Form C. 2118.

WAR DIARY
or
INTELLIGENCE SUMMARY.

August 1918

(Erase heading not required.)

Instructions regarding War Diaries and Intelligence Summaries are contained in F.S. Regs., Part II. and the Staff Manual respectively. Title pages will be prepared in manuscript.

Place	Date	Hour	Summary of Events and Information	Remarks and references to Appendices
FONTAINE-LEZ- CROISILLES.	31st.		at 9.30 pm. vide 52nd D.A. Order No. 34.	App. 39.

[signature] Capt/ro
Officiating B.R.A., 52nd Division Lieut. Colonel R.A.

APPENDICES TO WAR DIARY OF

52ND DIVISIONAL ARTILLERY H. Q.

FOR

AUGUST 1918.

52nd D.A. No. X/414.

9th Brigade.   (5)
56th Brigade. (5)
277th Brigade. (5)
311th Brigade. (5)
================

Southern Divisional Boundary has been adjusted as follows:-

B.30.a.2.3 - H.3.b.8.2 - H.3.a.0.0 - H.2.c.0.8 - G.6.c.0.9 - G.3.b.7.3.

N. Beresford-Peirse
Major R.F.A.
A/Brigade Major R.A.
52nd Divisional Artillery.

3rd August 1918.

Copies to:-   156th Infantry Brigade.
              R.A., XVII Corps.
              R.O.R.A. (2).

52nd Divisional Artillery Intelligence Summary.
6 am. August 1st to 6 am. August 2nd 1918.

1. OUR ACTIVITY.
   Harassing fire on trenches, roads, tracks during the night.

   Rounds fired -
   18 pdr.   1973.   4.5" How.   512.   6" T.M. Nil.

2. HOSTILE ACTIVITY.
   (a) Artillery.   10.45 am 5 minutes intense bombardment of front line in B.28.a. & B.27.d. by 10.5 cm and 77 mm.
   10.30 to 11.30 am heavy shelling on H.4.c. and H.4.d guns firing from a direction and bearing 82° to 1000 from H.3.d. 70.98.   At 9.30 am the battery position at H.1.d.30.75 was shelled by 20 rounds 10.5 cm and 50 rds 15 cm - one pit being damaged.

Date.	Time.	No. of Rds.	Calibre.	Area shelled.	Remarks.
1st.	9.30- 10 am.	20.	10.5 cm.	H.1.d.30.75.	
	9.30- 10 am.	50.	15 cm.	H.1.d.30.25	
	10- 11 a.m.	56.	10.5 cm.	B.28.c.& d.	
	10.30-11.30am	150.	?	H.4.c. & d.	
	10.45 am.	50.	10.5 cm.	B.28.a. & B.27.d.	
	2 pm.	50.	10.5 cm.	H.1.d.4.0.	Gas -Blue Cross.
	3 pm.	20.	15 cm.	H.1.d.20.20.	
	3.0- 5.0 pm.	20.	77 mm.	H.3.d.	
	9.10 pm.	26.	10.5 cm.	BAILLEUL.	
	3.37 am.	20.	77 mm.	B.27.a.	Gas.
	4.0 am.	100.	10.5 cm.	B.28.a. & 27.d.	
	4.0 am.	40.	77 mm.	B.28.a.	Gas.
	4.10 am.	80.	10.5 cm.	B.27.d.2.9.	
	5.25 am.	15.	15 cm.	B.23.a.	
	5.25 am.	20.	77 mm.	B.27.b.	
	5.25 am.	20.	15 cm.	H.4.d.	

   (b) Work   Nil.

   (c) Movement.   Considerable movement at I.2.c. & d. and C.27.c. during morning of 1st.   4 men seen going East on road B.30.b.3.5. at 4.15 am.

   (d) Aerial.   Normal.
   9.30 am., 1st.   2 E.A. flying over our lines appeared to be conducting a shoot.
   E.A. brought down by M.G. fire 7.5 am.   Bombing 'planes active between 11 pm and 1.0am.

3. GENERAL.   Visibility fair.
   12.50 pm Hostile Dump blown up on bearing Grid 97° from H.3.d.70.98.

Lieut. RFA,
for Reconnaissance Officer 52nd D.A.

2 August 1918.

52nd DIVISIONAL ARTILLERY INSTRUCTIONS No.2.

9th Brigade.
56th Brigade.
277th A.Brigade.
311th A.Brigade.

1. At 10 am. August 2nd the following Liaison arrangements will come into force on 52nd Division taking over command.

2. (a) 9th Brigade in liaison with 156th Infantry Brigade (H.Q. at B.20.b.2.3) and one Officer with each Battalion in the line.
Right Battalion - 1/7th Scottish Rifles. H.3.c.6.7.
Left Battalion - 1/7th Royal Scots. B.21.a.8.2.

(b) 56th Brigade R.F.A. in liaison with 157th Infantry Bde (A.28.b.8.8) and one Officer with 1/6th H.L.I., 1/7th H.L.I. in the line (location not known)

(c) 311th Bde RFA in liaison with 155th Infantry Bde (B.14.a.6.1.) and one Officer with 1/4th K.O.S.B., B.8.b.62.25.

2. Brigade Liaison Officer should be a Captain or reliable Subaltern. Battalion Liaison to be arranged by Brigades concerned.

3. 277th Bde RFA should be in close touch with 311th Bde RFA in order to co-operate if necessary.

4. Barrages will remain as at present allotted pending re-grouping of Batteries.

N. Beresford-Peirse
Major RFA.
A/ Brigade Major R.A., 52nd D.A.

1st August 1918.

Copies to -
R.O.R.A. (4)
R.A. Signals.
52nd Division 'G'.
155th Infantry Brigade.
156th Infantry Brigade.
157th Infantry Brigade.

SECRET.

52nd Divisional Artillery Instructions No. 3.

9th Bde RFA.
56th Bde RFA.
277th Bde RFA.
311th Bde RFA.

Reference XVII Corps G. 4/3 dated 31/7/18 and maps 1/20,000 sheets 51-b N.W., 44-a S.W.

At 10 am August 2nd, the following will come into force.

52nd Division will assume command of LEFT SECTOR of XVII Corps front - from H.5.a.70.60 - WESTERN Road in T.28.d.
Divisional Headquarters will be near MAROEUIL.
52nd D.A. Headquarters at F.27.b.80.90.

Artillery covering 52nd Divisional Sector.
    (a) Field Artillery.
        9th Bde RFA.
        56th Bde RFA.
        277th Bde RFA.
        311th Bde RFA.

    (b) Affiliated R.G.A.
        Left H.A. Group. - Lieut. Colonel MAGEE, CGA.
        30th Bde R.G.A.
        2nd Bde C.G.A.

Counter Battery Zone of XVII Corps.
    Northern Boundary - T.29.c.00.60 - U.19.c.00.00 - U.23.c.00.00
between XVII and VIII Corps - U.29.c.00.60. - thence due East.

    Southern Boundary - M.30.c.70.85 - N.34.c.00.00 - due East
between XVII and VI Corps.   (Map 51-b S.W.)

Numbers 13 and 5th Squadrons R.A.F. will work with XVII Corps.
The boundary for C.B. work between the Squadrons will be an East and West line between the 'AI' and 'IC' Zones on Counter Battery map.

Harassing Fire Zones, 52nd Division.
    (1) Heavy Artillery -
        Outer Zone - East of a line H.34 central - I.13.c.00.00
along Grid to U.19.c.00.00.
        Distant Zone - East of above.
        Northern Boundary as for Northern Counter Battery Zone boundary.
        Southern Boundary - due East from H.5.a.60.70.

    (2) Field Artillery -
        T.29.c.0.6. - U.19.c.00.00 - I.1.a.00.70 - N.5.c.60.70

Infantry Headquarters are situated as under -
    155th Bde at B.14.a.6.1. - Battalion in the line - 1/4 Bn.
    (WILLERVAL SECTION)   K.O.S.B. at B.8.h.62.25

    157th Bde at Aa28.b.8.8.   Not yet known.
    (OPPY SECTION)   5th H.L.I. Rt.
        7th H.L.I. Lt.

    156th Bde at B.20.b.2.3.   1/7th Royal Scots - B.21.a.8.2. Lt.Bn.
    (GAVRELLE SECTION).   1/7th Scots Rifles at H.3.c.6.7 (Rt.Bn.)

Ammunition to be kept at guns:-
    18-pdr. - 550 rounds per gun.
    4.5" Hows. - 400 rounds per gun (includes 50 rounds chemical shell).
No proportion of shrapnel to H.E. is at present laid down in the Corps.
    18-pdr. Batteries should maintain 50% of "A" and "AX" and if over 4,000 yards from S.O.S. line all "AX" should be with 106 fuze.
    4.5" How. Batteries should maintain 75% of their H.E. with 106 fuze.
    3" Newton T.M's should maintain 200 rounds per gun in defensive positions.

-2-

7. Trench Mortar Grouping will be issued later, at present T.M's will work with Infantry Brigades in whose areas they are situated. The T.M. sited to the South of the Divisional Boundary working with 155th Infantry Brigade.

The D.T.M.O. will be responsible for the tactical control of all heavy T.M's on the Divisional front.

8. Barrages and Mutual Support remain as at present as laid down in 4th Canadian D.A. No. G.17/288 dated July 30th 1918 with Map "G" attached.

A trace shewing new Barrages will be issued later.

9. Divisional Refilling Point is TIMBERYARD DUMP at A.20.d.50.50.

10. Artillery Brigades and D.T.M.O. to ACKNOWLEDGE.

N Beresford-Peirse
Major R.F.A.
A/Brigade Major R.A.
52nd Divisional Artillery.

1st August 1918.

DISTRIBUTION.
52nd Division "G". (1).
R.O., R.A. (4).
B.M.R.A. (1).
S.C.R.A. (1).
R.A. Signals. (1).
9th Brigade R.F.A. (5).
56th Brigade R. A. (5).
277th A.Brigade R.F.A. (5).
311th A. Brigade (5).
D.T.M.O. (1).
R.A., XVII Corps. (1).
155th Infantry Brigade (1).
156th Infantry Brigade (1).
157th Infantry Brigade (1).
Loft H.A. Group. (1).

LEFT DIVISIONAL ARTILLERY (XVII CORPS) INTELLIGENCE SUMMARY.
6 am 2nd August to 6 am 3rd August 1918.

(1) OUR ACTIVITY.
  (a) Operations. Registration carried out by day and harassing fire by night.
    Movement at I.1.d. and H.6.b.4.4 engaged and parties dispersed.
    "Retaliation Right" called for and responded to at 6.5 pm.
    Total rounds fired:-
    18-pdr. - 1470.   4.5" How. - 490.   6" T.M. nil

(2.) HOSTILE ACTIVITY.
  (a) Artillery. B.29.d. and B.27.d. were heavily harassed by 10.5cm. and 77mm from 7 to 9am.
    H.2.a. was shelled by 77mm gas shell during afternoon and evening.
    T.M's fired 30 rounds on H.4.b. at 12.30am.

Date.	Time.	No. of rds.	Calibre.	Area shelled.	Direction.	Remarks.
2nd.	9.50am.	20.	77mm.	B.20.b.		
	10am.	6	10.5cm.	BAILLEUL.		
	10am.	20	77mm.	B.15.d.	GAVRELLE.	
	10am.	50	10.5cm.	H.2.b.		
	10am.	25	10.5cm.	B.21.d.		
	10.10am.	60	77mm.	B.15.d.		
	10.15am.	20	10.5cm.	H.2.a. & b.		
	10.15am.	60	10.5cm.	B.27.b.		
	10.45am.	15	10.5cm.	B.28.d.		
	11.12am.	10	10.5cm.	B.15.d.		
	2.30pm.	20	10.5cm.	B.15.d.		
	3.20pm.	52	77mm.	H.2.a.		Gas, BLUE CROSS.
	6.47pm.	60	77mm.	B.27.a & c.		
	6.50pm.	100	77mm.	H.2.a.		Gas, BLUE CROSS.
	8.45pm.	12	10.5cm.	H.1.d.30.75.		
	9.15-10.42pm.	40	77mm.	B.20.b.		
	9.30pm.	50	4.2.	BAILLEUL.		
	10.30pm.	15	10.5cm.	B.28.d.		
	10.30pm.	10	15cm.	B.16.b & d.		
	10.30pm.	40	?	A.30.c.		
	11.0pm.	50	77mm.	A.17.		
	11pm.	20	77mm.	B.27.a & c.		
	11.15pm.	40	10.5cm.	A.29.d, A.30.c.		GAS.
3rd.	12.15am.	15	10.5cm.	BAILLEUL.		
	12.30am.	30.	T.M.?	H.4.b.		
	1.5-1.15am.	3.	15cm.	B.14.a.	OPPY.	

  (b) Work. Nil.
  (c) Movement in I.1.d. engaged
    Party of 25 men seen at H.6.b.4.4 engaged and dispersed.
    Small parties seen at I.2.c.6.2, C.16.d., I.3.a.2.9.
    Movement in trenches seen at C.26.d.9.6, B.18.c.55.10, B.18.c.6.2, B.24.a.85.65.
    One limber seen on road at C.15.a. proceeded to NEUVIREUIL.
  (d) Aerial Activity. Normal.

(3). GENERAL. Visibility poor owing to mist and rain.

3rd August 1918.   Lieut: R.F.A.
                       for Reconnaissance Officer 52nd Div: Arty.

SECRET.   52nd D.A. No.Z/404.

9th Brigade.
56th Brigade.
277th A. Brigade.

Reference 52nd Divisional Artillery Instructions No. 2.

1.   Cancel para. 2 (a) and (b).
     Substitute:-
          56th Brigade and 9th Brigades R.F.A. will share Brigade liaison with 156th Infantry Brigade.
          56th Brigade will be in Battalion liaison with left battalion.
          9th Brigade will be in Battalion liaison with Right Battalion.
          9th Brigade assumes Brigade liaison duties August 2nd.
          Relief every 7 days provided that liaison Officers tours of duty do not coincide with Infantry reliefs.

2.   Cancel Para. 3.
     Substitute:-
          277th Army Brigade will keep a Brigade liaison Officer with 157th Infantry Brigade and with battalions in the line of the Centre Brigade.

                                        M. Beresford-Peirse
                                        Major R.F.A.
                                        A/Brigade Major R.A.
                                        52nd Divisional Artillery.

2nd August 1918.

Copies to:-   311th Army Brigade.
               52nd Division "G".
               R.O.R.A. (4).
               R.A. Signals.
               155th Infantry Brigade.
               156th Infantry Brigade.
               157th Infantry Brigade.

April 6. W.D. 6

LEFT DIVISIONAL ARTILLERY (XVII CORPS) INTELLIGENCE SUMMARY.

From 6am 3rd to 6am 4th August 1918.

1. **OUR ACTIVITY.**
   (a) **Operations.** Registration carried out by day and harassing fire by night.
   Dump at I.3.a.40.20 shelled, and men seen to run away from this vicinity at 8.30pm.
   6" T.M's fired on ARLEUX LOOP S, at 2.0pm. Junction of FIRED ALLEY and ARLEUX LOOP N, at 7pm, and on the trench in H.6.a.
   Total rounds fired:-
   18-pdr. - 2265.   4.5" Hows. - 861.   6" T.M. 79.

2. **HOSTILE ACTIVITY.**
   (a) **Artillery.** Above normal.
   Considerable harassing fire on B.13 and 14 throughout the day and night.
   At 9.15 pm. H.2 central was shelled by 80 rounds 77mm.

Date.	Time.	No. of rds.	Calibre.	Area shelled.	Direction.	Remarks.
3rd.	6.5am.	30.	77mm.	H.10.a.		GAS.
	7.10am.	30.	10.5cm.	B.14.d.	OPPY.	
	7.10am.	10.	15cm.	B.21.c.70.70	NEUVIREUIL.	
	7.20am.	30.	77mm.	B.21.c.		
	8-9.15am.	60.	77	B.13 & 14 d.		
	8.25-9am.	20.	77mm.	Road B.16.a.		
	8.55 am.	50.	77mm.	B.4.a & c.		
	9.15-10.45am	30.	77mm.	B.7.b & d.	FRESNOY WOOD.	
	9.30am.	60.	10.5cm.	B.13.b.		
	10-11am.	75.	77mm.	B.13 & 14.		
	11am.	20.	10.5cm.	Road A.30.a.		
	11am.	14.	10.5cm.	B.27.d.		
	11.45.	15	15cm.	B.19.		
	11.50am to 12.5pm.	30.	10.5cm.	A.18.d. & B.13.a.	ARLEUX.	
	1.10-1.45pm.	30.	77mm.	B.14.b.	GAVRELLE.	
	1.15pm.	20.	77mm.	Dugout B.15.c.	FRESNES.	
	2.0pm.	10.	10.5cm.	B.14.d.	NEUVIREUIL.	
	2.30-3.30pm	40.	10.5cm.	B.13.a & b.		
	3.30.pm.	20.	77mm.	A.18.d.8.2.		
	5.30. pm.	55.	77mm	B.23.c.		
	5.50pm.	32.	10.5cm.	A.18.b & d.		12 duds.
	6.0pm.	50.	10.5cm.	B.19.		
	6.45pm.	20.	10.5cm.	B.13.b.		
	7.0pm.	40.	10.5cm.	B.29.a.		
	9.15pm.	80.	77mm.	H.2.central.		
	10.5pm.	30.	77mm.	H.1.a.		GAS.
	10.10pm.	20.	77mm.	A.24.c.		
	10.20.	50.	77mm.	B.20.a.		GAS.
	10.30pm.	10.	10.5cm.	B.27.a & b.		
	11pm.	50.	77mm.	B.23.a & b.		HE. & GAS
4th.	1.30am.	25.	77mm.	H.3 central.		
	3.10-4.50am	300.	4.2.	B.13.b.		

   (b) **Work.** Nil.
   (c) **Movement.** 30 men in single file seen on road at I.7.c., engaged and dispersed.
   Movement at I.1.d.7.5 fired on and dispersed at 1pm.
   8.45am. 2 mounted men seen going east from GAVRELLE.
   2.30pm. 15 men seen going west from FRESNES.
   Movement observed at C.14.b.8.5, B.24.b.5.0, C.25.c.9 C.21.b.5.4, C.21.a.2.8, C.25.b.0.5, C.20.c.1.9, I.8.c. and I.12.a.
   (d) **Aerial.** Normal activity.

3. **GENERAL.** Visibility Fair.

H.A.Everet

(XVII Corps)

LEFT DIVISIONAL ARTILLERY/INTELLIGENCE SUMMARY.
6am 4th to 6am 5th August 1918.

(1) OUR ACTIVITY.
    (a) Operations. Registration carried out by day and harassing fire by night.
        Movement engaged at B.3.a., H.1.c., I.1.b.60.05, I.1.d.25.45., I.1.c.78.48.
        6" T.M.'s fired on HARRY TRENCH, NEWTON TRENCH and ARLEUX LOOP S.
        Total rounds fired:-
        18-pdrs. - 2,114.   4.5" Hows. 489.   6" T.M. 37.

(2) HOSTILE ACTIVITY.
    (a) Artillery. Normal.
        BAILLEUL was shelled during the morning with 70 rds. 10.5cm.
        From 10.15pm. to 11.10pm. A.14.c.7.4 was shelled by 100 rds. 10.5cm GAS.
        From 10.50pm. to 1.0am. A.17.c. was shelled by 150 rounds 10.5cm. GAS, and 30 rounds 15cm. H.E.

Date.	Time.	No. of rds.	Calibre.	Area shelled.	Direction.	Remarks.
4th.	6.15am.	10.	10.5cm.	Road A.30.b.1.2.		
	6.15am.	30.	10.5cm.	F.L.B.28.d.		
	6.30am.	20.	77mm.	B.16.a.	82°G from B.8.c.8.3.	
	6.35am.	9.	10.5cm.	B.21.d.		
	7.15am.	20.	10.5cm.	BAILLEUL.		
	9.30am.	10.	10.5cm.	B.13.		
	9.40am.	30.	77mm.	B.4.c.6.0.		
	9.40-10.30.	30.	10.5cm.	B.16.a.1.6.	82°G from B.8.c.8.3.	
	10.15am.	10.	10.5cm.	A.30.b.1.2.		
	10.30am.	30.	10.5cm.	A.13.c. & B4.b.		
	10.30.am.	6.	10.5cm.	B.27.a.		
	10.30-11.40am	30	10.5cm.	? B.19.c.	Bursts appeared similar to 18-pdr. 106 fuze.	
	11.0am	50.	10.5cm.	BAILLEUL.		
	11.10-11.20.	12.	10.5cm.	Railway Track A.24.d.		
	11.15am.	12.	10.5cm.	B.28.d.		
	11.30am.	50.	10.5cm.	B.20.		Area shoot.
	11.30am.	20.	10.5cm.	B.13.		
	11.40am.	12.	10.5cm.	B.22.d.		
	12 to 1.30pm.	40.	77mm.	B.22.d.		
	12.10pm.	10.	15cm.	B.16.b.		
	1.20pm.	9.	15cm.	B.28.a.		
	1.30pm.	8.	10.5cm.	B.27.a.4.5.		
	2.30-4pm.	28.	10.5cm.	B.19.c.		
	2.45-3.5pm.	20.	10.5cm.	A.24.d.8.4.		
	3.10pm.	15.	10.5cm.	B.21.a.		
	3.10-3.30pm.	25.	15cm.	B.19.d.		
	6.5pm.	6.	10.5cm.	B.15.c.		
	10.15-11.30pm.	100.	10.5cm.	A.14.c.7.4		GAS.
	10.30pm.	50.	77mm.	A.30.		GAS.
	10.30.pm.	30.	10.5cm.	A.18.b & d.		GAS & H.E.
	10.50pm - 1am.	150.)	10.5cm.)	A.17.c.		GAS.
		30.)	15cm.)			H.E.
	11-12pm.	30.	10.5cm.	A.24.d.		
5th.	3.30-3.45am.	20.	10.5cm.	B.13.b.		

    (b) Work - Nil.
    (c) Movement. Movement in vicinity of CHEZ BONTEMPS throughout the morning. Movement seen about U.26.b., B.30.d., B.30.a.,30.19, B.30.a., H.1.c., I.1.b.60.05, I.1.d.25.45, I.2.d.0.5, I.2.a., I.4.c. and I.10.a.
        At 7.15pm 18-pdrs. obtained direct hit on dugout at I.1.c.78.48, men were seen coming out of dugout and a thick volume of smoke was rising from it.
    (d) Aerial. - Normal.

(3) GENERAL.
    Visibility - Fair.

5th August 1918.
                        Lieut: RFA.
        for Reconnaissance Officer, 52nd D.A.

LEFT DIVISIONAL ARTILLERY (XVII CORPS) INTELLIGENCE SUMMARY.
6am 5th to 6am 6th August 1918.

(1) ACTIVITY.

(a) **Operations.** 18-pdrs. fired on movement in I.2.a., H.6.b.40.11, I.1.c.78.48, B.30.b. & d. and near CHEZ BONTEMPS.

Three bursts of fire during afternoon on Trench junction at B.12.a.65.50.

Usual harassing fire carried out by night.

6" T.M's fired 29 rounds on Sunken Road B.5 central at 5pm, 15 rounds on Dugout in HUMID Trench H.6.a.3.0 and 19 rds. on movement & work at ANTELOPE ALLEY, partly dispersed.

Rounds fired:-

18-pdrs. 2694.   4.5" Hows. 643.   6" T.M. 88.

(2) HOSTILE ACTIVITY.

(a) **Artillery.** Rather below normal.
Battery CC.60 reported active.

Date.	Time.	No.of rds.	Calibre.	Area shelled.	Direction.	Remarks.
5th.	7am.	20.	10.5cm.	A.14.c.70.40.		
	8.45-10.20am.	110.	77mm.	B.27.a b & c.		
	9.25am.	35.	77mm.	A.24.b & d.		FAMPOUX.
	9.25am.	25.	10.5cm.	A.24.c.4.2.		
	9.25am.	50.	10.5cm.	A.30.d.		
	9.25am.	15.	10.5cm.	G.5.b.		
	9.35am.	50.	10.5cm.	A.30.b & c.		.... GAS.
	10.30am.	10.	10.5cm.	A.14.c.7.4.		
	10.45am.	50.	10.5cm.	H.5.a & c., H.11.a.	G.B. 110° from H.10.b.01.79.	
	11.45am.	15.	77mm.	B.4.b.		ARLEUX.
	12.20am.	60.	77mm.	B.21.d.		
	12.20.	40.	10.5cm.	B.15.c.6.6.		NEUVIREUIL.
	12.30.pm.	55	77mm.	B.15.d.		of ARLEUX.
	1.50pm.	20.	15cm.	B.13.b. & d.		
	1.50pm.	30.	77mm.	B.8.a.		
	1.50pm.	20.	10.5cm.	H.2.a.5.5.		
	2.30pm.	50.	77mm.	B.26.d.1.8.		
	2.40.	10.	10.5cm.	B.27.b.		
	2.50pm.	10.	10.5cm.	H.4.c.		
	3.20pm.	12.	10.5cm.	BAILLEUL.		
	3.20pm.	20.	77mm.	B.27.d.		
	3.30pm.	9.	15cm.	Cutting B.26.b.		
	4.15pm.	10.	77mm.	B.28.a.		
	4-4.40pm.	30.	15cm.	B.8.c.		Right of ARLEUX.
	4.45 pm.	9.	77mm.	B.27.c.		
	5.30pm.	20.	15cm.	G.5.b.		
	5.40pm.	15.	10.5cm.	A.19.c.		
	5.40pm.	20.	77mm.	A.24.b.		NEUVIREUIL.
	5.45pm.	20.	10.5cm.	A.30.a.		
	6.15pm.	8.	10.5cm.	B.27.c.		
	6.15pm.	9.	15cm.	B.25.b.		
	9.15pm.	13.	77mm.	B.27.a.		
	10.25pm.	22.	77mm.	B.26.b & c.		
	10.50pm.	20.	10.5cm.	H.9.b.		.... GAS.
	11.0pm.	50.	10.5cm.	H.4.b.		.... GAS.
6th.	1.0am.	16.	15cm.	B.27.a.		
	1.20am.	20.	10.5cm.	BAILLEUL.		
	2.15am.	50.	10.5cm.	B.13.d.		

(b) **Work** - Nil.

(c) **Movement.** 3 Huns seen walking about in C.19.b. and then seen to go to CHEDDAR TRENCH.

Enemy signalling lamp (red) observed in G.B. 84° from B.27.b.30.97. at 7.15pm.

Individual Movement seen in B.30.b & d; round CHEZ BONTEMPS, in C.1.c.0.8, U.20.c., Quarry in C.16.d., MANVILLE FARM, I.2.a., H.6.b.40.11, B.30.c & I.1.c.78.48.

(d) **Aerial Activity.** Below normal.

(3) GENERAL. Visibility poor owing to mist and rain.

At 9pm. 1 red light bursting into 2 reds went up opposite centre sector. No action followed.

6th August 1918.

for Reconnaissance Officer,   Lieut.

52nd D.A.No. A/423.   Appx II

9th Brigade (4).
56th Brigade (4).
277th Brigade (4).
311th Brigade (4).
D.T.M.O. (3).
================

Reference Gas Beam discharge known as "ROBIN" issued under 4th Canadian Division G.28/8-17 of July 28th and repeated to 13th and 14th Brigades C.F.A. under G.50/9/537 and to 3rd and 4th Brigades C.F.A. under G.8/269/38.

1. All future messages reference "ROBIN" will be issued reference the number of this letter - (A./423).

2. The zero hour for ROBIN is 2.0am.

3. The discharge point is B.16.b.0.8.

4. The wind limits for the operations are S.West through West to West North West, Velocity between 6 and 15 miles per hour.

5. Code words will be used as follows:-

    (1). Operation will take place tonight .... ROBIN.
    (2). Operation will not take place tonight .... IMSHI.
    (3). Cancel operation previously ordered ...... SPRAY.
    (4). Discharge complete .... KVG.

6. In conjunction with the above Gas Beam, a harassing programme will be carried out by the Divisional Artillery and Left Group Heavy Artillery.

7. The code words for the Gas Beam as laid down in Para. 5 above will also apply to the Artillery harassing scheme.

Case I or Case II will be ordered on the wire notifying the code word.

8. Tasks are allotted as follows, for forward guns and howitzers.

CASE I. If the wind is from S.W. to West.
    311th Brigade. Forward 18-pdrs. harass communications, trenches, roads and tracks, squares B.18.a., B.18.b., C.13.a., C.13.b.
    Forward howitzers on track junction in B.12.d. and B.18.b.

    277th Brigade. Forward 18-pdrs. - Roads and communication trenches in Squares B.18 and C.13.
    Forward Hows on Trench junctions in B.18.b.

    56th Brigade. Forward 18-pdrs. harass Roads, tracks and trenches in squares C.13.c., C.13.d., C.19.a. & C.19.b.
    Forward howitzers on Road through OPPY.

CASE II. Wind from West to West North West.
    311th Brigade. Forward 18-pdrs. harass communication trenches and roads in squares B.12, C.1., C.7.
    Forward hows. on trench junction in B.12.d. & B.18.b.

    277th and 56th Brigades. As for CASE I.

9. Artillery Programme will commence at Zero plus 10 minutes i.e. 2.10am.
The above active harassing programme will be vigorously carried out in bursts for 2 hours, until Zero plus 2 hours 10 minutes.
After Zero plus 2 hours 10 minutes Brigades will continue their normal harassing fire programme - paying special attention to gassed areas that fall within their zones.

Page 2.

10. 9th Brigade - from Zero plus 10 minutes to Zero plus 2 hours 10 minutes will carry out normal harassing fire with 100% increase of activity - after Zero plus 2 hours 10 minutes will revert to normal harassing fire.

11. All Brigades should carry out normal harassing fire up to Zero plus 10 minutes - avoiding any action likely to bring retaliation on to Square B.16.

12. F.A. Brigades to ACKNOWLEDGE.

N. Beresford Peirse
Major R.F.A.
A/Brigade Major R.A.
52nd Divisional Artillery.

4th August 1918.

Copies to:- G.S. 52nd Division.
R.A. XVII Corps.
Left H.A. Group.
R.O., R.A. (2).

SECRET.   52nd D.A. No. X/427/2.

277th Brigade (3).
9th Brigade (3).

       In continuation of my X/427/1.

1.   Moves of A/277, D/277, 19th Battery and D/69 will be from main positions only.

2.   Ammunition at main positions of the 9th Brigade Batteries will be handed over to 57th Divisional Artillery under orders of S.C., R.A.

3.   Ammunition at 277 Brigade positions will be taken over by 19th and D/69 Batteries.

4.   O.P's and forward guns will not move at present.

5.   A/277 and D/277 Batteries will draw ammunition from Refilling Point as required.

6.   On night August 8th/9th A/277 and D/277 will each move one Section into positions evacuated by one 18-pdr. Battery and one Howitzer Battery of 8th Divisional Artillery at B.13.a.14.76 (late 20th Battery R.F.A.) and A.18.d.96.77 (late D/69 Battery R.F.A.) respectively, completing the move on night August 9th/10th.
      Ammunition in these positions will be taken over from 8th Divisional Artillery under orders of S.C., R.A.

7.   Completion of reliefs will be notified to this office by code words as follows:-

          Night of August 5th/6th .... SLEEP.
            ,,   ,,   ,,   6th/7th .... REST.
            ,,   ,,   ,,   8th/9th .... AGAIN.
            ,,   ,,   ,,   9th/10th .... TIRED.

                                      N. Beresford Peirse
                                         Major R.F.A.
                                        A/Brigade Major R.A.
5th August 1918.   52nd Divisional Artillery.

Copies to:-   G.S. 52nd Division.
             R.A. XVII Corps.
             8th Divisional Artillery.
             57th Divisional Artillery.
             S.C., R.A.
             R.O., R.A. (2)
             56th Brigade R.F.A.
             311th Brigade R.F.A.
             R.A. Signals.

SECRET.

52nd D.A.No. Q/433/1.

My G.2/1/22 of August 4th:-

1. Ref. Para. 1. The 172nd Inf. Brigade will relieve that portion of 156th Inf: Brigade now occupying the area to be taken over by 57th Division, under arrangements to be made between G.O's C. Brigades concerned.

The 2 machine guns at H.4.c.0.8 will be relieved by two machine guns, 57th M.G. Battalion, under arrangements to be made between M.G. Battalion Commanders concerned. Completion of Machine gun relief to be wired priority by 52nd M.G. Battalion to 52nd Division Headquarters.

Ref. Para. (2) (a). The whole of OUSE locality will be inclusive to the Centre Brigade.

Ref: Para. (2) (b). The Brigade boundary will run from B.10.b.6.0 down the new unnamed extension of TIRED ALLEY leading from PLUMER extension to YUKON, thence down TIRED ALLEY as far as its junction with the GREEN line (the whole inclusive to the Left Brigade), and thence due Westwards.

2. It should be noted that the Divisional boundary on the North makes the Western Road inclusive to 52nd Division.

9th Brigade (5).
56th Brigade (5).
277th Brigade (5).
311th Brigade (5).
D.T.M.O. (5).

For information.

Major R.F.A.
A/Brigade Major R.A.
52nd Divisional Artillery.

5th August 1918.

SECRET.   52nd D.A. No. A/438.

9th Brigade (5).
56th Brigade (5).
277th Brigade (5).
311th Brigade (5).

Reference G.7/1/28 dated August 5th 1918 attached.

1. A wire will be sent from this office to each Brigade and to Left Group, Heavy Artillery, and 52nd Division for information, using the Code MARO (RIGHT - CENTRE OR LEFT) followed by the Zero hour.
   E.G. MARO LEFT - 9.53 am.

2. At this Zero hour all forward 18-pdrs. and forward howitzers which can bear will fire 2 minutes INTENSE and 3 minutes RAPID on the enemy front line and support trenches - opposite the Section of the Divisional Front indicated by the message.
   Fire from the LEFT, CENTRE or RIGHT Divisional Sections being brought to bear on the NORTHERN, CENTRAL or SOUTHERN portion respectively of the section opposite which retaliation is ordered.
   18-pdrs. will fire shrapnel.

3. Heavy Artillery Co-operation - which will be directed at the hostile batteries firing - will commence immediately on receipt of the order MARO.

4. Forward guns and Howitzers should be prepared to carry out their retaliations within 3 minutes of receipt of order. All switching being worked out previously.

5. The scheme will come into force at 12 noon, Tuesday, August 6th.

6. All previous retaliation Schemes are cancelled.

7. Acknowledge.

                                            Major R.F.A.
                                         A/ Brigade Major R.A.
5th August 1918.   52nd Divisional Artillery.

Copies to:- R.A. XVII Corps.
            52nd Div: "G".
            155th, 156th, 157th Inf: Brigades.
            R.O.R.A. (2).
            R.A. Signals.

Page 2.

G.7/1/28.

1.   Owing to the habit of the enemy in this Sector of laying down barrages on our lines, the following practice will come into force from 12 noon Tuesday, 6th August.

2.   A set piece retaliation will be arranged for the Field Artillery on the enemy's front and support lines, and for the Heavy Artillery covering the front on the enemy's Artillery positions.

3.   Brigades will call for these retaliations through their F.A. Liaison Officer. This Officer will apply to R.A., Divisional Headquarters in the code word MARO followed by the Brigade Section calling for retaliation (Right, Centre or Left).

4.   R.A. Div: H.Q. will thereupon fix a time about 15 minutes ahead for the Artillery to carry out a 5 minute bombardment.

5.   Schemes will be arranged by Field and Heavy Artillery forthwith.

9th Brigade (5).
56th Brigade (5).
277th Brigade (5).
311th Brigade (5).

52nd D.A.No. M/440.

1. The 52nd Divisional Artillery and attached Army Brigades R.F.A. will be tactically formed into three Groups for the support of the 52nd Divisional Front.

2. Dispositions (for August 8th - 10.0am).

LEFT GROUP. (In support of 155th Infantry Brigade).

Lieut:Colonel N.P.R. PRESTON, D.S.O., 311th Brigade R.F.A.
Headquarters 311th Brigade R.F.A.
A/311th Brigade - 18-pdr. Battery.
B/311th Brigade - 18-pdr. Battery.
C/311th Brigade - 18-pdr. Battery.
A/277th Brigade - 18-pdr. Battery.
D/311th Brigade - 4.5" Howitzer Battery.

CENTRE GROUP. (in support of 157th Infantry Brigade.)

Lt. Col. H.J. COTTER, C.I.E., D.S.O., 9th Brigade R.F.A.
Headquarters, 9th Brigade R.F.A.
19th Battery - 18-pdr. Battery.
20th Battery - 18-pdr. Battery.
B/277th Brigade - 18-pdr. Battery.
C/277th Brigade - 18-pdr. Battery.
D/69th Brigade - 4.5" Howitzer Battery.
D/277th Brigade - 4.5" Howitzer Battery.

RIGHT GROUP. (in support of 156th Infantry Brigade).

A/Lt.Col. J.M. INGRAM, 56th Brigade R.F.A.
Headquarters, 56th Brigade R.F.A.
28th Battery - 18-pdr. Battery.
A/56th Battery - 18-pdr. Battery.
B/56th Battery - 18-pdr. Battery
C/56th Battery - 18-pdr. Battery.
527th Battery - 4.5" Howitzer Battery.

3. Headquarters 277th Brigade R.F.A. will withdraw to Wagon Lines.
Headquarters 9th Brigade R.F.A. will be at A.29.a.30.40.
Details of move to be arranged between 9th and 277th Brigades R.F.A.

4. The 18-pdr. Barrage will be laid down continuously along the Divisional Front, covering the outpost line as at present; each Group covering the front of the Infantry Brigade which it supports and having its Group Boundaries the same as the Boundaries of the Infantry Brigade.
The 18-pdr. Barrage will be not less than about 200 yards from the Infantry line - 4.5" Howitzers 100 yards beyond 18-pounders.

5. The above Grouping and any adjustments to Barrage will come into operation at 10am. August 8th 1918 by which time Liaison and communications should be established.

6. F.A. Brigades to ACKNOWLEDGE.

N. Beresford-Peirse
Major R.F.A.
A/Brigade Major R.A.
52nd Divisional Artillery.

5th August 1918.

Copies to:- 52nd Div:'G'; R.A. XVII Corps; S.C.R.A.; R.A.Sigs.; R.O.R.A. (2) 155th, 156th, 157th Infantry Brigades; Left Heavy Artillery Group; D.T.M.O.

LEFT DIVISIONAL ARTILLERY (XVII CORPS) INTELLIGENCE SUMMARY.
6am 6th to 6am 7th August 1918.

1. **OUR ACTIVITY.**
   (a) Operations. Movement was fired on in I.1.a.& d., C.20 & C.26, B.24.b.& d., C.25.a & b.
   Harassing fire during the night on following targets:-
   ARLEUX SECTION. Tracks in C.1.c & C.7.a., B.5.b.60.65.
   OPPY SECTION. BRADFORD Trench, Tracks in B.12.a & b.,
   Road & C.T. in C.13, B.18.a & b. B.18.c & d.
   GAVRELLE SECTION. BELVOIR ALLEY, BRADFORD TRENCH, CAMPBELL TRENCH, CHUTNEY TRENCH, CURRY TRENCH; Roads & tracks in C.25.b & 26.a, C.19.c & 20.a, C.25.a to 19.c.,
   C.19.c.6.5 & C.19.d.75.38.
   Trench Mortars fired on dugouts in HUMID TRENCH H.6.a.C.9.
   Total rounds fired:-
   18-pdrs. 2623.   4.5" Hows. 843.   6" T.M. 19.

(2) **HOSTILE ACTIVITY.**
   (a) Artillery. Normal, Chiefly harassing fire especially on A.24, B.21, B.26, B.27 localities, together with a few rounds of gas shell. 230 rounds 10.5cm. were fired on our forward guns in B.13.b. between midnight and 4.0am, but no damage was done.

Date.	Time.	No. of rds.	Calibre.	Area shelled	Direction.	Remarks.
6th.	8-9am.	20.	10.5cm.	B.3.		ARLEUX.
	9.15.	6.	10.5cm.	B.12.c.		Grid 110° from A.24.c.45.20.
	9.15.	20.	10.5cm.	B.9.d.		Grid 89° from B.8.c.71.50.
	9.15.	10.	77mm.	B.21.c.		
	9.30.	10.	10.5cm.	BAILLEUL.		F/R 30 secs. G. 105° from H.3.d.70.93.
	9.40.	15.	77mm.	B.19.d.		GAVRELLE.
	9.40.	20.	77mm.	Track A.18.d. & 24.b.		
	9.45.	10.	77mm.	B.12.c.		G.110° from A.24.c.45.20.
	10-10.30.	30.	10.5cm.	A.24.b.7.3 to A.24.d.8.8.		
	10.50.	30.	77mm.	BAILLEUL.		
	11-11.30.	12.	15cm.	Road B.26.b.		G.105° from A.24.c.45.20.
	11.15.	11.	10.5cm.	A.24.b.		
	11.30.	5.	15cm. gun.	Back areas.		ARLEUX.
	11.45.	30.	10.5cm.	B.20.		
	11.45.	9.	15cm.	B.21.a.		F/R 20 secs. G.105° from H.3.d.70.93.
	12 noon.	24.	77mm.	H.2.b.2.0.		Gas, YELLOW CROSS.
	12.15pm.	13.	15cm.	Railway B.21.c.		
	1-2pm.	60.	77mm.	H.2. central.		
	1-1.45.	30.	10.5cm.	B.26.b.		
	2.0.	6.	15cm.	H.5.a.		
	2.30.	50.	10.5cm.	B.26.b & d.		.... GAS.
	3.45.	10.	10.5cm.	B.7.b.		ARLEUX.
	4.30.	5.	15cm.	H.5.a.		
	5.45.	30.	77mm.	A.16.d., 17.c & d.		ARLEUX.
	5.50.	20.	15cm gun.	A.18.a & c.		D/R 21 secs. G. 85° from B.8.a.4.3. Silenced by our 6" Guns.
	5.50.	40.	10.5cm.	A.24.a.		
	7.30.	20.	10.5cm.	B.21.b.		.... GAS.
	9.30.	7.	15cm.	B.29.b.		
	10.0.	10.	15cm.	B.27.d.4.4.		
	10.30.	30.	77mm.	B.20.b.		
	11.20.	20.	77mm.	H.5.a.		
	11.20.	12.	15cm.	B.21.a.		
7th.	12.30am.	10.	10.5cm.	B.20.a.		
	12.10-4.0.	230.	10.5cm.	B.13.b.		
	12.55.	5.	15cm.	B.21.c.		
	1.40.	20.	10.5cm.	A.18.		
	2.30.	8.	10.5cm.	B.21.a.		
	2.55.	25.	10.5cm.	B.27.c.a.		.... GAS.

Page 2.

(b) Work - Working parties seen repairing trenches at 11.30am
at B.24.b.& d. and at 2.0pm at C.25.a. & b., these were
fired on.

(c) Movement - Individual movement in U.20.c., C.20 and C.26.
Train seen moving South from BEAUMONT at 10.10am.

(d) Aerial. Normal.
1 E.A. over our lines at 4pm and 2 at 8.0pm.

3. GENERAL. Visibility - Poor, with good intervals.

Correct.

7th August 1918.
Lieut: R.F.A.
for Reconnaissance Officer, 52nd Div: Arty.

Appendix 17

9th Brigade (5).
56th Brigade (5).
277th Brigade (5).
311th Brigade (5).

52nd D.A.No. M/440/3.

Reference 52nd D.A.No. M/440 dated 5th August.

After RIGHT GROUP read (in support of 156th Infantry Brigade.)

6th August 1918.

M. Beresford-Peirse
Major R.F.A.
A/Brigade Major R.A.
52nd Divisional Artillery.

Copies to:- 52nd Div: 'G'; R.A. XVII Corps; S.C.R.A.; R.A.Signals; R.O.R.A. (2); 155th, 156th, 157th Infantry Brigades; Left Heavy Artillery Group; D.T.M.O.

LEFT DIVISIONAL ARTILLERY, XVII CORPS, INTELLIGENCE SUMMARY.
6am 7th to 6am 8th August 1918.

1. OUR ACTIVITY.
   (a) Operations. Movement at B.30.a & b. was fired on.
       Harassing fire during the night on following targets:-
   ARLEUX Section. C.3.c & d, C.3.a, U.25, Track from B.12.a.9.5
       to C.7.a.6.9 and track from B.12.b.1.6 to C.1.c.5.1.
   OPPY Section. Road from C.8.d. to C.9.c and C.9.c to C.15.a.
       EARL Trench, OUSE ALLEY (B.18.d.), BLANDFORD TRENCH, BEAM
       TRENCH, Trench from B.12.d.83.68 to C.7.c.0.4, MARQUIS
       TRENCH, B.11.b.68.28, B.12.d.44.43, Sunken Road in
       B.12.a & b. Trenches in C.13.a, b & c.
   GAVRELLE Section. C.27.c.2.9, C.27.c.2.2, GAVRELLE TRENCH, Road
       C.25.b. to C.26.a., Track C.19.d. to C.20 central, BELVOIR
       ALLEY, CHUTNEY TRENCH, Sunken Road C.25.a to C.19.a,
       C.19.c.6.5, C.19.d.75.38, B.30.a.80.84, B.30.a.30.34,
       B.30.a.86.93, B.30.a.60.55.
   6" TRENCH MORTARS - 12 rounds fired at 4.30pm. on work at
       ANTELOPE ALLEY.
   Total rounds fired:-
       18-pdrs. - 2457.   4.5" Hows. - 792.   6" T.M. 12.

2. HOSTILE ACTIVITY.

   (a) Artillery. Below normal.
       Hostile artillery was quiet during the day, except
       some harassing fire by 77mm. during the evening and
       night there was considerable shelling of H.2.a & b, H.4.a,
       B.13, B.20, B.21.b. and B.26.b.

Date.	Time.	No. of rds.	Calibre.	Area shelled.	Direction.	Remarks.
7th.	6.15am.	50.	77mm.	B.16.b.		
	6.20.	75.	77mm.	B.23.a.		
	6.25.	50.	77mm.	B.26.b.		
	10.30.	6.	15cm.	B.27.a.		
	11.20.	7.	10.5cm.	B.27.c.		
	11.30.	10.	77mm.	B.10.c.		
	11.55.	23.	10.5cm.	B.27.a.		
	12.15pm.	16.	77mm.	B.27.d.		
	1.15.	20.	10.5cm.	H.4.b.		
	1.30.	12.	77mm.	B.10.a.0.5		Registration.
	2.30.	20.	77mm.	A.30.b. & 24.d. FAMPOUX.		
	3.5.	9.	77mm.	A.24.d.7.5.		
	3.30.	20.	77mm.	B.22.a.		Registration.
	4.0-4.30.	50.	10.5cm.	H.4.b.		
	4.40.	30.	77mm.	B.23.b & 15.d.		
	7 to 9.0.	300.	?	H.2.a.		
	7.50.	60.	77mm & 10.5cm.	B.23.a. & 27.c.		GAS.
	8.20.	100.	77mm.	H.2.a & b.		H.E. & GAS.
	8.20.	50.	15cm.	H.2.a & b.		
	9.30.	25.	77mm.	B.20.		
	9.45.	60.	10.5cm.	B.18.b.		
	10.20.	60.	77mm.	B.26.b.		GAS.
	10.30.	50.	77mm.	H.2.b.1.1.		SHRAPNEL.
	10.30.	70.	10.5 & 15cm.	B.13.d.		
	11.0pm.	200.	77mm.	TOWEY ALLEY		
8th.	2.0am.	46.	10.5 & 15cm.	B.21.b.		
	3.15.	35.	10.5cm.	B.23.b.		
	3-3.30.	60.	10.5cm.	B.13.a & b.		

(b) Work.

(b) Work - Nil.

(c) Movement. Small parties seen at T.5.c.65.70, near CHEZ BONTEMPS, B.30.a & b, B.24.d.60.47. Telescope seen at B.24.a.95.47.

(d) Aerial. Normal.
8.15pm. 3 E.A's crossed our lines, but were driven off by A.A. & M.G. fire.

3. GENERAL.
Visibility variable, fair most of the day.
Flashes of an enemy A.A. gun were seen on G.B. 98° from B.14.b.3.7 at 7.2p.m.

H.J. Everett.

8th August 1918.

Lieut: R.F.A.
for Reconnaissance Office, 52nd Div:Arty.

APPENDIX

LEFT DIVISIONAL ARTILLERY, XVII CORPS, INTELLIGENCE SUMMARY.
6am August 8th to 6am August 9th 1918.

1. OUR ACTIVITY.
   (a) Operations. Movement was fired on in C.25.b & C.19.c and
       B.30.d.
       "MARO" LEFT was fired at 11pm, 12 midnight, 1.30am and
       "Maro Centre" at 5.0am.
       Harassing fire was carried out by night as follows:-
   ARLEUX SECTION B.5.a, B.6.a, T.29 and 30 and approaches
       to ARLEUX, SEVERN ALLEY and Junction of SEVERN ALLEY
       and BRITTANIA TRENCH.
   OPPY SECTION. KING STREET, MARQUIS TRENCH, EARL TRENCH,
       ERUMSTREET, BIRDPOST. Tracks B.12.a.8.5 to C.7.a.6.9
       and B.12.b.1.6 to C.1.c.3.1. BEDFORD ROW. Junction
       CLARENCE and BEALE TRENCHES and B.18.b.75.85.
   GAVRELLE SECTION All Roads and Tracks in B.24.d. and
       B.30.b. BELVOIR ALLEY, GAVRELLE TRENCH. Road C.25.a.2.8
       to C.19.a.0.0, C.19.c.6.5, C.19.d.75.38.
   6" TRENCH MORTARS fired 43 rounds on ARLEUX LOOP N and
       S. during the night.
   Rounds fired:-
   18-Pdr - 2717.   4.5" Hows. - 804.   6" T.M. 43.

2. HOSTILE ACTIVITY.
   (a) Artillery. Below normal, chiefly harassing fire on
       A.18, A.24, B.13, B.20 and H.3.

Date.	Time.	No. of rds.	Calibre.	Area shelled.	Direction. Remarks.
8th.	7.15-7.35am.	30	77mm.	B.23.a.	
	7.5-7.47	100	77mm.	B.20.c & 26.a.	
	7.37.	8	15cm.	Back areas.	
	7-8.30.	20.	10.5cm.	Back areas.	
	8.45.	20	10.5cm.	H.1.a.	61°G. from H.3.d.70.98.
	9.45.	20	10.5cm.	B.26.b.	
	10.0	10	15cm.	B.25.b.	115°G. from H.3.d.70.99.
	10.10.	4	15cm.	B.20.b.	
	10.45.	10	10.5cm.	B.20.b.	
	11.30	20	10.5cm.	B.23.c.	---do---
	11.50	10	10.5cm.	H.4.a & b.	---do---
	12.45pm.	26	10.5cm.	H.5.a.	---do---
	1-1.30.	12	10.5cm.	A.18.d.	75°G from B.20.b.05.55.
	2.40.	8	77mm	B.8.a.	ARLEUX.
	2.45.	50.	77mm.	B.9.b.	,,
	3.0.	20.	10.5cm.	A.18.d.	
	3.0.	40.	10.5cm.	B.14.b.4.7.	83°G from B.8.c.80.25 F/R 34 secs.
	7.30	10	15cm.	G.5.a & b.	
	7.30	6.	10.5cm.	B.27.a.	
	7.45	12	15cm.	H.1.a.	65°G from B.27.d.85.95. F/R 20 secs.
	8.0pm.	10.	10.5cm.	Back areas.	80°G from B.8.a.4.3.
	8.10.	50	10.5cm.	H.7.b.	68°G from B.27.d.85.95. F/R 21 secs.
	10.0	15	15cm.	B.21.b.	
	10.0.	40.	77mm.	H.3.b.	
	10.5.	25	77mm.	B.27.a.	
	11.0.	20.	10.5cm.	A.24.d.	98° G from B.14.a.51.70.
	11.30.	20.	10.5cm.	B.13.b.	
	11.55.	15	77mm.	B.27.b.	
	12mn.	30	77mm.	B.13.d.	.... GAS.
9th.	1am.	15.	10.5cm	BAILLEUL.	
	12.30am.	25.	10.5cm.	A.18.	.... GAS.
	1am.	20.	77mm.	B.13.c.	
	1.30-3.30.	50.	10.5cm.	B.13.b.	
	3.0.	15.	10.5cm.	B.21.c. cutting.	
	3.15.	20	10.5cm.	A.24.d.	G.98°from B.14.a.51.70.
	4.0.	6.	10.5cm.	BAILLEUL.	
	4.20.	26.	77mm.	B.22.c.	

(B).

Page 2.

(b) Work. Nil.
(c) Movement. 4 men seen walking N. in C.15.c & d. Parties seen in I.1.d.38.38 and B.30.d; 2 men seen at C.4.a.7.8, 5 men in C.9.b., 2 men seen to enter dugout at U.21.c.7.4, Individual movement in C.25.b. & 19.c., B.24.b.
1.55pm. Train seen to move N. behind DROCOURT and BILLY MONTIGNY.
(d) Aerial. Normal.
An observation balloon was brought down in flames by our aircraft at 10.30am.

3. GENERAL.

Visibility Good.

9th August 1918.

Lieut: R.F.A.
for Reconnaissance Officer, 52nd Div: Arty.

SECRET.   52nd D.A.No. F/470.

RIGHT GROUP.
CENTRE GROUP.
LEFT GROUP.

1. All previous S.O.S. Barrages are cancelled.

2. S.O.S. Barrage to come into operation at 12 noon August 9th as per attached tracing.

PROCEDURE.

S.O.S. call -05 minutes.   S.O.S. Lines.   INTENSE.
05 min - 15 minutes.   Barrage will creep   )
                           forward 100 yards   ) RAPID.
                           every 3 minutes.   )
15 min - 20 minutes.   S.O.S. lines.   NORMAL.

Repeating the procedure at "SLOW" Rate, until orders are received.

3. There is no intention of dropping the barrage back to cover the main line of resistance, owing to the presence of defended localities which will not be evacuated.

4. The gaps in the Field Artillery Barrages are filled partially by Machine guns and Medium trench mortars.
The Barrage of the Left Heavy Artillery Group being placed to strengthen gaps.

5. Trench Mortar and heavy barrages will be issued later.

6. Co-ordinates of Field Artillery Barrages, 18-pdr., are as follows:-

   4.5" Howitzer barrages being 100 yards outside 18-pdr. barrage

18 - 18-pdrs.) T.29.c.15.82 - T.29.c.10.27 - B.4.b.65.55 -
6 - 4.5" Hows) B.4.b.75.05.

12 - 18-pdrs.) B.4.d.98.25 - B.10.b.85.77 - B.11.a.02.55 -
6 - 4.5" Hows) B.11.a.07.04.

18 - 18-pdrs.)
6 - 4.5" Hows) B.17.a.53.52 - B.17.d.15.65 - B.17.d.20.32.

12 - 18-pdrs.   B.23.b.38.45 - B.23.b.50.00 - B.23.d.35.50.

12 - 18-pdrs.   B.29.b.05.65 - B.29.c.77.50.

6 - 4.5" Hows. B.29.b.32.90 - B.29.d.03.52.

7. GROUPS & D.T.M.O. to ACKNOWLEDGE.

                                        Major R.F.A.
                                        A/Brigade Major R.A.
8th August 1918.   52nd Divisional Artillery.

Copies to:- R.A. XVII Corps   1.   52nd Div: 'G'.   3.
             H.A. XVII ,,   1.   Left H.A. Group.   1.
             57th Div: Arty: 1.   8th Div: Arty: 1.
             RIGHT GROUP.   6.   CENTRE GROUP.   7.
             LEFT GROUP.   6.   R.O.R.A.   3.
             155th Infy:Bde.   1.   156th Inf: Bde.   1.
             157th Inf: Bde.   1.   D.T.M.O.   3.
             52nd Bn.M.G.C.   1.

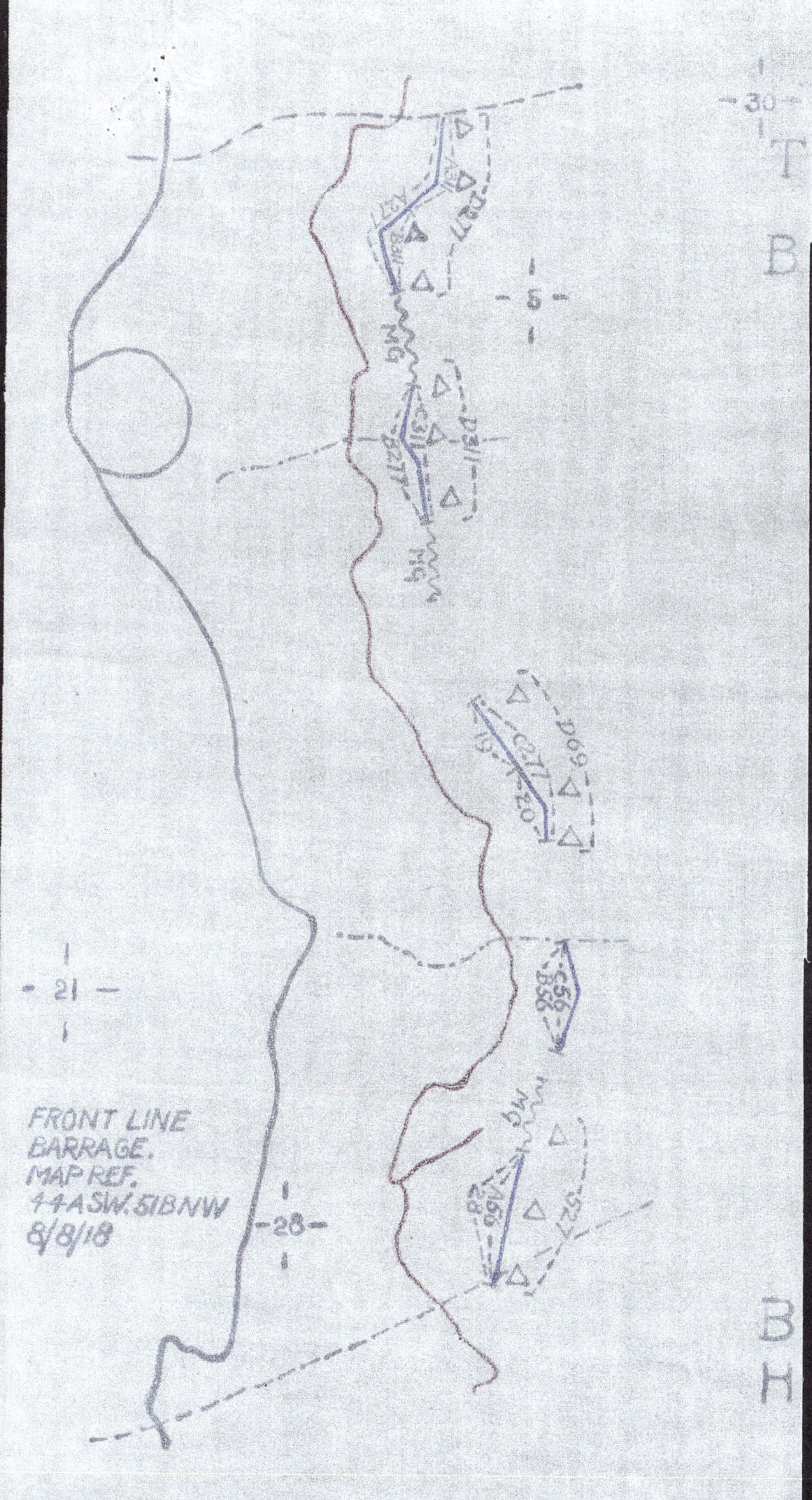

SECRET. 52nd D.A.No. M/471.

52nd DIVISIONAL ARTILLERY MUTUAL SUPPORT.

1. **WITH FLANK DIVISIONS.**

   (a) To assist Division on our LEFT.
   HELP ACHEVILLE.
   Left Group 52nd D.A. - 12 18-pdrs. T.29.c.00.30 - T.29.a.70.60.
                   3 4.5" Hows. T.29.c.20.25 - T.29.c.45.60
                                     - T.29.c.40.90.

   (b) To assist Division on our RIGHT.
   HELP FAMPOUX NORTH.
   Right Group, 52nd D.A.
       12 18-pdrs. - B.29.d.20.80 - H.5.b.80.40.
       6 4.5" Hows. - B.29.d.60.90 - H.6.a.15.50.

   (c) ASSISTANCE received from DIVISION ON OUR LEFT.
   HELP WILLEVAL.
   6 18-pdrs.   B.4.b.52.53 - B.4.b.61.19.

   (d) ASSISTANCE received from DIVISION ON OUR RIGHT.
   HELP GAVRELLE.
   12 18-pdrs. - B.29.d.20.80 - B.23.b.30.00.
   6 4.5" Hows. - 100 yards West of above.

2. **MUTUAL SUPPORT WITHIN THE DIVISION.**

   (a) HELP WILLEVAL.
   Action by LEFT GROUP, 52nd Divisional Artillery.
      Fires on its S.O.S. lines.
   CENTRE GROUP, 52nd Divisional Artillery.
      12 18-pdrs. B.4.b.75.05 - B.4.d.98.25.
      6 4.5" Hows. 100 yards west of above.

   (b) HELP OPPY.
   Action by CENTRE GROUP - 52nd Divisional Artillery.
      Fire on its S.O.S. Lines.
   LEFT GROUP, 52nd Divisional Artillery.
      12 18-pdrs - B.11.a.07.05 - B.17.a.60.50.
      6 4.5" Hows. 100 yards west of above.
   RIGHT GROUP, 52nd Divisional Artillery.
      6 18-pdrs - B.17.d.20.30 - B.23.b.40.45
      3 4.5" Hows. 100 yards west of above.

   (c) HELP GAVRELLE.
   RIGHT GROUP, 52nd Divisional Artillery.
      Fire on its own S.O.S. Lines.
   CENTRE GROUP, 52nd Divisional Artillery.
      12 18-pdrs - B.23.b.40.80 - B.23.b.40.40, and
                   B.23.a.40.50 - B.29.d.10.70.
      6 4.5" Hows. 100 yards west of above.

3. **RATES OF FIRE.**
         5 minutes INTENSE.
         5 minutes NORMAL.
         5 minutes SLOW.

4. The "MUTUAL SUPPORTS" will only be given provided guns can be spared from their own Group fronts.

Page 2.

5. All previous MUTUAL SUPPORT SCHEMES are cancelled.

The above comes into operation at 9.0 a.m. August 9th.

6. 52nd Divisional Artillery Units to ACKNOWLEDGE.

[signature]
Major R.F.A.
A/Brigade Major R.A.
52nd Divisional Artillery.

8th August 1918.

Distribution:-

52nd Division 'G'.	1.
R.A. XVII Corps.	1.
52nd Btn: M.G.C.	1.
155th Infantry Bde.	1.
156th Infantry Bde.	1.
157th Infantry Bde.	1.
Right Group.	6.
Centre Group.	7.
Left Group.	6.
D.T.M.O.	3.
Left H.A. Group.	1.
R.O., R.A.	4.
57th Div: Arty.	1.
8th Div: Arty.	1.

Appx XII 22

52nd D.A.No. M/471/1.

Reference 52nd Divisional Artillery No. M/471.dated 8/8/18.

Para.1 (d). Delete "West" - substitute East.

Para.2 (a). Delete "West" - Substitute East.

Para.2 (b). Delete "West" - Substitute East.

Para.2 (c). Delete "West" substitute East.

      Delete "B.23.a.40.50" substitute D.23.d.40.50.

[signature]
Major R.F.A.
A/Brigade Major R.A.

8th August 1918.   52nd Divisional Artillery.

SECRET.   REFERENCE 52nd DIVISION ORDER No. 119.
＊＊＊＊＊＊＊＊＊＊＊＊＊＊＊＊＊＊＊＊＊＊＊＊＊＊＊

1. Target 'A' is B.24.b.25.48. Zero hour 8.15pm.

   Target 'B' is B.24.d.25.45. Zero hour 9.30pm.

   Target 'C' is B.30.a.55.52. Zero hour 11.0pm.

2. Gas bombardment will be carried out by all 4.5" Howitzers of the 52nd Divisional Artillery.
   The M.P.I. should not be more than 30 yards to windward of the target.
   Ammunition. All ammunition of which few varieties are in hand should be used in preference to BNC, provided that chemical shells are kept in the following groups:-

   Group 1. BVN. BJBB. BJL. for Target 'A'.
   Group 2. BOBR. BOG.   for Target 'B'.
   Group 3. BNC. BPS.   for Target 'C'.

   All mixed lots of chemical shell should thus be expended.
   All future supplies will probably be BNC.

3. 6 18-pdrs. of RIGHT GROUP and of CENTRE GROUP will fire 50% 'A', 25% AX and 25% AS at each objective from Zero to Zero plus 2 minutes at INTENSE rates.

4. Reference Para. 4, 52nd Divisional Order 119.

   Right Group will carry out active harassing fire for Targets B & C and Centre Group for Target A.

5. The normal night harassing fire will also be carried out.

6. 52nd Divisional Groups to acknowledge.

                                         M. Beresford-Peirse
                                         Major R.F.A.
                                         A/Brigade Major R.A.
8th August 1918.   52nd Divisional Artillery.

                    DISTRIBUTION.

                52nd Division 'G'.   1.
                R.A. XVII Corps.   1.
                155th Infantry Bde.   1.
                156th Infantry Bde.   1.
                157th Infantry Bde.   1.
                Left Group H.A.   1.
                52nd Battn: M.G.C.   1.
                Right Group.   6.
                Centre Group.   7.
                Left Group.   6.
                R.O., R.A.   3.
                S.O.R.A.   1.
                D.T.M.O.   3.

LEFT DIVISIONAL ARTILLERY, XVII CORPS, INTELLIGENCE SUMMARY.
6am 9th to 8am 10th August 1918.

1. OUR ACTIVITY.
   (a) Operations. Some registration carried out and movement fired on during the day.
      Harassing fire by night as follows:-
      ARLEUX SECTION. Trenches and tracks in T.29.c, T.30.a & c, U.25.c, B.6.a.
      OPPY SECTION. BRADFORD TRENCH, tracks and trench junctions in C.13.c, B.12.d, C.13.b & d, B.12.b, C.7.b, Cross Roads at B.12.d.98.30, Trench junctions B.18.d.4.4 and B.12.d.96.30.
      GAVRELLE SECTION. Roads and tracks in C.25.a, C.19.b, C.19.c.
      6" TRENCH MORTARS fired 58 rounds on ARLEUX during the night.
      Rounds fired:-
      18-pdrs. - 2825.   4.5" Hows. - 677.   6" T.M's - 58.

2. HOSTILE ACTIVITY.
   (a) Artillery. Hostile artillery was normal, shelling being confined to harassing fire.

Date.	Time.	No.of rds.	Calibre.	Area shelled.	Direction.	Remarks.
9th.	4.45am to 1.30pm.	15	10cm gun.	WILLERVAL.	GB 53°30' from B.8.a.4.3.	Engaged by our heavies at 2.30pm.
	6.0.am.	33	10.5cm.	BAILLEUL.	GB 65° from B.27.d.85.95.	F/R 20 secs.
	8.20-8.40.	8	77mm.	WILLERVAL.	ARLEUX.	
	9.30.	20.	15cm.	B.26.c.		
	9.50.	20.	77mm.	A.24.		
	10.0.	30.	10.5cm.	B.26.c.		
	9.50-10.35.	10	10.5cm.	G.5.a.		
	12 noon.	40.	10.5cm.	B.10.a.	84° from B.14.b.50.70.	
	12.40pm.	10.	10.5cm.	B.2.c.)	NEUVIREIL.	5 min: bursts.
	1.5.	10.	10.5cm.	B.2.c.)		
	2.30.	10.	10.5cm.	WILLERVAL.		
	5.0pm.	18.	10.5cm.	B.26.b.	GB. 69° from B.27.b.21.71.	
	5.37.	8.	10.5cm.	B.28.d. & H.4.b.	120°	-do-
	5.50.	15.	15cm gun?	Back areas.	IZEL LES EQUERCHIN.	
	6.35.	30	10.5cm.	B.8.a.	94° G. from B.14.a.51.70.	
	7.0.	30.	10.5cm.	WILLERVAL.	84° G. ,, B.14.b.50.70.	
	9.42.	30.	10.5cm.	B.10.		
10th.	1.45-2.20am.	25.	77mm.	B.13.c & A.18.d.		
	3.30.	30.	10.5cm.	B.14.c.		
	3.30am.	30.	10.5cm.	BAILLEUL.		

   (b) Work - Nil.
   (c) Movement. Individual movement behind BLANDFORD TRENCH, parties of 4 seen in B.30.a, C.16.d, C.15.c; Considerable movement round CHEZ BONTEMPS, 2 men seen on road in U.20.c, 1 man seen laying a wire in U.21.d.
      Train movement in sidings in BEAUMONT throughout the morning
   (d) Aerial. Very little aerial activity observed.

3. GENERAL. Visibility fair to good.
   At 8.20pm. enemy dump in C.14 was seen to explode and continued to burn till 8.35.
   At 8.0pm propaganda leaflets were dropped in vicinity of BAILLEUL.

10th August 1918.

A/Reconnaissance Officer, 52nd Div: Arty:
Lieut: RFA.

SECRET.   52nd Division No. G.1/3/21.
                                  52nd Div: Arty: No. M/431.

PROVISIONAL DEFENCE INSTRUCTIONS.

LEFT SECTOR, XVII CORPS.

                                                    8th August 1918.

1.   Pending the issue of a complete Defence Scheme the following instructions are issued for guidance:-

2.   All 3 Brigades will be in the line, each Brigade having its three Battalions up.

3.   The Normal Dispositions in each Brigade for holding the line will be roughly, 2 Battalions in the front system and main line of resistance (Post Line), 1 Battalion in the Brown line.

4.(a)   The distribution of Battalions between the front system and main line of resistance (Post Line) is left to the discretion of G.O's C. Brigades. The front system must be held in sufficient strength to make the enemy believe it is our main line of resistance, and to provide adequate protection against raids. It follows that the strengths of the garrisons of the front system will depend upon local conditions, such as the state of the wire and the general defensibility of the trenches, etc.

(b)   In normal circumstances the Battalion in support in the Brown Line is at the disposal of G.O's C. Brigades for a counter-attack to restore a local situation either in the main line of resistance or the outpost zone.

5.   After the order "MAN BATTLE STATIONS".
(a)   The garrisons of the front system withdraw either into localities or into the main zone of resistance.
(b)   On the Right Brigade front there will be 2 localities; one about B.28.d.4.8 held by 1 Company (less 1 Platoon) and one about B.28.b.4.7 held by 1 Platoon.
       On the Centre Brigade front there will be 4 localities; one about B.16.d.9.2 held by 1 Company (less 1 Platoon); one about B.16.b.6.2 held by 1 Platoon; one about B.16.b.2.9 held by half-Company; one about B.10.c.9.6 held by half-Company.
       On the Left Brigade front there will be WILLERVAL - permanently held by 1 Company, and a locality about B.4.a.9.9 held by 1 Company; another about B.4.c.8.4 also held by 1 Company.

(c)   The remainder of the 2 Battalions in the front system of each Brigade will withdraw to the main line of resistance (Post Line).
       Each Company in the main line of resistance will have 1 Platoon in suitable trenches or shell holes in rear of the line, earmarked for an immediate and local counter-attack.
       The primary function of these platoons will be to counter-attack, the secondary function to stop an infiltration of the enemy through the main line by fire.
       Lewis Guns will be pushed forward from the main line, as necessary (roughly about 2 per Company) clear of our wire to provide a deeper zone of defence.

(d)   The Battalion in the Brown Line will similarly push forward Lewis Guns as necessary (roughly about 2 per Company) in front of their wire (if any) to provide a deeper zone of defence.

                                                    (e) After

(e) After the order "Man Battle Stations" has been given, the Battalion in support in the Brown Line is no longer at the disposal of the G.O's C. Brigades to counter-attack, and its functions will be purely defensive.

6. In all cases zones and localities must be fought for to the last. There will be no withdrawal.

7. There will be only one barrage - i.e., in front of outpost line of observation. It will go down for 5 minutes and then roll forward for 10 minutes, when it will come down again on its original line.
   The barrage will be at 45 yards per 18-pdr. gun.

8. 22 machine guns will thicken out the field gun barrage, 6 in the right section, 6 in the centre section, 8 in the left section.

9. The Field Companies R.E., will in case of attack form nucleus garrisons in Railway, Ridge and Spur Posts, one Company in each.

10. The Pioneers will stand by at Battalion Hd.Qrs. and will be in Divisional Reserve. Such working parties as are forward of the Green Line (exclusive) will place themselves under the orders of the nearest Battalion Commander.

****

RIGHT GROUP. (6): (277th B.de)
CENTRE GROUP (7):
LEFT GROUP (6). (D.A.G.O.)
D.T.M.O. (3).
52nd D.A.C. (3).

Forwarded for your information.

                                    M. Binsfor Pierse
                                    Major R.F.A.
                                    A/Brigade Major, R.A.
9th August 1918.   52nd Divisional Artillery.

Copies to :- R.O. (3).
            S.C.R.A. (1).

LEFT DIVISIONAL ARTILLERY, XVII Corps, INTELLIGENCE SUMMARY.
6am 10th to 6am 11th August 1918.

1. **OUR ACTIVITY.**
   (a) Operations. Movement in C.13.c. was engaged at 2.45pm.
   NF call at 9.45 am was answered and hostile battery at C.27.c.0.1 neutralised.
   "MARO RIGHT" was fired at 2.25am in retaliation for the shelling of our front trenches.
   S.O.S. was received at 3.9am and responded to.
   "HELP FAMPOUX NORTH" was responded to at 2.55am.
   Harassing fire on the following:-
   ARLEUX SECTION. Trenches and tracks, T.29.d, C.1, C.2, B.12.d, B.6.a.40.45.
   OPPY SECTION. B.19.b,20.75, C.7.c.25.00, C.7.c.75.50, B.12.d.6.4. Roads & tracks, C.13; T.M B.18.b.75.75. B.24.b.70.45, C.7.c.25.30, trench junction B.18.a.40.40, B.12.d.
   GAVRELLE SEC. Tracks and roads in B.30.b. & c. and C.19.d.
   6" TRENCH MORTARS fired 37 rounds on ARLEUX during the evening.
   Rounds fired:-
   18-pdrs. - 6670.   4.5" Hows.- 1673.   6" T.M. 37.

2. **HOSTILE ACTIVITY.**
   (a) Artillery. Below normal during the day, chiefly harassing fire on BAILLEUL & H.4.
   At 3.0am an intense bombardment of our trenches on the right commenced and continued for an hour.

Date.	Time.	No.of rds.	Calibre.	Area shelled.	Direction.	Remarks.
10th.	9am.	12	10.5cm.	H.2.d.		
	9.30am.	12	10.5cm.	B.26.c.		
	9.45.	10.	15cm.	H.3.b.		
	9.53.	9.	10.5cm.	B.23.c.		
	10.30.	20.	10.5cm.	WILLERVAL.		
	11-11.30.	20.	10.5cm.	B.20.		
	12.35.	5.	10.5cm.	BAILLEUL.		
	1-1.15pm.	30.	10.5cm.	H.4.a b & c.		
	1.30pm.	30.	10.5cm.	H.5.a & b.		
	1.40.	10.	10cm gun.	A.17.d.		Flash seen GB 85°30' from B.8.a.4.3.
	1.50.-2.15.	15.	10.5cm.	H.5.a.		
	2.30.	10.	15cm.	A.18 central.		
	4.3-4.23.	10.	10cm gun.	Back areas.		GB 95° from B.8.a.4.3.
	9.0	20.	10.5cm.	B.29.a.		.... GAS.
	10.15.	60	10.5cm.& 77mm.	H.4.a & b.		
	10.20.	10.	10.5cm.	BAILLEUL.		
	11.50.	20.	10.5cm.	BAILLEUL.		
	12-2.45am.	40.	10.5cm.	B.28.d.		
	3.5-4.5.		Intense bombardment on our trenches.			
	4.48.	15.	10.5cm.	B.25 central.		

   (b) Work - Nil. Working party in U.26 dispersed at 9.45am.
   (c) Movement. Movement in ones and two's round CHEZ BONTEMPS quarry, through the day. Movement also seen in trench C.13.c.
   Fires and smoke observed in back areas.
   (d) Aerial. Above normal. E.A. were active over our/back areas throughout the day. 8 observation balloons were up at one time.

3. **GENERAL.** Visibility - fair till noon, very good in afternoon and evening.

11th August 1918.   A/Reconnaissance Officer, 52nd Div: Arty.
                                                    Lieut: R.F.A.

APPENDIX VII War Diary

LEFT DIVISIONAL ARTILLERY, XVII CORPS, INTELLIGENCE SUMMARY.
6am 11TH to 6am 12TH August 1918.

1. OUR ACTIVITY.
   (a) Operations. Registration carried out by day & movement
   fired on at B.24.c.70.30 and on GAVRELLE-TRENNES ROAD.
   MARO RIGHT fired at G.35 pm.
   SK call on I.7.5.1.6 replied to at 2.30pm.
   Harassing fire as follows:-
   ARLEUX SECTION. Tracks and trenches in T.29.d., B.6.d.,
      T.30., U.25.a., C.1.b & c and B.5.
   OPPY SECTION.
      H.Q. at C.19.b.20.75, C.7.c.25.00, B.19.d.6.4, Roads
      and tracks in C.13.c., T.M. B.18.b.75.75, T.J. C.25.b.8.8,
      Road B.24.d 70.49, to C.13.c.15.60, H.Q. C.7.a.25.50,
      Track B.12.d.95.30 to C.13.d.5.9. Roads & track B.30.a.
      B.12.d.93.30, B.18.d.4.4, B.12.b.93.30.
   GAVRELLE SECTION. Trench and road junction B.25.b.6.8.

   Roads and tracks C.19.c., C.19.d., C.25.b.
   Rounds fired:-
      18-pdrs. - 2869.   4.5" Hows,- 756.   6" T.M. Nil.

2. HOSTILE ACTIVITY.
   (a) Artillery. Harassing fire below normal. At 4pm. trenches
   in B.23.c & d. shelled by 80. rds. 10.5cm.
       At 5.0pm. BAILLEUL was shelled with 100 rounds 15cm.
       From 3.15 to 5.0pm. a destructive shoot was carried
   out by aeroplane observation, on our forward guns in
   B.25. & B.26.
       300 rounds 15cm. mixed H.E. and BLUE CROSS GAS were
   fired, resulting in the destruction of one gun pit and
   damage to the gun, and casualties to the detachment. Later
   the same place was heavily shelled with gas shell.

Date.	Time.	No. of rds.	Calibre.	Area shelled.	Direction.	Remarks.
11th.	8.15am.	8	10.5cm.	SUGAR FACTORY.	B.16.a. 78° from B.14.b.3.7.	
	7.30-8.30.	10.	15cm.	B.26.		
	8-9.	26	10.5cm.	B.25.d.		
	8.0	20.	77mm.	BAILLEUL.	83° from B.14.b.3.7.	
	9.30.	15	10.5cm.	WILLERVAL.	68° from do.	
	10.10.	4.	15cm.	Back areas.	60° do.	
	10.25.	8.	10.5cm.	WILLERVAL.	72°	
	10.15-10.35.	20.	15cm.	B.25.d.		
	11.15-1.40.	15.	77mm.	WILLERVAL.	70° from B.14.b.3.7.	
	1.0pm.	10.	77mm.	Back areas.	85° do.	
	1.30-2.0.	50.	10.5cm.	K.5.a & b.		
	1.30-2.30.	20.	15cm.	B.23.b.		
	3.15-5.0.	300.	15cm.	B.25.d & 26.c.		...... H.E. & BLUE X GAS.
	3.10.	10.	15cm.	Back areas.		
	4-4.45.	80.	10.5cm.	Trench in B.23.c & d.	G.B. 89° from B.27.d.35.98.	4 gun salvos;
	4.5-5.20.	47.	10.5cm.	B.22.a. POST TRENCH.		
	5-5.30.	30.	77mm.	B.15. OPPY.		
	4.55-5.15.	100.	15cm.	BAILLEUL.		
	5.30.	20.	10.5cm.	BAILLEUL.	84° from B.14.b.3.7.	
	5.40.	25.	77mm.	BAILLEUL.	78° do.	
	8.15.	25.	77mm.	B.9.d.	62° from B.14.a.5.7.	
	9.10.	25.	77mm.	B.9.d.	-do-	GAS.
	8.pm-2am.	800.	77mm.	B.25.d.		H.E. & BLUE X.
	9-10.15.	150.	10.5cm.	B.26.		-do-.
12th.	12-12.27.	100.	10.5cm.	B.26.		-do-.
	2.50am.	10.	10.5cm.	B.26.	132° from B.14.a.5.7.	
	4.10.	10.	10.5cm.	B.28.	do.	
	4.0.	50.	77mm.	B.21.b.		

Page 2.

(b) <u>Work</u> - Nil.
(c) <u>Movement</u>. Individual movement in CHEZ BONTEMPS at 5.30pm.
    A man leading 2 saddle horses moved along the road from DROCOURT to CHEZ BONTEMPS.
    2.0pm. movement on GAVRELLE-FRESNES Road.
(d) <u>Aerial</u>. Above normal.
    8.15 to 8.25pm. an E.A. flew low over our front line and then over Battery position.
    Bombing planes active at night. 3 bombs were dropped near A.30 at 10.10pm.

3. <u>GENERAL</u>.

    Visibility fair to good.
    Enemy dump near MERICOURT seen on fire at 8.20am.

12th August 1918.   A/Reconnaissance Officer, 52nd Div: Arty: Lieut: R.F.A.

App XVIII War Diary

LEFT DIVISIONAL ARTILLERY, XVII CORPS, INTELLIGENCE SUMMARY.
6am 12th to 8am 13th August 1918.

1. **OUR ACTIVITY.**
   (a) <u>Operations</u>. MARO Right fired at 1.27pm. and 5.56pm.
   Movement in C.19.d. and B.30.b. fired on.
   Harassing fire at night as follows:-
   <u>ARLEUX SECTION</u>. Trenches and tracks in B.5.b, B.6, T.29.d., C.1.b, c, & d.
   <u>OPPY SECTION</u>. Headquarters at C.19.b.20.75, C.7.c.25.00, C.7.a.25.30, trench and road junctions at C.13.b.05.35, C.13.c, T.M. at B.18.b.75.75, C.13.a.4.6, tracks B.24.b.70.45 to C.13.a.20.70 and B.12.d.95.20 to B.12.b.25.40.
   <u>GAVRELLE SECTION</u>. Roads and tracks in B.25.b., C.19.c. and C.19.d.
   Rounds fired:-
   18-pdr. 2685,   4.5" How. 873.   6" T.M. Nil.

2. **HOSTILE ACTIVITY.**
   (a) <u>Artillery</u>. Quiet except for H.E. and Blue Cross Gas shelling in B.26.
   A trench mortar fired a few rounds on our lines in B.28.a and c, at 11pm and 2.0am.

Date	Time	No. of rds	Calibre	Area shelled	Direction	Remarks
12th.	6.45am.	5.	77mm.	WILLERVAL.		
	7.0am.	10.	10.5cm.	B.8.b.		
	8-8.30.	40.	77mm.	B.7.		
	11am.	10.	15cm.	FARBUS WOOD.		
	11.50-12.5.	15.	77mm.	B.1.b. Left of ARLEUX.		
	12 noon.	20.	?	Back areas.		2 guns firing from DROCOURT direction silenced by our Heavy Artillery.
	12.55-1.10.	80.	77mm.	H.3.b. & B.26.c.	80° from H.3.d.70.95.	
	12.55-1.10.	40.	77mm.	B.22.d. & B.26.c.	104° from H.3.d.70.90	
	1-1.15.	180.	77mm & 10.5cm.	B.26.b & d.		H.E. & BLUE X GAS.
	1-15pm	50.	77mm.	B.20.c.		
	5-5.30.	50.	77mm.	B.26.c.		-do-
	5.30-6.25.	130.	10.5cm.	B.26.b & d.		
	10.30-10.40.	20.	77mm.	BAILLEUL.		
	11.0pm.	10.	T.M.	F.L.B.28.c.		
13th.	2.2.15am.	6.	T.M.	F.L.B.28.a. & c.		

   (b) <u>Work</u> - Fresh earthwork in B.30.b & d.
   (c) <u>Movement</u>. Movement in trench C.19.d. seen at 2.40pm.
          "   "   "   B.30.b. "   "   11.10am.
       Movement seen at 3.35pm. at B.24.c.
   (d) <u>Aerial</u>. Normal.

3. <u>GENERAL</u>.   Visibility Good.

13th August 1918.

A/Reconnaissance Officer, 52nd Div: Arty.
Lieut: RFA.

appx XXIX War Diary.

LEFT DIVISIONAL ARTILLERY, XVII CORPS, INTELLIGENCE SUMMARY.
6am 13th to 6am 14th August 1918.

1. **OUR ACTIVITY.**
   (a) Operations. Registration carried out by day.
       Harassing fire at night as follows:-
       ARLEUX SECTION. T.29.c & d, T.30.a & b, B.5.b, B.6, C.19, U.25.a.
       OPPY SECTION. Trench junctions C.7.a.30.45, C.7.a.10.18, C.13.a.40.58, B.12.d.75.50, M.G. & Dugout B.18.b.85.80, Dugouts C.13.c.40.80, C.13.a.40.70.
       GAVRELLE SECTION: C.19.c & d. C.25.d.
       Rounds fired:-
       18-pdr. - 2711.   4.5" Hows. - 752.   6" T.M. Nil.

2. **HOSTILE ACTIVITY.**
   (a) Artillery. Quiet, Harassing fire chiefly on B.23, B.28 and B.16 & B.4.
       A 77mm Battery fired C.29.b.61.99 at 12.30pm. This position has not been active for some time.

Date	Time	No.of rds.	Calibre	Area shelled	Direction	Remarks
13th.	9.40am.	15.	10.5cm.	T.28.c.		
	10.15.	50	77mm.	F.L. in B.4.d.		
	10.45.	15.	77mm.	WILLERVAL.		Registration.
	11.20.	8.	15cm.	WILLERVAL.		
	12.15pm.	15	10.5cm.	B.7.b.		
	12.15-12.21.	20.	77mm.	B.28.c.50.50.		
	12.20-1.0.	8.	10.5cm.	B.22.c.		C.29.b.61.99. Bty.No.29.
	12.30-12.45.	40.	10.5cm.	FARBUS WOOD.		91°30' G from B.8.a.4.3. Silenced by our H.Arty.
	2.20.	10.	10.5cm.	BAILLEUL.		C.22.c.
	2.50-3.15.	32	10.5cm.	B.28.d.		
	3.27	13.	77mm.	B.29.c.		
	3.45.	50.	77mm.	B.16.		GAVRELLE.
	3.50-3.57.	25.	77mm.	H.3.b. & d.		
	4.50.	40.	10.5cm.	B.23 central.		
	4.50.	25.	77mm.	B.16.c.		
	7.55-8.0.	14.	77mm.	B.28.a.		
	8.30.	15.	77mm.	B.7.a.		GAS.
	10.20.	10.	10.5cm.	B.7.b.		
	10.25.	6.	15cm.	B.26.b.		
	11.22.	6.	77mm.	B.28.a.		
	11.50.	36.	77mm.	B.28.c.		GAS.
	12 mn-1.0am.	120.	77mm.	B.28.b.		
14th.	2.0am.	30.	15cm.	Back areas.		
	2.45-3.0.	12.	77mm.	B.28.b.		

   (b) Work. - Nil.
   (c) Movement. Only slight movement in U.20.c. observed.
   (d) Aerial. Normal activity.

3. **GENERAL.** Visibility good.
   At 7.0pm. flashes of a gun firing were seen on a bearing 84° from B.14.a.3.9.
   At 12.30pm. large fire was observed in B.17.b., it burned itself out by 2.45pm.
   At 1.35pm. dense black smoke was seen rising, apparently from a burning dump near LAMBRES in E.7.

                                                    Lieut: R.F.A.
14th August 1918.   A/Reconnaissance Officer, 52nd Div: Arty.

SECRET.

52nd DIVISIONAL ARTILLERY ORDER No. 30.

WARNING ORDER.

(1)   The 52nd Divisional Artillery will be relieved in action on the nights of August 14th/15th and 15th/16th.

(2)   Reliefs will be as drawn on Table "A" attached.

(3)   The forward Section of each Battery and one gun per Battery at main positions and all Anti-Tank guns will be relieved on night August 14th/15th.

The remaining 3 guns per Battery will be relieved on night August 15th/16th.

Maps, Orders and Aiming Posts will be handed over to relieving Units.

Units will retain their own guns and equipment.

Battery Staffs and B.C's of relieving Units will arrive on August 14th.
Guides will be provided on both nights by 52nd Divisional Artillery Units.
Gun teams and limbers to carry out relief will be provided on night 14th/15th by 52nd Divisional Artillery Units and on night 15th/16th by 51st Divisional Artillery Units.
Liaison Officers and Observing Officers will be relieved by 12 noon August 15th.
All reliefs will be complete by 12 midnight August 15th/16th.
All relief of guns will be carried out during the hours of darkness.

(4)   Incoming Units where no other accommodation is available will double up in wagon lines with outgoing units.

(5)   Trench Mortars
All reliefs will be completed by 12 noon August 15th.
Details to be arranged between D.T.M.O's mutually.

(6)   Divisional Artillery Gas Officer and Staff will hand over all information to incoming D.A.G.O. by 12 noon August 15th and then rejoin their Units.

(7)   D.A.C's and Dump reliefs will be completed by 12 noon August 15th.

(8)   51st Divisional Artillery will be responsible for accounting for Ammunition from 12 noon August 15th.

(9)   Completion of reliefs on each night will be wired to this Office by code words "INTELLIGENCE REPORTS" followed by the hour at which relief is completed.

(10)   Responsibility rests with 52nd Divisional Artillery Units to guide their relieving Units into the correct wagon lines.

(11)   This Warning Order will be confirmed to 52nd Divisional Artillery Units by wire

(12)   On completion of relief all Units 52nd Divisional Artillery will withdraw to their wagon lines.

Page 2.

(13) Command will pass to 51st Divisional Artillery at 9.0am August 16th.

(14) 52nd Divisional Artillery Units to ACKNOWLEDGE.

                                                  N. Beresford Pierse
                                                  Major R.F.A.,
                                                A/Brigade Major R.A.
                                             52nd Divisional Artillery.

13th August 1918.

Copies to:-   52nd Division "G". (1)
                R.A., XVII Corps. (1)
                51st Div: Arty: (6).
                9th Brigade (9).
                56th Brigade (9).
                52nd D.A.C. (4).
                D.T.M.O. (3).
                D.A.G.O. (1).
                311th Brigade (1).
                277th Brigade (1).
                S.C.R.A. (1)
                R.A. Signals.
                R.O., R.A. (3).

TABLE "A" issued with 52nd D.A. Order No.52.

Unit	Old Cell.	Win Line Locations	Relieved by	Location of 52nd D.A. Wagon Line to be This Wagon Line.	occupied by 51D.A. units	Remarks.
52 D.A. H.Q.	SEZA					
Stn.Bde.						
R.F.A.	SENA	A.22.c.5.4.				
15 Bty.	SEWA	A.29.c.45.20.	A/255 Bty.	A.27.c.8.4. *	Permanent W.L.(now empty)	
				A.27.c.	1 Anti-Tank gun on Charge *Permanent wagon line now empty.	
20th Bty.	SESA.	A.30.c.80.90.	B/255 Bty.	A.27.c.0.5.	A.27.c.	1 Anti-Tank gun on Charge. Move to A.27.c.2.3 when vacated by 20th Bty.
59thBty.	SEMA	H.1.d.50.75.	C/255 Bty.	A.25.c.20.95.	A.25.c.0. *	* Permanent wagon line now empty.
D/69.	TWRA.	A.30.c.74.70.	D/255 Bty.	F.24.c.7.6.	G.3.a.4.5.	Double up with A/287 Bty. till morning of 15th then occupy.
55th Bde. H.Q. SEMA.	G.5.b.50.15.	255 Bde.	A.6.c.5.9.	A.26.c.5.5. *	* Permanent wagon line now empty.
A/68.	SEMA.	A.50.c.50.00.	A/255 Bty.	E.2.b. temporary.		1 Anti-Tank gun on charge
B/68.	SMOA.	A.50.c.25.89.		A.26.c.4.2.		
C/68.		A.29.c.41.82.	B/255 Bty.	F.29.a.5. temp.	A.26.c.5.2.	
D/68.		A.29.d.41.70.		T.29.c.7.5. temp.	A.26.c.0.3.	
527 Bty. SEMA.				F.22.b.7.8. temp.	G.3.a.4.3.	527 Bty outside Div: Area. D/255 will occupy permanent lines at A.26.c.9.2 now 19th Bty
D.T.M.O. D.A.G.O.	} G.a.7.b.75.80.		51st Div: D.T.M.O. & D.A.G.O.			
52nd D.A.C. SEGA.			51st D.A.C.	F.20.b. & F.20.d.	F.15.c. & F.15.a. temporary.	

app XXI
31

LEFT DIVISIONAL ARTILLERY, XVII CORPS, INTELLIGENCE SUMMARY.
6am 14th to 6am 15th August 1918.

1. **OUR ACTIVITY.**
   (a) Operations. Movement at B.18.b.5590 and C.25.a.00.77 engaged and dispersed.
   Harassing fire by night on following targets:-
   ARLEUX SECTION. B.5.b, B.6.b, c & d, B.12.b & d, C.1.a b & c, C.25.a, T.29 d, T.30.a c & d, C.7.a.
   OPPY SECTION. BARON TRENCH, FRESNOY TRENCH, Dugouts

   C.13.c.50.75, Road junction C.13.a.85.60, C.13.b.00.35, C.13.c.40.10.
   GAVRELLE SECTION. Road and track & centres of activity in C.19.b, C.19.d, & C.25.b.
   Rounds fired:-
   18-pdrs. - 1893   4.5" Hows. 691   6" T.M. Nil.

2. **HOSTILE ACTIVITY.**
   (a) Artillery. Rather more active than for the last two days.
   Harassing fire chiefly on B.8, B.13, B.14, B.22, B.26.
   Some gas shelling in B.22, B.23.a & B.26.c.

Date.	Time.	No. of rds.	Calibre.	Area shelled.	Direction.	Remarks.
14th.	8-8.10am.	19.	10.5cm.	B.25.b.		
	8.5-8.20.	20.	77mm.	H.3.a.		G.B.83° from H.3.d.7.9, probably at C.30.a.5.9.
	9.2-9.10.	10.	77mm.	H.3.a.		
	9.5.	30.	15cm.	Back areas.		
	9-11.	27.	77mm.	B.27.c & d.		
	10.30-1pm.	50.	10.5cm.	B.13.a.7.0.		
	10.30.	5.	10.5cm.	B.8.c & 14.a.		FRESNES.
	10.45-11.10.	20.	77mm.	B.3.d. & 4.b.		,,
	11-11.45.	20.	10.5cm.	B.26.b.		
	11.30-12.15.	30.	10.5cm.	B.8.c & d & B.14.b.	GB. 105° from B.8.a.4.3.	? Battery OD 52. Registration.
	11.50.	36.	77mm.	B.26.c. } Gas, BLUE CROSS.		
	11.55.	14.	77mm.	B.23.a. }		
	11.55-12.15.	30.	77mm.	H.3.b & d.		
	12.30.	15.	10.5cm.	B.15.c.		NEUVIREUIL.
	12.47 pm.	40.	10.5cm.	B.14.a.9.4.		
	12.50.	3.	15cm.	B.28.d.		
	12.45-1.0.	40.	10.5cm.	B.8.d.		
	6.35.	10.	8" gun.	A.11.b.	GB. 86° from B.8.a.4.3.	
	6.45.	7.	10.5cm.	B.13.b.		
	7.35.	9.	10.5cm.	TIRED ALLEY in B.14.b.		
	9-12.0.	30.	15cm.	Back areas.		
	11-3am.	17.	10.5cm.	A.18.d.		
15th.	1.30am.	60.	77mm.	B.22.		.... GAS & H.E.
	2.35-3.0.	150.	77mm.	BAILLEUL.		
	3.0-5.0.	40.	10.5cm.	B.26.		

   (b) Work.- Fresh earth seen at B.2.a.9.8; smoke seen rising from here.
   (c) Movement. Small parties seen in C.25.a.00.77, B.18.b.55.90, I.4.d.
   (d) Aerial. Normal.

III. **GENERAL.** Visibility fair to good.
   At 7.40pm. flash was observed in G.B. 81°50' from B.27.b.21.71. Time F/R. 30 secs.

H.J. Ernest
Lieut: RFA.

15th August 1918.   A/Reconnaissance Officer, 52nd Div: Arty.

52nd DIVISIONAL ARTILLERY OPERATION ORDER No. 31.
===

1. 52nd Divisional Artillery Order No. 30 of August 13th holds good for 56th Brigade reliefs and Divisional Ammunition Column.

2. At 8.0pm tonight - August 14th - Grouping will be as follows:-

    LEFT GROUP - Headquarters; 4 Batteries 311th Brigade;
                 'A' and 'B' Batteries 277th Brigade.

    CENTRE GROUP - Headquarters and 4 Batteries 9th Brigade,
                   'C' and 'D' Batteries 277th Brigade.
    RIGHT GROUP - Hd.Qrs. & 4 Batteries 56th Brigade.
    Barrages for Groups remain as at present - Group Commanders to adjust Battery barrages by 8.0pm August 14th.

3. The 9th Brigade will be relieved in action by the 45th Brigade, 8th Divisional Artillery on nights August 14th/15th and 15th/16th.

    1 Section of Forward guns per Battery on night August 14th/15th and remainder on night August 15th/16th.

    All Batteries provide their own teams.

    9th Brigade H.Q. - relieved by 45th Bde. H.Q. August 15th/16th.
    19th Bty. RFA - relieved by 1st Bty. RFA. 14th/15th and 15th/16th.
    20th Bty. RFA - relieved by 3rd Bty. RFA. 14th/15th and 15th/16th.
    28th Bty. RFA - relieved by 5th Bty. RFA.   and 15th/16th.
    D/69th Bty. RFA - relieved by 57th Bty. RFA. 14th/15th & 15th/16th.

    Batteries retain their own guns and equipment.

    Maps, Orders and Aiming Posts to be handed over.

    Battery Commanders and Staffs of relieving Units will report at 9th Brigade Headquarters at A.29.a.3.4 at 10.0am August 15th.

    Guides from Units to meet them there at 10.0am.

    Guides to meet incoming Sections on nights of 14th/15th and 15th/16th August to be provided by 9th Brigade Headquarters and Batteries to be at MADAGASCAR CORNER A.26.d.8.2, at 8.30pm each night with written instructions. A.28.a.5.3   10pm

4. Anti-Tank guns of Centre Group will be taken over by 'C' or 'D' 277th Brigade on August 14th under Centre Group arrangements.

5. 8th Divisional Artillery Units will continue to use their own wagon lines North of 52nd Division Area until after relief is finished.

6. Trench Mortars.

    Guns and personnel will be taken over by 8th Divisional Artillery in OPPY and WILLEVAL SECTIONS and in GAVRELLE SECTION by 51st Divisional Artillery.
    (This is liable to alteration).

7. Completion of reliefs to be wired to this Office as in 52nd Divisional Artillery Order No. 30 of August 13th.

8. Commands to pass on completion of reliefs.

9. 52nd Divisional Artillery Units to withdraw to Wagon lines on completion of relief.

10.

10. 277th Brigade and 311th Brigade pass under control of 8th Divisional Artillery at 9.0am August 15th.

11. GROUPS to ACKNOWLEDGE.

[signature]
Major R.F.A.
A/Brigade Major R.A.
52nd Divisional Artillery.

14th August 1918.

Distribution.

52nd Division "G".	1.
8th Div: Arty.	6.
R.A. XVII Corps.	1.
Right Group.	3.
Centre Group.	14.
Left Group.	14.
277th Brigade.	2.
R.A. Signals.	1.
R.O.R.A.	3.
S.C.R.A.	1.
D.T.M.O.	3.
51st Div: Arty.	1.

App XXXIII

33

52nd. DIVISIONAL ARTILLERY ORDER NUMBER, 32.

(1) The 52nd. Divisional Artillery will concentrate in the ACQ-CHERVINCAPELLE area on August 15th.

(2) 52nd.D.A.C. will march to FREVIN CAPELLE on August 15th. on relief by 51st.D.A.C. going by ECOIVRES and ACQ.

(3) 56th.Brigade will march to Billets vacated by 255th.Brigade,R.F.A. at ACQ.

(4) 9th.Brigade will march to Billets vacated by 253 Bde.R.F.A. at ACQ.

(5) 56th.Brigade, R.F.A. to clear ANZIN CORNER G.1.d.50.00. by 9 am August 16th.
9th.Brigade,R.F.A. to clear G.1.d.50.00. by 10 am August 16th.

(6) Advance Parties to proceed under Brigade arrangements on August 15th

(7) Advance Parties will be responsible for guiding their own units into Billets.

(8) Units will halt for ten minutes at each clock hour --- no other halts will be permitted.

(9) 52nd.Divisional Artillery Units to acknowledge.
(10) 52nd.D.A.H.Q. will re-open at AUBIGNY CHATEAU at 9 am 15th.Inst.

                                    Major,R.F.A.
                                    a/Brigade Major,R.A.
                                    52nd.Divisional Artillery.

14th.August, 1918,

Distribution.

52nd.Division "G"	1.
8th.Div.Artly.	1.
R.A.XVII Corps	1.
Right Group	5.
Centre Group	5.
Left Group	1.
277 Bde.	1.
R.A.Signals	1.
R.O.R.A.	3.
S.C.R.A.	1.
D.T.M.O.	3.
51st.Div.Artly.	1.

appendix XIV
34

52nd D.A.No. Z/522.

CENTRE GROUP, 52nd Divisional Artillery.
LEFT GROUP   ,,   ,,   ,,

1. On night August 15th/16th, B/277 & C/277 Batteries R.F.A. will move to positions in the 8th Divisional Artillery Group, Commanded by Lieut: Colonel FORMAN, C.M.G., (Headquarters at A.C.C.S.7).

2. Ammunition will be left in SITU by B/277 and C/277 Batteries R.F.A.

3. Officers Commanding B/277 and C/277 Batteries should get into touch with Lieut: Colonel FORMAN as soon as possible.

4. CENTRE GROUP, 52nd Divisional Artillery, will make all necessary arrangements to put the Battery relieving 28th Battery R.F.A. into positions vacated by B/277 Battery R.F.A.

5. Ammunition in positions vacated by 28th Battery will be on charge of the RIGHT GROUP 8th Divisional Artillery (Lt.Colonel THACKERAY) until further arrangements are made between 8th Division and 51st Division.

6. Wagon lines of B & C 277th Batteries will not move.

7. B & C/277 Batteries will pass under command of 8th Divisional Artillery on vacating present positions.

8. Groups and 277th Brigade to ACKNOWLEDGE.

[signature]
Major R.F.A.
A/Brigade Major R.A.
52nd Divisional Artillery.

15th August 1918.

Distribution.

52nd Division G.	1.
R.A., XVII Corps.	1.
8th Div: Artillery.	2.
Centre Group.	2.
Left Group.	2.
51st Div: Artillery.	1.
277th Brigade.	3.
R.A. Signals.	1.
S.C.R.A.	1.
R.O.R.A.	3.

SECRET.   52nd.D.A.No.S.C. 1140

52nd. D.A.C.

    52nd.D.A.C. will be relieved by 51st. D.A.C. today, 15th. inst., and will occupy billets at FREVIN CAPELLE, vacated by 51st.D.A.C.

    Relief to be completed by 8 p.m. 15th. inst.
Time of march to be arranged direct between Os.C., D.A.Cs. concerned.

    52nd.D.A.C. will report to this office, hour at which they are marching.

                                                Captain R.A.,
15/8/18.   Staff Captain R.A., 52nd.Division.

Copies to 52nd.Division "G"
         R.A., XVll Corps.
         9th. Brigade R.F.A.
         56th. Brigade R.F.A.
         51st. Divisional Artillery.
         R.A., Signals.
         R.O.R.A.,
         52nd. Divisional Train.

Copy No. 19

52nd. DIVISIONAL ARTILLERY ORDER No. 33.

Reference Map 1/40,000, Sheet 51 c.

(1) 9th.Brigade, R.F.A. will move to billets in ACQ on 17th.inst.

(2) Units will not arrive in ACQ before 8-30 pm. With this exception, there are no restrictions as to time or route.

(3) Billeting Parties will report to Staff Captain R.A. at 56th.Brigade, R.F.A. Headquarters in ACQ at 10 am 17th.inst. and will take over billets from 256 Brigade, R.F.A.

(4) Two Lorries will be at Church at ANZIN (G.1.d.5/0) at 9 am 17th.instant, and will be met and taken over by representative 9th.Brigade, R.F.A. These lorries will do a double journey to ACQ, and should be freed as early as possible.

(5) Rations for 18th. will be carried on men and animals. Rations for 19th. will be delivered by train cagons at ACQ on morning of 18th.

(6) 9th.Brigade,R.F.A. to acknowledge by bearer.

[signature]

Captain, R.A.
Brigade Major, R.A.
52nd. Divisional Artillery.

16th.August, 1918

Copy No.
1 - R.A.XVII Corps.
2 - 51st Div: Arty.
3 - 52nd Division G.
4 - 52nd Division Q.
5-9 - 9th Brigade.
10 - 56th Brigade.
11 - 52nd D.A.C.
12 - D.T.M.O.
13 - S.C.R.A.
14 - R.O.RA.
15 - R.A.Sig: Officer.
16 - D.A.G.O.
18 & 19 - War Diary.

SECRET.   COPY No. 4

52nd DIVISIONAL ARTILLERY OPERATION ORDER No. 54.

Reference 51.C.

1. 9th & 56th Brigades and 52nd D.A.C. will march tonight 21st instant to BEAUMETZ (Q.35) and MONCHIET (Q.21).

2. Times of starting as follows:-

   56th Brigade .... 9.15pm.

   9th Brigade .... 10.15pm.

   52nd D.A.C. .... 11.0pm.

3. Advance parties (Mounted on bicycles) to meet Lieut. DANCEY at Cross Roads at E.22.a.3.2 at 7.0pm. tonight.

4. No restrictions as to route.

5. Rations for 23rd will be brought on train wagons, orders re which will issue later.
   Rations for 22nd on men and animals.

6. ACKNOWLEDGE.

                                        Captain R.A.
                                   Brigade Major, R.A.
21st August 1918.   52nd Divisional Artillery.

Issued at 5.20pm. 21st August.

DISTRIBUTION.

Copy No. 1 - 9th Brigade.
        2 - 56th Brigade.
        3 - 52nd D.A.C.
      4/5 - War Diary.
        6 - File.

SECRET.

52nd.D.A.No.A/540.

AMENDMENT TO OPERATION ORDER No. 54 of date.
_____

1. Cancel paragraph 4.
   Route ---- HAUTE AVESNES - WARLUS - BERNEVILLE.

2. Cancel paragraph 8.
   Timings ---- 35th.Brigade 8-30 pm.
                9th.Brigade 9-30 pm.
                52nd.D.A.C. 10-15 pm.

3. Transport. One lorry will be at 35th.Bde. H.Q. and one lorry at 9th.Bde.HQ. ------ ACO ------ as early as possible to-night to take extra kit.

4. Guides. Cancel my O.O.3a/1.
   Guides will be at Cross Roads, BERNEVILLE, Q.6.d.5.5.

5. Train Wagons will join units with rations for the 22nd. either to-night or to-morrow morning.

6. Acknowledge.

                                        Captain, R.A.
                                        Brigade Major, R.A.
                                        52nd.Divisional Artillery.

21st.August, 1918.

    Issued by S.D.R. at 6-10 pm. 21st.

SECRET. 52nd Divisional Artillery Copy No. 13
Order No. 34.

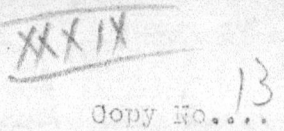

31st August, 1918.

1. 171st Infantry Brigade in conjunction with Right Brigade, 1st Canadian Division will carry out an operation tomorrow morning.
OBJECTIVES
171st Infantry Brigade - Capture and consolidation of HENDICOURT, exclusive of the Chateau and Grounds.
Canadian Brigade - CROWS NEST, HENDICOURT Chateau and Grounds, TRIGGER ALLEY and a line from U.12.d.2.6. to P.31.central.

2. ZERO HOUR will be 4.50 A.M. 1st September, 1918.

3. Field Artillery action will be as follows :-
(a) Left Group 18-pdrs. will fire a creeping barrage as under.
9th Brigade R.F.A. starting line U.11.c.77.80. - U.11.c.55.35.
56th Brigade R.F.A. starting line U.11.c.55.35 - U.17.c.15.75.
The barrage will remain on opening line for four minutes and then creep forward at the rate of 200 yards every eight minutes until it reaches finishing line as under, where it will form a protector barrage, which will continue till ZERO plus 90.
9th Brigade R.F.A. finishing line U.18.a.90.90 - U.18.a.35.05.
56th Brigade R.F.A. finishing line U.18.a.35.05 - U.17.d.70.10.
Rates of fire ZERO to ZERO plus 4 - INTENSE.
ZERO plus 4 to ZERO plus 50 - NORMAL.
ZERO plus 50 to ZERO plus 90 - SLOW.
Ammunition - Half shrapnel, half H.E.

(b) Left Group 4.5" Howitzers will act as under.
ZERO to ZERO plus 8 - Search areas 300 yards beyond 18-pdr. barrage
- Rate of fire - INTENSE.
ZERO plus 8 to ZERO plus 50 - 527th Battery search up HENDICOURT Trench from U.17.c.9.9. to U.18.c.4.0 keeping 200 yards beyond 18-pdr. creeper. Rate of fire - NORMAL.
ZERO plus 50 to ZERO plus 90 - 527th Battery DACHSHUND TRENCH - Rate of fire - NORMAL.
ZERO plus 8 to ZERO plus 30 - D/69th Battery GREYHOUND TRENCH - Rate of fire - NORMAL.
ZERO plus 30 to ZERO plus 90 - D/69th Battery DACHSHUND TRENCH. - Rate of fire - NORMAL.

(c) Right Group from ZERO to ZERO plus 90 put down flank barrage on the line :-
BULLDOG support U.23.a.50.27 Eastwards, Trench systems U.23.c and d East of North and South Line through U.23.c.central.
Western Defences RIENCOURT.

4. Heavy Artillery bombard HENDICOURT during night till 4.30 A.M. and from ZERO to ZERO plus 90 bombard RIENCOURT and its approaches.

5. 171st Brigade consolidate of line GREYHOUND AVENUE - U.17.a.70.00 - U.17.c.10.98.

6. Reconnaissance Officer will report to each Brigade Headquarters with synchronised watch between 9 and 10 P.M. tonight.

7. ACKNOWLEDGE.

Captain R.A.
C.C. Brigade Major R.A., 52nd Division.
Copies Nos. 1 - 5 9th Bde. R.F.A.
6 - 10 56th Bde. R.F.A.
11 File.
12 - 13 War Diary.

Issued at 9.30 P.M. 31/8/18.

CONFIDENTIAL.

ORIGINAL.

Vol 6

- W A R   D I A R Y -

of

HEADQUARTERS   ROYAL   ARTILLERY - 52ND DIVISION.

VOLUME , - V.
PART - IX.

FROM -
1st SEPTEMBER 1918.

TO -
30th September 1918.

Army Form C. 2118.

Instructions regarding War Diaries and Intelligence
Summaries are contained in F. S. Regs., Part II.
and the Staff Manual respectively. Title pages
will be prepared in manuscript.

WAR DIARY
or
INTELLIGENCE SUMMARY.

(Erase heading not required.)

SEPTEMBER

Place	Date	Hour	Summary of Events and Information	Remarks and references to Appendices
FONTAINE LES CROISILLES.	Sept. 1st		171st Inf. Bde. (57th Divn.) in conjunction with Right Brigade, 1st Canadian Division, attacked HENDECOURT at 4.50 am, our batteries firing a creeping barrage in support of the attack. All objectives were gained by 6.15 am. At 9 am the enemy were reported massing for a counter-attack, they were dispersed by our fire and the counter-attack did not materialise. At 6.5 am a further attack was made in conjunction with 52nd Division, and REINCOURT was captured by 7 pm. - vide 57th D.A. Order No. 30). A, B and C Batteries of 56th Bde RFA together with 56th Bde HQrs. moved forward after this attack so as to be able to cover a further attack to take place next morning. 285th Bde moved up into action at 6 pm. and cameu under Command of Left Group at 9 pm.	App:I.
	Sept. 2nd		At 5 am, 151st Inf. Bde attacked in conjunction with 1st Canadian Division on their Left and 52nd Division on their Right to break the QUEANT-DROCOURT Line - vide 57th Div: Order No.319 & 57th D.A. Order No. 51. - All objectives were gained by 8.30 am and the success exploited by 63rd Division advancing through the 57th Division in a southerly direction. Immediately after this attack the Left Group was broken up and the 9th and 285th Bdes RFA moved up in immediate support of 188th Inf. Bde of 63rd Division. 52nd D.A.H.Q. came under command of 63rd D.A. at 1 pm and moved up to CALLING CARD COPSE, 2,000 yards East of HENDECOURT. 56th Bde moved forward at 6 pm and with 9th Bde and 5th A.F.A. Bde were reformed into a Left Group under 52nd D.A.H.Q. All batteries were in CAGNICOURT AREA tonight. Owing to 188 Inf. Bde pushing forward to INCHY and PRONVILLE during the night no S.O.S. lines or harassing fire programmes could be given to the batteries. PRONVILLE was occupied during the night.	App:II... App:III,
	Sept. 3rd		9th, 56th and 5th A.F.A. Bdes moved forward into positions S.W. of BOIS DE BOUCHE in support of the Infantry who continued to push forward to INCHY and MOEUVRES. 52nd D.A.H.Q. moved forward to QUARRY, 1,500 yards N. of PRONVILLE. INCHY and MOEUVRES were in our hands by 4 pm and by 5 pm, 56th Bde RFA were in action 2,000 yards E. of PRONVILLE and 9th Bde RFA shortly after came in action 2,000 yards N.E. of PRONVILLE. 285th Bde RFA came under command of Left Group at 9 pm, the batteries being in action near BOIS DE BOUCHE. Harassing fire was carried out by batteries of the Group on the East bank of the CANAL DU NORD during the night. Enemy fire was greatly increased during day and night.	
PRONVILLE	Sept. 4th		Our Infantry pushed forward and gained a footing on the bridge heads E. of CANAL DU NORD during the morning but were unable to hold their positions and withdrew to the West bank 285th Bde were moved forward to positions close to 56th Bde during the afternoon. About 6 pm the enemy shelled INCHY and MOEUVRES very heavily and troops were seen advancing to counter-attack. Our batteries carried out considerable harassing fire fired S.O.S. but the main	

Army Form C. 2118.

WAR DIARY
or
INTELLIGENCE SUMMARY.
(Erase heading not required.)

Instructions regarding War Diaries and Intelligence Summaries are contained in F. S. Regs., Part II. and the Staff Manual respectively. Title pages will be prepared in manuscript.

Place	Date	Hour	Summary of Events and Information	Remarks and references to Appendices
	Sept. 4th		main attack was on the Division on our left. Only a small attack was made on our front resulting in the enemy obtaining a hold on the N.E. corner of INCHY. During the attack 56th Bde obtained observed shooting on parties advancing from BOURLON WOOD with excellent results. A short barrage was fired by 9th Bde at 9 pm and under cover of this our Infantry re-took INCHY. During the night our infantry tried to work forward but were unable to make good the bridgeheads. Our batteries carried out considerable harassing fire during the night. Hostile shelling was heavy both by day and night.	counter AAD AAD AAD AAD
	Sept. 5th		Our infantry continued by a process of infiltration to advance their line towards the CANAL; the Artillery were very active sniping enemy movement throughout the morning and by the afternoon visible movement had practically ceased. 5th A.F.A. Bde withdrew their wagon lines at night and thence proceeded the St LEGER Area to rest. Harassing fire continued at night. Hostile shelling was less than previous 24 hours.	AAD AAD
	Sept. 6th		Quiet day. Several small concentrations were fired on M.G. nests at the request of the Infantry. Usual harassing fire continued. Hostile Artillery were less active but INCHY was shelled frequently. The following points brought out during these operations are worthy of notice :- (a) The water arrangements were not made sufficiently quickly after the advance and consequently animals had frequently to be sent back a long way for water causing a lot of extra fatigue on the animals which were already overworked. (b) Ammunition re-filling points were much too far back and consequently ammunition supply involved long journeys for men and animals. During the counter-attack on the evening of the 4th fire had to be very carefully controlled, as in case of a long barrage being required, the ammunition supply would have been very critical	AAD AAD AAD AAD AAD AAD AAD AAD AAD AAD
PRONVILLE.	Sept. 7th		Quiet day - 286th Bde RFA moved into action after dark, B, C, and D batteries taking up positions close to 56th Bde RFA and A/286 taking up a position near BARALLE Wood ** to enfilade the CANAL DU NORD. This brigade came under command of 285thBde, forming a sub-group under 52nd D.A. A rolling barrage was fired on the slopes of BOURLON WOOD by all batteries of the Group, at 5.15 pm. 9th Bde.	AAD AAD AAD
	Sept. 8th		Quiet day - rolling barrage fired 5.15 am.	
	Sept. 9th		Quiet day- rolling barrage fired at 4.15 pm.	

Army Form C. 2118.

WAR DIARY
or
INTELLIGENCE SUMMARY.
SEPTEMBER.

(Erase heading not required.)

Instructions regarding War Diaries and Intelligence Summaries are contained in F.S. Regs., Part II and the Staff Manual respectively. Title pages will be prepared in manuscript.

Place	Date	Hour	Summary of Events and Information	Remarks and references to Appendices
PRONVILLE.	Sept. 9th		9th Brigade RFA became silent and attached to 56th Bde RFA, in case of necessity formed right B Group under Lieut. Colonel J.M. INGRAM. Left Group now consisted of - 285th and 286th Bdes RFA.	AFD
	Sept. 10th		Command of Left Group handed over to Lieut. Colonel DOOK - commanding 285th Bde RFA - at 10 am and 52nd D.A. Hdqrs withdrew to rest with Divn: H.Q. near CROISSILLES.	AFD
CROISSILLES	11th		Nothing of note occurred.	AFD
	12th		52nd T.Ms. rejoined the D.A. having been attached to 51st D.A. for past 3 weeks.	AFD
	13th 14th to 16th		Nothing to report.	AFD AFD AFD
QUEANT.	Sept. 17th		52nd D.A. moved to new headquarters near QUEANT and assumed command of the Artillery in the line. Consisting of 9th, 56th, 178th and 181st Bdes RFA. 52nd Division relieved 57th Divn: in the line. S.O.S. was fired from 10.30 to 11.18 am to repel a raid on one of our posts, the Corps H.A. assisting in the barrage. 52nd D.A. order No. 35 re cutting of wire on HINDENBURG SUPPORT LINE issued.- vide - At 6.50 pm, the enemy put down a barrage on the western shlf of MOEUVRES, at 7.15 pm the enemy attacked at MOEUVRES. S.O.S. was fired by our batteries and the Corps Corps H.A. Guards D.A. and 2nd C.D.A. gave assistance. S.O.S. was continued till 8.40 pm. Our line was forced back to the western out-skirts of MOEUVRES - vide - Daily report. -	AFD AFD App: IV. AFD AFD App: V. AFD App: VI. AFD
	Sept. 18th		Hostile activity was above normal throughout the day - vide Daily report - The enemy made further attacks in the MOEUVRES vicinity during the evening and S.O.S. was fired from 6.10 to 8 pm, the Corps H.A., Guards D.A., and 2nd CDA all giving assistance in the barrage - vide -	~~App: VII.~~ ~~App: VIII.~~ App:VII.
	Sept. 19th		Hostile activity less than previous 24 hours - vide Daily Summary - Barrage fired at 7 pm in support of attack on MOEUVRES by our infantry. Corps H.A., Guards D.A. and 2nd CDA all co-operated in this barrage. All objectives were gained by 8.45 pm, but a small pocket of enemy were left in the village - vide 52nd D.A. Order No. A/631. Order for movement of our brigades southwards, on the taking over of Left Brigade front by 2nd Canadian Division and subsequent re-grouping of Brigades issued - vide 52nd D.A. Order No.36.	App:VIII. AFD App: IX. AFD

9th Bdes

Army Form C. 2118.

WAR DIARY
or
INTELLIGENCE SUMMARY.

(Erase heading not required.)

SEPTEMBER.

Instructions regarding War Diaries and Intelligence Summaries are contained in F. S. Regs., Part II. and the Staff Manual respectively. Title pages will be prepared in manuscript.

Place	Date	Hour	Summary of Events and Information	Remarks and references to Appendices
QUEANT.	Sept. 19th		9th Bde RFA moved to positions N.W. of MORCHIES.	App: X.
	Sept. 20th		Normal day – vide Daily Summary.	
	Sept. 21st		178th Bde moved to positions 2,500 yards West of MOEUVRES at night. Considerable enemy movement was observed in the enemy lines and was engaged by our Artillery the Guards D.A., 2nd CDA and Corps H.A., assisting by a bombardment of the areas of activity. At 2.25 pm, the enemy put down a very heavy barrage in the vicinity of MOEUVRES and at 3.0 pm he attacked. Our batteries including the Corps H.A. and flank D.As. commenced counter- preparation at 2.45 pm and fired S.O.S. from 3.3 pm. The attack drove back 2 of our posts but an immediate counter-attack regained the lost ground. At 7.45 pm our posts were further advanced a small barrage being fired in support of this operation. Vide Daily Summary - 52nd D.A. Order No. 37-with reference to extending of front by taking over of one brigade front from the Guards Division and the consequent re-inforcing and re-grouping of our Artillery- issued – vide - 93rd and 2nd N.Z. Army Brigades marched into the Divisional area and occupied wagon lines near LAGNICOURT, coming under command of this D.A.	App: XI. App: XII.
	Sept. 22nd		Quiet day until the evening at 7.18 pm when a heavy barrage was put down in vicinity of MOEUVRES Our batteries fired counter-preparation with the assistance of H.A. At 8.51 S.O.S. went up on the MOEUVRES Sector and was replied to by our batteries and H.A., the Guards D.A. and 2nd CDA assisting. Situation was quiet again by 10.30 pm – vide Daily Report - 93rd A.G.A. Bde moved into action at dusk N.E. of BOURSIES.	App: XIII.
	Sept. 23rd		Normal day – S.O.S. was fired by our northern batteries at request of 2nd CDA at 7.45 pm - vide Daily Report - 72nd and 315th Army F.A. Bdes moved into wagon lines near LAGNICOURT and MARICOURT WOOD respectively and came under the command of this D.A.	App: XIV.
	Sept. 24th		Quiet day, nothing to report, usual wire – cutting and gas shelling by 4.5" Hows.	
	Sept. 25th		Day quiet – vide Daily Report - 52nd D.A. Order 38 – re operation in conjunction with 63 and 57 Divn: issued – vide - 72nd and 315th; 2nd N.Z. Bdes moved into action in positions N.E. of BOURSIES and the 2nd N.Z. Bde S.E. of PRONVILLE.	App: XV. App: XVI.
QUEANT.	Sept. 26th		Quiet day. At 6 pm the 52nd Divn: H.Qrs. moved to advanced positions in HINDENBURG Line, S.E. of PRONVILLE. Command of 178, 181 & 2nd N.Z. Bdes passed to 40th D.A., that of 93rd and 315th Bdes passed to Colonel GOVER; 9th, 56th, and 72nd Bde formed 52nd D.A.Group.	
	Sept. 27th		At 5.20 am 52nd Division attacked in conjunction with 63rd Division on the left and Guards Division on the right. By 6.10 am LEOPARD TRENCH and the line of the CANAL DU NORD had been	

Army Form C. 2118.

WAR DIARY
or
INTELLIGENCE SUMMARY.

SEPTEMBER.

(Erase heading not required.)

Instructions regarding War Diaries and Intelligence Summaries are contained in F. S. Regs., Part II. and the Staff Manual respectively. Title pages will be prepared in manuscript.

Place	Date	Hour	Summary of Events and Information	Remarks and references to Appendices
QUEANT.	Sept. 27th		been taken and the 52nd Division proceeded to mop up the Hindenburg line, the 63rd Division advancing on GRAINCOURT and ANNEUX. 56th Bde RFA omved up into positions close to West bank of CANAL DU NORD at 7.5 am. 72nd Bde moved forward to cross the Canal at 8.40 and came under command of 57th D.A.; owing to the Canal crossings not being completed they were unable to proceed until about 11.39 am. A M.G. nest at HOG POST was reported to be holding out at 9 am and C.O. 0th Bde was ordered to get in touch with C.O. 157th Inf. Bde and arrange to support his attack on it. This post was reported to be in hands of the Guards Divn: at 12.5 p.m. and 157 Inf. Bde attack was not made. At 11.20 all ground East of Canal du Nord between MOEUVRES and GRAINCOURT and BAPAUME = CAMBRAI roads was reported clear of enemy. At 1.15pm command of 9th Bde passed to 63rd D.A. 52nd Divn: reporting that they had no further need of their support. 52nd D.A.H.Q. then moved to 63rd D.A.H.Q. and later moved forward to a position in the Hindenburg line, about 1,000 yards E. of Canal.	APD APD APD APD APD APD APD APD APD
MOEUVRES.	Sept. 28th		D.A.H.Q. moved to join 189th Inf. Bde HQ, at Sugar Factory and thence moved with 170th Inf. Bde HQ. to E.30.a.5.1. and on to CANTAING MILL. 56th Bde moved into action in L.1.d. and 9th Bde to F.25. In the afternoon, 56th Bde supported an attack on the ESCAUT CANAL by 170 Bde. 9th Bde moved to L.2.b. with batteries in L.2.b., L.3.a. and F.27.d. The D.A. then came into action came under 63rd Divn: and supported 189th Inf. Bde who attacked through 170 Bde but did not progress. 52nd D.A.C. moved to E.21.b.	APD APD
CANTAING.	Sept. 29th		63rd Divn: crossed the ESCAUT river and secured the high ground on the eastern side. 52nd DAC moved to L.2.a.	APD
	30th		9th Bde assisted in a barrage for an attack by 63rd Divn: across the CAMBRAI-MASNIERES road at 6 pm. This attack anticipated by aquarter of an hour, an attack by the enemy, who were caught by the barrage. Our attack did not progress.	APD

[signature]
Brig: Gen'l RA.
Commanding R.A., 52nd (Lowland) Division.

APPENDICES TO

WAR DIARY OF HEADQUARTERS ROYAL ARTILLERY,
52ND DIVISION.

F O R

SEPTEMBER 1918.

SECRET.
****

Copy No. 4

D.A.7/479.

57TH DIVISIONAL ARTILLERY OPERATION ORDER NO. 30.

1st September, 1918.

1.   171st Infantry Bde., now holding the line GREYHOUND AVENUE - TERRIER ALLEY, will attack and capture RIENCOURT, EMU ALLEY and DACHSHUND ALLEY this evening.

    The 52nd Division will carry out an operation in conjunction with this simultaneously.

    Zero hour will be 6.5 p.m.

2.   Artillery co-operation will be as follows:-

    (a) An 18-pdr. creeping barrage opening at zero hour on the line U 12 c 80.00, U 17 d 38.55, U 23 c 25.00.

        Right Group - 6 18-pdr. batteries.
        Left Group - 6 18-pdr. batteries.
        Dividing line between Groups will be: HENDECORT Trench (sunken road), U 17 d 38.55 to U 24 b 80.20.

        Barrage will remain on opening line for 4 minutes. It will then lift back at rate of 200 yards every eight minutes until reaching the line U 12 d 20.00, U 18 d 50.10, U 24 b 35.20, U 24 d 45.10, U 30 b 46.60 - there forming protector barrage. Left of barrage will reach this line at zero plus 16. Right of barrage will reach it at zero plus 72.

        Protector barrage on line U 12 d 20.00 as far as U 18 d 50.10 will continue until zero plus 60.

        From U 18 d 50.10 to U 30 b 46.60 until zero plus 100.

        Ammunition: Half H.E., half Time Shrapnel.

        Rate of fire:
        Zero to zero plus 6   -   Intense.
        Zero plus 6 to zero plus 72 - Normal, except for batteries reaching Protector Line.

        Rate of fire on reaching Protector Line will be - SLOW.

    (b) Action for 4.5 Hows:

        One How. Battery, Left Group:
        Zero to zero plus 10 - DACHSHUND AVENUE, U 18 a 66.00 to U 18 c 50.00.
        Rate of fire - Normal.
        Zero plus 10 to zero plus 60 - Sweeping and searching U 18 b and d.
        Rate of fire - Slow.

        One How. Battery, Left Group:
        Zero to zero plus 20 - Searching up HENDECOURT Trench, from U 17 d 75.37 to U 18 c 60.00, keeping 100 yards beyond 18-pdr. barrage.
        Rate of fire - Normal.
        Zero plus 20 to zero plus 40 - That part of RIENCOURT in northern half of U 24 a.
        Rate of fire - Normal.
        Zero plus 40 to zero plus 60 - Searching up sunken road, U 24 a and c; keeping 100 yards beyond 18-pdr. barrage.
        Rate of fire - Normal.
        Zero plus 60 to zero plus 100 - TURTLE TRENCH and Trench line V 13 d 00.00 to V 19 c 40.90, paying particular attention to trench junctions.
        Rate of fire - Slow.

(Over

One How.Battery, Right Group:
  Zero to zero plus 30:
    3 hows. MORDEN Trench)
    3 hows. BULLDOG Support) Searching.
  Zero plus 20 to zero plus 40 -
    3 hows. BULLDOG Support)
    3 hows. STARFISH Trench) Searching.
  Zero plus 40 to zero plus 60 -
    RIENCOURT Trench - searching.
  Rates of fire for above - Normal.

  Zero plus 60 to zero plus 100
    Trench U 24 d 75.24 to U 30 b 45.65.
  Rate of fire - slow.

One How. Battery, Right Group:
  Zero to zero plus 30 - Portion of RIENCOURT in South half of
                          U 24 a.
                         OSTRICH Trench,
                  To keep 100 yards beyond 18-pdr.barrage.
  Rate of fire - normal.
  Zero plus 30 to zero plus 60. EMU Alley, sweeping from
                  U 30 a 82.65 to U 24 d 20.85.
  Rate of fire - normal.
  Zero plus 60 to zero plus 100. Trench from U 19 c 40.83 to
                  U 24 d 75.24.
  Rate of fire - slow.

(c) Left Heavy Artillery Group -
  Zero to zero plus 15 - Bombard RIENCOURT and OSTRICH Trench.
    Rate of fire - Intense until zero plus 5, afterwards normal.
  Zero plus 15 to zero plus 40 - EMU Alley and trenches U 24 b
                  and d.
    Rate of fire - slow.
  Zero plus 40 to zero plus 100 - Trench systems in V 13 and
                  V 19, paying particular
                  attention to trench junctions.
  Rate of fire - Slow.

3. Field Artillery Groups will synchronise watches with H.Q. 171st Infantry Bde. Left Heavy Artillery Group with H.Q., 57th Divl.Arty.

4. 285th Brigade R.F.A. will be in action in area U 9 and 10 by 6 p.m. this evening.
   Positions have been selected.
   This Brigade will come under orders of O.C., Left Group, at 9 p.m. to-night, but will not take part in the above operation.

5. Please acknowledge.

                                        W E Rudkin
                               Brigadier-General,
Issued at 1 p.m.   C.R.A., 57th Division.

Copies to: Nos. 1/3 Right Group
                3/6 Left Group
                  7 285th Brigade R.F.A.
                  8 57th Division "G".
             9/11 Left H.A. Group.
               12 XVII Corps R.A.
               13 57th Bn. M.G.C.
               14 H.Q. Right Divl. Artillery.
               15 H.Q., 1st Canadian Artillery.
          16/17 War Diary.
               18 File.

SECRET   Copy No. 30

57th DIVISION ORDER No. 119.

1st September 1918.

Ref. Sheet 51.B. SW. and 51.C. SE. 1/20.000 and attached map *

1. (a) The Canadian Corps on the left of XVII Corps assisted by Tanks, has been ordered to attack the QUEANT - DROCOURT Line on September 2nd, at an hour which will be notified later.

    1st Canadian Division is on left of 57th Division.

   (b) XVII Corps will co-operate by pushing forward its left with the object of gaining a position to attack QUEANT from the North.

   (c) The objectives of XVII Corps and 1st Canadian Division are shown on the attached map 'A'.
   Inter divisional boundaries are shown YELLOW on attached map.

2. 57th Division will be the left Division of XVII Corps and 52nd Division on our right will conform to our movements.

3. 171st Inf.Bde. is attacking the 1st objective today under orders already issued.
   172nd Inf.Bde. will capture the 2nd and 3rd objectives;
   63rd Division will pass through 172nd Inf.Bde. on 3rd objective to exploit success.

4. (a) 172nd Inf.Bde. will assemble immediately after dark on Sept. 1st near the left Divisional boundary so as to be able to take immediate advantage of a break through by the 1st Canadian Div.

    The closest and most bold touch must be kept with the progress of 1st Canadian Division: and G.O.C. 172nd Inf.Bde. must decide for himself whether he commits his brigade to the assault.

   (b) If the 1st Canadian Division succeeds in breaking through, 172nd Inf.Bde. will advance, and make good the 2nd or RED objective within the Divisional Boundary attacking it from the North.
   When the protective barrage in front of the 2nd (RED) Objective lifts, 172nd Inf.Bde will attack and capture that part of the 3rd (GREEN) objective which lies between the Southern Divisional Boundary and V.27.a.3.5. attacking it from the North.
   Strong Mopping up parties must be detailed for both objectives.
   63rd Division will then push through between V.27.a.3.5. and the Northern Divisional boundary.

5. 170th Inf.Bde will be prepared, should the attack of 171st Inf. Bde this evening be unsuccessful, to capture the objectives allotted today to 171st Inf.Bde. viz:- Min.SANS SOUCI (excl.) - East of RIENCOURT - DACHSHUND AVENUE.
   This attack would take place in the above event at   zero hour

   Should the attack of the 171st Inf.Bdea this evening be successful, 170th Inf.Bde. (less one Bn. at disposal of 171st Inf.Bde.) will be in Divisional Reserve with leading troops on the approximate line U.15.Central - U.10.central.

Sheet 2.

6. 171st Inf.Bde will hold the positions captured in their attack this evening.
As the attack of the 172nd Inf.Bde progresses from the North one Bn. 170th Inf.Bde. (placed at the disposal of 171st Inf.Bde.) will push forward to assist the attack of 172nd Inf.Bde. by cleaning up the trench system in U.24.b. and d. and V.19.a.

7. 57th Bn.M.G.C. with 2 M.G.Coys will act in close co-operation with the attacking troops of 170th Inf.Bde.

8. Artillery support will be as follows :-

(a) At zero a creeping 18-pdr barrage in conformity with 1st Canadian Division will come down approximately on a North and South line between U.13. U.24. and V.13. V.19. 10
This barrage will lift back at zero plus 5 and move at rate of 100 yds every 3 minutes until reaching the sunken road running S.W. through V.20 and V.25. Zero + 19. afterwards
rate with 100yds every 5 minutes until reaching sunken road.
On reaching this line batteries will engage trench system in V.13. V.19. and V.20. The above barrage will act as a flank protection to 1st Canadian Division and as a preparatory barrage for the advance Southwards of 172nd Inf.Bde.
barrage on a line 200ⁿ South of Corps Northern Boundary
At Zero plus 90 the above barrage will sweep southwards at and
rate of 100 yards every 5 minutes until reaching line HIPPO LANE POSSUM LANE where it will rest until zero plus 135 minutes. Fire will then cease.
Field Artillery support for the attack from the 2nd to the 3rd Objective will be notified later.

(b) From zero to zero plus 20 all heavy artillery will be employed on intense counter-battery work.
From zero plus 20 to zero plus 90 a portion of H.A. will bombard trenches in V.19. V.20.a. and V.20.c.
There will be no fire North of the line 500 yards South of and parrellel to Northern Corps Boundary.
At zero plus 1½ hours H.A. fire will lift Southwards.
There will be no fire North of Squares V.20. and V.26. after Zero plus 1½ hours.
At zero plus 2 hours 15 mins. H.A. fire will cease and Left Heavy Artillery Group will bombard targets allotted by the Division.

9. A contact aeroplane will call for flares as follows :-

(a) On the 2nd or RED Objective at Zero plus 3 hours.

(b) On the 3rd or GREEN Objective at Zero plus 5 hours.

10 Please acknowledge.

J.R.Wetherred
Lieut-Colonel
General Staff 57th Division.

Issued at 4.pm.

Distribution, see over.

Rates of fire normal up to zero +30
+30 & +84 slow from a batteries
+90 & +135 normal

D.A.7/481.

50th Divisional Artillery Operation Order. No.31.

Reference 57th Division Order No.119 of to-day.
Following are orders for Left Divisional Artillery in support of this attack.

1. Maps showing Corps and Divisional Boundaries, Artillery Group and Brigade Boundaries, Objective Lines and Barrage Areas have been issued to Group Commanders.

2. DISTRIBUTION OF ARTILLERY:

RIGHT GROUP. - Lieut.Colonel E.B.Cotter D.S.O.

        5th Army Brigade R.F.A.
        286th Brigade R.F.A.

LEFT GROUP - Lieut.Colonel H.J.Cotter C.I.E.,D.S.O.

        9th Brigade R.F.A.
        56th Brigade R.F.A.
        285th Brigade R.F.A.

3. 1st BARRAGE.

18-pdrs. (a) At Zero hour a creeping 18-pdr. barrage will open on the line U.12.d.8.0. to U.30.b.80.45.
It will remain on this line until Zero plus 10 and will then lift back at rate of 100 yards every 3 minutes until Zero plus 19, when rate will be 100 yards every 5 minutes until Zero plus 84.

The boundaries for this barrage are -
On the NORTH. - The Corps Boundary.
On the SOUTH - The Divisional Boundary.
On the EAST - The Sunken Road from V.21.a.50.66. to V.25.b.90.20.

When each battery reaches the Sunken Road (Eastern Boundary) or the boundary of its lane, it will continue searching all trenches in its particular lane until Zero plus 84, except in the area 200 yards South of the Corps Northern Boundary.

At Zero plus 84 - All 18-pdr batteries will cease fire and will switch their lines of fire on to a line 200 yards South of the Corps Northern Boundary with the exception of the 286th Brigade R.F.A. which will be held in readiness to advance.

Ammunition 45% shrapnel. 40% H.E. 15% Smoke.

Flank Batteries i,e, Left battery of Left Group and right battery of Right Group will only fire shrapnel and smoke.
Rate of fire Zero to Zero plus 24 - NORMAL.
Zero plus 24 to Zero plus 84 - SLOW.

(b) 4.5" Howitzers.
4.5" Hows. will open on a line 100 yards beyond 18-pdr. barrage and will lift back this distance searching all trench in their respective lanes until reaching barrage boundaries, when they will search back ceasing fire at Zero plus 84.

At Zero plus 84 4.5" How. Batteries will switch their lines of fire on to a line 500 yards South of the Northern Corps Boundary. Rate of fire - Slow throughout.
The above barrage will be a flank barrage to the Canadian attack and a preparatory barrage for the advance Southwards of the 172nd Infantry Brigade.

4. 2nd BARRAGE.
This will open at Zero plus 90 18-pdrs. on a line 200 yards South of the Corps Northern Boundary, 4.5" Hows. 500 yards South.

Brigades have been allotted equal portions from East to West
285th Brigade R.F.A., 9th Brigade R.F.A., 56th Brigade R.F.A.,
5th Army Brigade R.F.A.

This barrage will consist of a creeping switch barrage
moving Southwards at the rate of 100 yards every 5 minutes
until reaching a line HIPPO LANE - POSSUM LANE.

        The greatest care must be taken by Battery Commanders
that 18-prds. and Howitzers cannot shoot to the North (Left)
of the line on which the barrage opens.

        4.5" Hows. will switch their fire to the right at
the same pace as 18-pdrs. but must keep 300 yards to the South
(Right) of the 18-pdr. switch barrage. On reaching the line
HIPPO LANE - POSSUM LANE 4.5" Hows. will halt their fire on this
line until Zero plus 120, when they will cease fire.

        On reaching the line HIPPO LANE - POSSUM LANE 18-pdrs.
will cease fire at Zero plus 135 minutes.

        Ammunition - 18-pdrs. shrapnel only.
        Rate of fire for both 18-pdrs. and 4.5" Hows. - NORMAL.

5.   The 286th Brigade R.F.A. will advance at Zero plus 90
to the close support of 172nd Infantry Brigade. This Brigade
will act directly under the orders of the G.O.C. 172nd Inf. Bde.
to whom O.C. 286th Brigade R.F.A. should report for orders at
Zero plus 80.

6.   On the completion of the second barrage brigades must
be prepared to advance without delay by sections or batteries
to close support of 63rd Division which will pass through 52nd)Divi
57th Division.

7.   Left Divisional Artillery will come under the orders of
G.O.C.63rd Division when 63rd Division pass through 57th Division.
Command of Artillery will not change.

8.   Left H.A.Group will act under the orders of the B.G.,H.A.
XVIIth Corps until Zero plus 135 minutes when it
reverts to Divisional control.

9.   Orders for action and advance after Zero plus 135 minutes
will issue later.

10.   Every endeavour must be made by F.O.Os, Battery and
Brigade Commanders to get information as to the situation through
to Divisional Artillery as early as possible.

        In an operation of this nature, its success must depend
largely on accurate reports of the progress of the attack reaching
Divisional Headquarters without delay.

        Artillery F.O.Os. can assist very materially. Every
possible means of communication must be used and all previously
tested.

        C.W.Sets are being installed at U.19.d.8.6. and on
High ground at U.1.a. Messages can be sent by runner to these
stations for transmission.

11.   Note to 172nd Infantry Brigade. 172nd Infantry Brigade
must not advance South of the Northern Corps boundary before Zero
plus 90 when the creeping switch barrage will open.

12.   ZERO hour will be notified later.

13.   Please acknowledge.

Ammunition 9th and 56th Bdes.
Creeping barrage 50% A.
                 50% AX.
Flanking barrage 85% A.
                15% AS.
Smoke to be fired by left batteries of brigades only.
286th Bde on creeping barrage will fire smoke from its left battery.
Ammunition from this brigade 45% A.
                            40% AX.
                            15% AS.

Rates of fire -
   Zero to Zero plus 30 - Normal.
   Zero plus 30 to Zero plus 84. - Slow.
From Zero plus 84 to Zero plus 90 barrage forms on its Northern Line previous to switching.
   Zero plus 84 to Zero plus 135 - Normal.
   Howitzers stop at Zero plus 120.
When batteries reach the protective barrage they do not dwell on it but search communication and other trenches in their area until Zero plus 84.
The flanking barrage halts on the POSSUM and HIPPO lanes.
Zero hour will be 5.0 am.
Howitzers in the creeping barrage should jump from trench to trench as the 18-pdr. barrage comes up to the trench.
In the flanking barrage the Howitzers will keep 300 yards South of the 18-pdr. barrage and will stop at Zero plus 120.
The creeping barrage will remain on the opening line till Zero plus 10 and will then creep forward at 100 yards per 3 minutes, till Zero plus 19 after which it moves 100 yards forward every 5 minutes until it reaches protective line.
From Zero plus 90 to Zero plus 135 the barrage will move to the Right i.e. South at the rate of 100 yards per 5 minutes.
Batteries should be ready to move from Zero plus 2 hours 30 minutes with full echelon.

SECRET.

COPY NO. 18.

52ND DIVISIONAL ARTILLERY ORDER NO. 33.

1. The wire guarding the HINDENBURG LINE in E.21.a. and b. and E.22.a also that guarding the CANAL DU NORD line in E.15.c. will be destroyed by 52nd Divisional Artillery Group by the 23rd September.

2. D.T.M.O., 52nd Division will arrange to put a complete battery of 6" Newton Mortars into action in the MOEUVRES area, in addition to the 2 in action there.
    These 8 mortars will be responsible for cutting all the wire in E.21.a. and E.15.c. within range of the mortars using 4th charge.

3. The wire in E.21.b. and E.22.a. will be allotted as follows :-
    527th Battery - Wire in E.22.a.
    D/178 Battery - All wire in E.21.b. from Sunken Road inclusive Eastwards.
    D/181 Battery.- All wire in E.21.b. from Sunken Road exclusive Westwards.
    D/69 Battery - Will be prepared to deal with any wire in the Trench Mortar area, which the mortars cannot reach with 4th charge.

4. 527th, D/178th and D/181st Batteries will start work on 18th and Trench Mortars as soon as they are established.

5. A special allotment of 4.5" Ammunition for these tasks is being made and pending definite orders on this subject, the 3 Howitzer Batteries allotted definite tasks will fire 300 rounds per battery on the 18th.

6. Commencing evening 18th September, Groups will render a daily report on progress made, to reach this Office as soon after firing has ceased as possible.

7. Each brigade will arrange for one of its 18-pdr. Batteries to harass that portion of its 4.5" Howitzer battery task, that has been dealt with, during the night.
    This battery will fire 200 rounds during the night and will otherwise remain silent except for S.O.S.

8. D.T.M.O. will be responsible for informing the Right Infantry Brigade Commander as to what wire has been cut so that it may be kept under fire by Machine Guns during the night.

9. ACKNOWLEDGE.

Captain R.A.
Brigade Major R.A., 52nd DA.

17th September 1918.

Distribution :-

Copy No. 1. Right Group.
        2. Left Group.
        3. 9th Bde RFA.
        4. D.T.M.O.
        5. 52nd D.A.C.
Copy No. 6. 52nd Division 'G'.
        7. XVII Corps R.A.
        8. XVII Corps H.A.
        9. 52nd Bde RGA.
       10. Guards D.A.
       11. 40th D.A.
Copy No. 12. 155th Inf. Bde.
       13. 156th Inf. Bde.
       14. 157th Inf. Bde.
       15. S.C.R.A.
       16. R.O.R.A.
       17. R.A. Signals.
    18/19 War Diary.
       20. File.

52ND DIVISIONAL ARTILLERY.
INTELLIGENCE SUMMARY - 6.0 am 17th to 6.0 am 18th Sept. 1918.

OUR OPERATIONS.

S.O.S. was fired from 10.30 tp 11.18 am again from 7.10 to 8.40 pm.

A gas concentration was fired by the 4.5" Howz. batteries at 2.0 am in co-operation with H.A. on enemy battery positions.

At 10.16 am - movement was engaged between THREX TRENCH, E.16.c.2.0 and sunken road, E.16.c.6.5.

At 12.14 pm.- movement at bridge, E.15.c.20.35 engaged.

N.F. calls were answered on E.12.d.9.3., E.30.d.5.8. and E.18.d.4.4.

6" Trench Mortars - from 2.30 to 4.45 pm 65 rounds were fired in E.8.b.2.7. and E.8.a.1.9. and 40 rounds on E.8.b.30.35.

HOSTILE ACTIVITY.

Considerably above normal.

The INCHY-PRONVILLE VALLEY was heavily shelled with H.E. and Blue Cross Gas between 2.0 and 4.0 pm. HOBART TRENCH and D.24.a. also received considerable attention.

At 6.5 pm a heavy barrage, lasting for 25 minutes, was put down on MOEUVRES.

Some counter-battery work was also carried out during the attack.

WORK. N I L.

MOVEMENT. Observed in THREX TRENCH, bridge at E.15.c.20.35.

AERIAL ACTIVITY. Normal.

VISIBILITY. Fair.

Lieut. RFA.
For Commanding R.A., 52nd Division.

18th September 1918.

SECRET.

62ND DIVISIONAL ARTILLERY INTELLIGENCE SUMMARY.
6.0 am Sept. 18th to 6.0 am Sept. 19th '18.

OUR OPERATIONS.

S.O.S. was fired by the Right Group from 4.50 pm to 5.12 pm and again from 6.10 to 8.6 pm. Left Group fired S.O.S. from 5.0 to 5.35 pm.

Gas shell concentrations were fired on E.14.d.5.3. at 11 pm, midnight and 1.0 am, by 4.5" Hows.

Wire cutting was carried out on wire South of HINDENBURG Line in E.21.b. and E.22.a.

Movement was fired on in E.11.c.8.4., E.22.b. & c, E.5.a.5.3., E.10.b.5.0. and in THREX TRENCH E.16.b.

6" T.Ms. fired 40 rounds on E.8.d.05.88, E.8.d.25.80, E.8.d.5.5. and 49 rounds on E.8.d.35.65 to E.8.c.7.6.

HOSTILE ACTIVITY.

Considerable harassing with H.E. and Gas throughout the day on D.11.b., D.12, D.16, D.17, D.18, V.23 and V.29. Concentration of H.E. and Gas were put down on HOBART STREET twice during the evening.

Date.	Time.	No. of Rounds.	Calibre.	Area shelled.	Remarks.
18th.	10 to 10.30	40.	77 mm.	E.19.c.	Green Cross.
	12.15-12.42.	12.	10.5 cm.	E.13.d.	
	12.45-1.0 pm.	16.	10.5 cm.	E.13.c.	Blue Cross.
	6.45-7.15 pm.	?	10.5 cm.	TADPOLE COPSE.	
	10.30 pm	6.	10.5 cm.	E.13.c.	
	12 midnt.	6.	15 cm.	D.16.b.7.2.	and at intervals during night.

WORK. - None observed.

MOVEMENT. - 10.15 am - small party E.11.c.3.4.
    10.23 am - " " " "
    1.25 pm - " " E.5.a.5.3.
    4.0 pm - parties in E.10.b.3.0.
    4.15 pm &-) " " E.16.b. & E.17.a.
    4.45 pm)
    5.0 pm - large party of Infantry in full marching order

-2-

order and fixed bayonets observed in E.20.c. These were engaged by M.Gs.

GENERAL.   Visibility fair.

[signature]

Lieut. RFA.
for C.R.A., 52nd Division.

19th September 1918.

52ND DIVISIONAL ARTILLERY INTELLIGENCE SUMMARY
6.0 am 19th Sept. to 6.0 am 20th Sept.

OUR OPERATIONS.

From 11 am to 7 pm our 4.5" Hows. bombarded E.14.c. & d., and E.20.b. 4.5" Hows. cut wire in E.22.a., E.21.a. and E.15.c.

Barrage fired in support of attack on MOEUVRES from 7 pm to 8.45 pm.

Gas concentrations fired by 4.5" Hows. in E.15.d.3.1. at 4.0, 5.0 and 6.0 am.

Movement engaged in LYNX Trench, E.18.a. & c, E.22.b.0.3., X.27.c., E.40.

T.Ms. at E.20.d.5.5. to E.20.d.5.0. engaged by 4.5" Hows. at 9.5 pm.

Our 6" T.Ms fired with good effect, 22 rounds on M.G-emplacements at E.8.b.10.95 and 15 rounds on Canal from E.8.b.10.95 to E.8.b.3.4. between 3 and 5 pm.

From 12.30 pm onwards, 10 rounds on E.8.c.65.65 and 26 rounds on E.8.d.65.75.

HOSTILE ACTIVITY.

ARTILLERY.

Less active than during previous day, chief harassing was by 15 cm. on D.18.c. & d. and trenches in D.24.a. The barrage during our attack on MOEUVRES was light.

Date.	Time.	No. of rounds.	Calibre.	Area shelled.	Direction.
19th.	9.0 – 9.10 am.	4.	10.5 cm.	D.17.a.	
	10.0 – 10.30 am.	10.	15 cm.	D.14.b.	
	10.0 – 12 noon.	?	15 cm.	D.18.c. & d.	
	10.5 – 11.15 am.	4.	10.5 cm.	D.15.c.	
	10.50 – 11.15 am.	?	10.5 cm.(gun)	E.18.d.6.0.	4 guns firing
	2.20 – 3.0 pm.	6.	15 cm.	D.16.b.	
	3.30 – 4.0 pm.	40.	77 mm.	E.13.a.	E.24.a.5.5.
	6.0 – 6.20 pm.	50.	15 & 10.5 cm.	INCHY.	

WORK. – None observed.

MOVEMENT.   9.30 am small party LYNX Trench.
              9.45 am "   "   E.18.a. & b.

-2-

MOVEMENT. (contd.)
  10.30 am small party E.22.b.0.3.
  10.30 am party of 50 in X.27.b. & E.4.a.
  12 noon-
  1.0 pm. movement in E.15.b.
  2.30 pm 20 men in E.4.a.
  3.15 pm 20 men seen proceeding from QUARRY Wood to BOURLON Village.

AERIAL. Two E.As flying over our lines at 10.50 am driven back by M.G. & A.A. fire.

GENERAL. Visibility good.
  T.M. suspected at E.8.b. 3.5.
  Flashes observed at 10.10 am at E.18.b.3.3.
  Flashes observed between 5.18 and 6.50 pm at E.15.d.0.0., E.24.c.9.4., E.24.c.6.9., E.12.b.7.7., E.10.b.8.5., E.24.c.4.7., and E.10.b.9.0.

            Lieut. RFA.
           a/Reconnaissance Officer,
           for C.R.A., 52nd Division.

20th September 1918.

SECRET.

Right Group.
Left Group.

52nd D.A. No. A/331.

1.   155th Brigade will recapture MOEUVRES this evening and consolidate line ridge E.20.b., Cemetery Support in E.14.d. AAA 157th Bde will conform and consolidate Cemetery support as far as E.14.d.30.65 and capture railway line between HOBART and Cemetery ~~support as far as E.14.d.30.65 and capture railway line between HOBART and Cemetery~~ trenches.
Zero will be 1900 hours.
Artillery action will be as under -
     At zero, 52nd Divisional Artillery will put down a barrage on line E.20.a.05.45 to E.14.a.30.65 till Zero plus 5 and will then creep forward 100 yards per 4 minutes till the line of the Canal from E.20.d.0.35 to E.15.c.15.60. is reached.
     4.5" Hows. will be 200 yrds. ahead of 18-pdrs.
     At zero plus 45, 9th and 181st Bdes will cease fire the remainder will form protective barrage E.14.a.30.65 - E.15.a.0.2. - then along Canal to E.20.d.8.5.

2.   Zone tasks etc. will be as allotted by C.R.A. to Group Commanders.

3.   Rates of fire - Zero to Zero plus 10 - INTENSE.
                Zero plus 10 to Zero plus 45 NORMAL.
                Zero plus 45 to Zero plus 105 - SLOW.
                then as situation demands.

4.   H.A. continue to bombard Canal from Zero to Zero plus 20, then form blocks at Locks in E.8.d., E.20.d.8.5. and HINDENBURG LINE E.15.d.10.55 to E.21.B.10.80. till Zero plus 105 and concentrations on HINDENBURG LINE and Canal at irregular intervals during the night.

5.   Guards D.A. are forming a block barrage on lower half of E.26.b. West of Canal and 2nd C.D.A. are enfilading Canal in E.8.b. & d from Zero to Zero plus 105.

                                             W.R.Harris
                                             Captain R.A.
                                     Brigade Major R.A., 52nd D.A.

19th Sept. 1918.

52nd Division 'G'
155th Inf. Bde.
Corps H.A.
Guards D.A.
2nd C.D.A.

SECRET.   COPY No. 40
                                                              of 9

52ND DIVISIONAL ARTILLERY ORDER NO. 36.

1. 157th Infantry Brigade is being relieved by the 5th Canadian Brigade on the night 19th / 20th.

2. At 6 a.m. 20th instant the command of the present Left Brigade Front passes to 2nd Canadian Division.

3. On passing off command, the Northern Divisional boundary will be re-adjusted to
    E.14 central - E.14.a.0.2.- D.18.a.0.4.- D.17.a.0.6.- D.9.d.4.0.-
        D.3.a.0.0. - U.27 central - U.13.a.0.0. thence as before.

4. Consequent upon the above, Artillery reliefs and moves as in attached table will take place. Further details of reliefs will issue later.

5. In order to facilitate reliefs, the following regrouping will come into force :-

    RIGHT GROUP. Commander - Lt.Col. J.M.INGRAM,   R.F.A.
                                56th Brigade R.F.A.
                                181st.Brigade R.F.A.

    LEFT GROUP. Commander - Lt.Col. T. Mc.GOWAN, D.S.O.,R.F.A.
                                9th Brigade R.F.A.
                                178th Brigade R.F.A.

   S.O.S. lines will be redistributed accordingly forthwith, within present Group boundaries and reported to this office.
   The 9th Bde should take over the most northerly S.O.S. lines.

6. At 6 a.m. 20th instant, Lt.Col.Mc.GOWAN will hand over Left Group to O.C.,285th Bde RFA. but will not leave his present H.Q. till his own Brigade is relieved.
   The left group will then be composed as follows :-

                        285th Brigade R.F.A.
            2 - 18pdr.Batteries - 178th Brigade R.F.A.

7. After 6 a.m. 20th, till relief, the remaining two batteries of 178th Bde RFA. will be at disposal of Right Group.
   On arrival in their new positions, 178th Bde RFA will come entirely under Right Group.

8. 9th and 181st Brigades on arrival in their new positions, will be silent and directly under D.A.

9. Ammunition to be maintained in new positions will be as under :-

        56th and 178th Brigades, as at present.   18pdrs to maintain
        75% - H.E. and 25% - Shrapnel.

        9th and 181st Brigades.
            18pdrs - 300 rounds per gun, 75% Shrapnel and 25% H.E.
            4.5"Hows. - 200 rounds per 4.5" How.

   If Smoke is ordered, it will be at the rate of 1 round Smoke to 6 rounds Shrapnel or H.E.

10. During reliefs, there is on no account to be any movement before dark.
    i.e. 8 p.m.

11. No definite S.O.S. lines can be laid down, as the tactical situation will be changing during reliefs.
    Group Commanders must hand over S.O.S. lines adjusted to the latest requirements of the Infantry.

12. Brigade Commanders will report exact location of new Headquarters and Battery positions as soon as possible.

-2-

13. The 57th Division M.T.M. Battery in action in E.7.d. comes under 2nd Canadian Division 6 am 20th September.

14. Wagon lines will no notified by Staff Captain.

15. Completion of each relief to be reported to this Office.

16. ACKNOWLEDGE&

                                                          Captain R.A.
                          Brigade Major R.A., 52nd DA.

19th Sept. 1918.

Distribution.

Copy no - 1/5	56th Bde RFA	Copy no. 27. 62nd Bde RGA.
6/10	9th Bde RFA.	28. Guards D.A.
11/15	178th Bde RFA.	29. 2nd C.D.A.
16/20	181st Bde RFA.	30. 40th D.A.
21	52nd D.A.C.	31. 155th Inf. Bde.
22	52nd D.T.M.O.	32. 156th Inf. Bde.
23	57th D.T.M.O.	33. 157th Inf. Bde.
24	52nd Divn. 'G'.	34/35 57th D.A.
25	R.A. XVII Corps.	36 S.O.R.A.
26	H.A. XVII Corps.	37. R.O.D.A.
		38 R.A. Signals.
		39 D.A.G.O.
		40/41 War Diary.
		42 File.

TABLE TO ACCOMPANY 52ND DIVISIONAL ARTILLERY ORDER No.53.

SERIAL NO.	DATE.	UNIT.	FROM.	TO.	REMARKS.
1.	19/20 Sept.	9th Bde R.F.A.	Present position.	D.29.c.	Relieved by 285 Bde R.F.A.
2.	20/21 Sept.	178th Bde R.F.A.	"	D.19.c.	" Bde of Canadian Corps.
3.	21/22 Sept.	181st Bde R.F.A.	"	D.50.	" " "
4.	22/23 Sept.	56th Bde R.F.A.	"	D.17.b.&d.	" " "

S E C R E T.

52ND DIVISIONAL ARTILLERY INTELLIGENCE SUMMARY
6 am 20th Sept. to 6 am. 21st Sept. 1918.

OUR OPERATIONS.

4.5" Howitzers cut wire in E.21.b. & 22.a. by day and fired gas concentrations in conjunction with Heavy Artillery during the night.

77 mm guns fired Yellow Cross Gas Shell on Sunken road in E.17.d. & 24.a. at 3.0 am.

Harassing fire carried out by night on centres of activity.
Movement was engaged as follows :-
    8.0 am small party E.15.d. Road.
    8.50 " " " E.16.d. Road.
    9.5 " 2 parties of 20 - E.16.c. Road.

HOSTILE ACTIVITY.

Normal, but harassing fire rather heavy between 9.0 am & 4.30 pm

Date.	Time.	No. of rounds.	Calibre.	Area Shelled.	Direction.
20th.	8.30- 9.5 am.	30.	5.9.	E.14.a. & E.20.b.	BOURLON Village.
	9.30- 9.55 am.	30.	77 mm	D.17.a.	E.29.a.
	10.25- 10.50 am.	26.	4.2.	E.13.a.	BOURLON Wood.
	10.50- 11.30 am.	30.	5.9.	E.19.a.	BOURLON Wood
	11.35 am- 6.0 pm.	Intermitt:	4.2 & 5.9.	INCHY.	BOURLON Village.
	8.0- 8.15 pm.	20.	4.2.	B.18.a.	

WORK. None observed.

AERIAL. 10 am to 12 noon, 5 E.As. flew over ~~our front line~~ E.24 and E.30. Did not cross our lines.
    2.0 pm. to 4.0 pm - 2 groups of 5 flew over our front line.
    3.20 pm - 3 E.A. crossed our lines, engaged by M.G. and A.A. fire One British and an E.A. collided - both crashed. Enemy airman jumped out and came down safely in parachute.
    4.10 pm one E.A. driven back across our lines by our machines.

MOVEMENT. 8.0 am small party road E.15.d.
    8.50 am. " " " E.16.c.
    9.5 am. 2 parties of 20 Road E.16.c.

GENERAL. Visibility good with intervals of fair visibility.

Lieut. RFA.
Reconnaissance Officer,
for C.R.A., 52nd Divn.

21st Sept. 1918.

SECRET.

52ND DIVISIONAL ARTILLERY SUMMARY OF INTELLIGENCE,
6 am 21st Sept. to 6 am 22nd Sept. 1918.

OUR ACTIVITY.

4.5" Hows. carried out wire cutting in E.21 & E.22 by day and fire gas concentrations in conjunction with the H.A. by night.

77 mm guns fired Yellow Cross Gas Shell on southern position of BOURLON WOOD.

Concentration fire on HINDENBURG line E.21.b. at 11.45 am

At 2.45 pm counter preparation was commenced owing to the heavy barrage put down on MOEUVRES by the enemy.

At 3.3 pm S.O.S. was fired in response to call from the Infantry in E.20.b. & d.

At 7.45 pm a slow rate of fire was fired on E.14.b.1.1. and later lifted to Canal Du Nord in support of minor operation of Infantry.

Usual harassing fire by night.
Movement fired on as follows -
11.10 am men on crest in E.20.b.
11.30 am party in THREX Street.
11.35 am large party of enemy in sunken road E.21.b. walking towards trenches in E.21.d.
1.0 pm party in THREX Street.
1.45 pm party in LYNX St.

HOSTILE ACTIVITY.

Artillery. Chief activity was on front line in E.14 and 20. The bombardment of this area which commenced about 2.25 pm was extremely heavy.

Date	Time	No. of Rds.	Calibre	Area shelled	Direction
21st.	10--				
	10.20 am	30.	10.5 cm.	E.20.b.	Bourlon Village.
	11--				
	11.20 am	20.	77 mm	E.20.d.	" "
	12--				
	12.50 pm	23.	15 cm.	D.24.a.	" Wood.
	2.25--				
	2.45pm	Hy. Bdt.	10.5 &15 cm.	MOEUVRES.	
	4.0--				
	6.0 pm	50.	77mm & 10.5 cm.	D.15,16,17,&18.	Bourlon Vlg

MOVEMENT. 11 am - party on road E.18.c. & d.
11.10 am - party on crest E.22.b.
11.35 am - large party from sunken road E.21.b. to trench E.21.d.
Considerable movement in trench in E.17.a. & c throughout the day.
1.0 pm - small party in THREX Trench.
1.45 pm - "   "   "   LYNX Trench.

AERIAL.- 6.10 pm - 1 E.A. brought down in MOEUVRES in flames. A number of bombs were dropped in vicinity D.30 & J.5. during the night.

GENERAL. Visibility fair to good. 8.0 pm Red signal was observed bearing 109° grid from E.15.c.5.4. Flashes seen on grid bearing 85°, 88°, 77° from E.15.c.4.5.

Lieut. RFA

S E C R E T.

COPY No. 39.

52ND DIVISIONAL ARTILLERY ORDER NO. 37.

One battalion 157th Infantry Brigade is relieving 1st Guards Brigade in the line, from Southern Divisional boundary as far south as line D.23.a.0.7. - D.30.b.0.5.- K.3.c.0.8.- K.11.b.0.7. thence due East.

This battalion comes under the orders of G.O.C., 156th Infantry Brigade from 6.0 pm 22nd.

Consequent upon above the Artillery will be re-grouped as under :-

RIGHT GROUP - Lieut. Colonel J.M.INGRAM, RFA - Commanding.
        56th Bde RFA - active.
        178th Bde RFA - active.
        181st Bde RFA - silent except S.O.S.

RIGHT SUB-GROUP - Lieut. Colonel H.J.COTTER, C.I.E.,D.S.O.,R.A. - Commanding.
        9th Bde RFA - active.
        93rd Army Bde RFA - silent except for S.O.S.

The Right Group will support the present front, the Right Sub-group the new front.

The Right Sub-group will be under the Right Group in order to carry out the wishes to the G.O.C., 156th Brigade, as regards any fire he wants etc. but will deal direct with this Office, as regards intelligence summaries, etc.

O.C. 9th Brigade will arrange to see O.C. 74th Brigade RFA, D.20.d.8.0. who is at present covering the front to be taken over and will take over the S.O.S. lines at present in force.

At 6.0 pm 22nd, 9th Brigade RFA will take over the new S.O.S. lines and no longer be super-imposed on the present Right Group front.

93rd Brigade RFA (3- 18-pdr. batteries), will move into action at J.8.a. & B, leaving wagon line 7;30 pm, on 22nd and after arrival in action will be super-imposed on the 9th Brigade RFA for S.O.S. purposes.

Except for S.O.S., they will not fire.

9th Brigade RFA will find a Liaison Officer with the battalion taking over the front.

The location of the battalion Headquarters will be wired as soon as settled.

Time at which command of new front passes to 52nd Division will be notified later.

Right Sub-group will answer S.O.S. calls on the new front after 6.0 pm 22nd.

Right Sub-group will forward tracing of S.O.S. line taken over, to this Office.

Fire on new front will be as in my A/646 of date, after completion of relief.

ACKNOWLEDGE by wire.

Captain R.A.
Brigade Major R.A., 52nd Divn.

21st September 1918.

DISTRIBUTION.
    Copies 1/5 to 56th Bde RFA.   Copies 6/10 to 9th Bde RFA
1/15 to 178th Bde RFA. 16/20 to 181st Bde RFA 21/25 to 93rd Bde RFA
to 2nd C.D.A. 27 to Guards D.A. 28 to R.A. XVII Corps. 29 to H.A.XVII Corps
to 62nd Bde RFA 31 to 52nd Divn. 'G'. 32 to 156th Bde. 33 to 52nd DAC.
to D.T.M.O. 35 to D.A.G.O. 36 to R.A. Sigs. 37 to S.O.R.A. 38 to R.O.R.A.
39/40 War Diary. 41 to File.

SECRET.

62nd Divisional Artillery Intelligence Summary
6 am Sept. 22nd to 6 am Sept. 23rd 1918.

OUR ACTIVITY.

4.5" Hows. cut wire in E.21b and E.22.a. during the day and fired gas concentrations in conjunction with H.A. at night.
6.59 Movement fire on as follows -
Movement in E.10.a.
10 am movement in E.15.d. and a small party walking from THREX Street eastwards.
E.16 central, E.18 central and E.22.a. were harassed during the day. Centres of activity were harassed by night.
At 11.30 am and 2 pm, 2 minute concentrations were fired on HINDENBURG Support line from Canal Du Nord eastwards 900 yards.
7.12 to 7.32 pm counter preparation was fired.
S.O.S. was fired from 8.41 to 10.30 pm on MOEUVRES Sector.
6" T.Ms. fired 85 rounds on wire in E.21.a. from 5.15 pm onwards.

HOSTILE ACTIVITY.

<u>Artillery.</u>   Harassing fire below normal.
Heavy barrage in E.20.b. & d between 7.18 and 7.27 pm and again at 9 pm.
Intermittent shelling of D.12,16 & 17, during the night.

Date.	Time.	No. of Rounds.	Calibre.	Area shelled	Direction.
22nd.	10 to 11.20	20.	77 mm.	INCHY.	BOURLON.
	11.30 to 5.0 pm.	40.	77 mm.	E.20.b. & d.	" "
	7.18 to 7.27 pm.	Barrage.	77 mm & 10.5 cm.	E.20.b. & d.	

WORK. None observed.

MOVEMENT. 8.30 am small party E.10.a.
9 am to 5 pm - occasional parties of 2 and 3 seen on road E.18.b. and d and going into BOURLON Wood.
10 am small party seen walking from THREX St. in direction of BOURLON Wood.

AERIAL. 1.30 pm one E.A. brought down by our Aircraft and crashed at K.7.a.2.2.

GENERAL. Visibility fair.

Lieut. RFA.
for Commanding R.A., 62nd Dn.

23rd Sept. 1918.

SECRET.

62ND DIVISIONAL ARTILLERY INTELLIGENCE SUMMARY,
6 am 23rd Sept. to 6 am 24th Sept. 1918.

OUR OPERATIONS.

At 5.15 am we fired a counterpreparation for 10 minutes as the enemy was shelling MOEUVRES heavily, this was repeated at 6.12pm & 7.45pm.
4.5: Hows. carried out wire cutting in E.20.a & at request of 2nd C.E.
b., E.21.a & 15.c. and at night fired gas concentration in conjunction with H.A.
77 mm fired YELLOW CROSS gas shell into BOURLON WOOD.
Usual harassing fire at night.
6" T.Ms fired 155 rounds on wire in E.21.a. during the day.
Retaliation by enemy 77 mms was heavy.

HOSTILE ACTIVITY.

Artillery: Normal, except for heavy shelling of front line near MOEUVRES at about 8 am and 6.15 pm 23rd and 5.45 am today, and shelling of BOURSIES from 6.45 to 8 pm with 77 mm.

Date.	Time.	No. of Rds.	Calibre.	Area shelled.	Direction
23rd.	8 - 9 am.	?.	77 & 10.5 cm.	K.1.N & S.	BOURLON.
	9.30- 9.50 am	20.	77 mm.	D.2d.a.4.6.	
	11.30-11.50 am.	10.	77 mm.	TADPOLE COPSE.	"

WORK.   None observed.

MOVEMENT.   Train observed moving East on GB 90° from J.5.c.6.8.
            5 pm small party seen behind QUARRY WOOD.

AERIAL.   At 5.30 pm, 7 E.A. flew over our lines going west.
          Some bombs were dropped in J.5.a. & D.29.c. during the night, but no damage was done.

GENERAL. Flash observed near North end WISE WOOD - GB 92° from J.5.c.6.8. and on bearing 80°30' from same place.
          H.G. located at E.20.d.7.6.
          Visibility fair.

H.J. Everet
Lieut RFA.
for Commanding R.A., 62nd Divn.

24th September 1918.

SECRET.

62nd DIVISIONAL ARTILLERY INTELLIGENCE SUMMARY,
6 am 25th Sept. to 6 am 26th Sept. 1918.

OUR OPERATIONS.
Wire cutting continued by 4.5" Hows. in E.21.a. & b., E.22.c.,
E.15.c.   Gas concentrations fired in conjunction with R.A. during the night.

Harassing fire on centres of activity by night.
Movement engaged :-
    10.45 am party of 30 men in Sunken road E.17.b.
    1.0 pm party of 20 men.
    2.0 pm movement E.22.a.9.4. to E.22.b.1.0.
    4.10pm movement E.22.a.0.6. to E.22.a.3.6.
6" T.Ms. fired 70 rounds on wire in E.21.a. with good effect.

HOSTILE ACTIVITY.
Quiet day, only slight harassing fire by day.
INCHY &Wood in D.12.c. & d harassed by night.
Considerable T.M. activity in HOUVIERS vicinity at 10.15 pm.

Date.	Time.	No. of rounds.	Calibre.	Area shelled.	Direction.
25th.	11-1.30 pm	10.	77 & 10.5 cm.	D.12.b.	
	3.0 pm	6.	10.5 cm.	D.17.a.	
	6.0 - 10 pm	16.	10.5 cm.	D.11.c. & d.	

WORK. None observed.

MOVEMENT. 10.45 am party of 30 men in sunken road E.17.b.
walking towards BOURLON WOOD; at 1.0 pm party of 31 men seen at same place
    2.0 pm - movement between E.22.a.9.4. & E.22.b.1.0.
    4.10pm -   "   "   E.22.a.0.6. & E.22.a.3.6.

AERIAL. Normal.

GENERAL. Visibility fair.

Lieut. RFA.
for C.R.A., 62nd Division.

26/9/18.

S E C R E T:

COPY No....

52ND DIVISIONAL ARTILLERY ORDER NO. 38.

1. On a day and at a zero to be notified later, the British First and Third Armies will attack.

The Canadian Corps (1st Army) on our left, attacking BOURLON WOOD from the North, and West will direct.

In conformity with their action, the 63rd R.N. Division of the XVII Corps will attack with its left on the Corps North boundary and its right on the MOEUVRES - GRAINCOURT road (E.21.c. E.27.b. E.28.c. & E.5.a.) exclusive.

The 52nd Lowland Division will conform to the action of the 63rd R.N. Division and attack with its left on the MOEUVRES - GRAINCOURT road inclusive.

On our South the Guards are also attacking but not as part of the concerted movement of the Canadian and XVII Corps.

2. The objective tracing issued to brigades gives the objectives of the various phases.

The 63rd R.N. Division clears the HINDENBURG Support Line and captures GRAINCOURT and ANNEUX. The 157th Inf. Bde., 52nd Division clears the HINDENBURG Line and CANAL DU NORD working southwards along them to the southern Corps boundary and the 156th Inf. Bde clears the area shaded pink on the objective map.

The 57th Division eventually goes through and captures CANTAING and FONTAINE NOTRE DAME.

3. The Artillery Grouping at the commencement of operations till end of first phase will be :-

63rd Divisional Artillery.
    40th D.A. Group.   Comdr. Lt. Col. T. McGOWAN, D.S.O., RFA.
        170 Bde. RFA.
        181 Bde RFA.
        2nd N.Z. Bde RFA.
    Army Bde Group.   Comdr. Lt. Col. GOVER, D.S.O., RFA.
        93rd Bde RFA.
        315 Bde RFA.

52nd D.A. Group.
    36th Bde RFA.
    9th Bde RFA.   Group Comdr. Lt. Col. H.J. COTTER, C.I.E., DSO.
        9th Bde RFA.
        72nd Bde RFA.

4. The details of the Artillery barrage covering the attack have already been issued to the Brigades concerned.

50% of the 18-pdrs. open on the plus 15 line and 50% on the West bank of the Canal.

At zero plus 15 the barrage moves forward in accordance with the barrage table i.e., guns on the Canal remain there until the rest of the barrage joins them and the whole then moves forward together.

The 4.5" Hows. will be used on special points as notified and will always keep 200 yards ahead of the 18-pdr. barrage.

The 72nd Army Bde does not take part in the barrage but puts down smoke screens and carries special bombardments as ordered.

The 9th Bde RFA fires a shrapnel and smoke switch barrage on the HINDENBURG Line and Canal Du Nord in E.26 and K.2, in support of 157th Inf. Bde.

After ceasing fire according to programme, Brigades continue to support the attack by group liaison with Infantry Brigades and the engaging of special areas.

The 9th Bde RFA is detailed to support the operations of the 52nd Division and after ceasing fire on the switch barrage at zero plus 95 minutes, will support by observed fire only.

The southern corps boundary must be carefully watched as the Guards in taking their first objective move northwards.

Rates of fire will be as in XVII Corps Artillery Instructions issued to Brigades with following exceptions :-
    9th Bde RFA. - during switch barrage,
        Zero to plus 5 minutes - 4 rds per gun per minute.
        Plus 5 minutes to plus 15 minutes - 3 rds per gun per min.

-2/-

(9th Bde during switch barrage)
        plus 15 onwards - 2 rds. per gun per minute.
       Howitzers half the above.
    73nd Bde RFA for bombardment tasks,
       18-pdrs. - 2 rds. per gun per minute.
       4.5" Hows.- 1 rd. per gun per minute.

    Unless specially ordered, ammunition will be fired in the proportions which it has been dumped.
    4 Newton Mortars in E.25.d. will engage Canal from E.26.b.8.0. to E.27.c.1.4. from Zero to Zero plus 45 minutes, as arranged by D.T.M.O.

5.   Liaison will be as under :-

    40th D.A. Group will be in liaison with the attacking Infantry Brigade of the 63rd Division.
    9th Bde RFA will keep a liaison Officer with 157th Inf. Bde H.Q. and another with the Right attacking battalion of the brigade.
    The latter will establish himself as soon as possible on the ridge in E.28.a. and open up Visual communication with his brigade.
    Divisional and brigade headquarters will be as under, from Zero onwards :-
    52nd Division advanced - D.29.b.1.7. rear - D.7.a.5.7.
       155 Inf. Bde - D.15.b.7.7.
       156 Inf. Bde - E.19.a.2.9.
       157 Inf. Bde - D.28.b.0.2.
    57th Division.   - D.7.b.3.3.
       171 Inf. Bde - D.18.a.8.2.
       172 Inf. Bde - D.18.a.9.2.
    63rd Division.   - D.17.a.8.2.
       188 Inf. Bde.- E.15.b.2.8.
       189 Inf. Bde - E.13.b.3.6.
       190 Inf. Bde - E.19.a.4.7.

6.   During operations, each brigade will maintain one brigade O.P. manned by the following personnel :-
       2 Observing Officers.
       2 Telephonists with instruments.
       3 Linesmen with wire.
       2 Pigeon men with pigeons.
       6 Signallers with Lucas lamps.
    All efforts will be concentrated on keeping one O.P. in good communication with the brigade.
    These O.Ps. must be provided with a director.
    The importance of getting back information about the enemy guns must be impressed on all concerned.
    It is very important that O.Ps. be established as soon as possible on the high ground in E.28 and K.4.
    Visual communication or a combination of visual and a short telephone line, should be established to these O.Ps.

7.   The attached advance table shows the order in which brigades are to advance.
    As soon as possible, after the attack starts, each brigade will send out an officers' patrol to reconnoitre the canal crossings, positions, O.Ps. etc and clear up the situation.
    On his reports, the Brigade Commander must base his decisions and keep as closely to time table as possible.
    Each brigade will select advanced Wagon Lines close to the battery positions.
    Teams and wagons of 2nd N.Z.Bde, 56th Bde, 172th Bde and 181st Bde will be in position by Zero minus one hour.
    Remaining brigades will have their teams and wagons up by Zero.
    All animals will be watered before going to advanced Wagon Lines. Brigades will take priority at mutual watering points according to their place on the advance Table.
    Canal Crossings will be made at E.20.d.8.7., E.26.b.6.3. and possibly on the Cambrai Road.

8.   Attention is called to XVll Corps Artillery Instructions No.2 regarding the co-operation of Artillery and Aircraft.
    In addition to the calls legislated for, Field Artillery will answer N.F.calls with 12 rounds from each battery that can bear, during mobile warfare.

9.   Watches will be synchronised by an officer of these H.Q.

10.   Acknowledge.

                                            [signature]
                                            Captain R.A.,
25th Sept. 1918.   Brigade Major R.A., 52nd D.A.,

Distribution :-

Copy No.1 - R.A., XVll Corps.   No.2 - R.A., XVll Corps.
     3 - 52nd Division "G"   No.4/8-63rd D.A.
     9 - 40th D.A.   No.10 - Guards D.A.
    11 - 2nd C.D.A.   No.12/16-9th Bde RFA.
 17/21 - 56th Bde RFA.   No.22/26-178th Bde RFA.
 27/30 - 181st Bde RFA.   No.31/34-93rd Bde RFA.
 35/39 - 72nd Bde RFA.   No.40/44-315th Bde RFA.
 45/49 - 2nd N.Z.Bde RFA.   No.50 - D.T.M.C.
    51 - 52nd D.A.C.   No.52 - S.C.R.A.
    53 - R.A.Sigs.   No.54 - R.O.R.A.
 55/56 - War Diary.   No.57 - File.

S E C R E T.

ADVANCE TABLE.
TABLE 'A'.
To accompany XVII Corps No. G.(O) 100.

Time of advance (approx)	Brigade.	Advance to.	Time of getting into action in advanced pos: (approx)	Prepared posns.	Tasks on arrival.	On arrival come under orders of -	Remarks.	Route.	Probable posn.
Zero plus 85 mns:	No.2 N.Z. A.Bde R.F.A.		Zero plus 130 mns.	Prepared posns: W. of C. Du NORD.	Barrage on left flank astride Sunken Rd. in E.17.d.- E.24.a.& b, which starts at Zero plus 155 mins; covering Left flank of 63rd Divn: in its advance on ANNEUX.	C.R.A., 63rd Divn:	Remain under 63rd Divn: during 3rd phase.	'A'.	E.19.d. E.25.b.
Zero plus 105 mns:	56th Bde RFA. (52 D.A.)	W. bank of C. Du NORD: about E.26.a.	Zero plus 160 mins:		Super-imposed barrage formed by 515 and 93 A. 's on special points & corpses to be selected by CRA., 63rd Divn:	C.R.A., 52nd Divn:	Comes under 63rd Div: at same time as 9th Bde at Zero Plus 230 mins:	'A'.	E.26a. 527 Bty. to move first.
Zero plus 121 mins:	178th Bde RFA.(40 D.A.)	E. bank of C. Du Nord: (or if this is impracticable to W. bank of Canal.	Zero plus 210 mins:		ANNEUX & points in vicinity, lifting in conformity with barrage on either flank.(see barrage map). Tasks to be allotted by CRA, 63rd Divn:	C.R.A., 63rd Divn:	To come under 63rd Divn: when this Divn: pass: es thro' 63rd Div:	'A'.	K.1.b. L.4.d.
Zero plus 168 mins:	181 Bde RFA.(40 DA)	E. bank of C. Du Nord: (see above)	Zero plus 250 mins:		As detailed by CRA, 63rd Divn:	C.R.A., 63rd Divn:		'A'.	L.5.b. L.4.d.

Bty: Brigade.	Time of getting into section arrival. in adv: pos: (approx.)	Tasks on arrival.	On arrival come under orders of	Remarks.	Route.	Probable positions
515 A. Bde E. of C. Du Nord. RFA.	Zero plus 540 mins:		As detailed by CRA., 57 Divn:	C.R.A.; 57th Divn:		
9th Bde E. of C. Du Nord. RFA.	Zero plus 280 mins:		As detailed by CRA., 63rd Div:	C.R.A.; 63rd Div:		K.3.b. 'B'
72nd A. Bde E. of C. Du Nord. RFA.	Zero plus 390 mins:		As detailed by CRA., 57th Div:	C.R.A.; 57th Div:		
93rd A.Bde E. of C. Du Nord. RFA.	Zero plus 500 mins:		As detailed by CRA., 63rd Div:			K.3.b. 'B'

SECRET.

D.A. 7/506.
Copy No. ....

57th Divisional Artillery Operation Order No. 39.

30/September/1918.

1. 170th Inf. Bde. will relieve the 171st and 172nd Inf. Bdes. in the line tonight.

2. On completion of relief the inter-divisional boundary will be from F.23.central to A.22.a.0.0., thence along road to A.23.central, thence along road to A.23.b.8.0. Road throughout inclusive to 57th Division.

3. If the Canadian Division is still holding Railway Junctions at A.9.a.3.0. it is intended to push forward 57th Division line from the above point to A.15.c.0.0.

4. We now hold PROVILLE.

5. S.O.S. LINES TONIGHT.

35th HEAVY ARTY. GROUP: From road A.16.c.7.6. to A.22.a.1.0.
Road running East and West through
A.22.c. & d. (60-pdr. Shrapnel)
Trench in A.16.c. (6" Hows.)
Trenches about A.15.central. (6" Hows).

FIELD ARTILLERY. From A.8.d.30.30. to A.14.central to
A.15.c.D.2. to A.15.c.95.00. thence along
Trench to A.22.a.0.0.
Hows. on special points behind as selected
by Brigade Commanders.

Two Brigades R.F.A. will be transferred from 63rd D.A. Group to 57th D.A. Group tonight. These two Brigades, when transferred, will be responsible for line from A.8.d.30.30. to A.14.central to A.15.c.0.2.
40th D.A. will be responsible for S.O.S. from A.15.c.0.2. as above to A.22.a.0.0.

6. It is possible that a few of our men are in trench in A.21.b. Should this be the case an amended order will be published.

7. 52nd Division will relieve 63rd Division in the line tomorrow night.

8. N.B. THE TWO BRIGADES R.F.A. TRANSFERRED FROM 63RD D.A. GROUP TO 57TH D.A. GROUP WILL BE :-

93RD ARMY BRIGADE R.F.A.
No. 2 N.Z. ARMY BRIGADE R.F.A.

S.O.S. LINE, 93RD ARMY BRIGADE R.F.A. - FROM A.8.d.30.30. to A.14.central.
No. 2 N.Z. ARMY BDE. R.F.A. - FROM A.14.central to A.15.c.0.2.

9. ACKNOWLEDGE.

Issued at 8 pm.

Brigadier-General,
C.R.A., 57th Division.

(over)

Copy No. 1/10. 40th Div. Arty
11/15. 35th H.A. Group.
16/18. 170th Infantry Brigade.
19. 171st Infantry Brigade.
20. 172nd Infantry Brigade.
21. 57th Division "G"
22. XVII Corps R.A.
23. 57th D.T.M.O.
24/34. 63rd Div. Arty. (For Brigades to be transferred)
35. 3rd Canadian Div. Arty.
36. 52nd Div. Arty.
37. File.
38/39. War Diary

CONFIDENTIAL. ORIGINAL.

WAR.DIARY.OF.52ND.DIVISIONAL.ARTILLERY.

HEAD QUARTERS.

****

VOLUME.- V.

PART. - X.

FROM - 1st October 1918.   TO. - 31st October 1918.

Army Form C. 2118.

WAR DIARY
or
INTELLIGENCE SUMMARY.

OCTOBER 1918.

(Erase heading not required.)

Instructions regarding War Diaries and Intelligence Summaries are contained in F. S. Regs., Part II and the Staff Manual respectively. Title pages will be prepared in manuscript.

Place	Date	Hour	Summary of Events and Information	Remarks and references to Appendices
CANTAING.	1st		9th Brigade moved forward to the positions in F.27.d.,L.2.b. and L.3.a. and at 5.40 pm with 56th Brigade supported an attack by 155th Inf. Brigade on FAUBOURG DE PARIS and the MASNIERES Road. After this attack, which first reports indicated successful, 52nd Division took over from 63rd Division and the 52nd Divisional Artillery took over from 63rd D.A. assuming command of 72nd and 315th Army Brigades RFA which were constituted into a Group under O.C. 72nd Brigade RFA. 155th Infantry Brigade attack was not successful and a further attempt was made at 5.20 am to secure the strong point in A.27.a. but without success.	App.
	2nd		During the afternoon reports were received from F.O.Os that some of our men could be seen in the FAUBOURG DEPARIS. Fire of the Heavy Artillery which was being directed on this area was stopped and 155th Inf. Bde received orders to work up the trench in A.27 and to get in touch with any party holding out in FAUBOURG DE PARIS. During the night 155th Inf. Bde secured the strong point in A.27.a.	App.
	3rd		Hostile Artillery was less active, the vicinity of the Canal being intermittently shelled by 10 cm guns. A series of gas concentrations were fired in the afternoon on the FAUBOURG DE PARIS. At 2300, 155th Bde unsuccessfully attacked the FAUBOURG DE PARIS, artillery support being given as in 52nd D.A.Order No.40. The enemy fire in reply was slight but prompt. - vide App. Harassing fire during the night was directed on road A.22.d. to A.28.c. and trenches in A.28.	App. E. App.
	4th		4.5"Hows. engaged M.G.nest in house at A.27.d.l.7. partially destroying the house. There was a slight increase of hostile fire which was mostly harassing on back and forward areas and was chiefly from the N.E. M.Gs.in the FAUBURG-de-PARIS were inactive during the day.	App.
	5th		Gas concentrations were fired during the night on Sunken Road A.28.c.,and 4.5"Howitzers carried out shoots with balloon observation during the day. Hostile fire was greater than during previous day,particularly from 0500 to 0530. Fire was chiefly from east at long ranges. E.A.were active bombing on night 4th/5th.	App.
	6th		Hostile fire was somewhat greater than on 5th but all guns were firing at long ranges and there was no indication that many batteries were employed. 56th Bde moved into action in L.6 and L.12 on night 6th/7th.	App.
	7th		52nd D.A.Order No.41 issued vide App.2.	App.II
	8th	0750	Enemy artillery active during afternoon on Battery areas and CANTAING. Barrage fired for 63rd Division attack under instructions of 63rd D.A. At 0750 M.G.	App.

Army Form C. 2118.

OCTOBER 1918.

WAR DIARY
or
INTELLIGENCE SUMMARY.
(Erase heading not required.)

Instructions regarding War Diaries and Intelligence Summaries are contained in F.S. Regs., Part II. and the Staff Manual respectively. Title pages will be prepared in manuscript.

Place	Date	Hour	Summary of Events and Information	Remarks and references to Appendices
CANTAING.	8th		At 0750 M.G. in sunken road A.28.c. was engaged at request of 57th D.A. At 0842 searching fire was directed on enemy concentrations in A.23.c. At 1050 the enemy counter-attacked from H.2 northwards with captured tanks. S.O.S. was fired and enemy repulsed. Line along CAMBRAI-FORENVILLE Road. 24th Division relieved 63rd Division, 63rd D.A. remaining in command of Artillery.	ATD
AWOINGT.	9th		Attack of 24th Division at dawn met with no oposition. AWOINGT captured and/got into AWOINGT. 52nd D.A. moved to AWOINGT.	ATD
CAGNONCLES.	10th		Attack continued - 73rd Brigade attacking at 0500. Line pushed forward to ridge north of AVESNES LES AUBERT. 52nd D.A. moved B.6.c.	ATD
AVESNES LES AUBERT.	11th		D.A.H.Q. moved up to AVESNES LES AUBERT. Enemy shelled St.AUBERT heavily and harassed AVESNES. No advance was made by the infantry.	ATD
ST.AUBERT.	12th		D.A.H.Q. moved to St.AUBERT with 17th Inf.Bde. 93rd Army Brigade being in close support of the infantry followed by 178th Bde and 9th and 56th Brigades. The infantry pushed forward and at 1820 attacked under a barrage to secure the crossing of the SELLE river.	ATD
	13th		E.A. brought down by L.G. fire of batteries and observer captured. 178th Bde RFA passed from group and 306th Bde and 307th Bde came under 52nd D.A. The D.A. with its 5 Brigades working under 61st D.A. 9th, 56th, 93rd and 306th Bdes being in action east of St.AUBERT and 307th Bde remaining in rest.	ATD
ST.AUBERT.	14th		VILLERS EN CAUCHIES, KK St.AUBERT, HAUSSY and MONTRECOURT WOOD shelled. At 2000 a barrage was fired in support of operation by 72nd Bde who captured 3 prisoners. An A.A. gun at Q.31.b.8.2. was engaged by 4.5"How. and a 2.2"How was engaged at P.36.c.8.3. At 1240 and 1420 enemy moving to counter-attack toward HAUSSY was caught by our fire and many casualties were in flicted.	ATD
	15th		D/307 moved into action under 93rd Bde during night 14th/15th. Enemy shelled Battery areas particularly 19th Battery who had 4 guns hit. Enemy fire was much more from N.E. and E. and chiefly from RWS D'HARPIES. 52nd D.A. Order No.42 ** issued vide Brigadier General G.T. MAIR, D.S.O. assumed command of 52nd D.A. vice Brigadier General A.D.MUSGRAVE, D.S.O. 307th Bde moved into action east of St.AUBERT night 15th/16th.	App.III. ATD

Army Form C. 2118.

OCTOBER 1918.

WAR DIARY
or
INTELLIGENCE SUMMARY.
(Erase heading not required.)

Instructions regarding War Diaries and Intelligence Summaries are contained in F.S. Regs., Part II. and the Staff Manual respectively. Title pages will be prepared in manuscript.

Place	Date	Hour	Summary of Events and Information	Remarks and references to Appendices
	16th		0610 barrage fired in support of attack on railway and sunken road between SAULZOIR and HAUSSY. The attack was successful except on the left and many prisoners were taken. During the afternoon the enemy bombarded HAUSSY heavily. S.O.S. was responded to and our line was re-adjusted west of the river SELLE.	
	17th		Enemy Artillery fire less. 9th and 56th Brigades RFA were relieved by 76th and 315th Brigades RFA vide 52nd D.A. Order No.43.	App:IV. AP
	18th		24th D.A.,H.Q. relieved 52nd D.A.,H.Q.	App:V. AP
	19th		52nd D.A.,H.Q. moved to PROVILLE vide 52nd D.A. Order No. 44.	
	20th		52nd D.A. moved to MORCHIES area, Headquarters being at LAGNICOURT. FREMICOURT,	
	21st to 23rd		52nd Divisional Artillery entrained for VIII Corps area.— 9th Bde. at VELU, 56th Bde. FREMICOURT, vide Administrative Instructions No. 13.	App:VI.
MONT ST ELOI.			N I L.	
	24th		52nd D.A. marched to COURCELLES, AUBY area – vide D.A.O. No.45.	App:VII. AP
BLANCHE MAISON.	25th 26th		52nd D.A. marched to WAZIERES – FRAIS MARAIS area – vide D.A.O., NO.46.	AppVIII.
FRAIS MARAIS.	27th to 31st		N I L.	
			D.A. Order issued ordering relief of 12th D.A., by 52nd D.A., – vide D.A.O. 47.	App:IX.

Brig: General R.A.
Commanding R.A., 52nd Division.

APPENDICES. TO. -

WAR . DIARY . OF . 52ND DIVISIONAL . ARTILLERY . HEADQUARTERS.

OCTOBER 1918.

SECRET.   COPY NO. 29

52nd DIVISIONAL ARTILLERY ORDER NO. 40.

1. 155th Infantry Brigade will attack and capture FAUBOURG DE PARIS this evening.
   The attack will take place from the south-west, the forming up line being A.27.a.4.2. to A.27.c.9.0.
   The objective is the FAUBOURG DE PARIS, as far north as line A.21.A.? – A.22.c.2.6.

2. The attack will be supported by a switching bombardment of Heavy Artillery and 4.5" Howitzers and covered by a protective barrage of 18-pdrs.
   Tasks for this are shown in bombardment table attached.
   57th D.A. are co-operating by firing on trenches in northern half A.21.c. and on trench A.15.d.0.0. to A.21.b.9.6. from Zero plus 10 to Zero plus 100.

3. Zero hour will be 2300.

4. Watches will be synchronised from this Office.

5. S.O.S. lines after attack will be :-

       18-pdrs – A.21.b.3.2. – A.22.c.5.9. – A.28.c.4.0. – A.27.d.?.?.
       4.5" Hows. – 200 yards outside 18-pdr line.
   9th Brigade Group will be super-imposed on 72nd Brigade Group.
   Heavy Artillery – road A.28.c. A.28.a. A.29.b. A.22.d.

6. ACKNOWLEDGE.

                                                    (signature)
                                                    Captain R.A.
                                        Brigade Major R.A., 52nd Divn.

3rd October 1918.
Issued 8.10 pm.
DISTRIBUTION.
    Copies No. 1/10 9th Bde RFA.
             11/20 72nd Bde RFA.
                21 52nd Division 'G'.
                22 32nd Bde RGA.
                23 XVII Corps R.A.
                24 XVII Corps R.A.
                25 2nd D.A.
                26 57th D.A.
                27 155th Inf. Bde.
             28/29 War Diary.
                30 File.

TIME.	HEAVY ARTY. TASKS.	9th BRIGADE GROUP TASKS.		??? BRIGADE GROUP TASKS.		RATE OF FIRE.
		4.5 Hows.	18-pdrs.	4.5 Hows.	18-pdrs.	
Zero to plus 10	A.27.b.50.45 - A.27.b.55.70.	A.27.b.40.20 - A.27.b.50.45.		A.27.b.40.20 - A.27.b.50.45.		
Plus 10 to plus 25.	A.27.b.3.8.- A.21.d.7.0.	Hedge rows A.27.d.25.35.- A.28.a.20.40. & A.27.d.7.2 tp A.28.a.4.4.	A.27.b.55.70.- A.27.b.60.85.	Hedge rows A.27.d.25.35.- A.28.a.20.40. & A.27.d.7.2 tp A.28.a.4.4.	A.28.a.1.6.- A.28.c.5.9.& A.28.a.0.4.- A.28.a.9.3.	4.5" Howitzers.
Plus 25 to plus 40.	Factory and road A.21.d.7.3.- A.21.d.8.4.- A.21.d.7.0. to A.21.d.8.2.	---do---	A.21.d.7.0. to A.21.d.8.2.	---do---	fire to move N.lvrral with 4.5 Hows.after plus 35.	0 to plus 75 - Normal. plus 75 to plus 110 - SLOW.
Plus 40 to plus 75.	A.22.c.1.9.- A.22.a.1.1.	---do---	A.21.d.8.4.- A.21.d.95.70.	---do---	---do---	18-pdrs. 9th Bde Group. plus 10 to plus 25 - NORMAL. plus 25 to plus 90 - SLOW. plus 90 to plus 110 - VERY SLOW.
Plus 75 to plus 110.		A.22.c.1.9.- A.22.a.1.1.	---do---	A.22.c.1.9.- A.22.a.1.1.	---do---	72nd Bde Group. guns on southern half plus 10 to plus 35 - NORMAL. plus 35 to plus 90 - SLOW. plus 90 to plus 110 - VERY SLOW.
				guns on northern half.		plus 10 to plus 90 - SLOW. plus 90 to plus 110 - VERY SLOW.

SECRET.   Copy No. 30

52ND DIVISIONAL ARTILLERY ORDER NO. 41.

1. At a date and zero hour to be notified later, the XVII Corps will attack in conjunction with the operations of Corps to south.

2. The 63rd R.N. Division will attack on a front of 1700 yards in a N.E. direction from a line G.4.c.0.1. to G.17.a.25.55.
   The first objective will be the trench running through G.8.a., c., & d. and G.12.b.
   The second objective is the road from H.1.d.0.4. to B.28.c.05.80 and the WOOD in A.30.c.
   The 57th Division will co-operate on the left, their objective being the trench from G.4.a.0.8 to G.4.b.6.6.
   The 2nd Division will co-operate on the right, their objective being the same road as the 63rd Division, extending S.E. and including the village of FORENVILLE.

3. The 52nd D.A. Group consists of :-
   9th Brigade Group   ....   9th and 56th Brigades.
   72nd Brigade Group   ....   72nd and 315th Brigades.
   This Group will form the Right Group supporting the Right Brigade of 63rd Division (188th Inf. Bde.).
   315th Brigade RFA (less D/315) supports 57th Division till zero plus 60.
   The tasks and barrages for the above brigades are as shown on barrage tracings already issued.

4. 72nd Brigade RFA will be in liaison with 188th Inf. Bde.
   O.C., 72nd Brigade will report to G.O.C., 188th Inf. Bde on YZ night at MONT SUR L'OEUVRE.
   63rd Divisional Signals are laying a line from 188 Inf. Bde to 72nd Brigade RFA, HQ.

5. At zero plus 30 mins., 1 18-pdr battery 72nd Bde RFA crosses the river and moves forward in close support of 188 Inf. Bde.
   As soon as batteries reach 7,000 yards range on barrage, the remainder 72nd Bde will commence advancing to positions about G.10.b. or G.4.a. in support of 188th Inf. Bde.
   This brigade will cross the canal by bridge F.29.b.7.6.
   72nd Bde RFA will detail advance sections to work in close liaison with each attacking battalion of 188 Inf. Bde.
   When first objective has been taken, one section 315 Bde RFA will advance in close support of 57th Division, under instructions issued by CRA., 57th Division.
   Further advance of Brigades will be ordered as situation developes and wagon lines will be at an half hours notice to move from zero plus 5 hours onwards.
   On the 72nd Bde moving, 315 Bde will come directly under this Office

6. Each brigade will detail one O.P. to act as Brigade O.P. Once this has been established, battery O.Ps will be established as soon as possible.
   Every effort must be made to push O.Ps forward to newly captured ground without delay. Visual and a combination of telephone and visual communication must be used to the fullest possible extent and arrangements made to supplement telephone communication by all other available means.
   It is hoped to issue 4 pigeons to each brigade. These will be disposed as Brigade Commanders consider best, so that information can be got back in event of communications being down.

7. Co-operation with R.A.F. will be as laid down in XVII Corps Artillery Instructions No.2.
   Brigades must erect their Wireless as soon as possible after a move and put out ground signals.
   Code Ground Signals at present in force are :-
       9th Bde RFA.   A I
       56th Bde RFA.   A II
       72nd Bde RFA.   B III
       315th Bde RFA.   B IV
   GF Calls will be answered by two 18-pdr batteries and one 4.5" How. batt of 9th Bde Group, till completion of advance of 72nd Bde.
   On arrival in action, after advance, of 72nd Bde RFA, it will detail one 18-pdr and one 4.5" How. battery to answer GF Calls and 9th Bde Group 1 18 battery

2/-

8. Each brigade will detail one Officers' Patrol to go out and get in touch with the situation.
Only one patrol from 9th Bde Group will be out at a time.
Importance of getting their information back to Brigade and D.A. HQ. must be impressed on these Officers.
In addition, O.Ps must report all the information they can gather and look-out men will be sent up to assist observing Officers in keeping a general watch on the situation.

9. All enemy movement will be engaged at once by visual observation. On no account is the enemy to be allowed to show himself above ground unmolested.

10. Ammunition re-filling point for 52nd D.A. Group will be F.25.b. situation permits.
Arrangements for supplies and water will be as at present until situation permits of watering at the Canal.

11. Headquarters of formations at Zero hour will be as under :-
63rd Div: H.Q.   L.10.d.9.3.
188, 189, & 190 Inf. Bdes. MONT SUR L'OEUVRE.
57th Div: H.Q.   F.15.c.0.2.
170 Inf. Bde   F.19.c.6.1.
171 Inf. Bde   F.21.b.C.2.
172 Inf. Bde   F.22.b.7.2.
52nd DAHQ.   CANTAING MILL.

S.O.S. lines after attack will be the line of the protective barrage.

Watches will be synchronised from this Headquarters.

F.A. Brigades to ACKNOWLEDGE.

(signed)
Captain R.A.
Brigade Major R.A., 52nd Division.

Issued at 1550.
7th October 1918.

Distribution.

Copies No. 1/5   9th Bde RFA
            6/10   56th Bde RFA.
            11/15 72nd Bde RFA.
            16/20 315th Bde RFA.
            21   Staff Captain.
            22   R.O., R.A.
            23   R.A. Signals.
            24   217th Coy. A.S.C.
            25   52nd D.A.C.
            26   52nd D.T.M.O.
            27   63rd D.A.
            28   57th D.A.
            29/30 War Diary
            31   File.

SECRET.

ADDENDUM NO: 1
TO
52ND DIVISIONAL ARTILLERY ORDER NO. 42.

S.O.S. lines for 83rd Brigade RFA after attack will be :-

1 - Battery   search and sweep valley P.34.

1 - Battery   search and sweep valley V.5.d.

1 - Battery   at disposal brigade Commander, to engage all moving or other targets as situation permits.

                                                    Captain R.A,
15th October 1918.   Brigade Major R.A., 52nd Division.

Same distribution as D.A.O. 42.

SECRET.

AMENDMENT No: 1 TO
52ND DIVISIONAL ARTILLERY ORDER NO: 42.

1. The scope of the attack has now been enlarged to include the village of HAUSSY.
   The attack will be carried out by 3 battalions -
   The 9th East Surreys will be on the right. The 8th R.W. Kents in the centre and the 1st North Staffords on the left.
   The final objective will be Sunken road P.33.d., P.34.d., V.5.a. & d and the village of HAUSSY.

2. The Artillery covering the attack will be the 5 Brigades of the 52nd Divisional Artillery Group and the Guards Divisional Artillery Group who are providing the fire on the new portion of the front of attack.
   The amendments, consequent upon the change in the plan of attack, to the tasks issued in 52nd D.A. Order No: 42, are given in the attached table.

3. Rate of fire from Zero to zero plus 90 plus 74/ - VERY SLOW.

4. 306th Brigade RFA will have a liaison Officer with the 9th East Surreys whose Headquarters will be at V.11.d.1.8. by 1800 hours this evening.
   This Officer should be in telephonic communication with his Brigade Headquarters.

5. Zero hour will be 0510 hours 16th October.

6. S.O.S. lines after attack will be :
   18-pdr.   9th Bde RFA.   - P.33. central to P.34.d.0.9.
              93rd Bde RFA. - P.34.d.0.9. to P.35.c.8.2.
              56th Bde RFA. - P.35.c.6.2. to P.35.d.1.0. to V.5.d.8.9.
              306th Bde RFA. - V.5.d.8.9. to V.6.c.0.6. to V.12.b.0.7.
              307th Bde RFA. - V.12.b.0.7. to V.12.b.3.0. to V.12.d.5.4
   4.5 Hows: - Selected points in Brigade Zones, paying particular attention to Sunken roads.

7. With the exception of the above changes the orders already issued hold good.

8. ACKNOWLEDGE.

                                                    Captain R.A.
                                    Brigade Major R.A., 52nd Divn:

15th October 1918.
Distribution, same as 52nd Div: Arty: Order No: 42.

TIME.	UNIT.	No: OF GUNS.	SERIAL NO:	ALBERT MAP.
Zero plus 40 to Zero plus 90.	58th Fd. RFA.	3 -18pdr Btys.	3.	Creep forward 100 yards per 4 minutes to protective barrage P.34.d.0.9. to P.35.c.0.6. and then search and sweep 200 yards outwards till Zero plus 90.
Zero to 305 Bde RFA. Zero plus 74.		1 -4.5 How.Bty. 1 Sect: remainder	3.	P.35.c.8.1. searching N. as far as Mill P.35.c.6.0. 200 yards beyond 18-pdr. protective barrage.
Zero plus " " 40 to Zero plus 90.		3 -18pdr.Btys:	5.	Creep forward 100 yards per 4 minutes to protective barrage P.35.c.0.6. to V.5.b.5.6. and then search and sweep 200 yards outwards till zero plus 90.
Zero to 307 Bde Zero plus RFA. 40.		1 -4. How:Bty. 4 guns. 2 guns.	8.	V.5.a.35.80. to V.5.b.5.6. V.5.d.2.0. to V.11.h.4.3.
Zero plus " " 40 to Zero plus 74.			8.	200 yards beyond 18pdr. barrage.
Zero plus 40 " " to Zero plus 90.		3 -18pdr.Btys:	7.	Creep forward 100 yards per 4 minutes to protective barrage V.3.c.0.5. and then search and sweep 200 yards outwards till zero plus 90.
Zero to 95rd Bde 1 -18pdr.Bty. Zero plus RFA. 2.			10.	HAUSSY CHURCH.
Zero plus 2 " " to Zero plus 40.			10.	Smoke barrage V.5.a.5.0. to V.6.c.3.0.

Zero plus 40 to Zero plus 74.	307th Bde R.F.A.	7.	Creep forward 100 yds. per 2 minutes to protective barrage V.5.b.0.4. to V.5.d.2.0. and then search and sweep 200 yds. outwards till zero plus 74.
Zero to Zero plus 10.	93rd Bde 2 -18pdr Btys: R.F.A.	8.	Search and sweep area east of railway in V.4.b.
Zero to Zero plus 40.	" " 1 -18pdr.Bty.	10.	Smoke barrage V.6.a.5.0. to V.6.c.5.0.
Zero plus 10 to Zero plus 40.	" "	9.	Smoke barrage V.5.c.5.0. to V.12.a.5.0.
Zero to Zero plus 74.	Div: Arty on our left.	11.	Flank barrage P.33 central to P.34.b.0.5.- this barrage to include smoke.
Zero to Zero plus 7.	53rd Div: 2 -6" Newton T.M. Mortars.	12.	Road and railway junction P.34.d.

TIME	UNIT	NO. OF GUNS	SERIAL NO:	TASKS
ZERO to Zero plus 10.	306 F.A. N.F.A.	3 – 18pdr Btys:	5.	Railway V.4.b.5.0. to V.4.a.9.2.
Zero to Zero plus 74.	" "	1 – 4.5 How. Bty. 1 Sect: remainder	3.	P.35.c.3.1. 200 yds. beyond 18-pdr protective barrage.
Zero plus 10 to Zero plus 40.	" "	" "	6.	Sunken road P.35.c.0.0. to V.5.a.3.1.
Zero plus 40 to zero plus 74.	" "	" "	5.	Creep 100 yds. per 2 minutes to protective barrage. P.35.c.0.6. to V.5.b.0.4. and then search and sweep 200 yds. outwards till Zero plus 74.
Zero to Zero plus 10	307th Bde R.F.A.	3 – 18pdr Btys:	7.	Sunken road V.4.b.3.0. to V.5.a.9.2.
Zero to Zero plus 74.	" "	" "	8.	V.5.a.35.80. to V.5.b.5.3.
Zero plus 10 to Zero plus 18.	" "	" "	7.	Sunken road V.4.a.9.9. to V.5.c.0.3.
Zero plus 18 to Zero plus 26.	" "	1 – 18pdr Bty. 2 – 18pdr Btys:	7.	V.5.a.8.1. to V.5.a.7.3. V.5.c.2.5 to V.5.c.9.3.
Zero plus 26 to Zero plus 34.	" "	1 – 18pdr Bty. 2 – 18pdr Btys:	7.	V.5.c.3.2. to V.5.c.8.3. V.5.a.6.1. to V.5.c.8.5.
Zero plus 34 to Zero plus 40.	" "	" "	7.	V.5.a.6.1. to V.5.c.9.2.

TIME.	UNIT.	NO: OF GUNS.	SERIAL NO:	TASKS.
Zero to Zero plus 10.	9th Bde RFA.	3- 18pdrs.Bty. 1- 4.5 How.Bty. 1 Sect: remainder.	1. 2.	Railway P.34.a.0.0. to P.34.c.7.0. P.34.a.9.2. P.33.d.6.8. to P.34.c.0.6.
Zero plus 10 to Zero plus 40.	"	"	1.	Sunker road P.34.a.9.2. to P.34.d.0.3.
Zero plus 10 to Zero plus 74.	"	1 Section	2.	P.34.a.9.2. practice trenches P.34.a.
Zero plus 40 to Zero plus 74.	"	remainder	1.	practice trenches P.34.a.
Zero to Zero plus 10.	56th Bde RFA.	3- 18pdr.Btys: 1- 4.5 How.Bty.	5. 4.	Railway P.34.c.7.0. to V.4.b.3.0. P.34.c.0.3. to P.34.c.5.5.
Zero plus 10 to Zero plus 40.	"	"	3.	Sunker road P.34.d.0.3. to P.35.c.0.0.
Zero plus 10 to Zero plus 74.	"	"	4.	200 yards beyond 18-pdr protective barrage.
Zero plus 40 to Zero plus 74.	"	"	3.	Creep 100 yards per 2 minutes to protective barrage P.34.c.0.3. to P.35.c.0.6. and then search and sweep 200 yards outwards till zero plus 74.

SECRET.   COPY NO: 35

52ND DIVISIONAL ARTILLERY ORDER NO: 42.

Reference map 1/20,000 - 51 A. S.E.

1. On 16th October at a zero to be notified later, 72nd Brigade will attack and capture railway and sunken road P.34.d. and V.5.a. & c.
   The 8th R.W.Kents will be on the right and the 1st N. Staffords on the left.
   They will be formed up east of the LA SELLE river by zero hour.

2. The attack will be supported by 5 Brigades of Field Artillery, the tasks for which are given in the attached tables.
   H.A. will co-operate by engaging selected points and known hostile batteries.

3. Rates of fire will be :-
   Zero to zero plus 44 - NORMAL.
   Zero plus 44 to zero plus 59. - SLOW.
   Zero plus 59 to zero plus 74. - VERY SLOW.

   Ammunition - 18 Pdrs. 50% H.E. - 50% P.S.
   4.5" Howitzers engaged on Serial No. 3 and 4 from zero to zero plus 10 will not fire 106 fuzes.

   93rd Brigade in smoke barrage will open with 2 minutes RAPID smoke shell only and then fire at NORMAL using 1 smoke shell to 6 percussion shrapnel.

   9th Brigade will have a liaison Officer with North Staffords Hqrs. and 58th Brigade with Royal West Kents Hqrs.

   Watches will be synchronised from this Office

   S.O.S. lines after attack will be the line of the protective barrage

   ACKNOWLEDGE.

                                                    [signature]
                                                    Captain R.A.
                                              Brigade Major R.A., 52nd Div:

15th October 1918.

DISTRIBUTION.

    Copies No. 1/5   9th Bde RFA.   Copies No. 32   S.C.R.A.
              6/10 58th Bde RFA.   33   R.O.R.A.
              11/15 93rd Bde RFA.   34/35 War Diary.
              16/20 306th Bde RFA.   36/37 File.
              21/25 307th Bde RFA.
              26/   72nd Inf. Bde.
              27/29 61st D.A.
              30   52nd D.A.C.
              31   52nd D.T.M.O.

SECRET.   COPY NO:

52ND DIVISIONAL ARTILLERY ORDER NO: 43.

1. The 52nd Divisional Artillery will be relieved in action the 72nd and 315th Brigades RFA on night 17/18th.

2. The 72nd Brigade RFA will relieve the 9th Brigade RFA and 315th Brigade RFA the 56th Brigade RFA.

3. On completion of relief the 52nd Divisional Artillery will march to area west of CAMBRAI, squares A.8 and A.14, pending transfer to First Army by road on 20th inst.

4. The 2 Trench Mortars in action will be withdrawn on the night 17th/18th instant. Arrangements for the disposal of Mortars and personnel are given in the Administrative Instructions attached.

5. The 2 howitzer batteries may be relieved in daylight, one gun at a time.
    The 18-pdr batteries will be relieved one section at a time after dusk, there being no movement East of ST AUBERT before 1730 hours in these reliefs.
    All 1/20,000 maps and orders, re pending operations and S.O.S. grenades will be handed over on relief.
    All other details will be arranged direct between Brigade Commanders concerned.

6. Command of Brigades and batteries will pass on completion of reliefs.
    On completion of Brigade reliefs, command of the Artillery covering the front will pass to O.C. 306th Brigade RFA.(Lieut Col. TACOKE, C.M.G.,D.S.O., R.F.A.)

7. 52nd D.A.C. will march to new area starting 1400 hours.
    Brigades will march on completion of relief, by individual batteries if desired, 40 yards between sections will be kept and strictest march discipline observed.
    No restrictions as to route.

8. Instructions for advance parties have been already issued.

9. Administrative Instructions for move are attached.

10. Completion of reliefs will be wired to this Office, using the code word 'CANDLES'.

11. Location of this Headquarters after completion of relief will notified later.

12. ACKNOWLEDGE.

                                                    Captain R.A.
                                        Brigade Major R.A., 52nd Divl.

17th October 1918.
Distribution.
    Copies No. 1/5   9th Bde RFA.
              6/10   56th Bde RFA.
              11   52nd D.A.C.
              12   52nd D.T.M.O.
              13   217th Coy. A.S.C.
              14   72nd Bde RFA.
              15   306th Bde RFA.
              16   315th Bde RFA.
              17   61st D.A.
              18   72nd Inf. Bde.
              19   S.O.R.A.
              20   R.O.R.A.
              21   R.A. Signals.

SECRET.   Copy No.

52nd Divisional Artillery Order No. 44.

1. Reference sheet 57 C NE., map 1/100,000 LENS.

   52nd Divisional Artillery will march to the MORCHIES area on 19th inst.
2. Order of march will be -
   - 217th Cy: ASC. ... starting 0900 hours.
   - 52nd D.A.C. ...   "   1000   "
   - 56th Bde RFA. ...   "   1030   "
   - 9th Bde RFA. ...   "   1100   "

   Starting point for each Unit will be a point in present area to be selected by Unit concerned.
3. Route will be -
   Canal crossing F.30.a.5.5. - CANTAING - outskirts FONTAINE - NOTRE DAME, thence along CAMBRAI - BAPAUME road.
4. Brigades, 52nd D.A.C. and 217th Cy. ASC will march independently, Unit Commanders arranging their own halts etc.
5. 40 yards between sections will be maintained and every precaution against blocking roads taken.
   March discipline will be carefully supervised.
6. Advance parties will report to S.C.R.A. 1400 hours, 19th inst. at the junction of the CAMBRAI - BAPAUME and the MORCHIES - BEAUMETZ roads.
7. D.T.M.O. and all trench mortar personnel will march with and be under orders of 52nd D.A.C. till further notice.
8. Rations for the 19th will be carried on man and animal.
   Rations for 20th will be carried on train wagons under arrangements O.C., 217th Cy. ASC and delivered to Units in new area on the evening 19th inst.
9. Entraining programme for 20th will be issued later.
10. ACKNOWLEDGE.

(sd/) W.G.HARRIOTT, Captain R.A.
Brigade Major R.A., 52nd Division.

18th October 1918.
Distribution.
9th Brigade RFA.
56th Brigade RFA.
52nd D.A.C.
52nd DT.M.O.
217th Company A.S.C.
R.A. Signals.
S.C.R.A.
R.O.R.A.
War Diary.
File.

Copy No. ...13.

Appx VII

52ND DIVISIONAL ARTILLERY ORDER NO: 45.

1. 52nd Divisional Artillery will march to HENIN LIETARD area on October 24th.

2. ROUTE. LIEVIN - LENS - SALLAUMINES.

3. HOURS OF START.
   - 56th Brigade RFA. ... 0800 hours.
   - 9th Brigade RFA. ... 0800 hours.
   - 52nd D.A.C. ... 0900 hours.

   Units will arrange their own starting points in present billeting area and march independently.
   Trench Mortar personnel will march with 9th Brigade RFA.

4. Advance parties will report to Staff Captain R.A. at office of Town Major, HENIN LIETARD, which is situated in that town on the ROUVROY Road, at 1200 hours. Units will be notified if a lorry is available.

5. Unless a more easterly railhead is allotted, rations on the 23rd will be drawn by horse transport from THELUS railhead and thereafter by M.T. from the same place. Divisional Train are making the necessary arrangements.

6. 52nd D.A. H.Q. will move to HENIN LIETARD (old 52nd Div: H.Qrs.)

7. Brigades, D.A.C., L.T.M.O. to ACKNOWLEDGE.

                                         Captain R.A.
                        Brigade Major R.A., 52nd Division.

23rd October 1918.
Distribution.
Copy No.	1	9th Bde RFA.	Copy No.	7	R.A. Signals.
	2	56th Bde RFA.		8	B.G.R.A.
	3	52nd L.A.C.		9	S.C.R.A.
	4	D.T.M.O.		10	R.A. VIII Corps.
	5	217th Coy: A.S.C.		12/13	War Diary.
	6	52nd Division 'G'.		14	File.

SECRET.   Copy No. 11

ADMINISTRATIVE INSTRUCTIONS NO.13.

1. The 52nd Divisional Artillery will entrain tomorrow in accordance with the programme already issued.

2. 56th Brigade R.F.A. will entrain at FREMICOURT and 9th Brigade R.F.A. at VELU.

3. Vehicles, animals and personnel for loading must be at entraining station ready to load, three hours before the train is due to start and railway authorities will endeavour to have train ready for loading 3 hours before they are due to start.

4. Each Brigade will detail a Captain to be in charge of the whole entrainment from each station, and this officer will leave by the last train from that station.   Copy of entrainment programme is being forwarded to Brigades for these officers.

He will report by wire to Corps, repeating to 1st Army, giving details of personnel, animals and vehicles entrained as each train departs and will also give train No. and hour of departure.

When the last train is ready to start he will report completion of entrainment to 17th Corps and First Army.

5. Rations for consumption 20th inst are being delivered to units tonight and unexpired forage portion of which will be loaded on the train by units.

Rations for consumption 21st inst will be delivered at VELU and FREMICOURT Stations at 8.30 a.m. tomorrow by Train Wagons and will be taken over by units representatives at that hour on the station.

Unexpired portion of rations for 20th inst will be carried on the men and rations and forage for 21st will be carried on each train.

6. All horses will be watered prior to entrainment.   There is an ample water supply and troughs at both stations.

7. Each Battery and Section D.A.C. and also 217th Coy A.S.C. will send an officer representative and 1 O.R. to proceed by the first train leaving the station from which they are entraining, to act as an advance party for camps at ECURI and ACQ.   These officers will be met at ECURI and ACQ by a Staff Officer of this Headquarters and they should remain at the Stations until the Staff Officer arrives.

8. Each Battery and Section D.A.C. will detail 2 men to assist the party of pioneers provided by the railway authorities for roping vehicles etc.   These men should report to the Artillery officers in charge of entraining as detailed in para 4.

9. All tents and Shelters lent to 9th Brigade R.F.A. by Area Commandant, BOUCHIES, will be returned to Area Commandant before unit moves tomorrow.

All trench shelters drawn tonight by units from supply dump will be returned to supply dump by 9 a.m. tomorrow without fail.

10. The journey is expected to occupy about 5 hours.

11. There are good platforms at both stations and loading is from the side.

Horses can be walked straight on to the train but ramps are provided if required.

P.T.O.

- 2 -

12. Teams should not be unhooked until the train is in the Station and the exact position of the "flats" is known.
   Each train contains 17 "flats" capable of holding about 58 pairs of wheels.

13. The Mortars and all personnel etc of D.T.M.B. will be entrained at VELU.

14. ACKNOWLEDGE.

19th October 1918.

Captain R.A.,
Staff Captain R.A., 52nd Division.

DISTRIBUTION :-

    Copy No. 1 - 9th Bde RFA.
            2 - 56th Bde RFA.
            3 - D.A.C.
            4 - R.A.Sigs.
            5 - R.O.R.A.
            6 - 217 Coy A.S.C.
            7 - D.T.M.O.
            8 - Officer i/c entraining at VELU.
            9 -   " " " " FREMICOURT.
      10/11 - War Diary.
          12 - File.

CFS.

SECRET.   COPY NO. 27

52ND DIVISIONAL ARTILLERY ORDER NO. 46.

Reference map - sheet 36.J.

1. 52nd Divisional Artillery will march to WAZIERES - FRAIS MARAIS area 26th instant.

2. ROUTE.   AUBY - FLERS - DOUAI.

3. TIME OF START.
   - 53th Brigade R.F.A.   0930 hours.
   - 9th Brigade R.F.A.   0945 hours.
   - 52nd D.A.C. &)   1100 hours.
   - T.M.Personnel.)
   D.T.M.O. will march with 52nd D.A.C.

4. Advance parties will report to Staff Captain R.A. at Cross Roads W.18.d.1.9. at 1000 hours, 26th instant.

5. Rations for 26th instant will be carried on men and animals, for 27th on Train Wagons, under Train arrangements.

6. 52nd D.A.Headquarters will close at present location 1000 hours 26th instant and re-open at FRAIS MARAIS on arrival.

7. Brigades, D.A.C. and D.T.M.O. to acknowledge.

26th October 1918.

Captain R.A.,
Brigade Major R.A., 52nd Division.

DISTRIBUTION :-

- Copy No. 1/5   9th Brigade R.F.A.
- 6/10 58th Brigade R.F.A.
- 11/13 52nd D.A.C.
- 14   D.T.M.O.
- 15   217th Coy. A.S.C.
- 16   52nd Division "G".
- 17.   R.A., 8th Corps.
- 18   S.C.R.A.
- 19   R.O.R.A.
- 20   R.A.Signal.
- 21/22 War Diary.
- 23   File.

SECRET.

52nd DIVISIONAL ARTILLERY ORDER NO. 47

Reference Map 1/40000
Sheets 44 and 44a.

1. 52nd Divisional Artillery will relieve 12th Divisional Artillery between November 1st and 3rd.

2. 56th Brigade R.F.A. will relieve 63rd Brigade R.F.A. in the line under orders of 12th Divisional Artillery.
   9th Brigade R.F.A. will move up into Divisional Reserve, releasing the 82nd Brigade R.F.A.
   D.A.Cs. will relieve each other.

3. Details of the approach march are given in attached March table.
   Usual distance will be maintained on the march.

4. Train Wagons of No.2 Section D.A.C. and 56th Brigade R.F.A. will accompany units on 1st, loaded with rations for the 2nd.
   Remainder 217th Coy A.S.C. will relieve No.1 Coy, 12th Divl. Train at LANDAS on November 2nd, after delivery of rations for the 3rd, under arrangements between Coy. Commanders concerned.
   Rations for the 4th will be delivered to 9th Brigade Headquarters and No.1 Section D.A.C. after their arrival in new area on the 3rd.

5. 52nd D.A.H.Q. will assume command of the artillery covering 32nd Division at 1200 hours 3rd instant.

6. 52nd Divisional Artillery to ACKNOWLEDGE.

WG Marriott
Captain R.A.,
Brigade Major R.A., 52nd Division.

31st October 1918.

DISTRIBUTION -

```
Copies No. 1/5   9th Brigade R.F.A.
         6/10   56th Brigade R.F.A.
        11/13   52nd D.A.C.
           14   217th Coy. A.S.C.
           15   52nd Division "G"
           16   12th D.A.
           17   R.A., VIII Corps.
           18   52nd Division "Q"
           19   D.A.P.M. 52nd Div.
           20   R.A. Sigs.
           21   B.G.R.A.
           22   R.C.R.A.
        23/24   War Diary.
           25   File.
```

MARCH TABLE.

Serial No.	Date.	Unit.	From.	To.	Route.	Remarks.
1	Nov.1st.	56th Bde RFA.	WAZIERES.	ROSULT area.	FLINES - COUTICHES - ORCHIES. To be clear of FLINES by 1030 and NOT to enter ORCHIES before 1045.	Take over Wagon Lines vacated morning 1st by 62nd Bde RFA.
2		No.2. Sect. D.A.C.	FRAIS MARAIS.	H.12.d. west of RUESNES.	FLINES - ORCHIES - LANDAS - VIEUX CONDE. To follow 56th Brigade and to be clear of FLINES before 1100.	Take over Wagon Lines No.1 Sect. 12th D.A.C.
3	Nov.2nd	58th Bde RFA.	ROSULT area	Line	Route as ordered by 12th D.A.	Relieves 63rd Brigade in Line but remains in 62nd Brigade RFA Wagon Lines.
4	Nov.3rd.	9th Bde RFA.	WAZIERES.	ROSULT area.	..... FLINES - ORCHIES and to be clear of FLINES by 1015.	Takes over Wagon Lines vacated Morning 3rd by 63rd Brigade RFA.
5	Nov.3rd.	H.Q.and No.1 Sect.D.A.C.	FRAIS MARAIS.	ROSULT area.	FLINES - ORCHIES to follow 9th Bde RFA and be clear of FLINES by 1100.	Take over Wagon Lines vacated morning 3rd by Headquarters and No.2 Section, 12th D.A.C.

CONFIDENTIAL.

ORIGINAL.

Vol 8

WAR DIARY OF 52nd D.A., H.Q.

Vol: V.
Part XI.

From -
1st November 1918.

To -
30th November 1918.

Army Form C. 2118.

WAR DIARY
or
INTELLIGENCE SUMMARY.   NOVEMBER 1918

(Erase heading not required.)

Instructions regarding War Diaries and Intelligence Summaries are contained in F.S. Regs., Part II. and the Staff Manual respectively. Title pages will be prepared in manuscript.

Place	Date	Hour	Summary of Events and Information	Remarks and references to Appendices
FRAIS MARAIS.	1st		56th Brigade RFA moved to ROSULT area.	App
	2nd		56th Brigade RFA relieved 63rd Brigade RFA in action near NIVELLE.	App
SAMEON.	3rd		9th Brigade RFA moved to RUE DE BEAUME, 52nd D.A. Headquarters moved to SAMEON relieving 12th D.A. at 1200 hours, 56th Brigade RFA and 277th Army Brigade RFA being in action and 9th Brigade RFA in Reserve. 52nd Divisional Artillery Order No.49 - re possible move advance issued vide	App: I. App
	4th		9th Brigade RFA relieved 277th Army Brigade in action vide 52nd D.A. Order No. 48. 52nd D.A. Order No. 50 issued re relief of 8th Division by 157th Infantry Brigade and consequent alteration of Artillery Command - 33rd Brigade RFA in action, coming under orders of C.R.A., 52nd Division. Quiet day vide Daily Report	App: II. App:III. App:IV. App
	5th		52nd D.A. Order No. 51 re possible advance issued vide Quiet day vide Daily Report	App:V. App:VI. App
	6th		For Daily Report vide	App:VII. App
	7th		52nd D.A. Order No. 52 re proposed operation against FORT MAZY issued vide For Daily Report vide	App:VIII. App:IX. App
	8th		Enemy retirement followed up, some opposition being experienced from M.Gs. A/56th Bty. crossed CANAL DU JARD.	App
MONT DE PERULWELZ.	9th		52nd D.A. Headquarters moved to MONT DE PERULWELZ remainder of 56th Brigade RFA and 9th Bde having crossed the Canal in the early morning, 56th Bde moving to BON SECOURS, 9th Bde to HERCHIES.	App
SIRAULT.	10th		Advance continued, 52nd D.A. Headquarters moved to SIRAULT, 56th Bde to HERCHIES, 9th Bde to VACRESSE.	
	11th		52nd D.A.C. moved to SIRAULT. Orders for cessation of hostilities at 1100 hours issued vide	App

Army Form C. 2118.

WAR DIARY
or
INTELLIGENCE SUMMARY.
(Erase heading not required.)

Instructions regarding War Diaries and Intelligence Summaries are contained in F. S. Regs., Part II. and the Staff Manual respectively. Title pages will be prepared in manuscript.

Place	Date	Hour	Summary of Events and Information	Remarks and references to Appendices
	11th.		D.A. Order No. 53.	App:X. App
	12th} 14th}		Nil.	
SIRAULT.	15th		Army Commander entered MONS, A/56th Bty and D/69th taking part in the parade.	App
	17th		Second Army took over the responsibility for the front and outposts of 52nd Division were withdrawn.	App App App
GHLIN.	19th		52nd D.A. Headquarters moved to CHATEAU DE FESTINOY, GHLIN.	
CASTEAU	25th		52nd D.A. Headquarters moved to CASTEAU.	
	26th		52nd Division came under orders of XXII Corps.	
	27th - 30th		N I L.	

[signature]
Lieut. Colonel RA.
offg. Commanding R.A., 52nd Division.

APPENDICES TO

WAR DIARY OF 52nd D.A.,H.Q.

For

November 1918.

SECRET.　　　　　　　　　　　　　　　　　　　　　　Copy No.1.......

AMENDMENT No.1
to
52nd DIVISIONAL ARTILLERY ORDER NO.49.

Para 3.　　"For J.25.a.4.5. read K.25.a.4.5."

　　　　　　　　　　　　　　　　　　　　　(signed)
　　　　　　　　　　　　　　　　　　　　　　Captain R.A.,
3rd November 1918　　　　　　　　Brigade Major R.A., 52nd Divn.

Same Distribution as D.A.O. No.49.

52ND DIVISIONAL ARTILLERY ORDER NO.49.

1. When the enemy withdraws, the 52nd Division will follow at once.

2. The Brigade in the line, on the Left, with 2 Affiliated M.G. Coys. and a Field Cy. R.E., will cross the ESCAUT and JARD CANALS and make good the general line K.29 central to K.16 central.

3. The following bridges will be constructed at the earliest opportunity to carry H.T.
Bridges 'A' and 'B'   K.27.d.3.1. near JOUPORE.
Bridges 'X' to 'Y'   near PONT DE LA VERNETTE.
Approaches to these bridges will also be prepared.
A red flag will be hoisted on the high ground about K.31.b.8.5. when bridges 'A' and 'B' are open to traffic and a blue flag about J.25.a.4.5. when bridges 'X' and 'Y' are open.

4. As soon as either pair of these bridges is complete a squadron of Cavalry, 2 Platoons of Cyclists, supported by 2 Companies Infantry, 2 M.G. companies and 1 Battery R.F.A. will push forward and secure the following objectives :-
    (a) MONT JOPIE MONT.
    (b) MONT DE PEROWELZ and N.W. exits from BOIS DE HERMITAGE.
    (c) OOMIN - ROQUET - PEROWELZ Road.

5. The Artillery Action in support of the above operations after the relief of 277th Army Brigade RFA by 9th Brigade RFA will be as follows :-
    9th Bde RFA will be at 1 hours notice to advance to the old 277th Bde positions about the northern end of HAUTE RIVE and cover the opening stages of the advance.
All preparations for occupying these positions, even in the dark, will be made.
A/56th Bde RFA will cross in rear of the mounted troops and act entirely independently in their support.

6. As soon as A/56th Bde RFA is across, the remainder of 56th Brigade RFA will cross and come into positions of readiness on the east of the CANAL DU JARD.
They will work in a close liaison with the leading Infantry Brigade in support of the general advance.
This Brigade must act entirely on its own initiative, as the situation demands, and not await orders.

7. The 56th Brigade RFA will be followed across the CANAL by the Support Infantry Brigade which in turn will be followed by the 9th Brigade RFA. Orders for the subsequent action of the 9th Brigade RFA will be issued as the situation develops.

8. Should the withdrawal of the enemy take place tomorrow morning, before the relief of the 277th Brigade RFA is complete the following procedure will take place :-
    56th Bde RFA will advance to positions about HAUTE RIVE and cover the initial stages of the advance.
    The leading battery of the 9th Brigade, instead of carrying out the relief, will cross the river in support of the mounted troops.
    The remainder of the 9th Brigade RFA will cross in rear of its leading battery and carry out the role assigned above to the 56th Brigade RFA.
    The 56th Bde RFA will cross in rear of the Support Infantry Brigade and carry out the role assigned above to the 9th Bde RFA.
    277th Bde RFA will remain in their positions and eventually come into Divisional Reserve.
    It is to be clearly understood that the procedure detailed in this paragraph will only take place, should the enemy withdraw before the 9th Bde have completed their relief of the 277th Brigade.

9. Units not mentioned in the above instructions will stand fast, pending further orders.

-2-

10. Moves as detailed above will take place on the code word "HUNT". This will be wired to Brigades and sent by special D.R. to the Brigade Wagon Line Commander.

11. D.A.,H.Q. will move with advanced Divisional Headquarters to MARNE DE NIVELLE as soon as leading Infantry Brigade is east of JARD CANAL.

12. Artillery Brigades to ACKNOWLEDGE.

[signature]
Captain R.A.
Brigade Major R.A., 52nd Divn:

3rd NOVEMBER 1918.
Distribution.
Copy No. 1/5   9th Brigade RFA.
        6/10   56th Brigade RFA.
        11   277th Brigade RFA.
        12   D.A.C.
        13   52nd Division 'G'.
        14   155th Inf. Bde.
        15   156th Inf. Bde.
        16   157th Inf. Bde.
        17   VIII Corps R.A.
        18   VIII Corps H.A.
        19   58th D.A.
        20   S.C.R.A.
        21   R.O.R.A.
        22   R.A. Signals.
     23/24 War Diary.
        25   File.

SECRET.

App II

Copy No. 23

52nd DIVISIONAL ARTILLERY ORDER No.49.

1. 9th Brigade R.F.A. will relieve the 277th A/Brigade R.F.A. in the line on 4th instant.

2. Relief of A/277 Brigade R.F.A. and forward section D/277 Brigade R.F.A. will be complete by 0700 hours.
   Remainder of relief will be carried out by Sections at 30 minutes intervals and be complete by 1500 hours.

3. Movement EAST will be by road through I.30.a & b., J.25. and J.26.
   Movement WEST will be by roads through J.33, J.32, J.31 and I.36.

4. Wagon Lines will also be exchanged and on completion of relief, 277th Army Brigade R.F.A. will be in billets in the RUE DU BAUGY and RUE DE BALLORE, preparatory to marching to another Corps.

5. All telephone lines, S.O.S. rockets and 1/20000 maps, air photos and documents giving information as to the front will be handed over.
   277th Army Brigade R.F.A. will march with full echelons.

6. Command of Batteries and Brigades will pass on completion of reliefs. All other details will be arranged between Brigade Commanders concerned.

7. Major H.H.E.House R.F.A. will be in command of 9th Brigade R.F.A. during absence of the Brigade Commander.

8. Completion of relief will be reported by priority wire to this office.

9. R.F.A. Brigades to ACKNOWLEDGE.

Lieut.Col.
Brigade Major R.A., 52nd Division.

3rd November 1918.

DISTRIBUTION :-

Copies	1/5	9th Brigade R.F.A.
"	6/11	277th Army Brigade R.F.A.
"	12	35th Brigade R.F.A.
"	13	52nd D.A.C.
"	14	158th R.F. Brigade.
"	15	52nd Division "G"
"	16	R.A., 9th Corps.
"	17	H.A., 9th Corps.
"	18	77th Brigade R.G.A.
"	19	R.E. Sigs.
"	20	S.C.R.A.
"	21	D.A.R.A.
"	22/23	War Diary.
"	24	File.

SECRET.   Copy No..... 36.

52nd DIVISIONAL ARTILLERY ORDER NO. 50.

1. 52nd Division are taking over the whole 8th Corps Front, the 157th Infantry Brigade relieving the 23rd Infantry Brigade on the night 4/5th November.

2. Consequent upon the above relief, the 33rd and 45th Brigades R.F.A. of the 8th D.A. come under orders of C.R.A. 52nd Division at 0600, 5th instant.

3. 16th and 87th Brigades R.G.A. will also be affiliated to the 52nd Division.

4. 33rd Brigade R.F.A. will be in liaison with 157th Infantry Brigade and will arrange Battalion liaison in direct consultation with G.O.C., 157th Infantry Brigade.
    56th Brigade R.F.A. will remain in liaison with 156th Infantry Bde.
    9th Brigade R.F.A. will be under direct control of this office, but, as they also are covering the 156th Bde front, O.C., 56th Brigade R.F.A. may call on them direct for fire if he wishes to.
    45th Brigade R.F.A. will remain in Divisional Reserve.

5. S.O.S. lines will remain as before unless the G.O.C. Infantry Bde wishes them altered, when the necessary modifications will be made and reported to this office.

6. The northern Divisional Boundary will be -
    I.18.a.5.5. - J.10.c.0.0. - J.10.c.9.8, along North East Bank of ESCAUT FLEUVE and JARD CANAL (inclusive) to K.19.b.7.9. and thence the VERGNE River (exclusive).
    Southern Divisional Boundary will be -
    Q.9.c.2.4. - Q.16.c.9.5. - R.13.c.5.4. - R.20.a.1.1. - R.9.c.9.1. thence along HAISNE River.
    <u>Boundary between 9th and 33rd Brigades R.F.A.</u>
        Line Q.4.central - K.36.central.
    <u>Boundary between 9th and 56th Brigades R.F.A.</u>
        Line R.20.a.0.8. - K.16.c.0.0.
    <u>Boundary between Heavy and Field Artillery.</u>
        Line K.14.b.5.0. - K.39.c.7.7. - R.2.central - R.10.d.0.0.

    Within these boundaries Brigades will be prepared to answer GF calls with 2-18-pdr and 1 - 4.5" How. Batteries.
    LL Calls will be answered by all Batteries that can bear, irrespective of zones.
    NF Calls will also be answered in these zones and 4.5" How. Batteries will be prepared to answer ANF Calls as well within the Bde zone.
    During counter preparations GF calls will only be answered by a section of the Batteries detailed.
    During S.O.S., G.F. calls will not be answered by Field Artillery and LL calls by 1 section only of all Batteries that can bear.
    Rates of fire for GF and LL calls will be 3 minutes INTENSE.
    The wireless receiving set from D.A.H.Q. will be sent to 9th Brigade R.F.A. for use with forward section D/69th Battery R.F.A.

7. The Divisional policy will be to keep close touch with the enemy by active patrolling and follow up any withdrawal as laid down in 52nd D.A. Order No. 49.

8. F.A.B rigades to <u>ACKNOWLEDGE</u>.

                                                                               Captain R.A.,
4th November, 1918.   Brigade Major R.A., 52nd Division.
Distribution - as over

DISTRIBUTION :-

    Copies No. 1/5   9th Bde RFA.
                  6/10   56th Brigade RFA.
               11/15   33rd Brigade RFA.
               16/20   45th Brigade RFA.
                 21   52nd D.A.C.
                 22   8th D.A.
                 23   58th D.A.
                 24   31st C.D.A.
                 25   52nd Division "G"
                 26   155 Infantry Brigade.
                 27   156 Infantry Brigade.
                 28   157 Infantry Brigade.
                 29   R.A., 8th Corps.
                 30   H.A., 8th Corps.
                 31   87th Brigade R.G.A.
                 32   16th Brigade R.G.A.
                 33   S.G.R.A.
                 34   R.O.R.A.
                 35   R.A. Signals.
               36/37   War Diary.
                 38   File.

SECRET.

52nd DIVISIONAL ARTILLERY.

DAILY REPORT.
from 0800 4th to 0800 5th November 1918.

1. **OUR ACTIVITY.**

   Bursts of harassing fire were directed on roads and tracks throughout the day.

   A M.G. at K.30.a.0.4. was engaged by 4.5" hows at the request of Infantry.

2. **HOSTILE ACTIVITY.**

   (e) <u>Operations</u> - NIL.

   (o) <u>Artillery</u> - The eastern outskirts of THUN and the NIVELLE - BUNISON road were harassed during the day by 77 m.m. and 10.5 c.m., H.E. and Gas.

   J.28.d. was shelled with 100 rounds 10.5 c.m. H.E. and Mustard Gas during the evening.

   (f) <u>Movement</u> - NIL.

   (g) <u>Aerial</u> - 2 observation balloons were brought down in flames at 1130 hours.

3. **GENERAL.**

   Visibility - Good.

5/11/18.

Lieutenant R.A.,
for Commanding R.A., 52nd Division.

SECRET.

Copy No. 3/

appx V

52nd DIVISIONAL ARTILLERY ORDER NO. 51.

1. 52nd D.A. Order No. 49 is cancelled.

2. When the enemy withdraws, 52nd Division will follow up to gain and maintain touch with his main forces.

3. (a) The Infantry Brigade in the Right Section, with one affiliated M.G. Company, will cross the ESCAUT and JARD Canal and make good the general line Q.6.a. - K.29.central.
   (b) The Infantry Brigade in the Left Section, with two affiliated M.G. Companies, will cross the ESCAUT and JARD Canal and make good the general line K.29.central - K.16.central.

4. (a) The 8th Corps Cyclist Battalion (less 1 Sdy.), will cross immediately in rear of the Left Brigade and push forward and secure the following objectives :-
   (i) VIEUX CONDE - PERUWELZ Railway (R.1, L.31, L.25, L.19, L.13.
   (ii) CONDE - MONT DE PERUWELZ - PERUWELZ Road (L.32, L.26, L.20, L.14, L.8.)
   (iii) CONDE - CH. de L'ERMITAGE - BOQUET Road (L.33, L.27, L.21, L.15, L.8.b. and d.)

   (iv) The line LORETTE - BONSECOURS - PERUWELZ.

5. As soon as the line Q.6 - K.16 has been made good, Infantry Brigades will push on in accordance with para 2.
   Right Infantry Brigade Headquarters will move along the road RIEUX DE CONDE - GD. QUENOY - CHENE RAOUL.
   Left Infantry Brigade Headquarters along the road HERGNIES - MONT-DE-PERUWELZ.

6. At the earliest possible moment the following bridges will be made :-
   (a) Near COUPURE K.27.d.3.1.
       (Bridges HERGNIES "A" and HERGNIES "B")
   (b) Near PONT DE LA VERNETTE.
       (Bridges VERNETTE "X" and VERNETTE "Y")

7. As soon as these bridges are ready, a squadron 4th Hussars will cross and move forward to co-operate with the cyclists.

8. Artillery action in support of the advance will be as follows :-
   (a) As soon as information is received that the enemy has withdrawn, 9th Brigade Batteries west of the River SCARPE will advance to the old 277th Brigade R.F.A. positions about HAUTEVIVE and support the initial advance of the left Infantry Brigade.
   All arrangements must be made to occupy these positions at short notice in the dark.
   Wagon Lines will in consequence be at an hour's notice to move.
   (b) A/56th Brigade R.F.A. will move forward in close support of the leading troops of the left Infantry Brigade, with whom it will work in close liaison in rear of the Cavalry and cross the canal.
   56th Brigade R.F.A. (less A Battery) will follow and support the advance of the Left Brigade, working in liaison with the G.O.C. Infantry Brigade.
   (c) 19th Battery R.F.A. will follow the 56th Brigade across the Canal, get into touch with and support the leading Battalion of the Right Infantry Brigade, working in liaison with the Battalion Commander.
   (d) 33rd Brigade R.F.A. will support the advance of the Right Infantry Brigade as long as possible, from present positions.

9. With the exception of the moves detailed in the preceding paragraph units will not move without further orders.

10. The Moves will take place on the code word "HUNT", which will be wired to Brigades and sent by special D.R. to the Wagon Lines Commanders of 9th and 56th Brigades.

11. A central

11. A central visual station will be established about K.25.a.1.8.

12. D.A.H.Q. will move with Headquarters 52nd Division to MARIE DE NIVELLE as soon as leading Brigade is across the JARD Canal.

13. Artillery Brigades ACKNOWLEDGE.

                                                    Captain R.A.,
5th November 1918.   Brigade Major R.A., 52nd Division.

DISTRIBUTION -

Copies No.	
1/5	9th Brigade R.F.A.
6/10	56th Brigade R.F.A.
11/15	33rd Brigade R.F.A.
16	D.A.C.
17	155th Inf.Bde.
18	156th Inf.Bde.
19	157th Inf.Bde.
20	52nd Division "G"
21	9th Corps R.A.
22	8th Corps R.A.
23	58th D.A.
24	3rd C.D.A.
25	16th Brigade R.G.A.
26	67th Brigade R.G.A.
27	S.O.R.A.
28	R.O.R.A.
29	R.A. Sigs.
30/31	War Diary.
32	File.

SECRET.

DAILY REPORT - 52ND DIVISIONAL ARTILLERY.
0600 5th to 0600 6th November 1918.

1. OUR ACTIVITY.

Harassing fire was directed throughout the night on enemy posts.

60-pdrs. fired 20 rounds on house K.13.d.4.3. which was reported by 156th Infantry Brigade to contain an active gun.

2. HOSTILE ACTIVITY.
   (a) Operations.
               NIL.

   (b) Artillery. Very quiet. 77 mm guns and 10.5 cm Hows. fired on BRUILLE-THUN during the day; during the night, NIVELLE and BURIDON were lightly harassed with H.E. and Gas and 8 rounds were fired on BRUILLE.

A 77 mm battery was firing from the wood in K.9.d. during the afternoon.

   (c) T.Ms fired 12 rounds on J.21.d. at 2235 hours.

   (d) M.Gs did not fire on our low-flying 'planes but were very active at night on roads.

   (f) At 0730 horse transport on road K.29.a.10.30 to K.29.b. was dispersed by 6:" Hows. Considerable individual movement observed in K.28.c.

   (g) AERIAL NIL.

3 GENERAL.
Visibility poor.

A.F. Drifton

Lieutenant R.A.
for Commanding R.A., 52nd Division.

DAILY REPORT - 52nd DIVISIONAL ARTILLERY.
0600 6th to 0600 7th November 1918.

ACTIVITY.

4.5" Howitzers destroyed foot bridge at R.14.b.2.4. and completely demolished sniper's post in house R.14.a.4.6.
1130 hours, 4.5" Hows. engaged M.G. at K.13.c.6.0.
18-pdrs engaged hostile 77 mm Battery in E.23.
A suspected Company H.Q., R.15.a.3.8. was also engaged.
Harassing fire was directed at night on roads and tracks.

6" T.Ms. engaged enemy T.Ms. which fired on R.13 and Q.18.

HOSTILE ACTIVITY.

Operations.   N I L.

Artillery.   Greater activity than during previous 24 hours. During the day bursts of fire were directed on NIVELLE and ST. AMAND by 10.5 cm hows.   ODOMEZ and Q.1.a. were shelled by 77 mm Gun.
     At 1650 a 15 cm how fired 30 rounds in Chateau L'Abbaye.
     Increased harassing fire was directed on all roads in the forward area by 10.5 cm hows and 77 mm Guns during the evening and some gas was fired on NIVELLE.

T.M.   A few rounds light T.M. fired into Q.18. and R.13.

M.G.   Slight activity between 1900 and 1930 hours.

GENERAL.

Visibility - Bad.

Lieutenant R.A.,
for Commanding R.A. 52nd Division.

appx VIII

SECRET.   COPY NO. 2B

52ND DIVISIONAL ARTILLERY ORDER NO. 52.

1. The 157th Infantry Brigade will attack FORT MAZY and the COPSE immediately east of it, on 8th instant.
   Attack will be delivered from the south, from vicinity of R.20.a.5.1.

2. Attack will be supported by 33rd Brigade RFA and 16th Brigade RGA.
   Tasks for the above are shown in table overleaf.
   C.B.S.O. is arranging for C.B. Work.

3. RATES OF FIRE -
   ZERO to ZERO plus 5 - RAPID.
   ZERO PLUS 5 to ZERO PLUS 30 - NORMAL.

4. Zero hour will be 1300 hours 8th instant.

5. Watches will be synchronised from this Office at 0900.

6. R.F.A. Brigades and 16th Brigade RGA ACKNOWLEDGE.

                                                    Captain R.A.
                                    Brigade Major R.A., 52nd Division.

7th November 1918.
DISTRIBUTION.

   Copy No. 1   9th Brigade RFA.
          2   56th Brigade RFA.
          3/7   33rd Brigade RFA.
          8/12 16th Brigade RFA.
          13   87th Brigade RGA.
          14/15 VIII Corps H.A.
          16   VIII Corps R.A.
          17   52nd Division 'G'.
          18   58th Div'l Arty.
          19   3rd C.D.A.
          20   S.C.R.A.
          21   R.O.R.A.
          22   R.A. Signals.
          23/24 War Diary.
          25   File.
          26   157th Inf. Bde.

TABLE OF TASKS.

TIME	UNIT	SERIAL NO.	NO. OF GUNS.	TASKS.	REMARKS.
Between 0900 & 1230 hrs	33rd Bde RFA.	1.	6 4.5" Hows.	Houses R.20.d.5.9.; R.20.b.1.0., & R.20.b.5.0. and wire about R.20 central. Wire R.20.a.3.2.	Demolish. Cut Gap.
	16th Bde RGA	2.	4 6" Hows. 6 60 pdrs.	FORT MAZE R.14.d.25.30 S.W. Corner COPSE R.20.b.75.90. House R.20.b.70.85.	2 50 min: Bombardments & harassed irregularly till ZERO.
ZERO to ZERO plus 2.	16th Bde RGA.	3.	4 6" Hows. 6 60pdrs	FORT MAZE R.14.d.25.30. House R.20.b.70.85. Copse R.20.b.75.90	""""
ZERO to ZERO plus 2.	16th Bde RGA.	4.	2 6" Hows. 2 6" Hows. 4 6" Hows. 2 60pdrs. 4 60pdrs.	Houses R.15.a.85.00. Houses R.14.b.4.4. FORT FRANQUET. R.14.b.25.60 R.8.d.0.4. to R.9.c.1.2. R.9.c.1.2. to FORT du PIGEONNIER.	
ZERO to ZERO plus 2.	33rd Bde RFA.	5.	6 4.5"How. 3 18pdrs.	FORT MOULIN AVENT R.14.d.15.90. COPSE R.14.d., R.20.b.	Search and sweep paying particular attention to S.W. corner.
			3 18pdrs. 6 18pdrs.	FORT MAZE. R.15.c.40.45. to R.15.a.45.30.	
ZERO plus 5 to ZERO plus 6.	33rd Bde RFA.	6.	12 18pdrs. 3 4.5"Hows. 3 4.5"Hows.	FORT MOULIN AVENT. FORT FRANQUET. FORT du PIGEONNIER.	Keep 200 yds. clear of FORT MAZE.

S.O.S. lines after attack as at present.

SECRET.

DAILY REPORT - 52ND DIVISIONAL ARTILLERY.
from 0600 7th to 0600 8th November 1918.

OUR ACTIVITY.
    4.5" Hows. engaged M.G. at FOSSE in R.7.a. and Coy. H.Q. in house R.15a.5.8.
    Harassing fire was directed on roads and tracks during the night.

HOSTILE ACTIVITY.
    Artillery.   Enemy guns were fairly active on areas NIVELLE, HAUTE RIVE, PLANGIES, GUBRAY, FORET DE RAISMES and on back areas during the day but were very quiet during the night.
    Some 30 rounds GREEN CROSS Gas were fired at 1530 hours on J.28.d. and at 12.30 hours some PHOSGENE gas and H.E. was fired on J.29.c.

T.Ms.   A few rounds were fired by a light T.M. on Right Brigade front.

AERIAL.   NIL.

GENERAL.   During the night several explosions in enemy lines were heard. Several fires were observed in VIEUX CONDE. Floods between CONDE and FRESNES have fallen 3 feet in the last 48 hours.

VISIBILTY poor in the morning becoming fair in the afternoon. Poor on morning of 8th.

                Lieutenant R.A.
for Commanding R.A., 52nd Division.

App X

Copy No... 25.

52nd DIVISIONAL ARTILLERY ORDER NO. 63.

1. Hostilities will cease at 1100 hours on November 11th. Leading Troops will stand fast on line reached at that hour.

2. Defensive precautions will be maintained.

3. There will be no intercourse of any description with the enemy.

4. Acknowledge.

Captain R.A.,
Brigade Major R.A., 52nd Division.

11th November 1918.

DISTRIBUTION :-

```
Copy No. 1.   C.R.A.
         2/6  56th Bde RFA.
        7/11  9th Bde RFA.
       12/16  67th Bde RGA.
       17/20  52nd D.A.C.
          21  D.T.M.C.
          22  S.C.R.A.
          23  R.O.R.A.
          24  R.A. Sigs.
       25/26  War Diary.
          27  File.
```

OFS.

Confidential.

ORIGINAL.
****

WAR DIARY.

of

HEADQUARTERS ROYAL ARTILLERY 52ND DIVISION.

From.   Part XII.   To.
1st December 1918.   Vol. VI.   31st December 1918.

Army Form C. 2118.

WAR DIARY
or
INTELLIGENCE SUMMARY.

DECEMBER 1918.

(Erase heading not required.)

Instructions regarding War Diaries and Intelligence Summaries are contained in F. S. Regs., Part II. and the Staff Manual respectively. Title pages will be prepared in manuscript.

Place	Date	Hour	Summary of Events and Information	Remarks and references to Appendices
CASTEAU.	1st		Headquarters R.A., at Casteau.	
	11th			
THIEUSIES.	12th		Headquarters R.A. moved to THIEUSIES area.	
	13th		N I L.	
	31st			

Brig: General RA.
Commanding R.A., 52nd Division.

INTELLIGENCE SUMMARY.
or
WAR DIARY

(Erase heading not required.)

Summary of Events and Information

Place	Date	Hour		Remarks and references to Appendices

Army Form C. 2118.

Instructions regarding War Diaries and Intelligence Summaries are contained in F. S. Regs., Part II and the Staff Manual respectively. Title pages will be prepared in manuscript.

CONFIDENTIAL.

ORIGINAL.

Vol 10

WAR DIARY OF HEADQUARTERS ROYAL ARTILLERY,

52ND DIVISION.

From :-
1st January 1919.

To :-
31st January 1919.

Part I.
Vol. VI.

Army Form C. 2118.

WAR DIARY
or
INTELLIGENCE SUMMARY.

(Erase heading not required.)

Instructions regarding War Diaries and Intelligence Summaries are contained in F. S. Regs., Part II. and the Staff Manual respectively. Title pages will be prepared in manuscript.

JANUARY 1919.

Place	Date	Hour	Summary of Events and Information	Remarks and references to Appendices
THIEUSIES.	1st to 31st		Headquarters R.A. at THIEUSIES. N I L.	

J. Aubrey [signature]
Brig: General R.A.,
Commanding R.A., 52nd Division.

CONFIDENTIAL.　　　　ORIGINAL.

WAR DIARY OF HEADQUARTERS ROYAL ARTILLERY

52ND DIVISION.

FROM -
February 1st 1919.

TO -
February 28th 1919.

PART II.
VOL. VI.

Army Form C. 2118.

WAR DIARY
or
INTELLIGENCE SUMMARY.

FEBRUARY 1919.

(Erase heading not required.)

Instructions regarding War Diaries and Intelligence Summaries are contained in F.S. Regs., Part II. and the Staff Manual respectively. Title pages will be prepared in manuscript.

Place	Date	Hour	Summary of Events and Information	Remarks and references to Appendices
THIEUSIES.	1st to 15th		N I L.	
	16th		Captain G.K.STEWART, M.C., R.A, (Staff Captain,) left to take up appointment as Staff Captain IV CORPS. Captain W.G.HARRIOTT, M.C., R.A. (Brigade Major), is consequently carrying out the work of both Branches.	
	17th to 28th		N I L.	

Ashworth
for Commanding R.A., 52nd Division.
Brig: General R.A.

CONFIDENTIAL.

WAR DIARY OF

HEADQUARTERS R.A., 52nd (Lowland) Division.

From 1st March to 31st March 1919.

Vol. 5 - Part 3.

Army Form C. 2118.

HEADQUARTERS ROYAL ARTILLERY - 52nd DIVISION.

WAR DIARY

INTELLIGENCE SUMMARY

(Erase heading not required.)

Instructions regarding War Diaries and Intelligence Summaries are contained in F. S. Regs., Part II and the Staff Manual respectively. Title pages will be prepared in manuscript.

Place	Date	Hour	Summary of Events and Information	Remarks and references to Appendices
THIBUSIES.	1st to 17th		N I L.	
THIBUSIES.	18th		D.A.C. moved to SOIGNIES.	
"	19th		56th Brigade R.F.A. moved to SOIGNIES.	
"	20th		9th Brigade R.F.A. (less D/69th Battery) moved to SOIGNIES.	
"	21st		52nd D.A. Headquarters moved to SOIGNIES.	
SOIGNIES.	22nd to 28th		N I L.	
"	29th		Brigadier General G.T.MAIR. C.M.G., DSO., RA., ordered to assume command of Brigade Groups 52nd (Lowland) Division.	
"	30th 31st		N I L.	

31st March 1919.

Wagores C.M. RA
Brig:General R.A.,
Commanding R.A., 52nd Division.

CONFIDENTIAL.
****

WAR OF DIARY

HEADQUARTERS 52nd (LOWLAND) DIVISIONAL ARTILLERY
****

FROM 1st April 1919.

TO 30th April 1919.

Army Form C. 2118.

WAR DIARY

~~INTELLIGENCE SUMMARY~~

(Erase heading not required.)

Instructions regarding War Diaries and Intelligence Summaries are contained in F. S. Regs., Part II. and the Staff Manual respectively. Title pages will be prepared in manuscript.

Place	Date	Hour	Summary of Events and Information	Remarks and references to Appendices
SOIGNIES.	1/4/19 to 21/4/19.		NIL.	
"	22/4/19.		Brig: General G.T.Mair C.M.G., D.S.O. relinquished command of 52nd Divisional Artillery and proceeded to United Kingdom.	
"	"		Lieut. Col. J.M.Ingram assumed command of 52nd (Lowland) Cadre Division vice Brig: General G.T.Mair C.M.G., D.S.O. to U.K..	
"	23/4/19 to 28/4/19		NIL.	
"	29/4/19.		Headquarters 56th Brigade R.F.A., "A" and "B" Batteries, 56th Brigade R.F.A. entrained at Soignies en route for GAILES. (Scotland)	
"	30/4/19.		NIL.	

1/5/19.

[signature]
Captain R.A.,
for Commanding R.A., 52nd Division.

CONFIDENTIAL.
****

WAR DIARY

OF

HEADQUARTERS ROYAL ARTILLERY, 52nd (LOWLAND) DIVISION.

Part V.
=======
Vol. VI.

FROM -
May 1st, 1919.

TO -
May 31st, 1919.

Hdqrs., R.A., 52nd Division. Army Form C. 2118.

WAR DIARY
INTELLIGENCE SUMMARY.
(Erase heading not required.)

May, 1919.

Instructions regarding War Diaries and Intelligence Summaries are contained in F.S. Regs., Part II. and the Staff Manual respectively. Title pages will be prepared in manuscript.

Place	Date	Hour	Summary of Events and Information	Remarks and references to Appendices
SOIGNIES.	1/5/19 to 3/5/19.	))	NIL.	
"	4/5/19	)	"C" Battery, 56th Brigade R.F.A. and 527th (How) Battery R.F.A. entrained at SOIGNIES enroute for GAILES (Scotland).	
"	5/5/19 to 29/5/19.	))	NIL.	
"	30/5/19.		Cadres of Hdqrs., 147th A/Brigade R.F.A., A/147th Battery R.F.A., Hdqrs., 9th Brigade R.F.A., 19th Battery R.F.A. and 20th Battery R.F.A. entrained at SOIGNIES enroute for U.K.	
"	31/5/19.		Cadres of 28th Battery R.F.A. and D/69th (How) Battery R.F.A. entrained at SOIGNIES enroute for U.K..	

3rd June, 1919.

Wwams
for Commanding R.A., Captain R.A., 52nd Division.

www.ingramcontent.com/pod-product-compliance
Lightning Source LLC
Chambersburg PA
CBHW081424300426
44108CB00016BA/2297